Eat ir Harmony

A Feast of Life, the Arts, and Faith

Gregory S. Athnos

outskirtspress
DENVER, COLORADO

The opinions expressed in this manuscript are solely the opinions of the author and do not represent the opinions or thoughts of the publisher. The author has represented and warranted full ownership and/or legal right to publish all the materials in this book.

Eat in Harmony
A Feast of Life, the Arts, and Faith
All Rights Reserved.
Copyright © 2016 Gregory S. Athnos
v3.0

Cover Photo © 2016 Gregory S. Athnos . All rights reserved - used with permission.

This book may not be reproduced, transmitted, or stored in whole or in part by any means, including graphic, electronic, or mechanical without the express written consent of the publisher except in the case of brief quotations embodied in critical articles and reviews.

Outskirts Press, Inc.
http://www.outskirtspress.com

ISBN: 978-1-4787-7090-9

Outskirts Press and the "OP" logo are trademarks belonging to Outskirts Press, Inc.

PRINTED IN THE UNITED STATES OF AMERICA

Table of Contents

Prelude i

Introduction: Beginnings
1940 - 1945

Chapter 1 - *Reflections: A Conversation With the Stars*................3
Chapter 2 - 1940: The Music Begins...7
Chapter 3 - 1941: The Story of the Boy 10
Chapter 4 - *Reflections: A Conversation*
    With My Norwegian Uncle..15

Exposition: Formulations
1946 - 1965

Chapter 5 - *1946: Vaht Gut Qvestions Did You Ask T'Day?*..........20
Chapter 6 - 1950: A Life Changing Baseball Accident................26
Chapter 7 - 1953: College Days 35
Chapter 8 - 1958: "Are There Any Questions?" 43
Chapter 9 - *Reflections: What a Poet and*
    the Apostle's Creed Told Me.....................................47
Chapter 10 - 1958: Joining the Covenant Church......................51
Chapter 11 - 1965: A Stunning Summer in Europe 55
Chapter 12 - 1965: Sibelius in a Vegetable Garden....................61
Chapter 13 - 1965: On Stage With the Wagners in Bayreuth 69
Chapter 14 - 1965: What Cologne Are You Wearing?
    Dinner With Mendelssohn..98

Development: Living
1965 – 1998

Chapter 15 - *Reflections: What the Incarnation Tells Me About Art* 114
Chapter 16 - 1965: My Career at North Park College Begins ..116
Chapter 17 - *Reflections: What Moses Told Me About the Shadow of God* 119
Chapter 18 - 1966: My First College Conducting Position......121
Chapter 19 - 1966: The Varsity Singers Initiative 125
Chapter 20 - 1967: The Chamber Singers Initiative 138
Chapter 21 - 1967: International Summer School, Oslo, Norway 170
Chapter 22 - 1969: The Miracle of the House 187
Chapter 23 - 1969: Cranbrook and the "Rock Mass" 198
Chapter 24 - *Reflections: What I Learned From Beethoven and a Piece of Wood* 203
Chapter 25 - 1969: The New Song...213
Chapter 26 - 1972: The First Foreign Study Initiative 221
Chapter 27 - *Reflections: What My Imagination Told Me* 227
Chapter 28 - 1972: The Holy Mountain 230
Chapter 29 - *Reflections: What the Arts Tell Me* 244
Chapter 30 - 1974: Sabbatical: From Norway to the Catacombs 246
Chapter 31 - 1974: Almost Murdered in an Underground City .257
Chapter 32 - February, 1974: My Father's Funeral..................268
Chapter 33 - 1975: Building an Orchestra 275
Chapter 34 - *Reflections: What I See in the Mud and Scum of Things* 290
Chapter 35 - 1976: Hosting a Soviet Dissident 294
Chapter 36 - August, 1981: A Breakup 297
Chapter 37 - 1981: Medieval France Meets Country Western .300
Chapter 38 - November, 1981: A Healing..............................308
Chapter 39 - 1983: If I Forget Thee, O Jerusalem 311

Chapter 40 - *Reflections: When I Questioned Tertullian and Mentioned Beauty* 319
Chapter 41 - 1983: Another Harbinger 322
Chapter 42 - October, 1984: North Park College Chapel A Service of Commitment 327
Chapter 43 - *Reflections: What the History of Christianity Told Me* 331
Chapter 44 - 1985: Bach's Lunch 335
Chapter 45 - *Reflections: Bach, The Man Who Made All the Wrong Decisions* 339

Recapitulation: Culmination
1986 – 1998

Chapter 46 - 1986: The Reluctant Choirmaster 346
Chapter 47 - 1989: Hymnathon: Twenty-four Hours of Success 355
Chapter 48 - 1989: Hungary & Poland: Cathedral, Crucifix, and Congregation 359
Chapter 49 - Olga, Dimitri, Smolny: Soviet Union 1965, Russia 1993 390
Chapter 50 - Another Commitment Call 408
Chapter 51 - 1998: Departing North Park: All Good Things Come To An End 413
Chapter 52 - *Reflections: What Post-Modernism Tells Me* 429

CODA: Reflections
1998 –

Chapter 53 - *Reflections* 432
Chapter 54 - Looking Forward: Life After North Park............439
Chapter 55 - 2008: China and the Pre-Olympic Festival 440
Chapter 56 - Milwaukee Art Museum Lectures 468
Chapter 57 - Elderhostel/Road Scholar Lectures....................473
Chapter 58 - European Arts Tours..480

Chapter 59 - Author 483
Chapter 60 - Others Look Back: Notes and Letters 487
Appendix 499

Prelude

The 'Eat in Harmony' Cafe, La Crosse, Wisconsin

Part of who I am—a great part perhaps—is a result of my father's love for his restaurant. Apart from family he was driven, even possessed by his ownership of the *Harmony Café*. At least, that's how the locals referred to it: *"Let's have lunch at the Harmony"* (or breakfast, or dinner, or just a cup of good coffee). But there is a much deeper thought behind the name; actually, there is a much more descriptive name: the *Eat in Harmony Café*. Why he chose it he never said; I can only speculate that it had something to do with who my father was, how he had embraced his new life in America, and the way he treated his customers.

His dealings with all people, strangers included, were remarkable and inspiring.

During the Depression the *Eat in Harmony Café* became a household name throughout the hobo railroad network. As these men rode the rails looking for work, even temporary work or a day's wages, the word circulated among them that they would find a friend in La Crosse, Wisconsin.

"When you get to Chicago, take the spur that goes to La Crosse. Find the Harmony Café, but get there early, before it opens. Knock on the back door. The owner will answer. Tell him you're hungry. He'll ask you to wash his back steps and then knock again. 'I'll give you a breakfast you'll never forget', he'll say."

During those difficult years the back steps of the *Eat in Harmony Café* were being washed sometimes two or three times daily. He had the cleanest steps in the world! They didn't need cleaning; that wasn't the point. My father could have given them a great meal without the work being undertaken, but in his mind that would have been the worst thing he could have done. He was concerned about the men's dignity. Handouts would relegate them to inferior status and rob them of the pride that was constantly being drained from them because of the Depression. He chose to treat them as equals. They worked for their meals as well as their souls. They left with both full hearts and full stomachs; no one left his establishment hungry, physically or spiritually. *Eat in Harmony* was a philosophy and way of life, not merely a name.

That sentiment seems unfortunately quaint and antiquated in our entitlement world.

He treated each of his customers as individuals, not as a faceless crowd. But apart from one or two, he didn't know their names; rather, he knew them by what they ate and the way they liked it. *"Here comes two over easy"* I heard him say on more than one occasion. Everyone loved him, customers and employees alike. He had no enemies. He paid his bills on time. Rich or poor, politically powerful or just a plain working 'slob', all were treated as treasures. 'Harmony' was the motto he lived by.

He had three heroes. One was General Douglas MacArthur; we had a huge framed photo of him hanging on a wall. I don't know why. Perhaps it was my father's love of country, instilled first by dreams from his tiny village in the south of Greece, and cemented by his military service in France during the waning months of World War I, even before he became a U.S. citizen. All I know is, the portrait held a revered place in our home.

Elias the Boxer

Two of his heroes were African-Americans. Again, in a time before lunch counter sit-ins or 'freedom marches', before Rosa Parks and Martin Luther King Jr., my father treated everyone as equal in his mind and in the sight of God.

Because he had been an amateur boxer shortly after the Great War—as a child I marveled at his prowess with a punching bag—it stands to reason one of his heroes would be a boxer. But not Jack Dempsey or any other 'great white hope' like so many others idolized by the Caucasian populace. Joe Louis was his man—the 'Brown Bomber'. We gathered around the radio in our home and listened to every Joe Louis fight. Those episodes are most vivid in my memory, with my father unselfconsciously mimicking the announcer's commentary, punching the air with jabs and uppercuts.

Louie Armstrong was the other. Again, no explanation. My father wasn't a musician; he couldn't carry a tune. He rarely listened to music, nor did we have a single conversation about music or his trumpeter hero. My only guess is that here was another 'black man' who had succeeded in spite of the nature and condition of 'the age'. My father always rooted for the underdog.

Underdog. He would do anything to showcase how wrong it was for society to relegate groups to that status. He demonstrated such zeal during the 1940's when baseball was still segregated. Negro Leagues flourished in the Black communities of big-city America with perhaps some of the greatest players to ever grace the game. We'll never know for sure, though legendary figures abound: Josh Gibson, a power hitter who may have overshadowed the great Babe Ruth had he had the chance (his team-mates called Babe Ruth the 'white' Josh Gibson); Satchel Paige, whose exploits on the mound were mythic; and the young Henry Aaron, whom I saw play baseball when he joined the recently integrated Eau Claire, Wisconsin Class D team as a sixteen year old.

La Crosse, Wisconsin, was host every summer to at least one game between the local team and one of the Negro American or National League teams: the Homestead Grays, the New York Black Yankees, the Kansas City Monarchs, the Birmingham Black Barons, the

Indianapolis Clowns, and others. I faithfully was in attendance at every game and marveled at the power, speed, and grace of those players. There were no Black families in my hometown, zero, so these occasions were a revelation as well as a telescope into a sad chapter in our American history.

Negro League baseball games were the highlight of my summers, and cemented baseball's hold on my imagination and my dreams. Music was on the back burner in those years.

The *Eat in Harmony Café* was the preferred diner for the Negro League players. Whether or not other local restaurants would have fed them I don't know. All I know is that they always chose my father's establishment for their nourishment. I'd like to think it was the name of the restaurant that drew them. As a young boy I remember setting the tables and pouring water for them on each of their visits. I was always proud to serve them and, in retrospect, proud that my father exercised his motto of equality and personhood embedded in his *Eat in Harmony* dictum.

Patriot, friend of all, champion of underdogs—that sums up my father and his influence in my life.

I never heard my Greek immigrant father sing. If he ever listened to music on the radio or phonograph I was not aware of it. The only concerts he attended featured me, his son, playing cornet in a school band. My father was a cook; I was the musician. He served one kind of food; I served another. The stomach, or the soul? That was a false choice. It was both. He desired that no one leave spiritually or physically hungry; that was the song he sang. I desired the same symbiosis.

Eat in Harmony. Those words characterized my father and influenced me. It was a reflection of my father's attitude toward all the divisions and disputes that seem to permeate the fabric of life in the world, that also have the sinister capacity to disrupt local communities. He may have had little command of the English language but it appears he was fully 'in tune' with the universal human condition. He seemed to be saying,

"Gather at my table. Put aside all your differences and share a meal together. Savor your conversation. Find a common humanity. Leave as friends with newfound joy for the next hours of your life."

All this while drinking a cup of good coffee, or devouring flapjacks and eggs. That was the prevailing attitude in the *Eat in Harmony Café*. It became neutral ground for rediscovering a common humanity.

For him the word *Harmony* suggested *harmonious relationships*. It was the same for me in *my* 'eatery', my profession as a musician and teacher:

"Gather together with me. Explore beauty. Let the 'sounds' of art and faith course for a time in your veins and your heart. Think about life in all its bounty and promise. Leave my 'table' with a renewed sense of joy for your future and what is beautiful as you face tomorrow."

All this while listening to a Beethoven symphony or a Schubert Art Song.

Welcome to *my* banquet! The table is spread with dollops of faith, art, family, philosophy, miracles, life experiences, music history, and chance meetings. Some might say it's a 'potluck' with neither rhyme nor reason to the assembly of dishes. Others might call it a smorgasbord where one can pick and choose. But in my mind it *is* a banquet to be ingested course by course. I've invited you to this harmonious gathering around a table set with an array of 'dishes' to digest in pleasant union and conversation: *harmony* in the broadest sense. So, as my Greek immigrant father would say, "*Fàte se armoni: Eat in Harmony.*"

What better way for me to organize reflections on my life in music, art, and faith than to use the *Sonata*, a musical structure that inspired composers for nearly three hundred years. From the symphonies of Haydn and Mozart to the string quartets of Beethoven and Shostakovitch, the *Sonata* has proven its worth as a housing for inspired ideas in sound. It is, in my opinion, the best man-made organizer of musical ideas yet devised. It's something I know; why not give it a try to organize my life's story?

Sonata needs definition; it is derived from the Italian word *sonare*—to play. A *Sonata* is an instrumental piece; it has no words. The meaning contained in this structure is the pure joy of organized sound itself, allowing the listener to dig deep and attach personal feelings and responses to the music in a purely subjective manner: What does it say to me? How does it make me feel? What do I learn in the listening about myself and my place in the world? In reading my story I hope you'll discover your own answers to those questions.

The motivation for this book is the 'pure joy', the *harmony* of my life's experiences placed in a structure, the *Sonata*, to give them shape and meaning.

It is not always the 'facts' of life that impress us in our look back; it's what we were able to 'read' into them, the emotions that gathered around us as we lived out our days. It's not enough for me to say,

"Yes, I DID that."

The greater question is,

"Did it make a difference?"

Everyone's life is a *Sonata* played out against a cultural background of events that seem random until we re-gather our thoughts in reflection and discover an underlying purpose, a *first organizer* of sorts, guiding our journeys. That 'one moment' years ago—had I made a different choice the entire trajectory of my life would have been different. How many such junctures have formed our paths? I recount more than one in this book. Can we see the significance of those moments that seemed so insignificant at the time? Were they random? Accidents? Purposeful? Manifestations of a greater 'Hand' at work? I leave that consideration to you, the reader; I know where I stand and what I believe. I hope my position will not only become clear to you, but become convincing as well.

Within my life's *Sonata*, *harmony*, or *harmonious accord* has a rhythm, a pulse. How often have we felt our lives were careening by so quickly we couldn't catch our breath? (How like a *Finale* to a Mozart symphony!) Conversely, how often did we sense a slow unveiling of our existence? (Second movement *Adagios* are like that!) Time is measured more in emotions than in seconds. Sleep travels more quickly than our waking hours. Delight often seems too short; pain too long. Honestly, I don't know where all the years have gone. I only know I have lived two billion four hundred million seconds of invariable, uniform length, though I felt them in unequal portions—some interminable, others a sudden flash beyond my grasp, but all necessary to flesh out the story.

Sonata form has five parts: *Introduction, Exposition, Development, Recapitulation, Coda*. My story, my *harmony* fits rather comfortably into a corresponding five-part framework: *Beginnings, Formulations, Living, Culmination, Reflections*. The form dictates a chronological approach, but I've taken the liberty to superimpose and interject philosophic and artistic reflections and detours that I hope will add context to my spiritual journey. It is, after all, the *harmony*, those periodic chords framing the essence of life, those pillars supporting the roof of my existence—not necessarily the melody—that reign supreme.

The story is not mine alone to tell. I did not live it in a bubble, alone. Many countless people influenced what I would become and what I would contribute. Their voices deserve to be heard. Some will speak for themselves in their own words, while others will be heard only obliquely, in the margins, between the lines, or by inference. In truth, the story is more truly theirs, because what I did and how I lived, even perhaps without my always knowing it, was in response to who they were.

Not everything is revealed here. Only those moments in my musical career that appear, in retrospect, to have formed my heart, spirit, and mind in life-changing ways are told. Some may appear small and insignificant to the reader; others larger than life itself perhaps. I know the pieces of my *harmony's* puzzle—how they all fit, pieces large and small, irregularly shaped—and hope you will sense an inevitability and completeness in my choices.

Welcome to the five-course feast that has surrounded my life's *Sonata*! *Eat in Harmony*!

Introduction: Beginnings 1940 - 1945

A Higher Form of Music

A Boy and a Cello, His Memories and Dreams

1940: The Story of the Boy

Reflections: A Conversation With My Norwegian Uncle

CHAPTER 1

Reflections: A Conversation With the Stars

God said to Job, "Where were you when I laid the earth's foundations? Tell me, if you know and understand....
Who set its corner-stone in place, when the morning stars sang together and all the sons of God shouted for joy?"
(Job 38: 1-4)

Imprisoned for his faith, the 4th century philosopher Boethius wrote a treatise entitled *Consolation of Philosophy*. Within its pages he rather imaginatively suggested there were three kinds of music created by God in His consummate artistry. Of these three, the lowest form was *Musica Instrumentalis*, the music we hear (when I first read his work I wondered what other kind of music there could possibly be?). He said it is the music of our 'fallen state', a mere shadow of the glorious music intended for us before Adam and Eve, through their disobedience, were driven from the Garden of Paradise.

There was yet a higher form. Boethius called it *Musica Humana*, the music created by the perfection and symmetry of the body.

God, in His creation, made us in His likeness. Our bodies' pure symmetry—the miraculous workings of all our organs and members—produced heavenly music. But because of the sin of Adam and Eve, bringing about our 'fallen state', we were no longer allowed to comprehend the music God had placed in our fleshly creation. However, Boethius said, in the end time, when we once again receive the gift of reconciliation and 'wholeness', we will hear our bodies' wonderful music.

There was, finally, what Boethius called the highest form of music, *Musica Mundana,* sometimes referred to as the '*Music of the Spheres*'. (You may recall this phrase from the familiar hymn *This Is My Father's World*, where we sing the text '*and round me rings the music of the spheres*'). Boethius thought that God's creation of the stars and planets, suns and moons, their orderliness and beauty, produced a music that our 'fallen state' had caused us to forfeit. This sounds so outlandish to our modern sensibilities that we are prone to dismiss it as pure fancy for fear of being considered 'loony'. But I sometimes think we have heard this music, not in its fullness, but rather as a whisper of future promise.

Picture yourself in the middle of the woods by yourself on a crisp autumn night, away from city lights, looking up at the vast heavens saturated with stars. The Milky Way stretches like a broad ribbon of white as far as you can see. The stars appear so close you feel you could reach out and grab a handful to sprinkle on your Rice Krispies for breakfast. A lump rises in your throat. You stand there—transfixed, silent. Perhaps the words of the Psalmist invade your mind,

When I survey Your handiwork, what is man that Thou art mindful of him?

You see yourself as a mere speck of insignificance in the immeasurable sea of creation:

I am nothing. My existence is totally meaningless in the vastness of the cosmos. I have no more meaning than a single leaf in this endless forest.

But the Psalmist continues:

We have been made a little lower than the angels…

Almost angels? At that very same moment a conflicting thought arises:

I am special. From the foundation of the world God knew I would be standing here, moved in the depths of my spirit by the beauty and grandeur of His creation. He created this moment for me.

Perhaps, as one philosopher has suggested, our significance in the total scheme of things is validated precisely because we are able to recognize and contemplate our insignificance.

Then the spell was broken. Later, when trying to describe your experience to your friends, you failed. No matter how eloquent, no matter your mastery of vocabulary, there were no words to convey the depth of your emotional response to what you had witnessed. To me what you experienced at that moment was a faint foretaste of *Musica Mundana,* the *'Music of the Spheres'*. I think the Psalmist had a similar experience, and he wrote:

"The heavens tell out the glory of God, the vault of heaven reveals His handiwork…and this without speech or language or sound of any voice. The music of the heavens goes out through all the earth, their words reach to the end of the world." (Psalm 19: 1-3)

Like *Musica Humana*, Boethius said, at the end of time, when there is no longer the possibility of sin, when in fact sin and death are abolished, we will hear it. I'm counting on it!

> *Shouts the far flung sky*
> *Fearing tales of emptiness*
> *"Hear my cosmic heart"*
>
> (GA)

CHAPTER 2

1940: The Music Begins

The young boy watched as the old man stumbled purposefully across the stage, struggling to keep his balance. One foot stepped gingerly, the other dragged behind. The people gathered in the large room held their collective breath and clapped as he made his way slowly. The boy wondered why they were clapping—he hadn't done anything but try to walk! He didn't understand. In one hand was a big wooden box the old man held by a long neck attached to it. In his other hand was a long, skinny piece of wood with what looked like thin strings stretched from one end to the other. The boy had never seen these objects before. He leaned against the balcony railing, magnetized by the sight.

The old man sat down on a chair in the center of the stage and put the big box between his knees. The long neck reached up over his shoulder, nearly touching his ear. The clapping stopped. Everything became silent. Taking the long stick in his other hand he put it on strings the boy could see were attached to the box. Slowly he pulled the stick across the strings.

Music! Beautiful music. The boy had heard music before, but nothing like this!

A high note, followed by another just below it, then another a short distance below that, all in one movement of the stick. Something magical was whispering to him. Only three notes, moving downward as if coming from a place beyond anything he had ever known. They were coming to him, just him, he thought, and he embraced them. Pushing the stick in the other direction the man repeated another similar three-note pattern starting just below the sound of the first pattern: it was an imitation of the first perfection. Another three notes moved upwards instead of the downward pattern of the first two. Then, reaching down to a low note he began to move the stick slowly while the fingers of his hand on the long neck moved from the top of the neck downward toward the big box. As his fingers moved downward the sounding notes moved upward, reaching higher than any notes he had played. This irony of direction was not lost on the boy: "If the fingers move down why does the sound go up?" This was a world of 'other', and the boy was immediately drawn to it. The confusion between sight and sound created a confection that, in spite of his tender age, made all the sense in the world.

It couldn't have been more than twenty notes in all (it was actually nineteen, though the young boy wasn't able at that age to count that high).

It was his first live concert, and it changed his world forever. He knew at that moment these sounds, this beauty, this *'other'* had to be in his life—not only *in* his life, but life itself. The future—his future—was revealed to him, slowly at first, just a trickle of a stream that would eventually flood his sensibilities. He didn't even know what it was that had made these magnificent sounds, or how. He only knew it was his destiny; he absolutely had to have it.

The music continued, though the boy was lost in that *'other'* world after those first few notes. He would be immersed in this world for good; he knew it then.

1940: The Music Begins

I was that young boy. I was just barely four years old.

Greg at age four

Before long I learned the performer was Leigh Elder, director of the La Crosse Symphony Orchestra. The instrument was a cello, and the piece was "The Swan", from *Carnival of the Animals*, by Camille Saint-Saens. Strangely enough (fittingly enough) that very piece was one of the last orchestral compositions I would conduct forty-six years later as director of the North Park University Chamber Orchestra, bringing my moment of inspiration full circle. My soloist was cello major Christopher French who went on to become principal cellist for the Houston Symphony.

CHAPTER 3

1941: The Story of the Boy

My Norwegian immigrant Grandma, Ronnaug Nordlien Lee, was sitting next to me on the hard concrete steps overlooking the shipyard. I was barely five years old. The rest of my family—mother, father, and two older brothers, along with an aunt and uncle—were there, but I don't remember them in my recollection of the event. It was 1941: war-time in Europe. We were witnessing the launching of a ship from the Manitowoc ship-works into Lake Michigan. My older cousin had helped build it. I was too young to be caught up in all the terrible events that made this day and this event important in the total scheme of things. I only know now, from the slippage of time; but in spite of the global consequences and responses of that moment, the singular image of the day is that I was with my Grandma (I didn't even know her name; she was just 'Grandma'), and her quiet and large presence comforted me.

If she spoke to me I don't remember the words. If she embraced me, I don't remember the touch. She was simply sitting next to me. It is one of the few vivid remembrances I have of her, ever, as she died that same year, when I was five.

The steps were concrete bleachers overlooking the launching ramp.

Whatever their size, I have forgotten, but my legs dangled over the edge of one step, not long enough to reach the step below.

My fascination was focused on a large spider making its way toward me. I first spied it a number of steps below. It would appear over the edge of a step and then disappear in the shadow the higher step cast. Even though I couldn't see it I knew it was still coming toward me. My eyes were fixed, riveted on its projected path. It seemed ages between its appearances over the edge of the next closest steps. Each time it appeared, a step closer to me, its size seemed larger to my imagination than it actually was. Each appearance met with interesting responses: yes, I was afraid of it; but its recurring appearances meshed with my predictions of its progress, causing a certain detachment and rationality to blend with my apprehension. Fear was balanced by order and control, like a stalemate on a teeter-totter. The nearness of Grandma was my security even though I made no gesture toward her, nor did she seem aware of the encroaching creature. Her attention was compelled by the noiseless sliding of the ship into Lake Michigan; it was a symbol of human indignation rising to meet the challenge of evil, a response from the reasoned ones of the world in the face of unreasonableness, saying, "*Rise up against the enemy, don't wait until he knocks on your door.*" In my own little world a tiny enemy encroached and, mesmerized by it, yet securely in the presence of Grandma, I let it.

Caught between the macrocosm and microcosm of global and personal existence there was a dilemma calling for a response. The big people of the world were rising up in action. My child world's fascination was hypnotic, and deep inside I think I hoped my adversary would simply go away. If I pretended it wasn't there, perhaps it wouldn't be. And then it wasn't. It never reappeared over the edge of the step nearest me, just under my dangling legs.

Only one family memory predates this, and it is not linked with a specific time, but seems woven into the fabric of my first three years. I was always in the arms of my mother, and not in our home, but rather in our little basement church. I have no memories of home in those years, only the church. I had two older brothers, neither of whom is in my mental picture. It is only the old folding wooden theater seats, the small and, in my memory, dark basement church, the hymns and altar calls, and the security of my mother's arms.

I am truly a child of the Church, whatever good or ill would later be associated with that fact. My birthdays were always celebrated by putting one penny for each year in the Sunday School Lighthouse Bank in front of all gathered in the opening exercises, and watching it light up. Over the years I progressed from being an angel to a shepherd to Joseph in the annual Christmas program, growing from silent to speaking roles, even though one year the pageant had to be cancelled because the Athnos boys, comprising all the main male characters, had the measles.

I loved volunteering to take the offering, and was excited when I had finally become old enough. Margaret Reschlein and I always seemed to battle each other in the Bible drills in Lois Brieske's Sunday School class. How I looked forward to the annual Church picnic on a Minnesota farm south of La Crescent, the throwing of horseshoes seeming to get easier each growing year, and the red 'bug juice' remaining its same, sweet and satisfying delight.

The Church also prompted painful memories. As a small child, not yet grown into an understanding of most of the words preached, the images of judgment and the condemnation of unrepentant sinners nonetheless loomed large in my memory and populated my dreams.

One dream played itself out often in my childhood over many years; I remember it vividly. I was standing outside my father's restaurant, the *Eat in Harmony Cafe*, on Third Street at the corner of State Street. The heavens were collapsing, stars colliding, and the sun was screaming closer and closer to the earth. It was the *Apocalypse*, the end of the world. People were crying hysterically, running through streets knee deep in blood. Chaos surrounded me; yet in spite of it all, and alone, I stood quietly observing the destruction of time and space. The dream never changed over all the years of its playing out. Panic hovered around me like a dense fiery fog. I could almost feel the heat but it never touched me. Aware of the dread around me I nonetheless was possessed by calm—at least in my dream. Fear invariably came over me in my waking state, and I desired never to live through the dream again. But it came back again and again, and along with it, to my continual relief, a spirit of calm assurance.

My dream (I call it my dream because I seemed to possess it and live it as if it were a piece of my existence) was almost like the spider and Grandma Lee, both events marked by an encroachment, both alive with the capacity to invoke fear, both filled with a sense of aloneness, yet covered by an inner calm and detachment, and both engraved with an awareness of a larger presence of security. In one it was my Grandma. In the other, though much more subtle, it was the supporting faith which came through my growing up in the Church. How strange that while the Church seems responsible for the dream and all of its attendant frightfulness, it also had prepared me to discover a way of escape and deliverance.

As I looked back over the years I began to comprehend how it is that my entire life is prefigured in these two childhood experiences. They are who I am, for better or worse. It is not the best thing about me that I often have remained detached hoping that problems would go away if I pretended they didn't exist. I am not always pleased when I think how often I have isolated myself or allowed myself to be and act alone when there have been others who love me and would have willingly made sacrifices on my behalf. But my recognition that there is a secure haven to be found in my faith, a present and ultimate protection from the final consequences of evil, an assurance that I need not fear, a conviction that even death itself has already been overcome even if heaven and earth disintegrate as in my dream, gives me peace. In this light my story begins.

I am what I am
Touched by God, sprinkled with dreams
A certain madness
(GA)

CHAPTER 4

Reflections: A Conversation With My Norwegian Uncle

The Psalmist penned: "Sing to the Lord a song of thanksgiving.... He gives the cattle their food and the young ravens all that they gather."
(Psalm 147: 7, 9)

I was a young child sitting in my Uncle Enoch's barn up on Buckeye Ridge near La Farge in rural Wisconsin. It was milking time. Though Uncle Enoch never talked about it, and never came to realize it, in one brief encounter he taught me as much about the power of music and art as anyone else. Uncle Enoch and Aunt Palma, offspring of Norwegian immigrants, loved American Country Western music decades before it became popular. Their home was never without it. In all my Sunday afternoon visits to the farm their parlor was filled with this strange, twangy music that I never heard anywhere else. And I must confess that even as a child I didn't care for it. I was still possessed by *The Swan; that* was the beauty ringing in my ears. But the barn was different. That odiferous haven, filled with the scent of hay and cattle breath, silent and empty during the day, became vibrant with music at milking time. I would sit on a mound of hay enthralled by the sound of warm milk hitting the sides of metal pails, Uncle Enoch and my older cousins sitting on three-legged stools milking by hand, while beautiful orchestral music haloed the hour.

"Uncle," I remember asking, *"why do you play 'twangy' music in your house, and this pretty music in the barn?"*

Uncle Enoch chuckled softly without cracking a smile, then said, *"When I play this 'pretty' music the cows give more milk."*

Uncle knew what the cows liked. Though he didn't understand it or much care for it himself, classical music was what the cows got: earthy music in the house, otherworldly music in the barn. From Aunt Palma's Country-Western parlors to Bach's barn was a fifteen second romp for my short legs, yet the gravel road separating them could just as easily have marked the borders between distant kingdoms or galaxies.

Cows were not the only charmed creatures on those occasions. Decades before I knew of Boethius' *Music of the Spheres* I sensed something cosmic, something spiritual about art, and understood in my tender mind that even cud-chewing beasts were not immune to it. Had I not visited that *'other'* dimension at my first concert? What I later came to know about the power of art through the warrior Joshua, the Psalmist David, the unknown architects of the great Gothic cathedrals, the artist Michelangelo, the poet/theologian John Donne, the composers Bach and Beethoven, and the playwright Shakespeare only confirmed what I had already learned as a child huddled against the cold in my Uncle Enoch's barn—art is immensely spiritual, powerful and transforming.

"Cornsilk sundown"

Up on the ridge when the wind blows cold
Folks collar up weather-creased necks
And lean resolutely into the westerlies

Cattle breath steams their hay-homes
Huddled in the barn

Rusty old weathervanes creak a sad tale
To the tune of dark humming pines

Skies get all gold and purpley
Like can only happen in a cornsilk sundown

Barren furrows shadow long and silent
In cyclic sleep, while

Wrinkled creation returns to its clay
Wistfully awaiting the New Day
(GA)

Soli Deo Gloria

Exposition: Formulations
1946 - 1965

Expositions introduce the major themes forming the substance of the music to follow

Questions

Two Loves

More Questions

Discovered

Providential 'Accidents' in Europe

CHAPTER 5

1946: "Vaht gut qvestions did you ask t'day?"

There she was, standing with her hands on her aproned hips, waiting for her son to appear around the corner. It was my friend Terry Sharp's mom, a Jewish immigrant, ever vigilant in her pursuit for Terry's success.

Terry had become my best friend in fifth grade. While in earlier elementary school years my friends were from my own neighborhood, I was drawn to Terry because of his interest in music. He was taking cornet lessons at Washington Elementary School. I wanted to be like Terry. It would prove to have far more lasting consequences for me than for him, though neither of us knew it at the time.

We practiced together. One day we would go to my house following school, and the next day to his. I suppose this shared practice venue made it fair to each of us, but the greater good was that it spared our parents half the noise coming from these novice beginners!

The two practice sites were anything but equal. At my home our family gathering around the dinner table was quite noisy, what with six boys jockeying for the largest portions of their favorite dishes.

1946: "Vaht gut qvestions did you ask t'day?"

What I remember most is that every dinner hour began with the same question coming from one or the other of my parents:

"What did you learn in school today?"

That is probably the most ubiquitous question asked throughout the homes of the school children of America. And I dare say it is also the least answered question across the country. I remember my brothers and I would respond in the same manner, day after day:

"Oh, nothing special," or, *"Just the same stuff as yesterday"* (which we hadn't elaborated on either).

I have asked many adults about this type of inquiry, and everyone nods in agreement both to the question and to the evasive non-answers. Most of us who suffered under those questions turned around and asked the same of our own kids, and were always filled with chagrin at the lack of answers, having forgotten, I suppose, that we had frustrated our parents in just the same way.

This was not the case on the alternate days at Terry's home. His mother knew when to expect her son to appear across the street four houses to the north, rounding the corner with the large bush at the edge of the sidewalk. In my memory Mrs. Sharp was always standing on the public sidewalk: short, stocky, wearing an apron, looking in our direction. When Terry appeared she would cup her hands to her mouth and shout in a very loud, high-pitched voice colored by an immigrant's accent:

"Terry, vhat gut qvestions did you ask t'day?"

Terry grew up with the attitude that the secret of success was to be found in the ability to ask a good question. It was reinforced in my hearing every other day, but I'm sure on the alternate days, when he

21

arrived home after practicing cornet at my house, the same inquiry was made. That it took root in Terry is borne out by what we all saw of his academic progress throughout the remaining years of his public school education.

I remember in seventh grade, when the Math teacher was absent, Terry taught the class. He was especially good in Math, to the point that he could even play tricks with numbers on the blackboard in very elaborate and complex equations, 'proving' to the rest of us gullible and less math-minded students that 'one plus one can equal three'. We all believed him.

It didn't hurt that he had a photographic memory; everything he read he remembered. But it wasn't that he simply remembered; he could easily recall pertinent information at the drop of a hat. It appeared to me even then that his 'information recall' was different from mine. I was smart, too. I had a lot of information stored in my brain, but it was just a tower of information which seemed to float in the ether, untethered, and wasn't always at my fingertips when I needed it. No, with Terry it was different. It was as if the questions he had been encouraged to ask became the *Velcro*, or the sticking place for the answers. Put another way, it was as if the questions were file drawers or file folders housing the answers that followed. In other words, the answers in Terry's world had a place to go; they had a purpose framed by the question. In my world, where questions were not the genesis of information, information had no place to land. Information was simply information, and because there wasn't a question that prompted the quest for answers, the information simply didn't seem to have any importance. From my vantage point later in life, I realize that this is precisely the problem with education in general: too much information, not enough *Velcro*. Too many answers, not enough questions.

1946: "Vaht gut qvestions did you ask t'day?"

In High School Terry was President of the Spanish Club and the Latin Club. He was on the debate team, played in the marching band, the symphonic band, the pep band, and was the scorer for several of the athletic teams, all the while maintaining a perfect academic record. Upon graduation he received a full ride scholarship to Carnegie Institute of Technology in Pittsburgh, where he majored in Nuclear Physics.

How well I remember the next time I saw Terry, and it would unfortunately be for me the last time. We both had headed off to college, Terry to Pittsburgh, and me to Minneapolis. Four years later we both returned to our hometown for the summer. I had my baccalaureate degree in Music. Terry had his Ph.D in Nuclear Physics! At age 21! There was a long article in the local daily newspaper about his incredible accomplishment. He had gone through the entire academic program with a straight perfect score!

When my parents congratulated him, he simply turned the accolade around and focused his attention on what I had accomplished, which was really nothing by comparison. That was Terry. He was never full of himself though there was plenty of reason to be, and he would more than likely have been excused if he had been. He was self-deprecating, to a fault.

I remember asking him somewhat jokingly how many hours he had in his day, seeing I had only twenty-four and often that had not been enough to get everything done. His reply startled me:

"I limited myself to two to three hours of study a day, because I wanted to have time for my other interests."

Now I know that simply starting with the *Velcro* questions doesn't account for all of Terry's success; he was perhaps a certifiable genius and was certainly aided by his photographic memory. Nonetheless, to do what he did was to my mind superhuman. I was and will always remain in awe of him.

I never saw Terry again. Some years later I returned to our hometown and inquired after him. His parents were long deceased. Terry had left for California, but no one knew exactly where. I went to his Synagogue but could never find an answer to my question (those were the days before the Internet). There were other families in town with the same surname but none were related to him. He was not at our tenth High School reunion. At subsequent reunions I always inquired whether Terry would be coming. The answer was always negative. No one knew anything about him. I stayed away from the reunions; he was really the only one I desperately wanted to see. Forty years later I relented and went to my fiftieth reunion. It was said that Terry had died, but no one knew any more than that. Not seeing him after that final meeting in 1957 remains one of the great disappointments in my life.

In a way what I learned from him has played a very large part in my life. One should be willing to ask questions of anything at all. The result of the question may not alter the field of inquiry, but it may lead to a greater understanding of why the answer is what it is. Then again, a new way of seeing or understanding may be achieved. I have become a sort of *iconoclast*, always wondering if perhaps there is a better way to do things or think about things than the ones I inherited. By asking the questions which some may think inappropriate I put myself out on a limb; from there I must find a way to keep someone from cutting it off; I need to give evidence that there is another way or a better way. If not, I must return to the trunk of the knowledge tree, having discovered for myself that the traditional way is still the best way. In either case I benefit. As it turned out, my university teaching career would be marked by this *iconoclastic* posture resulting in a number of academic and performance endeavors that effected dramatic change in the music curriculum.

Terry remains to this day a sort of secular icon in my gallery of influences.

CHAPTER 6

1950: A Life Changing Baseball Accident

Baseball was my second love. It almost took over first place until an accident settled the score for good.

I had started school cornet lessons in fifth grade, practicing daily with Terry Sharp. From the beginning I was at the 'top of the heap', and from my first day in an organized band in elementary school I was the first chair player. That would remain the case all the way through undergraduate school. Ever since my experience as a four-year-old hearing *The Swan,* I had known, along with everyone else, that music was my first love and my probable destiny.

I was pretty good. All three years in High School I was chosen to represent Central High at the *Dorian Music Festival,* a TriState gathering at Luther College in Decorah, Iowa, with Weston Noble as conductor. Back home, all the solos were mine to play. I was going to be a professional musician; no one doubted that.

Also starting in fifth grade I became enamored of baseball. Along with three other neighborhood boys we made up our own system of playing the game, two on a side. Our field was the local skating rink, using the warming house as the backstop. The outfield six-foot chain link fence ran in a straight line parallel to the warming house, making center field the shortest distance from home plate. Left and right field foul lines were the longest reaches for home runs.

The fielding team had a pitcher and one fielder who could choose to play any position from infield to outfield. We put sticks in the ground to indicate the other defensive positions.

The hitting team had a batter and an umpire to call 'high' or 'low' on all the pitches; the pitcher called 'over the plate', 'inside', or 'outside'. Needless to say, there were arguments on almost every pitch! Each player took his turn, alternately, at the plate.

In the 1940's, when all of this took place, there were sixteen Major League teams, eight in each of two leagues, American and National. During the summer months we played two full games every day, one from each league, with days off when it rained. We knew all the players from all the teams: their hitting records, their batting tendencies, how fast they were. Records were kept.

One of the most challenging aspects of 'our game' was positioning the fielders for each of the hitters: how far to the right or left of the stick were they positioned? And, knowing the speed of the runner and the speed of the defensive player arguments were made on whether the fielder could have reached the spot where the ball was hit.

As we grew year to year and became stronger, more balls were hit over the fence, especially by Russell Wiedeking, the biggest of us. We grew so tired of climbing over the fence to retrieve Russell's home runs we made the decision that whoever hit a home run had to retrieve it. Basically, Russell became 'one' with the fence.

It was great fun. We continued this pursuit into Junior High School: it was always Harry Worth (the best pitcher and hardest to hit); Jerry Kreuzer (the best fielder); Russell Wiedeking (the slugger); and me (the fastest runner).

My favorite team was the New York Yankees. That was an odd choice. Even then Chicago's WGN broadcast all the Cubs' games on the radio; we often listened. I had visited relatives in Chicago, attending a game at Wrigley Field. I knew the names of the players. I still remember two: Andy Pafko, outfielder, and Phil Cavaretta, first baseman. There is no explanation for my infatuation with the Yankees, but love them I did!

I loved the Yankees so much I prayed for them every night of the baseball season!

Actually, I prayed two prayers. One was that I would never grow up. I was having way too much fun as a kid. Also, I had seen the 'adult world' in the headlines of the newspaper every day and on newsreels at the local cinema, what with the War going on. I remembered that as a preschooler at the outbreak of the war, the first word I learned to read on my own was 'Nazi', though I pronounced it 'Nazzy'. My Aunties, my mother's sisters, visited our home regularly and sat around our kitchen table drinking coffee and crying. My older cousins, their sons, were fighting in Europe and the South Pacific. We didn't know if they were alive or dead, as letters were infrequent. My favorite cousin, Roger Young, was a bombardier stationed in northern Italy flying bombing raids over the German oil reserves, a most dangerous mission. Many didn't return from those raids. I didn't like that world; I didn't want to be part of it: hence my prayer.

My other nightly prayer was that the New York Yankees would win. And win they did; every year it seems they were in the World Series.

1950: A Life Changing Baseball Accident

Years later, when I stopped the prayers, they were not as successful. Looking back from my adult years, when the team had fallen from its perennial lofty height, I thought perhaps George Steinbrenner should have hired me to bring them out of their doldrums!

With such a high level of interest in the sport, and with a growing talent in it, I entertained the notion of making baseball a career, if not as a player, then as a coach. I knew more about the background, history, and intricacies of the sport than I knew about the background, history, and intricacies of music. I continued both tracks but seemed more consumed by baseball.

That changed in ninth grade.

Nearing the end of a game I was on first base after a single. It was the third time I had been on base and each time I had stolen second, then third base. I was not a power hitter, but I was fast. No catcher at that level could throw me out. But they tried. On the very next pitch I stole second, much to the catcher's dismay. He knew I would be going to third. He called a 'pitch out' and stepped to the right side of the plate opposite the right-handed batter. I was on my way. This time he thought he had me, but he dropped the ball! In his anger he picked it up and threw it in disgust as hard as he could. I was unaware of the drop; I was simply heading to third and slid in, safe. As I was getting up, with my second knee barely off the ground, I looked up. There was the ball, right in front of my face. He hadn't intended to throw it at me, but there it was!

They say your life flashes before your eyes in moments like that. They're right. In that split second I knew I was in trouble. The ball hit me full force right in the middle of my forehead (there were no helmets in those days). As my movement was up and toward home plate the ball didn't knock me down. I didn't feel any pain. It just ricocheted off my head and half way back to the catcher who had thrown it. Everyone watching the game froze. I froze. It seemed at that instant the life of the world had stopped, and mine along with it. There was no sound, no movement. I thought to myself,

"So this is what it's like to be dead; the last thing you saw in life stays frozen for eternity."

After a few seconds I shook my head, grinned, chuckled a little sigh of relief, and observed that the spectators sighed along with me. I wasn't dead. It appeared I wasn't even injured.

The game continued. I don't remember if I stole home on the next pitch. I don't remember who won the game. All I remembered was that I had survived a monumental hit.

After the game my mother put me to work in the back yard. I began to have a tremendous ear-ache, increasing in pain rapidly. I asked my Mother to get me some ear drops. She asked when the pain started and I explained the situation of the game.

"Ear drops are not the remedy. Go next door to Dr. Walters' house and ask his advice."

As I was climbing our fence to cross the empty lot separating our house from his, Dr. Walters pulled out of his driveway and drove down the alley.

"Get on your bike and go to the hospital," she said.

The hospital was about a half mile from our home. My mother didn't drive, so I got on my bike and made the trip, leaving the bike on the lawn outside the entrance. I told the receptionist I needed to see a doctor for my ear-ache, then waited for attention. After conferring with the attending doctor, and after he examined the x-rays, he called my mother.

"Mrs. Athnos, I'm afraid your son Gregory is going to have to stay in the hospital for a while. He has a skull fracture, concussion and brain hemorrhage."

Though I had been hit in the forehead my skull had fractured down the back, a basal skull fracture, and I was bleeding in my left ear. How had I managed to finish the game, clean the yard, and pedal to the hospital?

After several shots the pain vanished and I really felt fine. I couldn't understand why I had to stay flat on my back in that awful hospital bed. School was still in session and I wondered if I would be able to complete my studies, pass, and continue on to High School.

I had really good friends, but they weren't the three from our 'made up ball games'; these were my friends from the music program, fellow band members: Charlie, Pete, and Ron. They were wonderful. Every morning they left home early, stopped by to say 'hello' and continued on to school. After school they came back with the assignments, and we studied together. After going home for dinner they returned and stayed long past visiting hours until the assignments were completed. The nursing staff was very caring, and allowed my friends to stay until everything was done. I guess that's the virtue of a small hospital. Though I was in the hospital for weeks, my friends never missed a day, and I missed no homework.

It came time for me to go home. For several days they propped me up in bed; I had not been out of the bed my entire stay. On the day of my release they brought in a wheel chair, placed it across the room and said they'd return to help me into it. *"What's to help?"* I thought, so I slid off the bed only to find I couldn't stand up or balance. When they returned I was lying in a heap on the floor.

"Didn't anyone tell you?"

I was then informed the part of my brain that controls coordination and balance had been affected by the injury and I would have to retrain myself to stand and walk. My oldest brother Don carried me from the wheel chair into our home.

My cornet was put away in my parent's bedroom closet. The doctors had advised against continuing to play it because the pressure build-up in my head from blowing against the small bore mouthpiece of the instrument would be detrimental not only to my recovery but perhaps even to my health.

What this meant was the curtailment of both my loves. Baseball was certainly out of the picture, given my future coordination and balance problems. Music might continue to be my destination, but my transportation, the cornet, was put in permanent storage. I had counted on being able to make a decision which love would win out in the competition. Now, it was out of my hands. I had no other loves than music and baseball. What did this mean for my future?

It didn't take long to choose a course of action. Every Sunday afternoon my father would take my mother out for a two-hour ride in the country. This was a much-needed break from the action of tending to her flock of six sons, the house, and meal preparation. It was like clockwork, every Sunday. We knew the path they would take as they left the house down Crowley Court; it was the same path by which they would return. I decided that during their absence each week the cornet would be 'resurrected' from their closet. Pledging my brothers to secrecy (no mean feat in itself, as we were quite competitive with each other), I took out the instrument and spent the better part of an hour practicing. Painful at first, nonetheless I persisted week after week. The discomfort subsided slowly and I began to return to my previous competency.

My parents eventually discovered my undercover operation. Their first response was anger. I convinced them that no damage had been done; they could see that for themselves. The pain was gone. I had survived. They acquiesced.

During the summer months I regained my strength as well as my equilibrium. I had a girlfriend, Nancy, who lived about two miles away. A railroad track ran between her house and close to mine. My plan was to establish balance by walking on one of the rails, incrementally increasing distances. At first it seemed impossible even to balance in place, much less put one foot in front of the other. Though I set a goal of walking the entire two miles without falling off the rail, it was never achieved. But I succeeded in covering ever-increasing distances between the falls.

In uniform on our front lawn in La Crosse, Wisconsin

After three long months of rehabilitation managed on my own, I returned for the start of fall classes. I was in a new school, a high school. Being somewhat shy and at that point lacking in confidence of my skills compared to the upperclassmen, I sat in the last chair of the cornet section with six players ahead of me. By the end of the first day of band rehearsals the director, Mr. Baker, had elevated me to first chair, principal cornet.

I ended up with the one love that had existed from the beginning. Camille Saint-Saens' *Swan* was still afloat! The only difference was that I now possessed a far greater determination and a much deeper commitment to becoming absolutely the best musician I could be: not simply the best cornet player, but the best musician. The cornet became my transportation to a far more significant and important destination. I desired to be a teacher and a conductor. And that is exactly what I became.

CHAPTER 7

1953: College Days

High School Graduation

There was never any question but that I would attend Northwestern College in Minneapolis. Walter Reschlein, a member of our small church family, was on their Board of Directors; I couldn't disappoint him by going elsewhere. Our church camp every summer employed students and staff from Northwestern. The only school ever mentioned in my circle was Northwestern. In addition, my older brother Bob had attended for two years before joining the Air Force, and raved about his experience. I had met some of his friends, Bill McKee and Hoopy McConkey (yes, that was his name), and thought my passage would be somewhat smoother simply because of those connections.

I never applied anywhere else, though I did visit the campus of

Trinity College in a downtrodden section of Chicago. It was grim. My direction was set: I was going to be a music major at that small, Christian college in Minneapolis.

After the first week of the fall semester I once again was assigned the first chair trumpet position in the College Band and was selected for the College Choir. Everything seemed pointed in the right direction.

Billy Graham was just beginning his International Crusade Ministry. He had been the President of Northwestern for a few years prior to my attendance, and his ministry headquarters was just a few blocks from the campus. Dr. Graham recorded his radio programs in our auditorium, and I was privileged to be trumpet soloist a number of times during my years at the college. George Beverly Shea, Cliff Barrows, and Dr. Graham were impressive in every way, and I feel blessed to have been invited to participate in their ministry in my own small way.

My very limited association with Billy Graham is one of the few highlights of my four years at Northwestern College. Another was my trumpet and voice teacher; Oliver Mogck was as fine a person as I have ever met and was a constant encouragement to me. As it turned out, there was a second equally supportive faculty member, Don Bisdorf, who conducted the Concert Band. He also started the *Carollons,* a small, seven member vocal/instrumental ensemble. We performed many of his sacred arrangements, and traveled extensively. Oliver Mogck and Don Bisdorf, with whom I worked most closely throughout my college days, were the people who made my life at the school at least a bit tolerable.

My piano teacher, a third great influence, was another story altogether. Reuben Johnson was a brilliant musician, to be sure, but his teaching style, at least in my case, was unique and often maddening. My baseball accident four years earlier had made playing the piano quite difficult for me. I could easily read the music, but when the signals left my brain they were scrambled before reaching the proper fingers. The brain injury had detrimentally affected my coordination, even to the use of my fingers; I always had trouble buttoning buttons. To think about the buttons was to make it impossible; if I didn't think about it the process was sometimes easier. That technique didn't transfer to my piano playing.

Mr. Johnson couldn't quite understand my problem. Neither could I. I only knew that after the baseball injury everything had changed. Try as I might, I couldn't do what he wanted of me. I didn't mind his or my frustration; it was his piano teaching methodology that drove me crazy.

He would stand behind me and grab a handful of my hair with his right hand.

"Play, boy. Don't look at the keys. Don't speed up. Don't slow down."

He always called me 'boy', never my name, at least not at first. I would begin playing. With a sudden, jerking motion he would pull my hair, causing my head to twist to one side or the other.

"Stop, boy. Did you look at the keys?"

"Yes, Mr. Johnson."

He had me stand up.

"Put one foot on the floor and one knee on the piano bench."

The ritual would begin again, only to be interrupted by another jerking of my head and hair.

"Stop, boy. Did you speed up?"

"Yes, Mr. Johnson."

Now he had me kneel with both knees on the piano bench. It was difficult to maintain my balance and reach the keyboard. Another jerking of my head led to another posture, this time putting one knee on the bench and the other on the writing desk of a chair that was slightly higher than the bench. The hair pulling continued.

"Stop, boy. Did you slow down?"

"Yes, Mr. Johnson."

He would go to a window, pull the cord of the wide venetian blinds, placing them in a horizontal position, reach through and extract a wooden ruler from the sill.

"Hold your hands out, boy; palms down."

Whack, whack, whack.

"OK, boy. Go to a practice room and stay there until you can play this piece without looking, slowing down, or speeding up. Then come back."

Lesson after lesson it was the same. Finally, in complete frustration I said,

"Mr. Johnson, I'm paying you for one half-hour lesson per week, and I don't want one minute more!"

He mellowed, took me out for a Coke and said,

"Do you know why I do this to you, Greg? (It was the first time he called me by name.) It's because you're talented—greatly talented. I don't do this to anyone else—just you."

That was nice to hear, but my lessons never changed, and I didn't improve. It wasn't that I didn't want to play the piano; it was that my brain condition didn't allow it. Mr. Johnson, in the most profound way a man of great heart, compensated and supported my musical efforts in other ways. He recommended me to several churches in need of an interim choral director, and hired me as lead trumpet in orchestras accompanying major choral works in his church. Deep down I knew even through those moments of frustration that he truly cared about me as a person as well as a musician. He was one of the few at Northwestern College that gained my trust. I admired him immensely; I grew to respect him, but I never liked those sessions in his studio. My hair, whatever is left of it, still hasn't forgiven him!

Years later I would meet Mr. Johnson again in Rockford, Illinois, following a performance by my North Park College Chamber Singers. Our conversation seemed to pick up right where we had left off while I was a student under his tutelage. His interest in my life and career had not wavered, not one bit. He wanted to know everything that had transpired in the intervening years. His was a genuine interest and it was clear he was proud of what I had become. I remember thanking him for his patience and encouragement during my college days, even mentioning the infamous piano lessons. We had a chuckle over that. My admiration and respect for him was confirmed that night, and I'm pleased we had the opportunity, as it was the last time I would see him.

I was not happy at Northwestern, and thought of changing schools at the end of my freshman year. The choral director, William

Berntsen, got wind of my intention and called me in for a conference. I told him I didn't think my education there would prepare me for a good job when I graduated. My goal was to be a teacher and a conductor. He made a promise to me:

"If you stay here at Northwestern I'll make sure you get the finest recommendation for a job and I'll personally assist you in finding one. I don't want to lose you; I need you here."

I stayed, and while I never was happy there, I relied on his promise. In my senior year I was elected President of the College Choir. That put me in the position of being the assistant to the director. But Mr. Berntsen never utilized me; he preferred to work with a younger student, a friend of mine, whose father was quite prominent in the Christian musical community. Though the student was a good musician it was a political move, and Mr. Berntsen didn't seem concerned over what that did to me.

Later in my senior year I asked for his support in looking for a job and giving me advise. He came back several weeks later with the prospect of a church job in Dallas, Texas, where I would be the assistant to the Music and Worship Director.

"Mr. Berntsen, I told you I was not interested in full time church ministry. I want to teach."

"If you don't take this job you're on your own. No more help from me."

I applied on my own for a school music position in Viroqua, Wisconsin, and then decided to go to graduate school. I didn't hold out much hope for being accepted because Northwestern College was not accredited; what decent music school would accept a student from such an institution? As long as I was going to attempt graduate studies I felt I should apply to the school I thought was the

1953: College Days

best in the Midwest: the University of Michigan. I expected rejection. They accepted me.

I graduated from Northwestern and very happily put those four years in my rear view mirror. Several years after I graduated, Northwestern College closed its doors because of a split over theology, and would not be 'resurrected' until many years later. It has since become a highly successful college. I only wish it had been, in my day, what it is today.

Northwestern College Graduation Photo

As with Reuben Johnson, I would meet Mr. Berntsen again when I returned to the new campus of Northwestern College. He was now the President. More than three decades had passed since I left determined never again to set foot on the grounds. In my heart of hearts I knew I needed to make my peace with the place and with him. I sought him out. Much to my chagrin and disappointment he expressed no interest in me as a person or as a professional. He asked nothing about what I had done since leaving Northwestern. My life, my family, my career never entered our conversation. Indeed, it was not a conversation; it was a sales pitch based upon what he had accomplished and what he wanted me to contribute to his endeavors. I know he deserves enormous credit for rescuing the future of the college and leading it to become a highly respectable institution, but I left with the same emptiness and disappointment I had while a student in my last year under his care. The sadness of that unfortunate conclusion remains with me.

Looking back, one often sees what was positive even in a negative situation. Oliver Mogck, Don Bisdorf, and Reuben Johnson were the 'saviors' in what was otherwise an unhappy four years. Yes, the promise that kept me at Northwestern College was broken. Yes, the school's lack of accreditation was a barrier. At the time it added up to a gigantic burden and hurdle. Now I see it differently. If I had not been there I wouldn't have met my first wife, who came to the school after graduating from the University of Michigan. Her influence caused me to apply for graduate studies at that prestigious institution. It was there I would find a part-time church choir position and be 'discovered' by the Covenant Church, and later be hired by that denomination's college in Chicago. There, after a painful divorce, I would meet Doy and my life would be wonderfully changed.

I'm sure that if I had left Northwestern my life, whatever it might have become, would have been rewarding and fulfilling. I would never have known anything else, and would have been content in whatever successes came my way. But having experienced life as it has unfolded, I can't imagine a more wonderful adventure.

Do I feel my unhappy years at Northwestern were part of an eternal 'plan'? Yes, without any doubt whatsoever.

CHAPTER 8

1958: "Are There Any Questions?"

He was a master teacher, Professor Hitchcock. Students lined up to take his courses, one of which was a requirement for my University of Michigan doctoral studies. Amazing to me was that students not a part of the program would risk taking and failing his course simply to sit under the masterful teaching of this campus legend. A course intended for about a dozen students ended up being held in a lecture hall seating nearly a hundred students. Being new to the campus I was unaware of the near mythic status surrounding the professor when I entered the hall for the first class.

The room was packed. An undercurrent of buzzing anticipation swirled around the room. Then he entered. The room fell silent, almost breathless. I was caught up in the intensity of it all. What happened next was radical, stunning, and brilliant.

Normally a class begins with the professor introducing himself and the course, pointing out the syllabus, the required texts and the first assignment. At least that is what I had experienced throughout my educational career. Not this day. His entrance and the ensuing silence held firm. It was as if we were suspended in mid-air uncomfortably waiting for some sort of soft landing. He stood there on that slightly raised platform in front of a sea of rapt faces, looking slowly across the room almost row by row, not saying a word. Finally, after what seemed a moment frozen timelessly, he spoke.

"Are there any questions?" Silence.

I don't know about the others; I only can speak for myself and for what was rolling around inside my own mind: "Questions? How can there be any questions when we haven't even been given the first of the anticipated answers regarding the course of study?" The stillness of the room remained unbroken, awkwardly. *"Will someone please speak up?",* I thought to myself. Nothing.

Professor Hitchcock looked around the room a second time, again slowly.

"Very well," he said, *"if there are no questions there can't possibly be any answers."* Turning abruptly, he left the room.

No one moved. No one spoke. Gradually, one by one, we got up and left, remaining in a shocked silence as the room emptied.

The next day, on a campus of nearly 30,000 students you could tell which one hundred were in Hitchcock's class. There we were, huddled in groups of three or four, or six or eight, scattered around the campus lawn or in snack shops, asking each other the same questions:

"What kind of questions should we be asking?" "What's important

about this class?" "What do we want to know?" "What do we need to know?"

It was time for the second class period and the room had the same electric, anticipatory, static silence as had been the atmosphere the first day. People often suggest the possibility of a deafening silence, and here we were, caught up in such a vortex. The professor entered the room and, just as had been his behavior the first day, stood silently on the platform surveying the multitude of faces. I wondered if he noticed anything different while he stared us down. Again, he broke the spell:

"Are there any questions?"

One hundred hands shot up instantly. He pointed to one of us, fielded the question, and the class took incredible flight. One by one the questions elicited answers calculated to draw us into an intensity of learning that was nearly miraculous in the energy pulsating back and forth like surf and undertow between the platform and the room. Questions and the subsequent answers generated more questions, building stone upon stone throughout the entire duration of the course until a gigantic cathedral of understanding had been erected. Here a pillar, there an opening for light, inside a central aisle directed toward the chancel of understanding, buttresses being established by the professor to hold up the counter-thrust from the cascading roof of inquiry. It was absolutely masterful.

"Are there any questions?"

The professor's provocative primer for educational success threw me back twelve years to the sidewalk in front of Terry's home, with his Mom's broken English piercing the air between their home and the corner: *"Vhat gut qvestions did you ask t'day?"* What I didn't really understand then I understood now in this doctoral class at the university. The confirmation of the secret to knowledge and understanding, so much a part of Terry's life, now became an important part of mine: the willingness and the ability to ask a good question. How magnificent.

CHAPTER 9

Reflections: What a Poet and the Apostle's Creed Told Me

The world is charged with the grandeur of God.
It will flame out, like shining from shook foil;
It gathers to a greatness, like the ooze of oil
Crushed. Why do men then now not reck his rod?
Generations have trod, have trod, have trod;
And all is seared with trade; bleared, smeared with toil;
And wears man's smudge and shares man's smell: The soil
Is bare now, nor can foot feel, being shod.
And for all this, nature is never spent;
There lives the dearest freshness deep down things;
And though the last lights off the black West went
Ah morning, at the brown brink eastward, springs—
Because the Holy Ghost over the bent
World broods with warm breast and with ah! Bright wings.
(Gerard Manley Hopkins, 1844-1889, "God's Grandeur")

The Apostles' Creed begins with the words, *I believe in God, the*

Father almighty, Creator of heaven and earth.... This succinct affirmation of God's handiwork in creation, in and of itself, provides a basis for a Christian view of art. Why? Because God in His wisdom created a material world—a world of sight, sense, touch, movement, and matter—all of creation becomes a worthy vehicle through which the truth about the Creator can be communicated. Our human dilemma is that we often remain unaware. We don't see God all around us, perhaps because we don't expect to see Him. The 'feet' of our minds are kept clean of the glorious 'mud' of things by virtue of being (metaphorically) shod. The Scriptures assure us that if we seek Him we'll surely find Him. Here, in creation itself, is a worthy and fertile field for artists dedicated to making Christ known. The first step is to remove the shoes of our blindness, the sandals of our reluctance, and begin to wallow in the 'stuff', the wonder of God's handiwork.

Caedmon, a late 7th century monk, wrote this Hymn, challenging us to make the Creator God known through His handiwork:

> *Now must we hymn heaven's Guardian,*
> *Might of the Maker and his mind's wisdom,*
> *Work of the glorious Father; how he, eternal Lord,*
> *Made the beginning of every wonder.*

Out of His own being, His own Spirit, God created in love all there is in the material universe. I believe that. Everything we see, hear, touch, taste and smell has within it both the remembrance and distilled essence of the Divine Creator.

Michelangelo's Sistine Chapel fresco of *The Creation of Adam* says it most powerfully. Picture it in your mind; I know you can—the spun energy of God and the coiled anticipation of Adam become fused at the point of fingertips. It is a slender point of continuity between Eternal God and Temporal Man, but speaks with forceful eloquence of Divine intention, Divine intervention, and Divine destiny: God has made from Himself a living soul! From His Spirit He has breathed into our flesh the breath of life. The two, spirit and flesh, have become 'One', and their union, as God said, was 'good'. Hear this: God declared from the very beginning the 'oneness' of flesh and spirit, the 'oneness' of mind and heart, the 'oneness' of the material world and the spiritual dimension, the 'oneness' of faith and reason.

In other words, God has given us all that makes us truly human. Yes, we are *physical creatures*, but our flesh is our housing, a container, only that. All our other attributes come from the spiritual nature of God Himself; they are His gifts to us. How ludicrous it is that we humans expend so much energy and money on the packaging, rather than the gifts it contains!

We are *intellectual creatures*—we have minds of tremendous potential.

We are *emotional creatures* who respond in pleasure and joy, or sadness and anger—a whole range of feelings—through all we experience around us.

We are *spiritual creatures*—we possess the sense that we have come from something much bigger, much greater than ourselves, something we cannot see, or measure, or even define clearly; but we know in our hearts it exists.

And we are *aesthetic creatures*—God Himself was the creative artist who made all things from Himself and nothing else. He created us in His image, and endowed us with the gift of that same creative spirit, as well as the gift to be 'touched' or 'moved' by created beauty. Through this creative spirit, I believe, we have our deepest understanding of the creative mind of God. We artists undertake the struggle of creativity: facing the challenging five-line staff or the formidable stone, or searching for the elusive word. Then, more than others, we are allowed to peer into the mind of the One who by His word alone brought everything into magnificent being.

My dog is also a physical creature. Like me, Jeeves has an intellect. He is emotional; he has feelings, and lets me know through his countenance and actions what he's experiencing. This is where our common attributes stop. My dog is missing two things that humans possess: the spiritual and aesthetic dimensions. These two attributes are what separate humans from other forms of animal life; they are what make us unique and different. Knowing this, it follows that we are only really, truly, fully human to whatever extent we exercise those differences—the spiritual and aesthetic.

In our growing arrogance, in our increasing separation from God, in our scientific age, we have split these attributes apart. Often we have pitted the physical, emotional, and intellectual against the spiritual and aesthetic, thinking that the physical and material side of each equation is all we need. One camp, the secular, declares that *empiricism*, or 'knowability' is the only basis for truth: if you can't prove it, it isn't worth considering. More recently, in our Post-Modern age, *empirical* truth itself has been cast aside; individuals have become cocooned in their own truth—truth is what they say it is. The other camp, most often those who call themselves Evangelical Christians, sees little need for evidence beyond the certainty of the heart. This was not God's intention in His creation: flesh and spirit, faith and reason, and the five human attributes were made 'One'.

Why is reconciliation between these warring worlds so difficult?

CHAPTER 10

1958: Joining the Covenant Church

In 1958, while I was a first year graduate student at the University of Michigan, my twin sons, Erik Timothy and Jonathan Gregory, were born. We were living with my in-laws at the time, half way between Ann Arbor and Detroit. Needing some additional income to help support my family, and not wanting to discontinue my studies, I took a position as Worship Leader/Choir Director in a local Baptist Church. Forty dollars a week wasn't much, but it helped. I also inquired about substitute teaching in that same town, and my name was put on their list of prospects. Both these endeavors would end up playing a significant role in my life.

That fall, two weeks into the new school year, my second at the university, I decided to check on my status as a substitute teacher. When I walked into the Personnel Office the supervisor looked at me and inquired,

"Don't I know you? Weren't you here a few months ago asking about subbing? Just twenty minutes ago one of our instrumental music teachers resigned. Are you interested in the position?"

So began my career as an instrumental music teacher! My assignment was in five Elementary Schools, recruiting and teaching young students how to play the various band instruments. I had completed one full year of Grad School, and decided to continue completion of the degree in Summer School.

Over the next eight years my public school teaching position would change, first taking up a Middle School Band program while continuing in several Elementary Schools. The last four years I became the assistant to the High School Band and Choral programs while retaining the Middle School Band. My undergraduate music degree had been in Choral Music. At Michigan I was pursuing an advanced degree in Instrumental Music. My Public School teaching experience now covered both fields. That would be critical to the next phase of my life.

The Church Worship Leader position at the Baptist Church had not been rewarding. I loved my work with the choir, but had misgivings about the Pastor, to the degree that it became important for me to abandon the job. But I needed the income. What was I to do?

Unknown to me, the Detroit Evangelical Covenant Church a few miles away was looking for its first paid Choral Director. Arthur Elander was a member of the Covenant Church denomination, but was serving as Choral Director in a large Lutheran Church. The Detroit congregation approached him about the job. He declined.

I knew of Art. He was the Supervisor of Choral Music in the school system where I was employed. I had never heard of the Evangelical Covenant Church, therefore I was not aware of their search.

1958: Joining the Covenant Church

Art told them he knew of this young musician, an Evangelical Christian, who had recently been employed by the school district. He gave them the location of my church.

"Before you talk with him, check him out to see if you like what he does."

I had no idea this was happening. The Detroit Covenant Church Chairman, Floyd Johnson, came one Sunday to 'spy' on me. The next week he called and offered me the position. I knew nothing about his church or his denomination, but at the same time felt this was another 'answer' to my dilemma. I told him I'd think about it.

The next week I decided to 'spy' on them! On Wednesday night I went to the church after their Choir rehearsal had begun and sat outside the door, listening. No one knew I was there. I liked the potential I heard. Their accompanist, Ruby Anderson, was excellent. I later learned she had her Master's in Organ from the University of Michigan, where I was a student. I liked the church building itself, and the wonderful pipe organ in the sanctuary. The only drawback was the seventeen-mile drive from my home. That turned out to be a small price to pay for leaving my questionable position at the Baptist church.

I accepted the position, and my 'new' church home became a blessing to me. Not only did the choir grow in size, it also grew in quality. My family was completely embraced by the congregation. For the next eight years our life in the Covenant Church would be filled with good friends and great spiritual and personal rewards.

Eat in Harmony

Detroit Evangelical Covenant Church Choir (1965)

This would not have happened without my walking into a school district Personnel Office twenty minutes after a resignation. Again I ask: coincidence, or Providence?

CHAPTER 11

1965: A Stunning Summer in Europe

Excitement was building for our first trip to Europe, traveling on our own for five weeks. In order to squeeze all the countries we hoped to visit into our time frame I arranged to fly from place to place. SAS offered a round-trip package from Copenhagen to Athens and back at a very reasonable price. It allowed us to stop at any city on the general flight path without advance reservations or additional charges. We could stop and go as we pleased. Flying instead of taking the train saved many hours otherwise wasted in travel, and the result was like adding two or three extra days to our trip. We also planned to fly at meal times, and this was a great savings. We would eat well on the flights, perhaps better than the meals we'd take on land.

The SAS package would begin following our travel to Norway, Sweden, Finland, and the Soviet Union. We arranged to travel on a Scandinavian Airlines charter flight from New York to Oslo, and would drive to New York with friends from our church in Detroit.

The Soviet Union had just opened up its borders to Americans, allowing visits for the first time since the Kennedy assassination two years earlier. It had been a tense two years preceded by the 'fingers on the red buttons' over the Cuban missile crisis. Kennedy's death fueled speculation that the Russians had something to do with it. Krushchev was filmed pounding his shoe on the table at the United Nations, shouting, *"We will bury you."* He was still in power during our initial plans but was deposed in October, 1964. People wondered why we would even want to go to the Soviet Union, much less be brave enough to risk it. I couldn't give them an answer; I didn't really know why. I simply wanted to see Leningrad and experience a bit of the Soviet Union for myself. What was it like to be a *Shostakovitch* or *Prokofieff* under an artistically repressive system? Questions; I had questions.

Visas were necessary. I wrote to the Soviet Embassy in Washington D.C. asking for the proper materials, which they sent. I completed the complex forms and mailed them back along with our Passports. It was two months before our New York departure: plenty of time. We continued to refine our plans for the rest of Europe.

Three weeks before our departure I had received nothing. I called. They assured me they were working on it. One week later I became quite nervous and called again. This time they looked up my file, returned to the phone, and said:

"You sent us the wrong application form."

"I sent you the form you sent me!"

"Well, it is not the proper form. We'll send you another."

"I only have two weeks."

1965: A Stunning Summer in Europe

"No problem. We'll take care of it."

Two days later the new forms arrived, I completed them and sent them *Special Delivery* back to the Soviet Embassy.

Early in the week leading up to our departure I called them again.

"Sir, at this point I don't care if you issue Visas for the Soviet Union or not. I need my Passports to leave the country. There isn't enough time for you to mail them to my home. I'm driving to New York, leaving tomorrow. I need you to send them to JKF airport in New York," and gave them the information.

Our drive to New York was fraught with anxiety. I called SAS several times each day to see if the Passports had arrived. They had not. I called when we arrived Saturday evening. No luck.

Arne Jennings, a service rep for SAS immediately took charge. He called the Soviet Embassy at midnight, woke up one of their agents and explained the situation. He was informed that the Visa and Passports had been mailed *Special Delivery* to the proper address.

We arrived at 3 p.m. on Sunday for the 6 p.m. charter flight. Nothing. We were in trouble. Without Passports we couldn't leave the country. Without them we would also lose our flight payments. It was a charter flight; miss it at your own peril and loss.

Boarding time was delayed for an hour. That was a hopeful sign; it gave us another hour to wait for the *Special Delivery* package. Shortly after 6:30 p.m. a carrier ran to the gate shouting,

"Special Delivery for Athnos."

57

We were elated! Opening the package we found the Visas necessary to enter the Soviet Union, but not our Passports! We couldn't leave the country. Our charter flight left without us. The once busy gate now held two extremely forlorn and stranded passengers.

Arne Jennings arranged a hotel for us and scheduled a regular flight the next evening direct to Bergen, Norway, which was to have been our first destination after arriving in Oslo on the charter. Sunday night was tough. We had missed our flight. We would have to buy tickets for the new flight. We were a day behind schedule.

We spent Monday in Manhattan. Michelangelo's early *Pietá* was on loan for the New York World's Fair; it was the first of many occasions I would stand in front of that masterpiece.

Back at the terminal another package arrived; it contained our Passports. We had been cursing the Soviet Embassy for screwing up our plans. Not only that, they had made the previous two months miserable. Now we discovered they had done what they promised to do. Following my call some days earlier they had sent the Passports *Registered Mail* while they continued working on the Visas. When the Passports arrived at Jamaica Post Office, New York, on Saturday morning, one of the clerks didn't 'register' it or put it in the mail to be delivered that day. It was put in the regular mail for Monday delivery. The Visas, sent *Special Delivery*, had arrived in time for the flight.

The package we received on Monday contained the following letter from Vladimir Sinitsyn, Attaché to the Soviet Embassy. It was dated June 25, 1965:

> EMBASSY OF THE
> UNION OF SOVIET SOCIALIST REPUBLICS
> CONSULAR DIVISION
> 1609 DECATUR STREET, N. W.
> WASHINGTON, D. C.

SAS
Customers Service
Kennedy Intl Airport
New York

June 25, 1965

Gentlemen:

Enclosed please find passports of Mr. & Mrs. Gregory Athnos which we are sending on their request.
It is our understanding that the Athnos couple is leaving the USA by SAS plane on June 27.
We will appreciate it if you keep their passports which will be picked up some time this weekend.

Sincerely,

Vladimir A. Sinitsyn
Attache

Letter from the Soviet Embassy

"Gentlemen: Enclosed please find passports of Mr. and Mrs. Gregory Athnos which we are sending on their request. It is our understanding that the Athnos couple is leaving the USA by SAS plane on June 27. We will appreciate it if you keep their passports which will be picked up some time this weekend."

In the end it was not the Soviets who messed things up; it was our own U. S. Postal Service!

Arne Jennings gave us the tickets for the new flight: $600! That was a considerable sum in 1965. Arne said,

"SAS will send you a bill. You'll get it when you return home after your travels. Don't pay it. It wasn't your fault. It wasn't our fault. It was the fault of the Post Office. Please don't think twice about not paying it. I'm already working to take it off the books. Have a great time in Europe."

We arrived in Bergen only a few hours later than our original plan had specified. The trip began, and it would be filled with 'wonders' and 'providential accidents', marvelous beyond our imaginations.

CHAPTER 12

1965: Sibelius in a Vegetable Garden

Where was it? We had arrived in Helsinki, the fourth country on our five-week venture in Europe. It was late evening. We were looking for the *Satakuntatalo Hotel*, which was really just a student dormitory in a residential area. The hill we were climbing was a bit steep and our luggage (no wheels in those days) was a bit heavy. We couldn't read the street signs and had no idea if we were even in the right part of Helsinki.

A tall, muscular Finn asked if we needed help. After telling him where we were headed he picked up our luggage, all of it, and charged up the hill. A quarter of a mile later he knocked on the door, informed the proprietor of our reservation, smiled and gave us a warm 'good bye' along with best wishes for a pleasant stay, and walked back down the hill. It was apparent he hadn't been going in this direction but simply acted in a gesture of good will. His kindness set the tone for a remarkable two days before we would leave Finland for the Soviet Union.

Finland was more than a jumping off point for the next leg of our trip. True, we had come here because it was the best way, perhaps the only way for us to cross the heavily guarded border into the country formerly known as Russia. Two days here suggested another reason behind our coming. My wife was of Finnish descent; this was a 'homecoming' of sorts for her. We also were in the land of Jean Sibelius, and for me as a professional musician that held a great attraction. Actually, my wife had been drawn to his music before me, so we together had hoped to find his home in the countryside before leaving Finland.

The next morning we intended to find our way on our Sibelius pilgrimage. To my dismay I would be the only pilgrim, as she decided to go shopping instead. Doubly disappointing: I would be a solo venturer and she would be spending money we didn't have.

I went to the bus station seeking directions to the home of Sibelius. I was told that his home, *Ainola*, was in the middle of a forest near Lake Tunsula, Järvenpää. The ticket agent wrote out directions in Finnish, telling me to give it to the driver. Before departure I purchased two pastries, then entered the bus. We set out, slowly leaving Helsinki behind and traveling on a two-lane road cut through the dense and lush forests that seemed to encroach upon the road itself.

I have no memory of the time or the distance we traveled, but eventually the driver stopped the bus and motioned for me to come forward. In halting English, and pointing, he said,

"Take path into woods. Soon you find home. I return this way one hour. If you by road I take to Helsinki." Leaving me roadside he journeyed on.

The Finnish woods were thick and beautiful. The light filtered through the trees more like a painting than anything I had ever seen. Years earlier I had been struck by these same images and felt the same emotions while viewing Ingmar Bergman's black and white films in Ann Arbor, *Wild Strawberries* in particular, where forests come alive with prismatic, filtered light, a pulsing *chiaroscuro*.

I soon came to a clearing. A garden was in front of me and to my left up a tree-filled knoll was a large home.

"This must be the place."

The path wound itself around the garden. Just past it was the stone, the gravestone of Sibelius, who had passed away eight years earlier. Large and rectangular, nearly flat against the ground, it held the raised bronze letters JEAN SIBELIUS. I sat on one of the benches, took out the pastries, and began mentally playing the familiar themes of his music while devouring the sweets.

Two of Sibelius' compositions played in my tonal memory. They both were bittersweet, a fitting contrast to my happy taste buds, and a portent of what I would be experiencing after crossing tomorrow's heavily armed and guarded borders into the Soviet Union.

The first was a *symphonic poem*—written in 1899 and revised in 1900—intended as a disguised protest against Russia. Titles under which the composition masqueraded were numerous in order to keep the piece from musical censorship; *Finlandia* would have been too obvious to the Russian censors. The turbulence of the first two thirds of the music reflects the national struggle of the Finnish people against the pre-Bolshevik Russians, finally giving way to the peaceful, hymn-like melody that has become familiar around the world. So familiar, in fact, that while it is one of the most important of the national songs of Finland it had also been converted into a Christian hymn, *Be Still My Soul*.

It was the final hymn-like portion that played in my head at the gravesite of the composer. I remembered not only the melody, but also the words of the Christian hymn:

> *Be still my soul, the Lord is on Thy Side!*
> *Bear patiently the cross of grief or pain;*
> *Leave to thy God to order and provide;*
> *In every change He faithful will remain.*
> *Be still my soul: thy best, thy heavenly friend*
> *Through thorny ways leads to a joyful end.*
> *Be still, my soul: thy God doth undertake*
> *To guide the future as He has the past;*
> *Thy hope, thy confidence let nothing shake;*
> *All now mysterious shall be bright at last.*
> *Be still, my soul: the waves and winds still know*
> *His voice who ruled them while He dwelt below.*

I am a Believer, and these words resonated a clear message of stability for the troubling days ahead: not only the immediate days, but my entire future as well.

In a previous chapter I mentioned my childhood memory of *The Swan*, music that set the course for my life. Now, twenty-five years later at age twenty-nine, sitting at the gravesite of Jean Sibelius, a different swan swam in my consciousness: a dark, brooding image possessed by a haunting song of exceeding beauty. This was the *Swan of Tuonela* from the Finnish mythological underworld, an orchestral setting by the Finnish composer. The swan sings wordless music depicting everything people long for and care about in their journey from birth to death. At once sad and magnificent, *Tuonela's* swan seems to know all the travails and questions of life.

My life's journey had been initiated by the earlier swan of my childhood, where one is first attracted to the grace, the elegance, and the

1965: Sibelius in a Vegetable Garden

slow, stately, seemingly effortless movement across the surface of the water. In youthful innocence one sees that which is above the surface, where all is calm and dreamlike.

Now, at this stage of my life, approaching age thirty, I had seen a different world. Continual wars throughout the years of my life—World War II, the Korean War, and now Viet Nam—had driven me below the surface to see that all is not as it appears. The gentle journey seen by the naïve viewer belies the turbulence in the depths, turbulence that is necessary if any progress is to be made. My adult awareness intimated that comfort and conflict were partners in life. We may prefer comfort, but comfort alone produces a sedentary, unproductive existence. We eschew turbulence, because a completely turbulent life becomes self-destructive. Where was the balance?

I had been content in my comfortable life with a good job, good family, good friends, and satisfying pleasure at my fingertips. Approaching that often-troubling thirtieth year I had begun to wonder what my future held in store. Would I simply continue being a successful public school music teacher? If so, would I be content? Was there something more, waiting for me to discover it? Would I be bold enough to grab it if and when it presented itself, or would I take the comfortable, easy road? And if I grabbed it would I have the talent, skill, and discipline to excel? Would the turmoil associated with change be tolerable to me? Sitting here, the pastries now but a memory, the sweetness of my life heretofore was also a shadow of things past. What would Sibelius' *Tuonela swan* have seen of my future concerns?

This was a more difficult tune than the hymn of *Finlandia*. The plaintive melody of an English Horn glides across turbulent waters, and its double reed sadness is evocative of death itself. No wonder so many composers use that instrument in their darkest depictions! The impossible quests imbedded in much of the mythology of Finland surface in this instrument, in this piece. *Lemminkäinen*, the hero in the *Kalevala* epic, fails in his quest for a beautiful maiden, overcome by the even greater, turbulent beauty of the *Swan of Tuonela,* the swan of death.

What was the immediate beauty of life I was seeking? Would it be overcome by an even more profound beauty, one of which I was now completely unaware? Where would it lead? All was frustratingly elusive, even in my reverie. The dark *Tuonela* melody persisted as the scene played out.

My quixotic inner visions of the two compositions were interrupted by a figure leaving the house on the knoll. An elderly woman was making her way down to the vegetable garden I had passed earlier. I watched. She was not aware of my presence. On impulse, I stood and made my way toward the garden, timing my walk so as to intersect her path as we both approached.

She smiled at me and we attempted a conversation. I told her how thrilled I was to have found this place, how moved I was to sit at the gravesite of Jean Sibelius and think of his music. She smiled even wider. Then she spoke.

Aino Sibelius, wife of Jean Sibelius

1965: Sibelius in a Vegetable Garden

She was the composer's wife, Aino: Aino Järnefelt Sibelius. The composer had named his home after his wife: Aino, *Ainola*! We talked about her husband for a time, with great joy for me, and pleasure for her as she expressed delight in my interest.

But now I had to get back to the road.

Aino Sibelius died four years later. She had been in her 90's when we spoke in the vegetable garden. Sibelius' home became a museum, having been designated as such in 1974. Tour buses descend on it year round, but it had been hard to get to in 1965, and I was the only one there. The solitude had been perfect.

I left for the Soviet Union the next morning, prepared for the unexpected through my meditations on the melodies of the famous composer, encouraged by the words of the *Finlandia* hymn, and open to whatever dark or glorious beauty lay ahead. The second swan of my memory had become a perfect companion to the first. The gentle sweetness of Saint-Saens' *Swan* was still my desire. Knowing that, I could tread with Sibelius' swan the *Tuonela* waters of turbulent beauty, come what may.

My two days in Finland had been bookended by kindnesses, beginning with the anonymous, tall, muscular stranger who climbed a hill and settled our nerves. Then, my last moments in the Finnish forest, with the calm, serene Aino Sibelius. Those treasured moments convinced me that life with all its twists and turns still leads to a lovely, ageless serendipity.

What I experienced at the gravesite of Sibelius—the two haunting melodies, the words, questions of the future, my future—led to a year of great turbulence and unexpected transition. It was the year of my 30th birthday and the year when every aspect of my life as a musician would change. What I was born for, soon to be discovered, would embrace me fully and never let me go. It was just as the *Finlandia* hymn text had said,

> *Thy hope, thy confidence let nothing shake;*
> *all now mysterious shall be bright at last.*

CHAPTER 13

1965: On Stage With the Wagners in Bayreuth

It came in the mail, December, 1964. A typed note was stapled to a brochure labeled *Bayreuth 1965*. It read: *"Tickets for all performances are completely sold out since months ago."*

That was not good news. Since my graduate student days at the University of Michigan I had become an ardent fan of the music of Richard Wagner. I breathed his music, I reveled in its power, I marveled at its revolutionary nature. I became eager to delve more deeply into both the craft and the emotion of his music, and began doing so.

The five-week European tour I had planned for the next summer had been centered around attending performances of the composer's *Der Ring des Nibelungen*, commonly called the *Ring Cycle,* in Bayreuth, Germany, site of its first performance in 1876. Needless to say, I was crushed by the bad news.

Part of my interest in the *Ring Cycle* emerged from my understanding of the Judeo-Christian Scriptures with their accounts of *Creation*, the *Fall*, and *Ultimate Redemption* in the *End Times*. I was and am persuaded by those accounts. But I was also aware of Creation mythologies from other cultures, beginning with the *Gilgamesh Epic* from the 2nd Millenium BC. While there were similarities in all of them, including accounts of a great flood and global destruction, there seemed to be only one creation account that had a truly positive and hopeful conclusion, and that was the New Testament account from the Holy Judeo-Christian writings. However, because of my musical profession I was drawn to explore the Creation Epic at the root of Wagner's *Ring Cycle*.

Earliest sources for the *Ring* date to the *Norse Ragnarök*, found in the *Poetic Edda*. It described future events including a great battle culminating in the fiery death of the gods, a world submerged in water, and the rebirth of the world, all similar themes found in other epics. Several stanzas described the future to the god Odin:

It sates itself on the life-blood of fated men, paints red the powers' homes with crimson gore. Black become the sun's beams in the summers that follow, weathers all treacherous. Do you still seek to know?

Brothers will fight and kill each other, sisters' children will defile kinship. It is harsh in the world, whoredom rife—an axe age, a sword age—shields are riven—a wind age, a wolf age—before the world goes headlong. No man will have mercy on another.

What a summation of the world as we have known it since *Adam's Fall!* It is the 'stuff' of history and continues to kidnap the news headlines in our own day.

Wagner's version was drawn from a similar myth drawing its inspiration from the *Ragnarök*: the *Nibelungenlied (The Song of the Nibelungen)*, a 12th century High German poem that rose to become part of the great German 'national epic'. It is a mix of mythology and pathology that holds us in its hypnotic spell while at the same time horrifying our sensibilities. In it the world is purified, but not by *Love*—rather by violence. Unlike the Judeo-Christian Jesus Christ, its 'savior' is anything but pure; he is greatly flawed, possessed of all our well-known human frailties. Yet, in spite of his flaws he brings about the death of the 'old order'.

My disappointment in not getting tickets was no small matter. I was determined to continue my pursuit of Wagner's work in whatever way I could. Perhaps just being in Bayreuth and standing outside his *Festspielhaus* would bring me some measure of consolation; that became my substitute plan. We re-invented our strategy. Our arrival in Bayreuth would now be just days ahead of the opening of the Festival. With that decision and our revamped itinerary we headed to Europe.

Norway and Sweden had occupied our first days. Then Finland and Sibelius. Following a nerve-wracking border crossing on a bus filled with Finns we entered into the Soviet Union and Leningrad for a week. It was just months after the Kennedy assassination, and we were among the first Americans allowed in. Back to Helsinki and by air into West Berlin, following the flight design of the plan that had broken the Berlin blockade after World War II. I spent one evening at *Checkpoint Charlie* talking with the American soldiers stationed at that critical junction between East and West Berlin. They amused themselves by holding up Playboy centerfolds to the binocular-wielding East German guards who were quick on the draw when the salacious photos were unveiled. We crossed into the eastern zone, showing our documents to those same guards, and wandered the nearly abandoned, rubble-strewn, pockmarked streets under Soviet control. The *Berlin Wall* was still being constructed, having been initiated in 1961 supposedly to keep Fascist elements from 'corrupting' the new East German State; in truth the wall was built to counteract the enormous flood of citizens fleeing to the West.

The contrast between East and West Berlin was striking, from the blight of the eastern zone to the bustling Kurfürstendam Boulevard of the west. We climbed the wooden platforms and looked over the broken glass embedded in the concrete atop the Wall into 'No Man's Land' littered with wreaths for those who had died attempting to climb the barricade into freedom, some just days before our arrival. Then we journeyed on to Nürnberg where I would have one of the most memorable experiences of my life a few days hence.

Wagner's *opus magnus* is monumental on a variety of levels. One can spend a lifetime with the work and not nearly begin to unravel its multiple strands of meaning. I had only begun to scratch the surface.

One way of approaching the work seemed the simplest: track the *Golden Ring*, from its original purity to its corrupted use, through the hands that possessed it and were destroyed by it, and finally returning to its original purity. Gold was power. The quest and greed for power led to theft and murder; multiple murders in fact. When the world had had enough the gold was returned to its primal state of innocence. That's at least one skin of the musical 'onion' known as the *Ring*.

Another was to track the essence of *Love*.

In the opening drama, 'Das Rheingold', Wagner begins with an expanding orchestral arpeggio on an **E-flat major chord** *with no modulation for 136 measures. It represents the creation of the world. Its 'Garden of Eden' is the Rhine River with the Rhinemaidens as caretakers and possessors of the gold.* **E-flat** *is, in Wagner's mind, the key of the original and pure Creation.*

Alberich, chief of the Nibelungen race of dwarfs, descends into the Rhine to acquire the gold. The Rhinemaidens tell him he may have it if he is willing to renounce Love, thinking no one would make such a decision. Love is, after all, the glue of the cosmos. Love is the stabilizing moral force of existence. Love is the source of redemption in human relationships, leading to a greater global redemption. Without Love the center cannot hold.

Alberich renounces Love. It is an 'Eden' disobedience of the moral law. The erosion of innocence begins. The 'Garden' will be abandoned. All the consequences of a world in turmoil will issue forth from his renunciation.

Alberich steals the gold. Wotan, the chief god, steals it from Alberich and gives it as payment to two giant brothers, Fasolt and Fafner, as payment for creating Valhalla, the home of the gods. Fafner wants sole ownership of the gold, kills his brother, fashions the gold into a Ring and turns himself into a dragon for the protection such a creature assures.

From this single event of Love's renunciation lies and deception, betrayal, corruption, mayhem and murder are loosed upon the world and all its inhabitants. Everyone who touches the golden ring will die. The world will need a savior. Alberich's renunciation will require sacrificial restoration. Love must in the end prevail for the salvation of the human race and all creation itself. In Wagner's conception the savior will be the flawed Siegfried, the unbeknownst grandson of the chief god Wotan. A less than perfect sacrificial love, tinged with hate, will spring forth from Brünnhilde, one of Wotan's Walküre daughters. Two purification rites, the flames of destruction—Götterdämmerung (The Twilight of the Gods)—and a watery flood will purify and re-establish Creation.

The day arrived, finally. Not only was it the middle of our five-week tour of Europe, it was also the centerpiece that formed the pinnacle event of our travel pyramid. In spite of our disappointment excitement had been building since December of the previous year, 1964.

We were going to Wagner's *Valhalla*—Bayreuth, Germany—and the *Festspielhaus*, the theater home of my favorite composer!

We had arrived in Nürnberg the previous afternoon. Our good friend from Detroit, Lt. Colonel Thomas Dixon, stationed in the military, was our host along with his wife. Tom served in the Intelligence arm of the U. S. Army. It was great to spend even these few hours with them. Unfortunately, we stayed up way too long that night catching up on 'old times'.

Morning came too quickly, and it began horribly. We overslept and missed the early morning train to Bayreuth; the next wouldn't depart Nürnberg until late morning, thus wasting half of this most precious day. How could I have let that happen?

My wife decided not to accompany me. I would be traveling alone. Strike two.

At the rail station the ticket agent refused my request for a second-class compartment; I had wanted to save some money. Also, a second-class ticket had open seating and I could choose my location. First class was considerably more than I wanted to spend and, in addition, seats were assigned. In spite of my insistence, he prevailed. Strike three.

I felt I was indeed 'out'. Nothing was as I had envisioned it for the last seven months. I felt like going back to spend the day exploring Nürnberg. Reluctantly, I boarded the train after finding the right first-class railcar. Entering the car I saw there was only one other person. Checking my seat assignment I realized the agent had placed me in the seat next to him! In an otherwise empty car! Racing through my mind were two considerations: one, find another seat—there were many to choose from. Two, sit where I was assigned. I weighed the options. This was Germany after all, known for its discipline and orderliness. If I sat in a different seat, the conductor might exercise his authority and force me to move to the proper location, causing me some degree of embarrassment—it would look like I was avoiding the person occupying the adjacent seat (which I indeed was).

If, however, I sat down next to him in a completely empty car what might he think? Would he feel it inappropriate?

I made the decision and plopped myself down right next to him. The train pulled away from the station with the two of us nestled together like 'peas in a pod', an otherwise empty pod no less.

He was seated next to the window. I faced straight ahead in silence. When Nürnberg was no longer outside the window he opened his briefcase and pulled out a *Time* magazine. "*Must be British or American,*" I gathered quietly. I decided to try to strike up a conversation; it was getting awkward sitting there in complete silence, with only the incessant rhythm of the track seams intruding on the stiffness of our space.

"*I'm going to Bayreuth. Where are you going?*"

"*Same place.*" It was a muttered response.

"*You know, the Wagner Festival begins next week.*"

"*I know.*" Again, muttering.

It was quite obvious he wasn't interested in communicating. I persisted anyway.

"*It's amazing,*" I said, "*I tried to get tickets last December, and they were already sold out for the entire festival. I couldn't believe it.*"

"I don't need tickets."

"You don't?"

"No."

"Are you involved with the Festival?"

"Yes."

I was being totally intrusive, and I knew it. He was being intentionally evasive; I knew that too. My better choice would have been to allow him his solitude, but I had gone too far to stop now.

"Are you in the orchestra? I hear it is quite wonderful."

"No."

"The chorus?"

"No."

"Well, then, what do you do?" By this time I was exasperated with his one-word answers.

"I'm singing the role of Siegmund in the Ring Cycle."

Here was one of the major roles in all of opera, requiring a great world-class singer, and I was sitting next to him!

The drama *Die Walküre*, second in the *Ring* and the only drama where *Siegmund* appears, synopsized in my mind even as he said, "Siegmund in the Ring Cycle."

Siegmund, offspring of the chief god Wotan mating with a mortal woman. Siegmund who, in the second drama of the Ring, 'Die Walküre', fled the forest storm caused by his disguised father, and pulled the imbedded sword 'Nothung' from the trunk of a tree, an event rich in foreboding for the gods. This was Siegmund, who impregnated Sieglinde not knowing she was his sister from the same parentage, or that she was betrothed to Hunding, whom she didn't love. Siegmund, killed by Hunding when the gods withheld their favor while attempting to stem the tide of their own destruction, and caused 'Nothung' to break in pieces. Siegmund, father to a child he never saw, one whose mother Sieglinde died in childbirth attended by the Walküre Brünnhilde, while giving the world its future promise in her son, the eventual savior and model for a new Creation: Siegfried.

I couldn't imagine my good fortune, and hoped he'd soon warm up to the conversation. He did. When he discovered I was a professional musician and a great fan of Richard Wagner's music, words began to flow. We talked about music and opera in general, Wagner's musical demands on singers, and a host of other related topics, including his own career. Born in Dodge City, Kansas, he began his career as a Baritone. Thinking he was more of a tenor he retrained himself for the repertoire of a *Heldentenor* ('heroic tenor' called for in Wagner's music dramas). I would later learn he was considered the premier American-born *Heldentenor* of his generation. He told me of his experiences in many opera houses of the world. I was also pleased to hear of his friendship with Dietrich Fischer-Dieskau, at the time my favorite tenor.

The train was hastening on to Bayreuth, and now I wished it would proceed more slowly; this was too good to have it end quickly.

We arrived too soon in Bayreuth and exited the train.

"Welcome back to Bayreuth, Mr. King." A small crowd had gathered

on the platform to greet him. He hadn't told me his name during our exchanges on the train. Now I learned it was James King.

James King

I thanked him for the conversation and wished him all good fortune for the next month of the Festival.

"I have the rest of the day free," he said, *"so why don't you spend your limited time here with me? I can show you exactly what you need to see before you head back this evening."*

He didn't have to ask me twice.

"Wonderful," I replied enthusiastically.

When I had been informed back in December of 1964 that tickets were no longer available I had decided to arrive here the week before the Festival began on Sunday, July 25th, guessing that the town would be alive with activity. Even without attending a performance it would be exciting to be here. Now I was about to see just how exciting it could be!

Mr. King checked into his hotel, then hailed a taxi and we headed out to the *Festspielhaus* near the edge of town.

1965: On Stage With the Wagners in Bayreuth

Bayreuth Festspielhaus

Wagner had designed it to house his operas because no other stage in Europe was large enough for what he had in mind. Some have called it Wagner's Temple, a 'church' for his 'musical religion'. Until World War II only the music of Wagner was performed here. During the war the Nazis took charge of the *Festspielhaus*. Wagner's music was used for Hitler's propaganda, and soldiers were required to attend lectures on Wagner in the hall. Bayreuth was nearly destroyed by Allied bombing, but the *Festspielhaus* was spared. At the war's end a *Festspielhaus* concert included music by Beethoven; it was the only time music other than Wagner's has been performed there.

Approaching the venerable Wagner 'shrine' we were met at one entrance by a guard. From the opening of the *Festspielhaus* in 1876 Wagner himself had declared that no one would be allowed into the theater except for performances. All other situations, including rehearsals, were to be limited to participants. For eighty-nine years that had been enforced by guards like this one.

"Good to see you again, Mr. King. Welcome back." Mr. King returned the greeting and we entered into the corridor ringing the auditorium itself.

We paused to take it in. As we stood there—Mr. King thrilled to be back, and me overcome with emotion for standing in such a hallowed space—an elderly gentleman approached us. Even at a distance I recognized him. *"I've seen his face on album covers,"* I remarked inwardly.

"Karl, Karl, come over here. I want to introduce you to a new friend of mine."

I was right. It was Karl Böhm, the great German conductor who would conduct many Wagner Festivals over the years, and was in charge this year for the first time. We shook hands. He inquired of me briefly, gave me his best welcome, and moved on.

"Birgitt, please come here. I'd like you to meet a new friend of mine."

I knew this face too, again from album covers. It was the legendary Birgitt Nilsson, the Swedish soprano who many consider to be history's greatest *Brünnhilde*, the heroine of the *Ring Cycle* and one of the most challenging roles in all of opera.

It was Brünnhilde, the favorite Walküre daughter of Wotan, responsible for bringing the bodies of noble warriors slain in battle to their eternal reward in Valhalla. Brünnhilde, who disobeyed her father and became emotionally involved with the lovers Siegmund and Sieglinde, intervening on Siegmund's behalf. This Walküre daughter attended Sieglinde while her son Siegfried was born. Her great 'aria', 'Mightiest of Miracles', spoke of the coming redemption Siegfried would bring. The same Brünnhilde who was awakened by Siegfried's kiss from her punishment of eternal sleep in the center of a ring of fire. Angry because of the death of her lover she would ultimately defy her father Wotan by calling down Loge's fire to consume the gods in their Valhalla home. She would sacrificially immolate herself in the fiery Götterdämmerung while returning the Ring to the Rhinemaidens. It was through the actions of Siegfried and Brünnhilde that Wagner's 'new world' would be born and Creation restored.

Nilsson's is a voice of great stamina; it has to be to sing over a 100-piece orchestra comprised of many brass instruments for as many hours as the role entails. It's like a laser beam with its power, reaching to the extreme upper balconies in any opera house in the world. Ms. Nilsson was a large woman, and her presence as we stood there shaking hands was both physically and emotionally intimidating, contrasting with her very warm and personable greeting to me. I thanked her for the ways her voice had thrilled me from the first time I heard it in recordings. She seemed genuinely pleased. It was again a short conversation, with Mr. King standing aside with a pleased grin on his face for the experience I was enjoying.

"Wolfgang!"

"Mozart?" Just kidding! I knew who Wolfgang was: Wolfgang Windgassen, history's most revered *Siegfried* from the *Ring Cycle*. If James King was America's finest *Heldentenor*, then Wolfgang Windgassen was the world's greatest, maintaining that distinction for his entire career and beyond. *Siegfried* is the consummate hero not only of the *Ring Cycle*, but a hero for the ages, even with his tragic flaws.

He who refashions Siegmund's broken sword 'Nothung', slays the dragon and tastes its blood. Siegfried, who understands what the birds sing and the forest whispers, following their voices to the sleeping Brünnhilde. Siegfried who, with the awakened Brünnhilde, will usher in a new era replacing the old Valhalla gods through his sacrifice and her immolation.

Siegfried, Hitler's model for the new Aryan racial supremacy based on his love of Wagner, the anti-Semite. Siegfried of the 'Siegfried Line', a supposedly impenetrable wall of defense around Germany's land acquisitions attained by sheer force, aptly named by Hitler for the 'superhero'.

The role of *Siegfried* contains about 20,000 words sung at a fever pitch with sky-scorching high notes for nearly eleven hours. That a singer can actually memorize all those words and the melodic lines that accompany them, all the while acting out a demanding choreography, is testament to the incredible capability of the human mind. Whoever sings this role becomes one of the most significant singers of his generation.

This year, in addition to the role of *Siegfried*, Wolfgang Windgassen would also sing the role of *Loge*, the god of fire in the first drama of the *Ring Cycle, Das Rheingold*. And I was talking with him here in the halls of the *Festspielhaus*!

In a span of less than ten minutes I had met some of the leading characters of Wagner's *Ring Cycle*, and about fifteen hours of the music drama had coursed through my veins in the same span. It was as if I was seeing the entire four-opera *Ring* as one would view a painting. First you comprehend the 'whole' and then proceed to its 'parts'. In music the 'parts' are observed in flowing sequence and you never comprehend the 'whole' until after-the-fact reflection. I found myself seeing it instantaneously. Remarkable.

"Would you like to see the orchestra pit?" Mr. King's question interrupted the scene as the last of the 'Wagner cast' proceeded down the corridor.

In any other theater or opera house in the world I would not have been interested. An orchestra pit is simply the space in front of and slightly below the stage where the 'accompanists', that is, the orchestra are seated. Musical theater and opera are 'voice driven'. The instrumentalists, while part of the package, are the platform from which voices are launched; voices carry the lyrics, hence they carry the 'meaning' that drives the drama. The audience sees the orchestra at the same time it sees the stage, but what happens on the stage draws the primary attention.

Here in Wagner's *Bayreuth Festspielhaus* it is different. Most of the orchestra is located *under* the stage, out of the sight lines of the audience. The stage is above the instrumentalists, not behind it. That would seem to place the orchestra in an even greater subservience to the singers. Just the opposite is true. There is a reason why the orchestra is hidden from view, and in Wagner's mind it is a psychological one. His operas, *Music Dramas* as he preferred them to be called, were in many cases intended by the composer to change your view of life and the world, not merely to 'entertain'. He had an *agenda*. What you saw on the stage was 'life' in all its reality or at least the reality he wanted you to embrace; the world evolved in your presence, and hopefully you along with it. You were to leave the theater a changed person. When the orchestra sits between you and the action it gives the impression of 'pretend' story telling, pleasurable for the short duration, but forgettable soon after as you returned to 'life' as you had always lived it.

Some say Wagner called this region below the stage—the home of the orchestra—the *mystical abyss*. Like the *Oracle at Delphi*, the 'instrumental vapors' rise from the abyss to intoxicate the *Oracle*, in this case, the singers. Thus, he treated the orchestra with greater reverence than the singers. The orchestra was the fountainhead, the wellspring from which the drama unfolded. He was quoted once as saying,

83

"Don't listen to the singers; they lie. If you want to know the truth, listen to the orchestra."

Wagner thought each instrument of the orchestra had an individual voice through its 'color'. Color is what makes a tuba and a flute sound different even when they play the same note, middle C for example, with 256 cycles or vibrations per second. He thought the *sound* of each instrument was like a vowel sound in spoken language. Since the *color* of each instrument was different from the others, he thought that difference could be considered a 'consonant'. Concisely, *sound* equals vowels, *color* equals consonants. In his opinion, then, the orchestra had a much more varied 'language' than the human voice, so that it could be even more expressive than human language. In other words, the orchestra has a vocabulary far more diverse and even richer than, let's say, Webster's Dictionary.

The orchestra achieves an even greater drama by pursuing an independent musical line that, while it indeed supports the singers harmonically, is at the same time making its own statement about 'reality'. *Leitmotifs* (leading musical motives or short themes) made orchestral independence possible. A *leitmotif* exists in Wagner's *Ring* for every person, place, object, event, and emotion in the drama. Hector Berlioz had begun this practice in *Symphonie Fantastique* by assigning an *Idée Fixe*, a fixed idea or single melodic theme to the image of 'the girl'. Every time the listener recognized the theme, 'the girl' was to come to mind. In that way Berlioz could unfold the story. Wagner carried that idea to the extreme. In the *Ring* at least eighty-three *leitmotifs* are found (some musicologists double that figure), each identifying its own object of attention. If you know them the story can be told even without words. Wagner's *Ring* could be told without the singers!

Wagner felt there should never be an attempt by the orchestra to completely blend with the singers. That Wagner succeeded in liberating the orchestra from domination by the singers is seen in the number of recordings over the ages that include the orchestral parts of his operas without the singers, even though they exist together in live performance. I have several of those recordings, and the music doesn't suffer a bit without the singers' lines.

Another evidence in support of the supremacy of the orchestra is borne out in Wagner's analogy of the 'musical sea'. He compared the singers' vocal lines to an open boat on the clear waters of a lake (the orchestra). The 'boat' is an object completely different from the 'lake', yet it has been crafted entirely for use on the 'lake' and with a great regard for the 'lake's' characteristics. If the 'lake' were different, the 'boat' would of necessity have to be different as well. The 'lake' determines the character of that which floats on it. The orchestra, in Wagner, is the 'lake', the supreme voice, and the singers are the 'boat'.

So, yes, I was truly eager to see the orchestra pit.

When an orchestra is placed on a normal stage each row of players from front to back is on a graduated, slightly elevated tier from the row in front of it. The back row of the orchestra is higher than the front row. Not here. Each row steps down a tier from front to back. The conductor stands or sits on a platform slightly in front of and below the lip of the stage, and slightly above the orchestra. He is shielded from the audience's view by a curved shell; they see neither him nor the orchestra. The conductor can see all the singers and all the orchestral members. Ingenious.

Wagner's orchestra was enormous, often at least one hundred musicians. Many brass instruments were used, including several of his own invention, providing not only a greater color palette but a greater power as well. The sound gathers in the pit, projects forward, is reflected off the curved shell behind the conductor toward the back of the stage, reflects forward again, mixes with the voices and hits the audience full force with a composite energy one would never forget. I was soon to experience that for myself, though I didn't know it at the time.

We climbed on to the enormous stage, one of the largest of the opera houses in the world. In the center of the stage a metal scaffold stood alone. Two middle-aged men were on stage, one of the floor and the other high up on the scaffold. The only object besides the scaffold was a large, rock-shaped prop with minimal backdrops. I wondered how this could be, seeing the Festival was to open in just a few days. Surely they must be in rehearsal. Where is the set?

"Wolfgang, please let me introduce you to a new friend of mine."

With that, Wolfgang Wagner, one of the grandsons of Richard Wagner and financial director of the Festival, moved toward us. He was the one at the foot of the scaffold.

"Wieland, come join us."

He came down quickly and completed our circle of four. It was Wieland Wagner, the other of the Wagner grandsons, and artistic director. His vision for the *Ring Cycle* that year, 1965, was revolutionary. There would be minimal movement on the stage in a sort of *tableau* format, with the action on and around that rock-like prop. The drama was to be achieved by light. It was, as I said, revolutionary, and future *Ring* productions would be measured against Wieland's 1965 staging.

By now I was on overload. This encounter with the Wagner grandsons was at the same time exhilarating and ominous, given the long

1965: On Stage With the Wagners in Bayreuth

history of the Wagner family's friendship with Adolf Hitler, including the two now standing next to me.

Their grandmother—Cosima, daughter of Franz Liszt and wife of Hans von Bülow, Wagner's conductor—had run away with Richard Wagner, living with him out of wedlock for many years before finally getting married. That was unheard of in 19th century Europe, but she and Richard continually flaunted convention. Much younger than Richard, she outlived him by four and a half decades. When Hitler came to power, enamored as he was of Wagner and his music, he became a close family friend of Cosima. She and the family were supporters of Hitler and entertained him at *Wahnfried*, the Wagner home in Bayreuth, many times before her death in 1930.

Winifred Williams, an Englishwoman raised by a musician friend of Richard Wagner, married Wagner's and Cosima's homosexual son Siegfried in 1915. It was an attempt to avoid scandals over his homosexual encounters. Between 1917 and 1920 she gave birth to four children, including Wolfgang and Wieland, who were now standing beside me. In 1923 she met Adolf Hitler, whom she cryptically referred to as USA (*Unser Seliger Adolf*, our blessed Adolf), sending him food and stationery during his imprisonment. The stationery may have been used for *Mein Kampf*, Hitler's autobiography. Ten years later, upon the death of her husband Siegfried, Winifred took over the *Bayreuth Festival*, running it through the end of World War II. While Winifred remained completely loyal to Hitler throughout her entire life she did not always condone his actions, particularly toward the Jews. After the collapse of the *Third Reich* she was banned from the *Bayreuth Festival*, passing the directorship to her sons Wolfgang and Wieland. Winifred was alive when I was in Bayreuth and died fifteen years later, in 1980.

I had seen photos of the Wagners with Hitler, including several with

Hitler with Wolfgang and Wieland Wagner

two teenagers—Wolfgang and Wieland—embraced by the demigod mass murderer himself. Here it was, twenty years later, and I wondered where their loyalties lay today? They had been Nazi sympathizers then. Were they now?

Our conversation centered on my admiration of their grandfather's music. It continued for at least a few minutes, until interrupted by the sound of a bell. Wolfgang turned to Mr. King and told him they had decided to have a working break in a *Bier Stube* just outside the *Festspielhaus*. Turning to me he extended an invitation to join them!

Gathered around an oblong table were a number of people including those I had met upon entering the hall one hour earlier: James King, Karl Böhm, Birgitt Nilsson, and Wolfgang Windgassen. In addition were Anthony Friberg, the Associate Conductor to Karl Böhm; Ron Rogers, voice coach to the solo singers; Mrs. Gillis, a Bayreuth Patron; and the two Wagner grandsons, Wolfgang and Wieland.

English was the *Lingua Franca* so I was able to understand everything that was being discussed. The question surrounded the scene in '*Siegfried*' where *Siegfried*, led by the song of the birds, is confronted by *Wotan* disguised as a wanderer. *Wotan* is trying to keep him from reaching the destination where the sleeping *Brünnhilde* lies surrounded by a ring of fire. If *Siegfried* discovers her, *Wotan's* doom is sure.

Siegfried takes the sword *'Nothung'* which he has re-crafted from the broken pieces gathered at the death of his father *Siegmund*, and smashes the spear of the disguised *Wotan*. This action is a pivotal moment in the entire *Ring Cycle*, as it demonstrates the superior power of *Siegfried* and the eventual destruction of *Wotan*. A new order of the gods will be created.

The question: How to give this event the actual and symbolic power it requires, when Wieland's vision for staging was in *tableau*, a rather un-choreographic style. Back and forth around the table one idea surfaced, followed by discussion pro and con, and then another. I was fascinated. I leaned in toward each opinion and my head felt like it was on a swivel as the opinions ringed the table.

"Greg, what do you think? You've heard all the suggestions. From the standpoint of an audience member what do you think would be most effective?"

I was flabbergasted. I was just an observer, honored simply by being invited to sit at their table. Now I was asked for an opinion. *"Well,"* I thought, *"as long as they've asked, I'll tell them what I think."* And I proceeded to do so. The conversations and responses continued.

I looked at my watch. I had a train to catch and not much time. I stood up, explained my situation, and thanked them from the depths of my heart.

"This has been the most exciting time I can remember, and I'll never forget it. Thank you for that. All my best wishes for a very successful Festival to each one of you."

With that I turned to go, when Mrs. Gillis, the Festival Patron, spoke:

"It's been a pleasure for us to have someone as dedicated to the music of our composer, and an American as knowledgeable as you. Perhaps if you could arrange to take a later train we could arrange a special surprise for you."

I said I'd see what I could arrange and left hastily. It began to rain. It didn't dawn on me to take a taxi; I began running through the rain all the way back to the station. I had arranged for Tom Dixon to pick me up when I arrived back in Nürnberg. I needed to call him and inform him of my change of plans. The phone number I had was for the military base.

"I need to talk with Lt. Colonel Thomas Dixon," I spoke to the receptionist at the other end. There was a long pause.

"Sorry, no such person is listed in the military here."

It crossed my mind that perhaps the reason for his not being listed was that he was in the Intelligence Wing.

"Please put me through to your superior."

To my surprise they patched me through, and eventually I reached Tom.

"Tom," I said, *"I'm not sure what's happening here in Bayreuth, but the train has now left. I don't know when the last train departs; perhaps there will be no more trains today. Don't go to the station until I call you."* He understood.

I now realized all of this may have been for naught. It was more than half an hour since I had left the *Bier Stube*. The meeting by this time certainly was finished. I would have to go to one of the guards at the door and say, *"Wolfgang and Wieland Wagner said I could come in,"* and have them believe me! It was Wagner's rule, after all, that no one would be allowed in except for performances. Dejection. What do I do now?

I left the station only to discover that Mr. King had come back to the station and was waiting for me in a taxi. He literally jumped out of the car when he saw me.

"This is really tremendous," he nearly shouted at me. *"The Wagners so enjoyed having you join our discussion today that they have decided to break their Grandfather's edict. They're running a dress rehearsal of Act II of Siegfried this evening, and you are to be their guest."*

This was exactly the Act that had been discussed around the table!

As we drove back to the *Festspielhaus* Mr. King implored me to stay another day in Bayreuth. He was expecting a friend from the Foreign Service Office, Cultural Affairs Division, in Washington D.C., he said, and wanted me to meet him. Mr. King thought I would be an excellent candidate to join their team that arranged exchange concerts between the United States and Europe, and wanted to present me with a good recommendation. I thanked him for his confidence in me. It was tempting to consider. Had I not two weeks earlier contemplated my future while sitting at the gravesite of Sibelius in Finland? Was this the path? I knew immediately it wasn't.

"Mr. King, my deepest desire is to be a teacher and a conductor. That has been my goal since I was a child. I don't think I can abandon my plans at this point." He honored my thoughts.

Sitting in the center seat of the first row in the *Festspielhaus*, seated next to Ron Rogers, Birgitt Nilsson, Wolfgang and Wieland Wagner, being able to reach out and touch the curved shell that shielded conductor Karl Böhm and the orchestra from view, staring directly on to the enormous stage, hearing the world's greatest Wagnerian singers including the *Heldentenor* Wolfgang Windgassen—it was almost like a command performance:

At the mouth of the dragon's cave Alberich boasts to Wotan of his plans for regaining the Ring and ruling the World. Alberich warns the dragon that a hero is coming to fight him, and offers to prevent the fight in return for the Ring. The dragon Fafner dismisses the threat. Siegfried confronts the dragon, they fight, and Siegfried stabs Fafner in the heart. Fafner learns Siegfried's name, and tells him to beware of treachery. (That will happen in the final music drama leading to Siegfried's betrayal and death). When Siegfried draws his sword from the dragon, his fingers are burned by the dragon's blood and he instinctively puts them to his mouth. On tasting the blood, he finds he can understand what the forest bird is telling him: a woman is sleeping on a rock surrounded by magic fire. Siegfried heads toward the mountain, confronts the disguised Wotan, and with the sword 'Nothung' breaks Wotan's spear. The end of the old order of gods is near.

I returned late that night by train to *Nürnberg*, playing the conclusion of the *Ring Cycle* in my head:

Siegfried's betrayal, Brünnhilde's cursing of the gods, mounting the body of the dead Siegfried on her steed Grane, throwing the Ring back into the care of the Rhinemaidens, immolating herself and flying off to be consumed by Loge's fire engulfing Valhalla. The orchestral music mounts even as the floods rise and the flames subside. Three themes intertwine: the 'Rhinemaiden's' undulating theme in the woodwinds; the 'Majesty of the Gods' theme in the brass; and the 'Redemption by Love' theme in the strings. It was this same redemption theme sung by Brünnhilde at the birth of Siegfried. Everyone is dead; everyone, that is, except Alberich! Alberich, the Nibelung who stole the ring at the beginning! Is the world destined to have the vicious cycle begin again? Will we never escape his renunciation of Love? Is no final and complete redemption possible?

The title of Wagner's opus magnus may be more confusing than we have previously thought: *The Ring of the Nibelungen*. Not the ring of the corrupt god *Wotan*. Not the ring of *Siegfried*, the flawed hero. Not the ring of the less-than-perfect redemptress *Brünnhilde*. The ring of a single *Nibelung: Alberich! Alberich!*

The final drama of the *Ring, Die Götterdämmerung*, has been translated 'The Twilight of the Gods'. The *Norse Ragnarök* is defined similarly. I now found myself questioning the appropriateness of that interpretation. *Twilight* suggests a slow, gentle fading of the light: an ending, yes, but one that seems to honor and revere those who move into the sleep of death. It grants them a peaceful demise.

The conclusion of '*Die Götterdämmerung*' is no *Dona Nobis Pacem*! Violence attends this conclusion, a complete wreaking of havoc on those who have brought all of Creation to its bleak and bitter consummation. There is no Love here for those who perish, nor is there a sense of loss: utter destruction through flood and fire, not purifying those who are being destroyed, but rather cleansing the original intent of Creation itself. It is not *twilight*, but *damnation* that reigns in these final chords emanating from the *mystic abyss*. The *Damnation of the Gods* is how it feels, both musically and emotionally.

How will Wagner avert a second catastrophe? As the three magnificent themes course their way to the conclusion, he does two things to symbolize that *Alberich* will not lead us into another world of despair. One is accomplished through subtle music theory that the average audience member will not comprehend. A cardinal rule of composition is that the key of the beginning of a work is also the key of the ending; in this case, *E-flat*, the key of the original *Creation*. That is exactly the destination of the themes we hear. They seem to be careening inexorably toward *E-flat*. But at the last instant Wagner dramatically changes course, moves away from *E-flat* and the composition ends in *D-flat*. He broke the cardinal rule! That is significant. Why?

The second Wagnerian gesture has to do with the three themes. Which of them will conclude the work? Will it be the *Rhinemaiden's* theme? They were present at the beginning of *Creation* itself. To return to the original purity of a psychological and musical *Eden* has merit. Is this the destination?

Or will it be the *Majesty of the Gods* theme? Of the three themes it is the most majestic and powerful with the full brass choir ringing in the hall. Do we want another world dominated by those gods whose behaviors were deceitful and self-serving, whose actions had led to so many deaths?

What about the *Redemption by Love* theme? *Love*, the moral glue of the cosmos? *Love*, the great healer of all that has become chaotically and chronically diseased? *Love*, that conquers all the anti-love forces in the universe?

Two themes give way at the end. 'Redemption by Love' alone remains. It was Brünnhilde's song to the dying Sieglinde as she gave birth to Siegfried. It is 'Redemption by Love', the 'Mightiest of Miracles' that sings beautifully above all other themes, and causes them to give way at the end to her solo wordless voice in the orchestra. And the key of 'Redemption by Love' is **D-flat**! *Alberich's fate is sealed. He successfully stood against the key of Creation,* **E-flat**. *The satanic Alberich, though still alive, has been rendered powerless in the face of Love's Redemption* *and Resurrection, resounding in the key of* **D-flat**. *We have not returned to the beginning after all! We are in a new heaven and a new earth, even here, even now, even as we continue to wait for the End Time reward. That may not have been the intent of the composer Wagner, but it is the truth of the greater Christian 'epic' I have embraced.*

I continued my travels to Italy and Greece. I never spoke with Mr. King again, nor was there any communication with those I had been privileged to meet. It was simply a once-in-a-lifetime event that was miraculous in and of itself, and fortuitous in the musical landscape of my life in music. I had a clearer view of Wagner and his major achievement. Above all, I had a much more profound respect and love for the true *Epic*, one that I had embraced from childhood, one that more persuasively stands alone as humankind's hope, and mine.

In recent years the Wagner Festival has begun selling tickets to attendees for dress rehearsals. But in 1965, through the kindness of the Wagner grandsons, I became the first person allowed to transcend the rules set down by their grandfather, the composer of the *Ring Cycle* and creator of the *Festspielhaus*.

Karl Böhm led a very successful Festival that year, including Wieland Wagner's innovative and revolutionary *Ring Cycle*. Though considered one of the giants of 20th century conductors, his legacy was tainted by unfounded accusations of Nazi affiliations. He was subject to a post-war two-year ban of 'de-nazification', following which he went on to conduct in all the major symphonic and opera houses of the world. He died in 1981.

Birgitt Nilsson retired from her singing career in the 1980's and returned to her farm in Sweden. She was heralded as the greatest *Brünnhilde* of her generation, a successor to the great Norwegian soprano Kirsten Flagstad. No one could match her shimmering yet explosive high register. It was said that during a performance in Italy, her high 'C' caused people outside the theater to think a fire alarm had been sounded! She was humble and maintained a self-deprecating sense of humor:

"Stay close to the earth; that way, if you fall you won't hurt yourself."

I still, to this day, remember her robust handshake in the corridor of the *Festspielhaus*. Birgitt Nilsson died on Christmas Day, 2005.

Wolfgang Windgassen was considered the most accomplished Wagnerian *Heldentenor* of the middle fifty years of the 20th century. In 1974, at the pinnacle of his world-wide fame, he died suddenly of a heart attack. How fortunate I was to meet him and hear him in Bayreuth in the role for which he was famous: *Siegfried*.

Wieland Wagner, Richard's grandson, became a sensation for his 1965 production of the *Ring Cycle*, the production I witnessed in part, where symbolism and psychology took the place of naturalism. Though his association with Hitler dated to his teenage years (he called the Führer 'Uncle Wolf') his reputation was not soiled as a result. He died one year after I met him, in 1966. Hitler and Nazi-ism aside, having had the opportunity to speak with him and see an Act from his seminal and transformative production remain among the musical highlights of my life.

Wieland's brother Wolfgang assumed full control of the Wagner Festival upon Wieland's death until he retired in 2008. As a boy he was a member of the *Hitler Youth*, though he never became a member of the Nazi Party. Son of Siegfried Wagner, grandson of Richard Wagner, great grandson of Franz Liszt, his heritage and legacy placed great burdens upon him. His productions were often criticized. He was considered autocratic, and was despised by the children of his brother Wieland. His daughter Eva (perhaps named for one of the leading characters of *Die Meistersinger von Nürnberg*) took over the Festival after his retirement. His son Gottfried wrote a scathing book about the Nazi affiliations of the Wagners, thus ostracizing himself from the family. Wolfgang died in 2010.

Following his retirement from the opera stage in the 1980's, James King taught voice at Indiana University for nearly twenty years. He died of a heart attack in 2005 at age eighty. I'm deeply indebted to Mr. King for giving me the opportunity to be more than a tourist in Bayreuth. He was exceedingly kind, and greatly generous to have given his free time to this stranger who happened to be seated next to him on a train, and who wouldn't leave him alone!

None of this would have happened had not everything gone wrong that day! If I had not overslept I would have been a tourist in Bayreuth like so many others. If my wife had decided to accompany me we would have experienced Bayreuth together but, again, would simply have been tourists. Had I been successful in purchasing a second-class rail ticket…. Had I chosen not to sit where I was assigned in that nearly empty rail car…. If I had been content to sit in silence, or to stop my attempts at conversation when it appeared my seat-mate was uninterested…. Any one of these 'ifs' would have eliminated my grand experience, and all five 'ifs' needed to coalesce to make this singular and remarkable 'meeting' possible. There is a powerful message imbedded here, one that became a central part of my manner of thinking from that moment forward:

"Treat nothing as coincidence; treat everything as a critical piece of your life's puzzle. Be bold. You will know what it all means in the end, and you will be the better for it."

CHAPTER 14

1965: What Cologne Are You Wearing? Dinner With Mendelssohn

It was still 1965, and I was thrilled to be in my Father's birth country for the first time.

We were on a bus headed from the airport to Athens, headed up the coast of Greece looking out toward the Mediterranean Sea. We had been in Europe for three weeks, having begun our trip in Norway, then Sweden, Denmark, Finland, the Soviet Union, East and West Berlin, Bavaria, Austria, Italy—we had been riding the whirlwind. It was easy to look back and see all our visited countries blurring and blending together into a single composite sameness called Europe, in spite of the varied experiences we had encountered.

Greece was immediately different—everything: the color of the sky bathing the scenery in a particular light like no other; the buildings gleaming under the brilliant sun, all whitewashed with tinges of medium blue; the shimmering arm of the Ionian Sea calm as a Classical temple. This was no longer the Europe we had become accustomed to seeing.

1965: What Cologne Are You Wearing? Dinner With Mendelssohn

And I was home! Mesmerized is a better word. I was mesmerized by the scenery flying by my window.

This is where my father was born in 1890. This is the country he had left behind fifty-nine years ago to flesh out the dreams and pictures he saw as a young boy in the short five years of school he attended. This is the place of his parents whom he had abandoned for his dream's sake, yet continued to love even though he would see his mother only once before she died, when he returned to Krestana after the Great War.

This is the home of all my ancestors on my Father's side, wedded for centuries to the silver green olive groves, my ancestors now long forgotten and lost even to my Father's memory—all my questions about family unanswered. There had been no contact since a black and white photo of my grandmother in her simple, wooden coffin arrived at our home in Wisconsin in 1946—she, who hid with her daughters in the woods during the German occupation, and ate roots and berries to survive—my grandmother who never fully recovered from the trauma and deprivation.

This was the home of Socrates, of Aeschylus, Pericles of the Parthenon, the Trojan War, the occupation by the Turks, ouzo and olives, calamari beaten to death on the rocks before being served on your seaside plate, of the Oracle of Delphi sniffing the vapors and giving ambiguous answers to life and death questions, of ruined temples recalling yesteryear's glory, of icons and incense. This was my Greece, and all these images cascaded through my mind while staring out the window.

Little did I know then, caught up in my ancestral roots, what would transpire several days later. Visiting Olympia on a four day Classical Tour I would decide to break from the group and venture to the village of Krestana, my father's birthplace. Leaving my wife behind to enjoy the sites of the first Olympic Games, I hired a taxi to drive the six miles to the village. Out to the coast we drove, and then back inland. The ride was frightful, as the driver spent most of his time looking at me in the back seat rather than keeping his eyes on the road, all the while spraying the air with unintelligible Greek. Leaving the road the driver careened, literally, across a field and up a hillside into the small hamlet. I had the feeling this was a wasted endeavor; he spoke no English, I spoke no Greek. What would I do once we arrived?

He had his own plans! Driving to the edge of a taverna in the town square, he grabbed several thirty-year-old photos of my father's family from my hand and charged into the middle of a group of old men drinking ouzo and playing backgammon. Within seconds the photos were changing hands as the arguments ensued. If it weren't so frustrating to behold it would have been comical. *"This is futile,"* I thought to myself. *"Why did I come here?"*

I decided to intervene. Pushing my way into the middle of the mob of old-timers I shouted the two family names with the best Greek pronunciation I could muster:

"Athanasopoulos, Mastaropoulos!"

All became quiet. One of the men approached me:

"Excuse me, do you speak English?" I was shocked.

"No one from your family still lives here, but I knew your father when we were young. We used to play together before I went to America. Come with me. I can show you the house where he lived."

We left the taverna and set out up a path along the hillside

1965: What Cologne Are You Wearing? Dinner With Mendelssohn

overlooking the village. A young boy of about fourteen years of age walked with us, excited to be with an American. The old man, just recently retired back to his home village, translated my questions for the youngster. Lucky for me, as he was the only one who spoke English.

My questions cascaded, followed by translations for the boy and then answers back to me. After a few minutes the young boy stopped with an astonished look on his face, and then took off running back down the path.

"He thinks you're related. He's going to get his family from the fields; they'll meet us back in the taverna."

In front of my father's birth home in Krestana, Greece

We continued on the path and soon stopped in front of a rude, simple house. It was small, the typical whitewashed adobe-like structure common to Greece. Its red clay tile roof had a hole in the center to let out the smoke from the small fires often necessary to give heat to the home in winter months, fires lit on the dirt floor in the middle of the house. The door was made of wooden planks painted blue, the only color other than white anywhere on the house inside or out. The old man told me an elderly woman lived in the house so we couldn't go inside.

We headed down the hill. Waiting for us in the taverna were a number of our long-lost family members—second- and third-cousins—along with a number of excited villagers, eager to see the first American visitor to their village in their lifetimes.

Taking out my camera, I was deterred by their wagging fingers. It was apparent they were embarrassed to be photographed in their field clothes. It was also too dark, they said. Through my new English-speaking friend I informed them my camera could take pictures even in the dark. Reluctantly, they lined up and the camera flashed. Cheers broke out. Children came running up for souvenirs of America; they had never seen flashbulbs before.

Haralambos, my second cousin, pointed to a woman seated off to the side, apart from the rest of the group. It was his wife Soula. She had a toothache, he said, and that was why she wasn't in the picture. I gave her two aspirins and a glass of water. Later she came smiling and thanked me for the miracle drug I had given her; they had never heard of aspirin!

Our 'party' was interrupted by an older woman, dressed in black, who came running and crying into the taverna. Grabbing my ears she lifted me up out of my chair and slobbered me on both cheeks with kisses and sobs. It was, I learned, my Aunt Theodora, who had been abandoned by her husband, one of my father's brothers who ran off to Germany. Senile, she was cared for by the villagers who smiled knowingly and lovingly at the scene. It was Aunt Theodora who lived in my father's birth home.

Two hours flew by. Here was a family remnant—an ancestral line wedded to the olive groves and the village of Krestana for untold centuries—being reconnected, having been broken by my father's emigration fifty-nine years earlier. This was my rediscovered 'blood' coursing and swirling around inside the dark space of the taverna. I felt whole and completed.

I promised I would see them again, a promise I would keep several times.

That fortuitous family event in Krestana was a surprise waiting for my discovery several days hence. But, having progressed ahead of my story, I was still seated on the bus groaning its way towards Athens. Another surprise was waiting and about to reveal itself, and soon.

My reverie was broken by my wife poking me on the shoulder.

"The man sitting in front of us. His cologne is fantastic. Ask him what it is," she whispered. I whispered back, somewhat annoyed,

"Are you kidding? I'm in my Father's birthplace and you're asking me to do what?" I returned to my window reverie.

"Yes, I mean it. Really. Ask him." I ignored that second request, so she insisted one more time.

"Alright, let me think about it."

This was embarrassing! Garnering some *chutzpah* I leaned forward, reached out and tapped him on the shoulder.

"Excuse me," I said in as pleasant a voice as I could muster given my aggravation with my wife, *"I have a strange request. Would you mind telling me the name of your cologne?"* I cringed even as I asked. He laughed.

"That is a strange request indeed."

I knew right away he was from England; the 'indeed' at the end of the sentence gave it away.

"It's a German cologne called Tabac."

"It is a quite nice scent indeed." I chuckled at my unspoken humor, thanked him, and turned once again toward the window.

"Is this your first time to Greece?" I responded in the affirmative.

"I've been here many times, so allow me to point out some interesting things along the way."

He turned toward the window, and all three of us were caught up in the passing landscape. We listened intently as he seemed to know this route quite well. As we approached the outskirts of Athens it became even more interesting. Then, when we were well into the city, he said,

"Up ahead we're going to make a left turn. When we do, look straight ahead. You'll get your first glimpse of the Acropolis. It will take your breath away."

It was as he said, and it did.

1965: What Cologne Are You Wearing? Dinner With Mendelssohn

We arrived at *Syntagma*, or *Constitution Square*, just outside the American Express Office. After retrieving our luggage I thanked him for his brief but helpful 'travelogue'.

"I've enjoyed talking with you as well," he replied. *"I have a free evening. Would you care to be my guests at dinner tonight?"*

We had no plans either, and said we'd love to join him.

"I'm staying at the Grand Bretagna Hotel," and he gestured in its direction.

I knew it was the most famous hotel in Athens, and also the most expensive, as it looked over the Square with the Acropolis in the distance. We were staying at a small, inexpensive hotel a few blocks away.

He gave me his business card. I read it silently: *R (period) H (period) Mendelssohn.*

"Mendelssohn!" I nearly shouted. *"I know a Mendelssohn."*

"So do I," was his reply, *"and we'll talk about him at dinner tonight."*

And so we did.

Our bus companion was Robert von Mendelssohn, a banker from England. I never was quite able to completely understand all the twists and turns of his Felix Mendelssohn lineage, but he was indeed a descendent. Our conversation was memorable. The Mendelssohn line is filled with striking people who made magnificent contributions to the world, sometimes during strident times. There was Felix's grandfather, Moses Mendelssohn, one of the most famous Jewish philosophers; and his very gifted younger sister, the composer and pianist Fanny. Of course Felix, born a Jew, reborn a Christian, was the object of our greater attention.

We talked about the nature of 'genius'. We talked about Mendelssohn the *Classicist* trapped in the age of the *Romantics*. Mendelssohn's Christian conversion entered our conversation.

Mendelssohn was a musical genius in the truest sense of the word. Often that designation is applied loosely. Too many are called 'geniuses' when they are not. One may be extremely gifted and prodigious and not be a true genius. One may create towering works of immense beauty, and yet not technically qualify for the title. Geniuses are rare, not common. Mendelssohn fits the profile perfectly. Like Mozart.

Regardless of his 'genius' stature Mendelssohn has not always garnered the appreciation his music deserves. It was a matter of 'timing'. He lived in the post-revolutionary period of early *19th century Romanticism*. The *Romantic* spirit was one given to great excess, gigantic egos, inflated musical ideas, and revolutionary thoughts about the forms, structures, and harmonies of music. In many ways the *Romantic* sentiment turned its back on the inherited past. *Classicism* was the language of Haydn, Mozart, and early Beethoven. *Classicism* sought balance between form—that is, the templates housing musical ideas—and content—the emotional characteristics of those ideas. The four-movement symphony devised by Haydn had a given structure that all who wrote in the form used to display their themes. The same was true of the Concerto, Sonata, and String Quartet, the major forms of *Classicism*. If you understood the structure of a first movement *Sonata-Allegro* from a Haydn symphony you could use that knowledge to listen to the first movement of a Mozart concerto. The structure was like a 'jello mold'; it was the 'form'.

The ingredients, the melodic ideas, were what differed; the ingredients were its 'content'.

After the French Revolution, with its quest for 'individual freedom', things changed. Individuals were now free to pursue their dreams apart from the dictates of the former 'aristocracy'. 'Individual freedom' led to 'individualism', or 'individuality'. No longer was there adherence to a single mode of expression or a single structure to display one's expressive ideas. Composers now expressed what they 'felt', free from the encumbrances of the past. Further, concert halls for the rising 'free and middle class' of Europe allowed thousands of the former 'peasant class' to revel in what had previously been reserved for the privileged few. This less sophisticated and relatively uneducated class found entrance into the music fundamentally easier through its emotional content, not its structures. They desired 'stories' painted in sound. The new wave in concert halls was *Program Music*: paint a picture, tell a story, describe a person or an event—that was the new medium. *Absolute Music*, where the 'meaning' was the sound itself devoid of a specific 'program', became relatively obsolete.

Mendelssohn did not possess that same *Romantic* temperament. He was a *Classicist* at heart. He loved order and restraint, hallmarks of the former style. His ego remained in check. He was not a revolutionary. He chose not to call attention to himself through radical musical ideas. He was intentionally 'out of date' and 'out of touch'; that was his problem.

Anyone who knows the scene in his oratorio *Elijah*, where Elijah meets the Prophets of Baal, can understand the contrast between Mendelssohn and his *Romantic* contemporaries.

Baal's prophets attempt to call down fire from their gods to ignite their sacrifice. Elijah ridicules their failed attempts, prompting the prophets to become more and more frenzied in their actions, including cutting themselves with knives and lancets. Exhausted by their efforts they collapse in humiliation. Elijah adds insult to their injury by dousing his sacrifice with water to demonstrate the absolute superiority of his God, Who sets the altar and its sacrifice ablaze. Then comes the slaughter of Baal's prophets.

We discussed what the extreme *Romantics* Franz Liszt and Hector Berlioz would have done with this drama! Not Mendelssohn. The control and order of his musical approach seems too restrained for the times. Genius, yes, but one wrapped in the refined and disciplined cloth of the past.

While I loved his music—*Midsummer Night's Dream*, the Oratorio *Elijah* (which I have performed as a chorister on numerous occasions), the gorgeous *Violin Concerto* with one of the sweetest melodies this side of heaven, and his *Italian Symphony* (which I later would conduct with my college chamber orchestra)—I had also admired him for his re-discovery of Johann Sebastian Bach, resurrecting the *Baroque* giant's music after nearly a century in oblivion. That in itself was a topic of some conversation.

During his lifetime Bach was not highly regarded as a composer. He had chosen the path of the Church during the *Age of the Enlightenment*. It was a wrong decision to be sure, at least by 'secular' sensibilities. In Bach's day no one 'with any contemporary sense' would sacrifice his talent on the altar of the Church! Bach suffered for that choice, as Mendelssohn did for his. After his death Bach's music nearly disappeared, with only rare church performances of some of his cantatas. His great orchestral opus, the six *Brandenburg Concerti Grossi*, given to the *Margrave of Brandenburg*, had remained unplayed even by the Margrave's orchestra.

Bach statue outside Thomas Kirche, Leipzig, Germany

Nearly seventy years after Bach's death a young man, age eighteen, came to Leipzig and its new and great Conservatory of Music. Bach had spent the last twenty-seven years of his life in this city.

Mendelssohn, the genius, was that teenager. He had converted from Judaism to Christianity, particularly the Lutheran religious position. One must grasp the inevitability, as we discussed it, of such seemingly unrelated events as these:

Mendelssohn, the musical genius—Mendelssohn the devout Lutheran Christian—Mendelssohn in a position of authority at the Conservatory—Mendelssohn in the city of Bach's spiritual pilgrimage. He was perfectly positioned and perhaps the only man of his era, precisely because of his spiritual commitment, who would be open to the 'discovery' of Bach.

There are various stories of how he came in contact with the music of Bach, including several apocryphal accounts. However it happened, when Mendelssohn first unfolded Bach's manuscript on the rack of his piano and played those magnificent sounds, Bach's world of oblivion was gone forever. It was Mendelssohn who sent out the word to look for manuscripts by the Kapellmeister of Leipzig and send them to him. It was Mendelssohn who mounted some of the first performances of Bach's music, unheard even in the composer's lifetime. It was Mendelssohn who declared that music students would learn how to set music to paper following the compositional practices of the *Baroque* master. That remains true today in all the music schools of the Western World. The 'nobody of his time' became the 'everyman for all time'. That is a towering tribute not only to Bach, but also to his emancipator Mendelssohn.

If Mendelssohn had never composed a note of music he would still deserve great honor for having 'resurrected' the music of Johann Sebastian Bach.

Our dinner conversation had traveled a long and wide road. It had been another of the 'markers' I would look back on as seminal in my growth as a musician, forcing me to consider approaches to music and culture in fresh ways. I learned to look closely at the *people* behind the music, to see them as 'real flesh and blood' like myself.

I felt privileged in having this opportunity for yet another encounter with the offspring or family of great composers: Aino Sibelius, wife of the composer, in Finland three weeks earlier; Wolfgang and Wieland Wagner, grandsons of Richard Wagner, one week earlier; and now Robert of the Mendelssohn line.

It could just as easily not have happened. If I had ignored my wife's request a third time…well, I'm thrilled I didn't, and all because of a German cologne called *Tabac*.

That was fifty years ago. Robert von Mendelssohn, whose business card I still possess, passed away in 1996 at age 94.

I use *Tabac* daily and think of both Mendelssohns each time.

Soli Deo Gloria

Development: Living
1965 – 1998

Themes are taken apart to reveal their substance and worthiness

A New City, a New Musical Career

Bold Initiatives

An Answer to Prayers

Journeys and Visions

A New Path

Devastation and Healing

CHAPTER 15

Reflections: What the Incarnation Tells Me About Art

The Word became flesh.
John 1: 14

In the incarnation of Jesus all flesh and everything in the material world was reaffirmed, reclaimed by God for His original purposes. Jesus in His flesh was still *of* God in His Spirit. Not lesser, not greater, not separate, but *of*. Wrap your mind around this: *an actual physical embodiment of God.* The early Church Father Iranaeus said:

"Born into his own created order which he himself bore."

God didn't just *wear* the creation as a cloak, but *became* the creation and participated fully in the realities of time, space, and history just as we do. Therefore, as another Church Father, Tertullian, said,

"...materiality [or the created world] *is a worthy vehicle for grace."*

Or, as the late Robert Webber put it:

"Just as God was embodied in human flesh, so also divine reality can be communicated through material reality."

In other words, the arts are not mere enhancers or illustrators of the Gospels but actual expressions of redeemed creation. In art the creation is not just an *illumination* of the message, it doesn't only *contain* the message; it, in some mysterious way, *embodies* the message. Art, as 'a worthy vehicle for grace', is fashioned into the praise of God.

In the mind of the Creator God, as we have said before, there was never intended to be any contradiction between the physical, intellectual, emotional, spiritual and aesthetic parts of our nature. To remain in our fractured state of being is not only unhealthy—it is unholy. In Jesus, the incarnate God-Man, lies the path for our return to 'oneness'. In that moment when God became Man, fallen creation was on the verge of being reclaimed to be what it was in the first creation—the 'good' of God's artistic and creative act.

The God who created *became* the creation in order to re-create the world. Webber said: In like manner,

...the arts function in a redemptive way. In the arts we release time, space, touch, sight, smell, sound, and movement from their bondage to sin. The arts then become examples of redemption and a foretaste of the coming kingdom of God, when all creation will be released completely from the effect of sin and be free to enter eternal praise. In this sense, the artist's work is to anticipate God's glory in the world to come.

CHAPTER 16

1965: My Career at North Park College Begins

In my twenty-ninth year those meditations and prayers from my summer in Europe were answered. Before my thirtieth birthday in March of 1966 I would sign a contract to join the Music Faculty of North Park College in Chicago.

I had become familiar with the Covenant denomination in 1958 and grew to love it. The Detroit Covenant Church introduced me to North Park College. Every two or three years the College Choir sang in our church. They were outstanding, and I grew in my admiration for the quality of the Music Department.

At least once a year we hosted a visit from an Administrator from Covenant headquarters, also located in Chicago. Little by little my understanding of the denomination grew.

In the winter of 1965, seven years after joining the Covenant Church, and just months after my inspiring and challenging experiences in Europe, the next phase of my life, the next in a series of 'answers' and miracles took place. It happened on a visit from

1965: My Career at North Park College Begins

another Administrator from Chicago. After the Sunday morning service he took me aside.

"Have you heard about the opening in the Music Department at North Park?" I hadn't.

"I think you should apply. In my opinion you have exactly what they're looking for." I asked just what that might be?

"Someone to head up their Music Education program, training future music teachers."

My experience over the previous eight years had prepared me for such a position as that. I had working knowledge of both the instrumental and choral fields from elementary grades through high school. I also had very definite ideas about what seemed lacking in public school music education, and had developed some programs I thought might improve the field.

I applied.

It was not a smooth process. North Park's Academic Dean, Dr. C. Hobart Edgren, didn't seem to know precisely what he and the Music Department were looking for. They appeared to be shuffling their current music faculty around to make the pieces fit, and were unsure which position might be available. I made several trips to the campus. I would receive a tentative offer; then it would be retracted, only to be offered again some weeks later. This went on for about four months, and I was extremely frustrated. Why would I want to leave my secure and rewarding position in Michigan for one as indecisive and lacking in focus as the position North Park seemed to be offering.

Finally a letter came, along with a contract to be signed. I decided not to accept it and stay where I was. I had recently bought a new home and a new car. In this interim period my position in Michigan was about to change with my elevation to a higher position with a salary increase. The North Park contract was nearly forty percent less! Coupled with the higher cost of living in Chicago, signing North Park's contract seemed financially inconceivable and ill advised.

Rather than a telephone conversation, I decided to turn down the position in person. That way, I felt, I would be keeping my options open for the future by declining this present contract in an honorable way. Once again, I drove to Chicago to speak with Dean Edgren; it was my fourth visit. I entered his office with every intention of politely declining his offer.

Without any persuasion on his part, I said 'yes', and signed the contract.

Fall, 1966, after joining the North Park College Music Faculty

CHAPTER 17

Reflections: What Moses Told Me About the Shadow of God

> *The Lord spoke to Moses and said, "Mark this: I have specially chosen Bezalel of the tribe of Judah. I have filled him with divine spirit, making him skillful and ingenious, expert in every craft, and a master of design. I have endowed every skilled craftsman with the skill he has. They shall make everything that I have commanded you."*
> (Exodus 31: 16)

In chapters 25 to 30 of Exodus God commanded Moses to build a tabernacle to Him, and gave specific instructions on how it should be done and what materials to use. A quick reading of these chapters should impress us with the quality of materials and artistry that God had in mind. Nothing is spared. Only the finest materials, the most precious were to be used, as the Scriptures repeatedly say, *For Glory and for Beauty.* How many stories or persons in the Bible are given as much space as this passage defining God's desire and definition for beauty?

Then, in chapter 31, God told Moses who would carry out the artistic endeavor. Bezalel—what a strange name! In Hebrew it means, 'in the shadow or protection of God'. Bezalel, the first great artist recorded in the Bible (after God Himself) is singled out for a lofty purpose—to make the truth of God known through the construction and artistry of the tabernacle.

So, then, like the *Word made Flesh*, the tabernacle didn't just *contain* the truth of God—it *became,* it *embodied* the truth of God, and the artist was gifted by God to enable this transformation of created material into praise. Think of it! God gave special gifts to artists in order to make Himself known. Think of it! God, our God was the first patron of the arts! This is the Christian artist's calling—to live in the shadow and protection of God like a modern day Bezalel. Bezalel's commission from God should encourage us to replicate the Tabernacle, so to speak, in our artistic endeavors in order to 'embody' the truth of our Savior.

That was my challenge in this new position at North Park. That was my quest.

CHAPTER 18

1966: My First College Conducting Position

The only conducting position included in my new college teaching position was as director of the *Oratorio Chorus*, an organization open to the campus and surrounding community without audition. The *College Choir* formed the 'backbone' of the ensemble, with a requirement to participate in it. *Oratorio Chorus* rehearsed once a week, and performed two major choral/orchestral works each year, with Handel's *Messiah* an annual performance in December.

A raging ice storm greeted the day of my first concert. I wondered if anyone would brave the elements to attend, and worried that my choir might also be decimated. Leaving my office in Hansen Hall out the south door I hit a patch of ice on the top step of the ten leading to the sidewalk, flew into the air holding my *Messiah* score and baton, did a complete 360 degree cartwheel, landed on my feet at the bottom, and slid into the snow at the edge of the sidewalk. After the adrenaline rush left my body I thought to myself, *"Today is going to be just fine,"* and made my way into a packed gym and a full choir!

Oscar Olson, a long time member of the North Park College administrative community, sent me the first congratulatory note I received for a performance in Chicago:

Your 'Messiah' was much more than a performance! I felt adoration and worship translated into action. There were many evidences of long and hard hours of your own preparation and of rehearsal discipline. A warm thanks, and many years of such ministry!

Sally Johnson, who sang tenor in that performance, also sent a note:

Dear Mr. Athnos, I want to thank you for the 'Messiah'. This was my first opportunity to sing in it, and each rehearsal was a great experience. As for the actual performance, I'll bet I was the only tenor who cried through the last page of the 'Amen'! Thanks very much, and I'm looking forward to another term of Oratorio.

The spring of my first year we performed Zoltan Kodaly's *Budavari Te Deum*, and Franz Joseph Haydn's *Lord Nelson Mass*.

The next year, 1967-68, in addition to the annual *Messiah* performance, the *Oratorio Chorus* performed Brahms' *German Requiem*. On April 4th Martin Luther King, Jr. was assassinated in Memphis, another of those tragic killings of American leaders from that fateful decade. Our performance was to take place four days later, on April 8th. It seemed fitting to make our performance both a memorial and a tribute, which I wrote. I asked a colleague to read the statement before we began:

The conductor of this afternoon's concert has asked me to make the following statement:

The performance today is a tribute to a martyred man and an eternal idea. Throughout his years of maturity, Martin Luther King Jr.

fought unceasingly for equality, brother with brother. His were positive deeds of kindness and love, not negative acts of violence and hatred. He brought a ray of future hope and promise to our world of dark despair inhabited by so many of our fellow citizens, black and white.

It is fitting, therefore, that Brahms' 'German Requiem' serve as a tribute to the man and his idea. It does not, like other Requiems, dwell on the future wrath of a vengeful God, striking us with fear and travail. Instead it speaks of hope—"Blessed are the dead which die in the Lord"—"But the righteous souls are in the hand of God"—and for the living it cries: "Our hope is in Thee".

Through the message of this work we again realize that the dead have life—their ideas live through us. The final statement of the 'Requiem' is a challenge to us all—"Blessed are they which die in the Lord, for their works shall follow after them". It is left to us to carry the torch he carried with zeal and with eloquence. In this spirit of peace and equality we offer our performance today.

Aline Jérôme, whose family had fled the dictator Duvalier's Haiti because of persecution, was in attendance. I knew her and her family from North Park Covenant Church, where I was director of the early service choir, working alongside Oscar Olson. She wrote in her very sensitive and beautiful style,

Dear Mr. Athnos, I would like to find the words to express to you my gratitude for all the trouble you went through to make it possible for us to listen, like for the first time, to the Brahms' 'German Requiem'. Listening to this masterpiece of Brahms, I was asking myself how can the human being attain these high peaks of art and understand and express so well, in a musical language so pure, the great truths of the Bible? But, what amazed me the most was to realize that you, Mr. Athnos, were able to capture so well in your spirit and in your heart that flow of harmony to pour it on the audience. What talent! Believe in my deep admiration.

While I didn't know it at the time, that tribute performance was to be my last as conductor of the *Oratorio Chorus*. A new Music Department Chairman, Dr. Herbert Pankratz, joined our faculty that summer and, much to my dismay and disappointment, decided that he wanted to take over the group. There was pain involved for me, obviously, but it was mitigated somewhat by my growing involvement with three other performance groups: the *North Park Academy Varsity Singers*, the *College Chamber Singers*, and the *North Park Covenant Church Choir*.

Sadly, the *Oratorio Chorus* was discontinued two years later due to lack of student and community interest.

CHAPTER 19

1966: The Varsity Singers Initiative

Part of my College assignment was to establish a Choral program at their private high school: North Park Academy. Years earlier such a program had existed, but due to lack of interest and poor leadership it had been abandoned, their choir robes gathering dust in a closet, and their choral library given away. I would be fighting more than a vacuum; it would be a challenge to overcome the negative attitudes.

I took a different approach to building the program than anyone expected. Two weeks before school began I 'hung out' at the athletic field watching the football team practice. I spoke to no one, but simply made sure the team saw me every day. My goal was to spot the outstanding players, and have them recognize me when the first school bell sounded.

In faculty meetings I inquired about student leaders. Who were the 'shakers and movers' on the Student Council? Who were the most academically advanced students? Who were the star athletes on all their teams? I took down their names and looked up their photos in the previous year's Yearbook.

On the first day of classes I stood in the main hallway looking for those 'familiar faces'. Pulling each one aside, I said,

"I'm starting a new program here this fall and I'm looking for the top students in the school. I've been told you're one of them." Or, *"I've seen you on the football team and I've seen what a great leader you are."*

"What kind of a program?"

"Varsity Singers." I didn't want to call it a choir; that still was a lingering bad taste in everyone's mouth. I wanted to use the word 'varsity'. It spoke of a kind of athletic quality that I wanted to apply to the new musical group. 'Varsity' also refers to the top tier rather than the subs of the 'junior varsity'.

"But I can't sing."

"No auditions. I want leaders, and you're one of them. I don't care if you can sing or not. We're building a team of leaders who are willing to do whatever it takes to succeed."

At our first rehearsal seventeen students showed up. They were leaders, but not enough to form a choir. I needed far more than that. On the next day's morning announcements, I had a student read:

The Varsity Singers had a successful beginning yesterday, but there are still openings for leaders. Our maximum will be forty-two, and we're rapidly approaching that number.

It wasn't exactly the truth—that is, the part about 'rapidly approaching'.

The next rehearsal we had forty-two leaders sitting on the risers. One of them was an excellent pianist/accompanist. Two could read music: one soprano and one tenor. Thirty-nine others were willing novices.

I knew the group would be successful because the leaders I was looking for were not accustomed to failure, and I had a room full of them. I brought them a picture of what they would look like on stage: navy blue blazers with a specially designed 'Varsity Singers' emblem on the pocket. Grey pants for the guys and grey-white herringbone skirts for the gals. It was a classy look. No robes for this bunch! They saw the future, and embraced it.

Varsity Singers, first year, 1966-67

Before we sang a single note of the first piece, I promised them a Spring tour to Wisconsin and Michigan. It was brash and bold, but how could I expect to take on any less 'risk' for myself than I was expecting from them!

With only a few 'singers' in the room rehearsal techniques were going to be tedious, but I had to make them exciting. Rapid pace. Constant encouragement. Physically active. Sopranos learn the first measure. Then Altos. Put the two together. Then Tenors. Then Basses. Then put them together in four-part harmony. Praise their success. Lead a cheer. Encourage applause. Then on to the second measure, and so on through the piece. It worked, and they were constantly engaged and excited. Sooner than I expected, they began to understand the printed page.

Our concerts were wildly successful—standing-room-only crowds, not just with parents and faculty in attendance, but also other students. Letters came to my box from everywhere:

Thank you for the tremendous concert last night. It's almost impossible to believe the miracle you have performed with the choir. They are great! I recommend a tour for them—they are that sort of material, I believe. Thank you. Inez Olander [Faculty]

To the Varsity Singers: Most of you know me well enough to know that I seldom find it difficult to have something to say. But I feel tonight the frailty of language in a way I rarely do. How does one convey with poor words his affection for you, for what you did for the school tonight, for your parents and friends, but especially for me. It's sometimes very difficult for an old man to enter your world, your joys, your dreams, your sorrows. But I think I was with you tonight. And although I find it very hard to verbalize, I think I understand vicariously your sense of togetherness, your affection for each other and for your director, your sense of pride in who you are. Thank you for what you did for me…. And I look forward with real anticipation to next weekend [our first tour]. *Bring your trigonometry books! Sincerely, Vernoy Johnson* [Vernoy was a beloved math teacher].

Dear Gregory: The concert Friday night was stunning. It seemed to me the youngsters sang not so much for us as for you, for each other, and for the joy of creating something of quality and splendor. As one of the audience I felt, at times, almost like an intruder. How can I thank you for giving our children this priceless taste of excellence? Signed, Rachel Ann Patterson [a parent].

This letter came to the group from another student not a member of the choir:

Never before have I spent so much time with one group and gained so much as I have with the Varsity Singers. As a member of the audience, whether surrounded by friends or strangers, I have always felt a sense of unity with these people…having been brought together by a common experience. For your singing truly has been an experience for me. I have never felt like an onlooker during one of your concerts, but always like a participant. I have laughed with you…cried with you…and in a way unseen by all…I have sung with you. It has been my privilege to profit from the words you have sung, an experience I'll always remember, because my life is one of the countless others that have been enriched by your singing. No one is capable of entering and leaving one of your concerts without becoming changed in some small, but significant way. And so it has been with me many times. I do not quite know how to express my appreciation to you for all that you've done—if for no one else, then just for me. So…thank you. Thanks for everything! Thanks for letting me 'sing my song' with you. Sincerely, Stephanie Boever

The spring tour was magnificent. These kids were a tremendous reflection of the quality of the Academy itself. The parents of one of my singers accompanied us on our first tour venture. Jennie and Eldred Erickson wrote to the choir:

Words are hard to find to express our 'thank you' to all of you for the wonderful weekend we had. As I'm sure you know, we are so proud of you as a group, and now after having been with you for three days, we're fairly bursting with pride. We're proud both for the fine way you conducted yourselves, and for the tremendous way you performed. We're so happy to be 'part' of this great first Varsity Singers group! Thank you again for asking us to come along! It was a wonderful vacation and privilege for both Eldred and me, and we enjoyed every minute of it. Thank you too for singing for me and making Mother's Day just that much nicer. That kind gesture will always be remembered…. Choir, make the most of your opportunity to sing under such a wonderful director! Lovingly…

Coming back at night after our final tour concert the three-hour bus ride was magical. Students took charge, taking it in turns to sing solos they had learned on their own, the same students who had never wanted to sing a note before the year began, alternating with pieces from our concert program. There were no dry eyes on the bus. It was one of those moments you never want to end.

Dear Mr. Athnos, Even though I've only been a Varsity Singer for one scanty year, I can say in all truth that I have felt so much pride and joy in being in Varsity Singers. I am completely overwhelmed. I for one would like to say thanks to you for making it all possible. You're terrific. I know I'll never forget Varsity Singers no matter how far away I go. It will always stay with me. I'm not very good with words—but I loved it. Please let us graduates know what's going on in years to come. Thank you so much for the great experience. Good luck always. With love, Jill

In the Spring I had Varsity Singer tryouts for the following year. Every student at North Park Academy auditioned. I wish I could have taken all of them! Alas, many fine kids didn't make the final cut. I received a very touching and moving letter from one of them, responding to an article that appeared in the campus newspaper:

I know the piece you wrote for the newspaper was not written to or for me, but for the Varsity Singers. It is odd, I suppose, that it held such a great emotional feeling for me. I could almost feel that final handshake and sense the sadness that came with the end of the tour.

In the last month or so I have come into close contact with Varsity Singers—not so much the singers individually, but the group, the unit, the idea. It started with an unsuccessful audition, but most certainly did not end there. I have never experienced quite as real and sharp a disappointment as when I did not make Varsity Singers. It was not so much that I did not expect the disappointment, for I really didn't expect to make it. It was just that, more than anything else, I wanted to be a part of that group—not for the glory of it, but for the indefinable feeling that would have come in belonging, being a part of Varsity Singers. I didn't know how much it meant to me, until reflecting on the fact, I realized that I would have given up Student Council or any other activity just to be a part of Varsity Singers.

This attitude came mostly, I suppose, after I knew you. I was so prepared to be laughed right out of that audition, but I wasn't. When I first came to interview you for the newspaper, it was, for me, a way to face the rejection of the audition and not making Varsity Singers. And when I left that interview, any hurt that I had ever felt about not being accepted was completely wiped away. Since then I have come to appreciate everything that the Varsity Singers do. Even though I am not a part of this year's or next year's Choir as a singer, I always will be in spirit.

I have never known any loss from which I gained so much. No one will ever know how much I wanted to be a part of that group, or how much a part of it I am right now, this minute. Anything that you or the Varsity Singers ever undertake has my full support. Perhaps that is a meaningless thing, but it is true.

You have been a complete success this year, Mr. Athnos. I hope with all my heart that every day and every year holds such great fulfillment for you. Good luck this summer in your studies and good luck with next year's Varsity Singers. I hope that they are as tremendous as this year's Varsity Singers have been…if that is possible. I regret that I could not be a part of it. But in a way I am, and always will be. Thank you, Mr. Athnos, for what you have done for me, but especially thank you for what you have done for North Park. Very truly yours, Martha Mulder

That fall I re-auditioned several students, including Martha. She had expressed herself with such passion that I knew, for my sake as well as hers, Martha absolutely needed to be part of the Choir. There had been no auditions the previous Fall, yet the success of the group was beyond my wildest imagination. So I didn't care if Martha could sing; I craved her desire, I loved her spunk. One month into the new school year I received another letter from her:

I just wanted to tell you how very much I am enjoying Varsity Singers. It's sort of a strange feeling for me to be a real part of the choir this year because I never thought I would be. It's really like a dream come true…. I don't know if my contribution to the choir will ever be that great, probably not. But I just want you to know that Varsity Singers is one of the greatest things that has ever happened to me, and it will always have my full support. I'm sure my family gets tired of hearing me talk about it, but they'll be there at Christmas for sure just to see if it's as great as I say it is. And that will mean a few tickets too, with seven kids in the family! But seriously, I think you're doing a terrific job, and I have a lot of respect for you as a musician and as a really great person. Yours truly, Martha

1966: The Varsity Singers Initiative

We had another outstanding year. Betty Nelson, the Assistant Principal who traveled with us on our second tour, wrote this:

Dear Greg. It is always difficult to describe deep emotions in words, but I do want you to know how keenly I feel the experiences of this past weekend. I'm convinced that the reason this trip with the choir was so exciting and memorable is because the group has such a respect and love for you as a person and as a director. You have brought them together as a group in a manner that is hard to match. They have brought honor and respect to North Park Academy in return. We are all sincerely in your debt! It's just plain fun and exciting to be with you and the choir. Thanks for asking me to join you for the trip. It is a wonderful experience for me to live with the students and know them under these circumstances. Many, many thanks for what you give to all of us!

Varsity Singers Small Group performs Santa Lucia Pageant

Our third year started with high hopes and ended in deep sorrow; the announcement was made that North Park Academy would close its doors at the end of the school year 1968-69. The news was not received well by students, faculty or parents. Its reputation was stellar throughout the Chicago area; it was in the top one percent of high schools in the nation whose graduates went on to earn doctorates.

Varsity Singers in their last year, 1968-69

Unfortunately, finances ruled the day and ruined the future. I felt, as did many parents, that, had the opportunity to create an endowment been granted, the Academy would not only survive, but thrive. The parents were not given that opportunity; North Park College needed the space inhabited by the high school and was willing to let it fade away.

Our Spring Tour went on as planned, and it was a roller coaster of emotions night after night. Our final concert of the tour took place at a Covenant Church in Rockford, Illinois. Tears flowed; you might say tears 'reigned', and it was remarkably sad and beautiful at the same time. Bob Hjelm, Senior Pastor of the Church, wrote to me the next week:

Dear Friend: As this week begins for me, I am still deeply moved by Sunday night's concert and all of the meanings it held for you and for the young people.... We really didn't know what we were in store for Sunday night here. We had received the announcement, of course, of the closing of the Academy. It never dawned on us that the last concert sung by "The Singers" would be here at our church. Consequently, we were unprepared for the involvement we would have in such a meaningful time in the lives of the young people and yourself. We came expecting just the singing. We received a very unselfish sharing of your lives. It was really a rare and wonderful and tragic experience all wrapped up into an unforgettable evening.

So I wanted to express something of my personal feelings of gratitude and shared concern today. It is a shame beyond words to express it that the Academy now shall end its ministry, its life. I've been in on some dyings along the way, as a pastor. This particular one has tugged in a particular way at my heartstrings, and I want you to know that I share it as much as I can with you.

So, thanks for an unforgettable evening on Sunday for many reasons. It was top-flight music, but even more it was an outpouring of the heart and the life of the young people and of yourself.... God bless you and all of your "kids".

One final letter came to me following our campus concert on May 23rd, the last we would ever sing together. It was from Sarah Olsson, one of our singers and the daughter of North Park College president Karl Olsson. The last paragraph reads:

As the last note was sounded, and the audience rose up in a standing ovation, I felt completely drained of everything. I wanted to cry—but I couldn't. I wanted to cheer and laugh—but I couldn't. I could only stand there and stare at our choir. I refused to believe that this was it, and that the Varsity Singers had ended their short history on such a fantastic note. It had been a perfect concert and for that reason it should have been able to go on and on. I left after the standing ovation. I couldn't stay any longer. I just wanted to remember that last song and the looks on our faces as we sang it.

The singers needed to hear from me; what could I say that hadn't already been said and, even more than that, experienced. The Academy doors had closed for the last time. Summer was upon us; it felt like winter. I took the pain of seventy singers upon myself and, coupled with my own, found it unbearably sad. It had been too short a life to have to experience a death. They needed not only consolation, not only closure, but a renewing pride in what they had accomplished, a pride that would sustain them into their growing and passing years. I sent this letter to each of them:

Dear Singers: I am indeed the most fortunate of all men. You have given me a measure of life and love, pleasure and reward beyond estimate and without equal.

Together we have experienced joy and sorrow, anxiety and relief, heights and depths. We have laughed together—and cried together. There has been mutual trust and admiration. We have shared with each other, and have given greatly of ourselves. We have found the meaning of and necessity for self-sacrifice and self-discipline. We have founded a community, an identity, one spirit built on personal relationships.

Our pride is fierce—because we struggled and strove in constancy, without wavering, to establish it. We guard jealously our tradition—because we created it with the sweat of our bodies, the ferment of our minds and the nobleness of our spirits. We lovingly cherish our memories—because they alone constitute our future.

Time is the great healer of the infirmities of the spirit. Names eventually fade from consciousness. Faces change and are reluctantly forgotten. But we have more and greater things to remember. Our hearts and lives have been shaped and fashioned into a more promising instrument of God's creation. Together we have positively shaped and influenced thousands of people in our own unique way. No one, on this campus or elsewhere, has ever conveyed joy, love, and exuberance as have we. No one ever will. I'll never forget what you have done for me. My heart and affection belong to all of you: "God keep you safe. God keep me, too, and bless us both...." With thanks, your director.

CHAPTER 20

1967: The Chamber Singers Initiative

The Chamber Singers were not my idea. Early in the Fall of my second year on the faculty seven students pulled me aside:

"We understand you have an interest in Renaissance choral music. The College Choir doesn't sing any of that repertoire. We're wondering if you would start a group."

"How many of there are you?"

"Just seven."

It turned out they had two sopranos, two altos, one tenor, and two basses. Two

Founder of Chamber Singers & Early Music Consort, 1967

were voice majors; the others were majoring in other fields but had outstanding musical skills and a strong interest in singing.

"I'll be happy to work with you, but not as a conductor. I'll sing tenor and we'll work as a team without someone standing in front of us."

We began rehearsing at my home by candlelight around the dining room table, with my eighty-five pound Golden Retriever *Falstaff* curled up under the table across our feet. It felt as if we were in a Renaissance Venetian Palazzo.

Our first concert was at Christmas in the Seminary's *Isaacson Chapel*, an intimate setting with perfect acoustics for Renaissance music. We sang by candlelight, mixing Scripture readings and Renaissance poetry with the music of Des Prez, Vittoria, Hassler, Palestrina and others. The Chapel was filled.

Chamber Singers, 1968-69

From then on the Chamber Singers *Christmas Concerts* were a campus and community favorite. In subsequent years we added instruments, eventually moving toward Renaissance instruments, and finally with the singers also playing those same instruments.

I preferred not to include voice majors, though there were always several in the group each year. That allowed me to work the voices into the character most fitting for the *genre* without apologizing to the voice majors for 'mistreating' their voices. Auditions were by invitation. The size of the group varied from year to year, determined by the choral literature to be included in our programs. One year five singers participated; that was the fewest. Our largest group was eighteen. I always sang with them, standing in the center of the group. They learned musical attacks, tempo, and dynamics through listening to my intake of breath. The Chamber Singers reveled in the organic unity developed through this process and enjoyed the opportunity to focus directly on their audiences rather than staring at a conductor.

Our programs at first had been limited to the campus. The College Choir toured every other year during Spring Break. The Development Office planned their tours and paid for them. It was considered a worthy and necessary expense to keep our 'public', the Covenant Church, engaged with the college. In our fourth year I thought it was time for our group to represent the school to our denominational constituents around the country. I spoke with Vice President LeRoy Johnson, who headed up the Development Office.

"Mr. Johnson, I'd like to make a proposal. Our denomination has churches in Florida; most of them are small and are not able to host the College Choir. They can't afford the honorarium necessary to cover tour costs, and they don't have enough homes to house the singers. We're *a small group. I think we should be sent to those churches who never get any representatives from North Park."*

"Do you think our churches would like the music you do?" he asked.

He had seen the attendance at all our campus concerts, including many people from local Covenant churches. He himself never missed our performances and always expressed his delight. Why that question?

"Mr. Johnson, I know you pay for the tours of the College Choir, picking up the shortfall. I also know they have never raised enough through offerings to cover their costs, yet the college thinks it's worth the expense. Why not give us a chance?"

He was still struggling with the proposal.

"Alright. Let me offer this. Give us permission to concertize in Florida and if the offerings don't cover our expenses, including airfare, I'll pay the difference out of my own pocket. The tour will cost you nothing. We'll see if the Chamber Singers will garner any interest and have any positive impact for the school."

He finally agreed.

Our first off-campus tour paid for itself through the Florida church offerings, and had money left over. It was the first tour in North Park's history that had been self-supporting, much less ended up with a surplus.

Chamber Singers Florida Tour

Upon returning to the campus I was called in to President Lloyd Ahlem's office.

"Look at this," he said, and handed me a stack of letters.

"What do you mean?"

"These letters," he replied. *"Read them."*

I wondered if he had received complaints about the students, the nature of our musical program, or me. I read several. They were glowing in their praise of the Chamber Singers, one after the other. There must have been thirty letters or more. Here is a sampling:

Those Chamber Singers are exactly what I believed them to be—a mighty organ of voices. You just don't know how well they did in everything—not only in the absolute perfect artistry of the music but also in their relating to our people.... The charming formality that a presentation like that requires was not missing, and then at the same time, the touch of human-ness so intimate and real. Professor Athnos was absolutely a master of all the arts, not only of singing and directing, but winning our people.... The Artists of last night gave a glimpse of the finer things of the college.... I just cannot say anything too great about Professor Athnos and his excellent leadership—without ostentation, without pride.

We heard the Chamber Singers last night in the Vero Beach Covenant Church. We were rightfully proud of how they represented North Park College not only with their singing but their communication with the people of our church.... We are glad to see that the college is making an effort to relate to the denomination.... Thanks also to Greg Athnos and the kids for a wonderful evening.

Thank you so much for sending us the North Park Chamber Singers. It was a pleasure and joy to hear such fine singers, and to meet such delightful young people. Please send them to us again.

"Are you sure you didn't tell them what to say?" I knew the President was not a music aficionado, though to his credit he always attended our campus concerts, sitting in the front row. There were times I wished he wouldn't come, both for his sake and mine, because his discomfort showed. But to be fair, Dr. Ahlem always came to my defense and the defense of the Chamber Singers when, on occasion, constituents complained about the character of our music. He never ceased to do what was right for us; I appreciated him for going beyond his own preferences on our behalf. I assured him the letters were just as much a surprise to me as to him. He was satisfied.

That was how our tour history began! Over the thirty-one years I led the Chamber Singers we ended up touring almost every year, either during Spring Break, alternating with the College Choir, or during the summer months.

After one of our East Coast tours we heard from the Covenant Church in Rochester, New York:

I am writing in the afterglow of our concert with the Chamber Singers.... I believe that Rochester with its Eastman School of Music influence provides a rather sophisticated audience, and last night was no exception, with many from the community of music in attendance. The total response to the Chamber Singers was, 'absolutely beautiful'.

"Of the People" Chamber Singers Poster

We did a five-week Midwest tour in 1976 featuring a Bicentennial musical drama I compiled and wrote, entitled, *Of the People, By the People, For the People.* Excerpts were shown on the CBS-TV affiliate in Chicago upon our return. Again, letters flooded the President's office:

I believe OF THE PEOPLE, BY THE PEOPLE, FOR THE PEOPLE may well be the best and the most interesting and celebrative program of the Bicentennial year. The outstanding music and dramatic presentation was enhanced by the extent of research which was apparent and summarized in the hand-out program. The humorous notes entertained while the serious provoked deep thought. Thanks for a well-spent evening.

It was an excellent portrayal that carried a pertinent, thought-provoking message in the midst of all the hoopla of this Bicentennial year. All the feedback I received was glowing with praise. The people were greatly impressed with the students and with the great piece of work done by Greg Athnos. One rather conservative 'old-timer' in the congregation said, "It made me grateful to be an American."

What an excellent program! No flag waving, no cynicism, just an honest and straight-forward appraisal of our National strengths and weaknesses. I personally was deeply moved by the presentation and have heard nothing but positive comment from all who attended.

Chamber Singers "Of the People" Tour, 1976

Dear President Ahlem: You perhaps have heard this excellent group acclaimed by various people and various sectors of our country, but we would like to add our word of appreciation for the beautiful and meaningful evening they gave us. We had a number of Bicentennial activities in the Twin Cities which added significance to this fateful year of '76, but the appearance of the Singers added a dimension of history and honesty that gave us a clearer perspective of where we have been and are going as a nation.

In this year of our 'Buy Centennial', with 'Happy Birthday America' an excuse for selling everything from red, white and blue toilet seats to star-spangled caskets, I was totally refreshed, renewed, and in a sense, repatriated by the masterful performance by the Chamber Singers on July 4th. Sometime in the midst of their program the thought broke upon me: "I have never been/felt so unequivocally proud to be associated with this college, with the name North Park, as I am because of this performance." To be blunt I felt 'proud as hell' to be part of an institution which could produce something like this…. This was the Liberal Arts at their finest…. I found myself enthralled, totally captured by their message…flawless technical expertise combined with a genuine human naturalness and warmth…. Was it their skill as singers? As versatile musicians? As dramatists with a gift for Square Dance? Or simply being the finest of my peer group, giving their all to express through their finely-honed gifts and talents, ideas and ideals significant to them and to all of us as Americans, as human beings…. At a gut level I recognized that so much of what I think this school should be all about, and has the raw material to become, was made manifest on July 4th…. Encore! Encore!

We toured the western United States and western Canada for eight weeks another summer, giving 60 concerts of Renaissance Choral and Instrumental music, traveling 12,000 miles in one un-air-conditioned school van! The pastor of the Tucson Covenant Church was upset with North Park for not providing a suitable means of travel for the southwestern states in the summer:

The North Park Chamber Singers gave an outstanding program last night in Tucson.... Mr. Athnos did an outstanding job of preparing our people with his comments and I wish to commend him.... However... it is unrealistic to ask a group of young people to travel in a van without air conditioning from Albuquerque to Phoenix in one day and be bright and positive for a concert in the evening. The same is true for their travel from Tucson to San Diego, a distance of about 425 miles with daytime temperatures between 110 and 120 degrees.... The positive job these young people are doing is being undermined by poor planning at the school.

As it turned out, we stayed 'cool' during the trip to San Diego by putting ice cubes down the backs of our shirts while singing Christmas carols! I had told them the first week would be tough, with long travel days, concerts every night, and incredible heat to overcome.

"If we survive the first seven days, we'll have a tremendous summer together. If not, if we let the circumstances overwhelm us, it will become intolerable."

I shouldn't have been concerned. They were 'troupers' in every sense of the word.

The group assembled a library of art, philosophy, and Native American culture, housed in a box. We took turns reading the books and leading lively discussions every day. We never ate in a fast food restaurant the entire summer! College students! Imagine that! The radio in the van was never turned on! Our cultural conversations were exciting enough.

Our program was indeed esoteric, but audiences loved it. The first half consisted of Renaissance sacred music and poetry, telling the story of Christ entitled, *Christus: A Renaissance Portrait*. The second half featured Renaissance instrumental music played by the singers on Period instruments.

Again, letters poured into the college:

One of the greatest experiences to come my way.... If we had had any idea of the quality of this program in advance we certainly would have encouraged everyone in the Occidental College music department to come.

Last night our church was ministered to in music by one of the finest groups that North Park has ever sent out.... It was a treat to be introduced to this Renaissance music by such a well-trained and totally musical group. It was evident that these young people really love the music and enjoy performing together.

On Monday I called Mission Springs to get the Singers on the Family Conference program. They had already received a half dozen calls from other churches with the same request.

I attend Stanford to hear their Medieval group... the NP group tops the Stanford group! Another

"Christus, A Renaissance Portrait" Program Cover

1967: The Chamber Singers Initiative

family who also attend the Stanford concerts independently came up with the same comparison, and they are not died-in-the-wool North Parkers like we are.

People felt they had worshipped God in a new way, one that excited them.

The finest program ever! To use the word 'program' is not being fully descriptive. They represent a worship experience that makes us thankful and proud to be a part of the family of God.

Playing Renaissance instrumental music on Fisherman's Wharf, San Francisco, on our free day

This morning I woke up early and…picked up the program of your 'Renaissance' performance. I looked at your pictures, your names, and read through the poems. As I did I replayed the performance in my mind.... I

am a junior in high school and haven't decided whether I will major in music or not when I go to college because of the competition and flooded market. But when I heard you sing that night, I wanted very badly to become a music major.

The Chamber Singers presented a concert in our church last Sunday night which in my judgment was the finest musical presentation that I have heard at the college level.

After that tour was over we made a side trip to *Ancilla Domini Convent Chapel* to record the program we had lived with for eight weeks. We arrived at noon and, with a short break for dinner, finished recording at 2 a.m., then returned to Chicago. Later we sent a few records to the Convent, and received this letter from Sister M. Angelita:

I feel I owe you a special note of thanks, since I am the happy recipient of one of the records.... I am the Sister who serves as main organist here.... Besides its artistic beauty and religious inspiration, your new record is special to me since it was recorded in our chapel. Naturally we are very happy that you and your students enjoy so much performing your music in our place of worship. You as the director are certainly to be commended in the way you influence and inspire your Chamber Singers to perform music of such difficulty and high caliber. We hope you will treat us again to the glorious sound of your very competent and admirable singing group.

Another program was taken to Norway and Sweden on a four-week tour. It was our first foreign excursion. The ten singers, including me, were received with great enthusiasm by the Scandinavians. I was asked to write an article for the November, 1987 edition of the *Covenant Companion*, the denomination's monthly news magazine, on my thoughts regarding our experience with the 'Mother Church' in Sweden:

It was June of 1987 and our seat belts were fastened. The SAS DC-10

1967: The Chamber Singers Initiative

was gathering speed on the O'Hare runway. Several hundred pounds of concert programs were in the cargo hold along with the luggage for eight of my students who were seated all around me.

I was trying to convince myself that the North Park College Chamber Singers were really on their way to Scandinavia at last! All the work—itinerary planning, fund raising, program preparation, correspondence, phone calls, travel and housing arrangements, car rentals, ferry crossings—was finally finished. I should have been relieved and excited. Why did I have an uneasy knot in the pit of my stomach?

In spite of our thoroughness, it occurred to me that we didn't really know what to expect from our hosts. How would we be received by the churches? Would they enjoy the program of American music we had prepared? Would our stay in their homes be pleasant? We were, after all, foreigners from an institution most of them had never heard of before. Even silly questions kept me from sleep. Would we really be served herring at every breakfast? How would we ever survive lutefisk?

Uneasiness should not have plagued my thoughts, for I had been associated with the North American offspring of the Swedish Mission Church for a long time. I first heard of the Evangelical Covenant Church thirty years ago when I was hired as music director of the Detroit church. My immediate impression centered around its ethnic roots and heritage. Scandinavian ways were not foreign to me, as my mother's parents had come to America from Norway in the late 1800's. It was a re-baptism, so to speak, to be thrown again into a church family where so many people shared the same last name (with a name like Athnos you notice such things).

Joining the North Park College music faculty twenty-one years ago, I came to know the wider Covenant family. I have performed or spoken in almost 200 of our churches throughout the country. While the names have

151

changed to the point where 'Athnos' no longer stands out, I am still amazed at the closeness and kindred spirit that marks our constituency. We are a family held together by a strange and wonderful glue, which is for many of us our heritage and for many others an adopted second heritage.

There is a certain stamp that marks Covenanters, even in our growing diversity. I feel I know it quite well, though definitions are elusive. There is the closeness, but beyond that a spirit of quiet graciousness and hospitality often charms me. Then there is the Nordic reserve that can either speak of self-confidence or of a reluctance to really give one's self completely to another. The conservative streak in us can be prudent, but has sometimes struck me as being a little too 'safe'. We are not often bold enough for this half-Greek's taste.

The humility of spirit that is a trademark of the Covenant is genuine and admirable. But it, too, has a less desirable face. How many times have we been so quiet about our successes or our gifts that very little ever comes of them beyond our own small gathering? For example, I am amazed at how few people who have lived for decades within the shadow of North Park even know we exist. I have experienced the same lack of community recognition of a number of our Covenant churches. The Covenant and North Park College have never been very good at blowing their own horn. It seems we are occasionally 'in' a community but not 'of' it. Our cities and towns often remain untouched by or unaware of our presence.

For years I have been possessed by a curiosity about the "Mother Church" in Sweden—the Mission Church. If we have sprung from their roots does that mean they are like us? Do they resemble us in their spiritual concerns? What about their social consciousness? How are they viewed by others in their communities? Do others know anything about them? What do their churches look like? What is their cultural or aesthetic posture? Is the diversity of spiritual postures that marks our American churches part of their experience? Now I was about to discover some of the answers to these questions.

The North Park College Chamber Singers were celebrating their twentieth anniversary season by touring Norway and Sweden. As their director, I was responsible not only for the idea, but also for making all the travel and concert arrangements and raising the nearly twenty thousand dollars necessary to cover our expenses. I was starting from ground zero. I had only been in Sweden for twelve hours twenty-two years ago on my way from Norway to Finland. I knew no one. I had no idea how many Mission churches there were, their size, or where they were located. This was indeed going to be an experience, not to mention a lot of work. But here we were, ten months later, hours away from an idea's realization.

After landing in Oslo and picking up our two rental vehicles, we set out for Dalen, a small village halfway across Norway. One is never really prepared for the beauty of that country, no matter how much has been said about it or how often it has been visited. We had five days before our first concert to stand in awe of God's creation, and so we did.

Chamber Singers explore the Norwegian Fjords

Our first concert was for the Annual Meeting of the Norwegian Mission Church being held in Stavanger. We greeted them by singing one of their patriotic songs in Norwegian, and then proceeded into our own musical heritage of American religious folk hymns, spirituals, and folk songs. When our final chord was released, six hundred of our family in Christ leaped to their feet. Any doubts or misgivings I might have had vanished in that instant. We were welcome, felt peacefully at home, and remained so through concerts in Haugesund, Bergen, Lillehammer and Oslo.

The friendliness of the Norwegians disarmed us. Contrary to the reserve I anticipated, these new friends in the Mission Church were outgoing, lavish in their compliments and praise, quick to smile and laugh, and almost eager to embrace us with hugs instead of handshakes. In spite of the breathtaking beauty of the mountains and fjords celebrated by us in our many free days in Norway, it seems we could hardy wait for our next opportunity to be with the people in the churches.

The Norwegian Mission Church, it appears, is more closely aligned with the Evangelical Free Church of America than with our Covenant body. They knew far more about them than us. Rare was the person who had heard of North Park College, and most parishioners seemed only dimly aware of the Covenant Church, though the ministers knew something of us. All the more reason for us to be amazed not only at the reception we received but also that we were invited to share with them at all. Yet, in spite of what I have just stated, our world proved once again to be very small indeed. As we boarded a sightseeing bus chartered by the Stavanger annual meeting, we struck up a conversation with one of the leaders of the Mission Church and discovered that his sister teaches Norwegian at North Park! I thought such things happened only in the Covenant here!

What impressed me most was the deep and abundant spirituality in the

Norwegian Mission church. These were people for whom the Christian faith was vital. Christ's command to live our new life in him was clearly evident. As we alternated between the Mission Church and the rest of Norwegian society we began to sense that it was almost possible to tell who was a Christian just by observing their behavior. The evangelical church in Norway is growing in quantum leaps. I wonder if it is because of the noticeable difference the Christian faith seems to make in its adherents, a difference at once observable and compelling.

My most indelible memory is of Geir Johannessen, pastor of the Mission Church in Haugesund, a tall rail of a man with a smile carved in eternity. We spent forty hours with him, traveling from Stavanger, worshiping and singing in his church, and sharing his table and his home. My students fell in love with him and his family. He became my friend and brother. As we drove from Stavanger to Haugesund Saturday night we talked of my interest in the centrality of the resurrection of Jesus. He invited me to preach the next morning in his church.

I believe the providence of God was at work in his request, not only for my chance to share what has become so important to me, but also because of the night he was soon to have.

No sooner had we settled into his living room than the phone rang. It was a woman from the town, not a member of his church, who once more had become the victim of a beating by her husband. She needed help. He spent the rest of the night taking her out of that horrible situation, consoling her, counseling her, tending to her wounds, taking her to doctors, and answering her cries in the night. In the morning his fetching smile was still in place. As he translated for me, phrase by phrase, it was as if he was my shadow. When I became caught up in my enthusiasm, so did he. Every nuance, every inflection, every shout, even every gesture was imitated as if he were my echo. He said he was inspired by me, but the truth is that who he was, what he had done through the night, and now his haloed presence as he translated lifted me up as I have rarely been lifted before. God is truly using that wonderful man. He stands in my mind as a symbol of the Mission Church of Norway.

On the twelfth day of our tour my wife Doy left for Chicago as planned to rescue Grandma, our babysitter, from Trifon, our two-and-a-half-year-old son. The next day the Chamber Singers left Norway and entered Sweden.

The landscape looked familiar. Though I had only been in Sweden a few hours years earlier I had seen this landscape many times driving through northern Wisconsin and the Upper Peninsula of Michigan. In our driving throughout the southern half of Sweden the landscape remained as we had seen it in the first hour. We were to spend seventeen days there, singing nineteen times. We wouldn't see the sun until the last day. Chicago was in the 90's; Sweden never passed 52. But we were neither bored nor depressed, thanks to our incredible hosts.

We were met at Säffle, our first stop, by Olle and Margot Engstrom, whom we had met the previous year on our campus. Olle Engstrom had spent an immense amount of time arranging our Swedish itinerary and now would be our guide for a total of seven days. Former dean of the Mission Church Seminary in Lidingö, he knew churches, people, ministers, Mission church history, and the American Covenant better than anyone else in the country. He is also a man of international stature, one who has given his retirement years to the quest for peace throughout the Third World. I had talked with him several times about his experience in El Salvador and Nicaragua. He is obviously a powerful man of God, given to social action. As we traveled together in those days, and as I became familiar with the 'Mother Church', I began to realize how Dr. Engstrom stands as a beacon of the spirit of many in the Mission Church in Sweden. I would learn how different in some ways they are from our own denomination.

1967: The Chamber Singers Initiative

It was Swedish Flag Day. We had been invited to participate in Säffle's celebration prior to our concert in the Mission church. Following our presentation we were given gifts from the Community of Säffle by their representative in the Swedish Parliament. An hour later we were singing to an overflow crowd in the church. The music critic from the newspaper gave us a stunning review titled "Uniquely Competent Choir":

"The choir, Chamber Singers, consists of nine extremely well-singing young people under the leadership of Gregory S. Athnos. He is also one of the singers and conducts the choir very discreetly, with small means. For my own part, I have never heard a choir with such a marvelous way of singing in a chamber music style. The singers sing in such a relaxed mood and so naturally, so purely and with such fine nuances. Their 'piano' and 'pianissimo' were almost heavenly.... To state it very simply, they sing extraordinarily beautifully! The conductor said they were tired after two weeks of singing in Norway. How would the choir then sound without such strains?

What is unique is that the members were both very competent soloists and in addition to that could produce such an exceptionally fine choral singing. It is difficult to combine the two. In a choir the individual voices must not be heard but be melted together to oneness. In this respect the choir succeeded completely! After the concert I learned that they had worked very purposefully in this direction.

During the time of studies in the U.S. the choir concentrates predominantly on Renaissance music. Maybe this is the explanation to the very special quality and color that the choir has.

There followed a section of American songs sung by soloists in the group. Lynette Johnson from Minnesota sang a song by Samuel Barber. Elizabeth Magnusson, with relatives in Arvika, sang in a wonderful way Gershwin's 'Summertime'.

But the audience was not satisfied with that. The applause would never end. The choir thanked them by singing a fine interpretation of '*Bred dina vida vingar*'. One had to be present at this concert to understand that these songs, often simple ones, were interpreted in such a wonderful way that they all could be considered as fine pieces of art."

It was only our first concert in Sweden, and we were struck by the difference in tone between our two Churches. In Sweden the Church faces squarely and boldly into the community, both gathering and providing numerous resources. What we witnessed in Säffle would be repeated at almost every stop. I became increasingly fascinated by the character of the Mission Church of Sweden. A number of impressions remain with me.

Our first action in arriving in a town or city was to stop in a service station and inquire about the location of the Mission church. No matter how large the city the first person we asked knew of it and how to get to it. The Mission church in Sweden looms large in the mind of its community. We discovered why in a hurry. Almost every church was in the very center of town. Rather than moving to the outskirts when the church facilities became outmoded or too small, they simply added on, or tore them down and built them larger.

As an artist and musician I was immediately impressed by the architecture, interior design, art work, and acoustics. The sanctuaries in Jönköping and Uppsala, to name only two of many, were visually stunning and creative and focused worship in a most dramatic and moving way. The acoustical environment for singing ranged from outstanding to superb. We never sang in a dull, dry, disappointing sanctuary. I wish the same could be said for the American Covenant Church.

Most churches we visited had a vast array of programs extending into the community. In one town of 13,000 people there were 800 young people involved weekly in various youth group activities in the Mission Church. We heard similar statistics in many places. I was amazed at how many congregations had cafeterias open to the public during the day. Business people, families, and travelers frequented them. Much of the food was prepared in the homes of the women of the church, who took their turns serving in the cafeteria. Low cost, high profit: good for the programs of the church. A number of churches also had within their building complex housing for the elderly or infirm. Several had hotels. Every church seemed to have a large house, gathering hall, sleeping facilities, and recreational space by a lake a few miles from town. Some were elaborate enough to be used as conference centers for the general public, again providing revenue for the local church.

The Church there is not merely another social institution. It was evident through conversations I had and messages I heard that the primary motivation that gave blossom to these myriad social concerns was the root of the good news of spiritual transformation. The command of Christ was being heeded: "Go into all the world." Though imperfect, as we all are, here was a Church forthrightly attempting to live out the Gospel in full view—a Church that cared for the whole person, not just the heart. Here was a Church where preaching and witness carried weight because it was acted out in the face of society. Dr. Engstrom and others spoke of the roots of the Mission Church in Sweden growing from the soil of social action as well as personal piety. The foundation has remained solid and secure. I was impressed and saddened, because I wondered whether in my own denomination back home—and I do love it—there were as many churches or institutions with similar commitment. In Scandinavia reticence and reserve often stop at the door of the Church, with its ministry and its programs.

Midsummer Eve had arrived. The Chamber Singers had sung for 6,000 people and received glowing praise from music critics in both countries. In three days we would return home. After singing in the Immanuel Church in Stockholm Sunday morning, we were invited by Gunno Södersten—their former organist and an outstanding composer—and his wife, Barbara, to their home for a farewell brunch. Gunno, such a sweet man he is, met us at his door and extended a formal, gracious 'thank you' and 'welcome'. The food was wonderful, just what we had come to expect from the Swedes. Gifts were given to all of us. I'll never forget Gunno's piano improvisation on the musical equivalent of my name. Dr. Engstrom spoke to us on behalf of the Swedish Mission Church and even more, for himself, as he had heard our concert at least seven times. How much he would miss it, he said, and how much he would miss the exuberant young singers who were such a delight to him.

That is how I felt about him—and Margot, Gunno and Barbara, Geir, all the many fine Christians who welcomed us into their homes and into their hearts—and about the Mission Church which had become in these four weeks a model of what the Church of the risen Jesus Christ could be. That is the ultimate song and it remains with me.

While in Sweden we had been invited to celebrate Desmond Tutu's *Nobel Peace Prize* for his fight against Apartheid in South Africa. It was a small group of people representing the Mission Church of Sweden, gathered in an outdoor park near Stockholm. We shared a major part of our concert program, including several Spirituals that fit the nature of the celebration. I had the privilege of meeting Archbishop Tutu, a moment I continue to cherish. That group of Chamber Singers ranks as one of the top two or three groups in my entire three decades as their director.

On that 20th anniversary in 1986 I was interviewed for an article, *"Creative Quality in Teaching",* in the school's quarterly journal, *The North Parker*. Steve Elde led the interview.

1967: The Chamber Singers Initiative

North Parker: *Tell me about the Chamber Singers. How did this group get started?*

Athnos: *We have always had a very fine choral program. In my second year here, I realized there was another dimension of music that would be better served by a smaller group. I found some students who were interested—or rather, they found me— and we got organized. Next year will be our twentieth year.*

North Parker: *Why did you select the music that you did?*

Athnos: *I thought we ought to specialize in Renaissance and early Baroque music, since the College Choir deals with the late Baroque, Classical, and Romantic periods. The music of the Renaissance came primarily out of the worship of God. There's a sense of purity about it, a linkage with the Christian faith that you can sense when you listen. It's like taking a 'spiritual bath'.*

North Parker: *There's a purity of sound…*

Athnos: *We try to treat our voices as very pure instruments.*

North Parker: *You sing with the Chamber Singers as you direct. Why?*

Athnos: *I started doing this for practical reasons. Tenors are always hard to find, so I decided to be the main tenor and find a person who could match my voice. I also have outstanding musicians in the group, people who understand the music in very sensitive ways, without having a director in front of them. I have found that just being a member of the group and allowing students to enter into the interpretive process works better. They have to anticipate entrances, releases, and color changes. They develop a sixth sense. These ten or twelve students become one voice and spirit. I tell them to get out of their music and make eye contact with someone in the audience, to draw people in….*

North Parker*: So you create a relationship with your audience...*

Athnos*: This is something larger groups can't do. Audiences get the feeling that we really love the music we sing and want them to love it too. I will often explain a piece of music the audience might not understand. On our most recent tour we did a piece by Charles Ives, with men singing in one key and the women in another. It was difficult to sing and difficult to listen to. I knew this, so I took a little time to talk about Charles Ives, how the music was put together, and what to listen for. After the concerts, this was always the piece that people wanted to talk about.*

North Parker*: What kind of students do you look for in Chamber Singers:*

Athnos*: I try to find students who are very personable, who enjoy meeting people, because that sells North Park. It's important to have people who love each other and get along well.*

North Parker*: You must have many memories.*

Athnos*: I've enjoyed every tour. Ten years ago, during the Bicentennial, the Chamber Singers toured the country for five weeks with a program of American music called, "Of the People". We've traveled almost 40,000 miles in 19 years. There have been some great moments. I remember sitting at the end of the cable-car line in San Francisco. We were all dressed in our formal wear, with our Krummhorns, Recorders, and Viola da Gamba. We sang and played those Renaissance instruments for an hour and a half, and several hundred people stopped and listened. We left the Gamba case open, and when it was over we had enough money to go to the best seafood restaurant in San Francisco. That was fun!*

North Parker*: Looking back on nearly twenty years, have you any final thoughts?*

1967: The Chamber Singers Initiative

Athnos: *I'm fortunate that I'm doing things I really enjoy, things that allow for creativity. With the exception of "Introduction to Music" classes, nothing that I teach at North Park existed when I came here. I sensed a need for them and helped create them. I'm proud of what I've done here, and I'm proud of North Park for allowing me to be creative and innovative. I don't think there are many institutions where such a thing would have happened.*

We traveled in Italy for two weeks. The President of the *Choral Society of Tuscany* called the Chamber Singers the best American chamber choir he had ever heard.

Chamber Singers in Italy

The Chamber Singers also joined the College/University Choir on their tours to Poland and Hungary in 1989, and Sweden, Russia and Estonia in 1993.

One solitary concert event in 1971 is deserving of attention. We were invited by Rabbi David Mersky of the *Emanuel Congregation* in Chicago. We shared our *Christus: A Renaissance Portrait* program with a number of young congregants at their Friday service, followed by a time of discussion. Putting the music into its context of 15th century Europe, about the time the Jews were being expelled from Spain and suffering persecution in every town and village across the European landscape, we talked about the incongruity they must have felt. On the one hand they were hearing beautiful choral singing emanating from magnificent stone cathedrals they were forbidden to enter. On the other hand, the music was being sung by people who were responsible for their day-to-day persecution. The people who sang the music of Heaven on Sunday gave them a taste of Hell the rest of the week. How difficult must that have been!

It was a lively discussion, filled with open and honest give and take. I was proud of my students that night as they embraced Jewish young people of their own age, breaking down at least for a short time the historic and religious barriers that truly have no place in our society. Rabbi Mersky sent me this letter:

I hasten to write to express more formally my gratitude to you and to the members of your group for the outstanding program which you shared with us.... I had no end of comment from the people who were with us that night, and I can only say to you what I have said to others: I was witness to a remarkable evening of beautiful music, in a beautiful setting, by beautiful people.

One of our most 'touching' or 'moving' tour experiences took place on one of our East Coast tours during Spring Break. The East Coast Conference of the Covenant Church has many upper middle class congregations and a number of affluent churches. There was

1967: The Chamber Singers Initiative

one exception—a church in the Bronx, one of the few African-American congregations in the denomination at that time. Situated in a blighted area, many of the congregants live in poverty. North Park had never made any arrangements to perform there because they would not be able to supply housing, nor would they have the funds to help defray the cost of the tour.

I was determined to share our music with them, whatever it took. I arranged our itinerary so that we would sing on a Saturday night in Connecticut, just a short drive from New York City. Our Sunday night concert was arranged in New Jersey. That freed Sunday morning to participate in the worship services of the Bronx church—that is, if they would agree to the arrangement.

In my phone call to their Pastor I explained that we simply wanted to worship with them because they were part of our 'family'. If they wished, we would sing two or three pieces. We didn't need housing or lunch. No 'honorarium' was necessary. We had cleared the morning and desired to gather to worship our Lord with them.

No one had ever asked him before. He was thrilled.

That Sunday we drove into the Bronx, past boarded up and burned out buildings bombarded with graffiti. Arriving at the Church we were met at their razor-wire-protected parking lot by four young men who took charge of our two vans, promising they would stay with them the entire morning.

The service began. The congregational members were dressed in their 'Sunday Best'. The woman running the service told visitors that God deserves our finest appearance, so, ladies—no pants; men—coats and ties.

The Chamber Singers were asked to sing; we chose one 'Spiritual' and, of all things, a High Renaissance Palestrina Motet! Even as I chose it I wondered, *"What on earth am I thinking?"* A most remarkable thing happened a few seconds into the Palestrina. The church's drummer and organist (a Hammond organ of course) began playing along with the *a cappella* motet. It took us by surprise; to our amazement, it worked! We loved it! *Soulful Palestrina*: talk about breaking down barriers between cultures and idioms! That rendition was one for the ages; I wished then that we had recorded it. I doubt Palestrina has ever sounded like that in the four hundred years since it was composed, and I'm sure the composer would have said a hearty 'yes' to the revelation.

An offering was taken. The doors to the sanctuary were locked and guards were posted at the doors; they had been robbed on several occasions during the taking of the offering. Everyone was told they had to come forward, even if they had nothing to put in the basket. The 'Hallelujah March' proceeded, accompanied by organ and drums.

Later, before the sermon, another offering was taken, doors locked, organ and drums filling the air while the march progressed.

Finally, after the sermon and at the conclusion of the service the Pastor called me to the platform. Turning to the congregation, he said,

"This professor and his students went out of their way to worship with us today. They asked nothing of us. This man said we were part of their 'family', and he is right. We are part of not only the Covenant, but also the Family of God. I want our church to bless these young people. We're going to take another offering, just for them."

It was the third offering of the morning! After the service the ladies of the church prepared a delicious lunch for us, including collard greens, the whole 'nine yards'.

The Pastor called me into his office and handed me the money collected in the third 'Hallelujah March'. I didn't want to take it, but he insisted. It turned out to be the largest offering of the entire East Coast tour, larger than even the most affluent Covenant Churches where we had performed. It was a humbling moment. The people who could least afford it gave the most, and did so with joy.

A few years later I heard of the passing of the pastor who had stepped out of his comfort zone, as we also had done, and crossed that artificial barrier that has no place in the Kingdom of God. I gave thanks for his life and his gracious generosity of spirit.

One of the joys that results from working closely with students is that they become as close as family. Over the years many have remained good and close friends. I have been both honored and blessed in the relationships, and treasure the letters that have come my way, as expressed in small measure here:

Dear Greg,

How can I ever thank you for all the things you have taught me this last semester in Chamber Singers?.... I am a changed person because of it.... Thank you as well for encouraging me to do my best with the gifts God has graciously given me. Thank you for helping me believe in more of who I am by reminding me of Whose I am. I will miss you and Chamber Singers. In Him, (Kelly Olson)

Dear Greg,

How can I even begin to tell you what is in my heart! The past four years have been the best and hardest years of my life. I remember the first time I met you. I was a freshman auditioning for the choir. I was so nervous but your warm smile just calmed me down. Well, here I am, four years later and still in choir and now Chamber Singers. It's been a joy and privilege to work with you.... You are a man of passion and you give 100% of yourself in all you do.... I admire you as a musician, teacher, and friend. You have inspired me spiritually, intellectually, and musically.... I can't thank you enough for all the time you've taken to listen to me and care about me. You've always been there for me, encouraging me and helping me out. You are a blessing in my life, and I "Thank my God every time I remember you." Love, (Nicole DiGrazia)

Dear Greg,

I cannot thank you enough for all the wonderful memories, for five years of singing, touring, laughing, learning, and witnessing. I have never been a part of something that I enjoyed more and felt more a part of. Your excitement about and love of music is contagious, and it certainly infected my soul.... You gave me a new sense of confidence when you invited me to be a part of the Chamber Singers.... You are a gift from God to all those who sing with you. My sincerest thanks, (Ann-Marie Olson)

Dear Greg,

The opportunity to be in Chamber Singers is one that has blessed us in many ways. We have seen our country like few people ever have a chance to.... Your adventuresome spirit and way with puns, though joked about, are remembered with love. All of our fondest memories come to their ultimate expression in the recording of our music.... I cannot find the right words to express the feelings experienced when we listen to it. It is so beautiful and filled with the spirit of our God. I am sending you my most sincere thanks for sharing your love and understanding of Renaissance music with us. God bless you, (David and Karolyn Rice)

Altogether the Chamber Singers undertook over fifty weeks of touring for the college. I arranged every itinerary, raised almost all of the funding, volunteered my time, and was not paid. It didn't matter; I felt privileged to do it. To see my students grow in maturity as well as musicianship and service was more than worth it. The Chamber Singers brought satisfaction in abundance to my life. I hold them close to my heart—all of them.

CHAPTER 21

1967: International Summer School, Oslo, Norway

Only months into my first year as a college music professor I became aware of a summer school opportunity in Norway. The topic was *Edvard Grieg and Norwegian Folk Music*. Half Norwegian myself, and having a keen interest in folk music of various cultures, I thought this might be a perfect way to satisfy several of my curiosities regarding music and culture.

The six-week *International Summer School* program was housed on the University of Oslo campus at Blindern. Students from America would be traveling together to Norway on Norwegian American Line's *M/S Bergensfjord*. The cost was prohibitive; my salary wouldn't stretch that far. To my surprise an anonymous donor paid for my entire trip. As I wasn't even aware anyone knew of my interest in the program, his gracious offer was both a mystery and a kindness. I later discovered the donor was Mr. Kristian Mohn, President of Norwegian American Line, to whom I wrote a letter of thanks upon returning from Norway.

On the morning of my flight to New York I received a phone call stating the flight had been delayed. There would be only a short window

1967: International Summer School, Oslo, Norway

of time to get from the airport to the ship. Arriving at JFK in New York I discovered TWA had lost my luggage! This put me in a quandary. Should I set sail on the high seas without any clothes other than what I was wearing? Hailing a taxi I told the driver the limited time I had to get to the pier. *"Impossible,"* he said. I urged him to try, and said if he made it I'd board the liner even without any luggage. If he didn't make it I'd return to the airport, wait for my luggage, and fly to Oslo.

The drive across Manhattan was hair-raising as he wove in and out of traffic at breakneck speeds. We arrived at the pier fifteen minutes late. The shed was empty. My heart sank. At the far end of the terminal a man yelled to me,

"Are you Athnos?"

"Yes."

"Hurry up. We've been holding the ship for you."

With that I walked up the gangplank, they pulled it away, and the ship left the dock: streamers flying, music playing, and the ship's air horn blasting. In the midst of the celebration I noticed who was standing next to me along the railing. It was the Reverend Otto Larsen, his wife, and twin daughters, from La Crosse, Wisconsin! I had been in his church many times as a boy. I knew the family well. We marveled at this chance meeting and discussed briefly our plans for the summer. That was the last time I saw them, not only on the entire crossing, but ever.

I had boarded the ship wearing a navy blue suit and carrying a briefcase with a few toiletries; that was the extent of my wardrobe for the trip!

After passing the Statue of Liberty I decided to check out the ship.

Going forward on the main deck I wondered why I was the only person there. Then I looked down and saw the signs: 'wet paint'. Looking further I saw that I had light grey paint on the legs of my navy blue pants from the knee down! I returned to my cabin and spent the rest of the day trying to get the paint out of the pants. I mostly succeeded—mostly.

Each night of the crossing I washed out my socks and underwear, hoping they'd be dry by breakfast, and continued working on the grey paint. I had the early breakfast call, and we lost one hour each night of the journey, so every morning I went slogging down to breakfast in wet underclothes. By noon body heat dried them. I undertook the same ritual every day.

Half way across the ocean I was asked, *"Are you someone famous?"*

"Why do you ask?"

"Because people are saying, 'He must be famous. At breakfast he's wearing a suit. At lunch he's wearing a suite. At dinner he's wearing a suit.'"

They evidently didn't realize it was the *same* suit!

The morning of our arrival, steaming up the Oslo fjord, I was the only one standing by the railing observing the beauty of the country. Everyone else was busy packing. I had survived the crossing with just the clothes on my back and was reaping the 'no luggage' benefits as I took in the landscape of Norway.

My luggage was waiting for me in my dorm room. TWA had lost it. SAS found it and had it delivered. But I hardly used much of it during the summer, as I had become accustomed to washing things out each night. All summer I traveled light on my weekend excursions out of Oslo into the hinterlands.

The students in the *International Summer School* were from around the world, including many Communist countries: North Viet Nam, the Soviet Union, Cuba, Hungary, and others. We learned each other's folk songs at our nightly gatherings; I was particularly impressed by the beautiful *Moscow Nights*, and learned to sing it in Russian.

My professors were outstanding: Dag Schjelderup-Ebbe, Kjell Skyllstad, and Liv Greni. Dag dealt with the theoretical aspects of Grieg's music; Kjell covered the historical and biographical components of the composer's life; and Liv was the expert on Norwegian folk music. Through them I became more greatly aware of the relationship between the music of Grieg and Norwegian folk music. Each weekend I went to various regions of Norway tape-recording folk music, sung and played by ordinary people, not professionals—mostly farmers. On the basis of some of my observations and discoveries Liv Greni invited me to do several broadcasts on Norwegian Radio.

Perhaps the most interesting folk music experience was the *Hardangerfele Competition* in Tuddal, Telemark. The *Hardangerfele* is the national instrument of Norway, in the shape of a violin but with extreme differences. It has eight strings, four under the fingerboard that vibrate sympathetically when the upper strings are bowed. Its bridge is rather flat, making double- and triple-stop playing (two or three strings bowed simultaneously) an integral part of the sound. The *Hardangerfele* is both a melody *and* harmony instrument. In addition, the body of the fiddle is inlaid with mother of pearl and ivory with decorative etching around the perimeter, making it quite beautiful to look at. Before the end of the summer I purchased a *Hardangerfele* in an antique shop in Bergen; it had been made in Grieg's hometown of Lofthus.

The players gathered from across Norway: self-taught and playing on instruments they themselves had made. The Friday session was to begin 'about 6 o'clock' according to the posters; that is, according to my interpretation, whenever the inhibited Norwegians were sufficiently 'lubricated' to lose their inhibitions! It appeared to me that everyone was quite intoxicated, even the Judges! At every wrong note loud groans issued forth from the panel; it had to be quite painful for the performers who had already left their 'comfort zone' to risk public display and potential humiliation. For two days I recorded their playing. Some were quite dreadful, others wonderful. *Hardangerfele* music is loved primarily by the 'country folk'. 'City folk' often ridicule the genre, comparing its sound to that of 'a cat being gutted without the benefit of anaesthesia'. Regardless of opinions, it was a tremendous learning experience, and I became quite knowledgeable about Norwegian folk music and the *Hardangerfele* culture.

I was privileged to research the Grieg archives in Bergen. This opportunity would play a significant role in my future path, but in unexpected ways. My research began quite innocently; then it turned into a compelling study project. But first, I had to make sure I understood just why Grieg was so important to Norwegian musical culture. My studies with the three professors had provided the foundation.

Grieg had attended the Leipzig Conservatory to pursue the Germanic tradition of composition. A classmate, Rikard Nordraak, had convinced him to 'look North'. This was the age of *Nationalism* and countries long out of the 'mainstream' of European culture were searching for their own distinctive voices. Why should they and their cultures remain inferior to the 'big Four': Italy, France, England and Germany? Was it possible the 'language' of their national folk traditions could become the 'stuff' of concert hall worthiness? And exactly what musical ingredients were unique or special to their various cultures that would provide an alternative to the others?

Norway had no one to represent them, nor had they the slightest concern for representation. Mountainous as it was, 19th century Norway lacked even so much as a cohesive language. Trapped in their individual valleys with no exit, dialects grew up that would make communication difficult when roads finally penetrated their isolation. They were not only isolated geographically from the rest of Europe; they were isolated from each other. What need did they have for the concert hall experience?

Nonetheless, Nordraak's words, coupled with those of Ole Bull, the famous Norwegian violinist, had great influence on Edvard. Ole Bull exclaimed,

Do you see the fjords over there—the lakes and streams, the valleys and forests, and the blue sky over all? They have made my music. Sometimes it seems to me as if I were only a silent listener while the soul of Norway sings within me.

Grieg decided to become the 'voice of Norway', a musical Nationalist. The time was right. Europe was struggling with post-Beethoven confusion in compositional styles as well as the struggle for 'national identity' from countries on the fringes. He could pursue the 'mainstream' or take the tributary called 'Nationalism'. He chose the latter. He wrote,

But we do not, like that Teutonic race, feel the desire to pour out our souls in broad rivers of words; we have always cared only for what was clear and full.

And again,

Artists like Bach and Beethoven erected churches and temples on ethereal heights. My aim in my music is exactly what Ibsen says about his own plays: 'I want to build homes for the people in which they can be happy and contented.

There were characteristics in Norwegian folk music that gave him the materials for an exclusive 'voice'. One was a *three-note motif* that is found countless times throughout the Norwegian folk idiom: a beginning note followed by another one half step lower and another two notes below that. For example: C-B-G, or A-G#-E, or any other such combination. All one has to do is listen to the opening of his *Piano Concerto in A minor*, the first composition written to express his 'nationalism', to see the profound way he introduces himself as the 'voice of Norway'. He thunders down the entire keyboard in octaves declaring that *three-note motif* over and over again. It is as if he is saying,

"Listen everyone. I am a Norwegian. This is my music. This is your music. Isn't it beautiful?"

Every subsequent musical theme in the three-movement concerto can be traced to that *motif*. Grieg let his public know in no uncertain terms he was a Norwegian! Anyone familiar with Norwegian folk music would have recognized the music as 'their own'.

Much Norwegian folk music is in a scale pattern dissimilar to those of Western culture. Not *Major*, not *Minor*, but a particular *Mode* that is foreign to the mainstream, called *Lydian*. It has a raised fourth note of the major scale. Instead, in the case of *C major* for example (c-d-e-f-g-a-b-c), the *Lydian* is c-d-e-f#-g-a-b-c. That one note difference (*f#* instead of *f*) distinguishes Norwegian music from all the other 'musics' of Europe. We should take the liberty here to become slightly 'theoretical' in our analysis, suggesting that *Lydian Mode* is a 'bi-tonal' mode. In *C Major, C*, the 'Tonic', is the fundamental tonal center of the scale. It is the 'sun' of its musical solar system. *G* is the second most important note of that scale, and is called the 'Dominant'. *Lydian Mode* reinforces Dominant *G* by raising *F* to *F#*. *G* is now is preceded by a half-step just like *C*. The *C* scale now has two 'tonal centers', not one. Grieg resorts to *Lydian Mode* frequently, giving his music a distinctly Norwegian flavor.

Interestingly, another Norwegian folk instrument, the *seljefløyte*, or 'willow flute', naturally plays in *Lydian Mode*.

Grieg's genius lies in his ability to completely capture the essence of folk music and at the same time maintain a high level of artistic integrity. But it appears Grieg was unhappy with his countrymen's lack of response toward his music. In a letter to his friend August Winding in 1877, he wrote:

Much as I love my Fatherland, I can't help longing to get away from here, since there is no understanding whatsoever of my art in my own home, and that is hard to bear as you can imagine.

He also appears to have been frustrated in his attempts to put his musical ideas into the large forms of symphony, concerto, sonata, and string quartet. His time at the Leipzig Conservatory had convinced him that to be successful one must become proficient in those larger formats. He was struggling. In a letter to another friend, Matthison-Hansen, during the writing of his *String Quartet* in 1877, he again complained,

Something I must do for my art. Day by day I am becoming more dissatisfied with myself. Nothing that I do satisfies me and though it seems to me that I have ideas, they neither soar nor take form when I proceed to the working out of something big. It is enough to make one lose one's wits.... My problem is want of practice and want of technique, because I've never gone further with it than to compose by fits and starts. But there must be an end to that now. I will fight through the great forms, cost what it may! If I go crazy on the way, you now know the reason.

He continued his 'fight' to no avail. He blamed his difficulties on his attempts to be 'Norwegian' through the writing of Nationalistic compositions. He appeared to be on the verge of abandoning his original desire to be the 'voice of Norway'. Furthermore, his *String Quartet* was not coming together as he had hoped:

You have no idea what a job I have had with the modeling—but that is because I had been near stagnation and that again was the result partly of many 'occasional' works (Peer Gynt, Sigurd Jorsalfer, and other stupidities), partly of too much popular stuff. To that I mean to say 'farewell, my shadow', if it can be done.

Understanding even this brief biography prepared me for my visit to the Bergen Archives. I discovered several loose sheets of manuscript just lying scattered on the floor. I determined to use them as my research project.

Grieg manuscript of Piano Trio

It turned out to be the first movement (*Andante con moto*) of an unfinished *Piano Trio* (Violin, Cello, Piano), dated 1878. I thought perhaps this abandoned composition might give me some clues and insights into the psychology of the distraught Grieg, coming as it did on the heels of his *String Quartet* frustration. Further research turned up letters referring to this period of his life. One in particular, written again to Matthison-Hansen in early 1878, caught my attention; it spoke again of his *String Quartet*. He wrote,

I needed to do it as a study [he was referring to the String Quartet]. *Now I shall make a start with another piece of chamber music. I believe I shall find myself again this way.*

I believed the 'piece of chamber music' was the manuscript I had discovered in loose pages on the floor. Grieg soon gave up on the chamber piece after writing the draft of the first movement. He wrote nothing for two years. This is not what a successful composer does. He was not 'finding himself' as he had hoped. The silence of his compositional pen appears to be a sign that a tragic crisis of confidence was overtaking him. What would bring him either consolation or renewed confidence?

In 1880 the composer found the poetry of Aasmund Olavsson Vinje. What he read mirrored his mental state; it is as if Grieg himself could have written the lines. Verse two of *The Youth* reads,

> *Now you know what it means dreams to forget,*
> *To die to hopes, to all on which your heart is set.*
> *The green you gathered withered fast as flowers to hay;*
> *That was the least; your young love too, alas, withered away.*

What dreams? What hopes? Those that drew him back to Norway to give his homeland a voice? Was the gathered 'green' those early works that successfully established him as a Norwegian Nationalist?

Now they had withered. Had the urgings of Rikard Nordraak and Ole Bull led him down the wrong path? Had he wasted the better years of his life pursuing the wrong musical channel?

The entire cycle of Vinje's poems, set to music by Grieg, reflects his disillusionment as well as his resignation. After the song cycle of 1880 Grieg wrote only a little, and made only a few further attempts at the larger forms. He seemed defeated by what he considered his failures:

To all appearances I am living a more peaceful life than ever before, but in reality it is a life full of inward struggle. I have no outward activities. I give few lessons, that is all. Yet I am both spiritually and bodily unwell and decide every other day not to compose another note, because I satisfy myself less and less. When one has to struggle for technique, as I must do—and strangely enough the fight becomes always more difficult—to bring anything to birth becomes so hard at last that all one's strength is exhausted.

Those words were penned in 1882; Grieg was just thirty-nine years old! The following year he continued,

Happy! Why should I be? In my art I ought to be completely happy, but am not, because I have not gone straight forward and so have not achieved what I was called to achieve.

The years flew by. Nothing in his outlook changed. At age fifty-one he wrote,

You see, the feeling that my life's work in all important respects should be at an end, I have not 'til now been able to believe in. It seems to me there is so much I ought to do, so much I feel both the power and the craving to do—in the few good moments. But now I begin to feel that I must try to get the position clear, resign myself, and rejoice over all the

1967: International Summer School, Oslo, Norway

good Mother Nature has meted out to me. In other words, I must say to myself, 'Be at peace and be thankful'.... The music I think of one day, I pluck out of my heart the next because it is not genuine. My thoughts are bloodless, like myself, and I lose faith in myself.

The works he was able to compose—short piano pieces in the Norwegian style—he despised:

To my shame I must confess that once again I have been lyrical.... I have done nothing but the so-called 'Lyrical Pieces', which are collecting around me like lice and fleas in the country.

In 1905, two years before his death, he expressed once again his 'spiritual defeat':

The mountain shook and brought forth a mouse, and my mouse is, moreover, a very little one, so small you need spectacles to see it. It is only a volume of piano pieces to throw into the maw of mammon. It is to be a bait to Peters in Leipzig [a music publishing house] *to make him print two orchestral scores without a murmur. But through this 'mouse' I have realized for the first time that I have grown old. Pegasus had to be treated in a very special way merely to make him docile enough to move at all. There are a couple of year-old Norwegian pieces that I like, otherwise it is not my hearts' blood that has flowed here.*

The works for which Grieg is known all date from the period *before* that 1878 unfinished *Piano Trio* I had discovered in Bergen. I wrote my research paper based on that work and submitted it to my professors. It was only the beginning. I knew that I would some day return to continue my study into the life and music of Grieg. I determined that my first Sabbatical leave from North Park seven years later would be directed toward this project; it was worthy of more in-depth research. In those few weeks at the University of Oslo I had become deeply moved by a story here-to-fore untold. What I had uncovered was just the tip of an iceberg I thought would reveal the true tragedy of Norway's most significant composer.

However, through a circuitous maze of events I would not end up in Oslo in 1974. Grieg's 'story' would have to wait for another day, and perhaps another person to do the telling. My own story was to involve Rome, via Athens and central Turkey, studying early Christian Catacomb Art.

Further study of *'The Psychological Tragedy of Edvard Grieg'*, the name of the paper submitted to my professors, would have enhanced my musical life most certainly; ending up in Rome and the Catacombs would alter the spiritual trajectory of my life most profoundly. That will be the subject of a subsequent chapter.

Near the end of the summer I was interviewed for an article published in the August 4th edition of *Aftenposten*, Norway's leading newspaper. It read,

Aftenposten newspaper article

"Grieg and I have become good friends this summer," says Greg Athnos with a satisfied face as if he was talking about a friend that sat by his side. A thick pink musical score with 'Edvard Grieg' written with big letters on it is as good as if Grieg was there, at least for Athnos. He has come to the International

Summer School at Blindern from his music teaching job at North Park College in Chicago, exclusively because of Grieg. It is the newly started course 'The Music of Edvard Grieg' taught by Dag Schjelderup-Ebbe that tempted him over the ocean.

"Grieg has more value than we usually accredit him," continues Mr. Athnos. It looks like Grieg, like so many other Nationalistic composers, has been forgotten because they did not strive to find values outside the national trademarks in their works. In America it is 'Peer Gynt' and the 'Piano Concerto' most people associate with Grieg.

Q.: You too?

A.: I must admit that I also viewed Grieg exclusively as a Norwegian Nationalist before I started this course. Today I view him as an international composer.

We need to inform you our friend Athnos is more than a teacher of music; he is also a conductor of orchestras and choirs.

Q.: Are you going to perform Grieg at North Park now?

A.: I'll at least put Grieg on my programs more often than before.

Q.: Shouldn't the Grieg course be taught in Bergen rather than Oslo?

A.: I would have loved to spend more time in Bergen, and I wish I would have been lucky enough to discuss Grieg with Saeverud [a composer and musicologist]. I would love to have asked him about the two-year period in Grieg's life, 1878-1880, when he didn't write anything. I would like to fill that gap.

Q.: Have you gained a lot of knowledge through this Grieg course at the Summer School?

A.: Without a doubt, though I wish there had been more time to spend with contemporary Norwegian composers. The course is still rather new, so that may come in time. We have analyzed many of Grieg's works, many of which are less known. Since many of my classmates have the same limited understanding of Grieg it has been interesting to hear their views and opinions. I was surprised how few students were in the class; it should have drawn much greater attention. Maybe you will have to make more of a 'fuss' about it.

Q.: You have Leonard Bernstein in America who makes a 'fuss' about music to the public.

A.: Bernstein has done a lot to increase understanding of music for the common man. If you're going to 'sell' something it has to be made more 'popular'. This is as true for music as for anything else. I would say that concert audiences are beginning to take a more serious approach to music. It is becoming less of a 'social' affair and more of a 'deeply felt experience'.

Q.: Do you have a course at North Park for such musical understanding?

A.: We are experimenting with a new path. We are placing music into the surrounding culture that gave it birth.

Q.: What was your best musical experience in Norway?

A.: Going to the Hardangerfele Competition in Telemark was simply extraordinary. That's where I became saturated in the nature and uniqueness of Norwegian folk music that was the basis for Grieg's music.

On our final night in Oslo we were hosted by the elected officials of Oslo in a marvelous banquet at City Hall. I was asked to represent North America in a short speech to the gathered dignitaries. Another American student wrote me in December:

1967: International Summer School, Oslo, Norway

Dear Greg: Ever since the farewell dinner at Blindern I have meant to write you a note to tell you I thought your speech was outstanding. As an American I was so proud to be represented by you and what you said! Thank you! Sincerely, Gladys Rucks

These were my brief remarks to the ceremony:

Your Excellencies and my fellow students,

I'm happy to be able to speak to you representing our North American participants. We are unique in that we represent the heritage and traditions of many nations—East and West, North and South. We find ourselves here in Norway for a variety of reasons.

Some because we seek to unite the broken bonds of common family— All for reasons of educational and professional growth.

Some for pleasure in traveling and seeing things we've heard and read about for so many years—All for the excitement of living and associating with representatives of a vast body of cultures and ideologies, and the challenge of facing and accepting the myriad viewpoints of others.

Some to re-focus our views of home in a more objective, detached manner—and All because we realize the future of the world is ours and we want in all earnestness to improve it.

I have come, believe it or not and in spite of my name, to unite family bonds broken almost one hundred years ago when my grandparents left Gudbrandsdal for the United States. To re-unite with this family was a real joy.

I've come, too, for professional reasons. Through research into the life of Edvard Grieg, and my newly found interest in Norwegian Folk Music, I've developed a growing curiosity that will, without a doubt, drive me to return to this great country.

To the professors who have been so helpful, and to the people in the mountains and valleys who offered kindness and hospitality, we owe a great debt of gratitude.

I have felt the challenge of responding to the great problems of the world in a communal way, listening to and respecting the opinions of others as they have in turn respected mine. In this six-week moment in time our paths have briefly crossed. Within the confines of this academic 'give and take' we have in our own way united the world.

We from America, and all of you as well in our mental and human frailty will sooner or later forget each other's names—but we hope our lives will reflect the profound impact this meeting has had upon us.

To all, we from North American offer our deepest thanks and continued good will and peace.

Seated at Grieg's piano in his Trollhaugen home near Bergen

CHAPTER 22

1969: The Miracle of the House

If I couldn't purchase a home in Chicago we'd have to move back to Michigan. No more renting, especially in our cramped, unsatisfying school apartment.

We had moved to the North Park neighborhood of Chicago three years earlier when I joined the Music Faculty of North Park College. I had taken a rather large reduction in salary in the move, and was willing to do so primarily because teaching at the college level was attractive to me. Furthermore, I felt 'called' to the position.

It had not been an easy move. My wife's parents would be left behind along with all the dear friends we had made through our church. A forty percent cut in salary, coupled with the increased cost of living in Chicago, meant we would be living much more frugally than we were accustomed. My new car would have to be traded for an older one in order to save on the monthly payments. We would be selling our recently purchased new home. Our rented residence in Chicago would be a steep downgrade. By the time we arrived in Chicago I had $300 in the bank; that was the sum total of our savings. Yet I felt 'called', and that trumped everything.

Our 'welcome to Chicago' moment was anything but welcoming. The moving van pulled up in front of our school rental apartment, and I pulled in behind it. We went into the apartment to get the 'lay of the land'. Less than five minutes later we returned to the truck only to discover someone had broken into it and had stolen my eight-year-old twin sons' bicycles. This was a bad omen. Returning to the apartment we found a dirty kitchen, a stove covered in grease, and a moldy refrigerator. We couldn't prepare any meals there. For the next week we had to 'eat out' while the school cleaned the wretched space. I was tempted to question my 'call'.

School began for my sons before it began for me. On their first day in third grade at Hibbard Elementary School they came home at mid-morning recess.

"We're not going back there," they said. *"No one speaks English. No one is friendly."*

Not quite true, though at the time there were over 60 native languages being spoken in the classrooms. We indeed had moved from a homogeneous native-born American community into one of the most diverse 'melting pots' in the nation. Someone had written a book entitled, *Lawrence and Kedzie*, described as the most diverse junction in the world; we were walking distance from that intersection.

On another occasion the boys came home for lunch carrying a small handgun they had found on the bridge over the North Branch of the Chicago River, a path they took daily. They thought it was a toy. It looked like a toy, but it wasn't a toy! I called the Police. The officer came, took one look at the weapon, and broke out into a cold sweat. It was fully loaded and had what he called a 'hair trigger'. He continued,

1969: The Miracle of the House

"What's the first thing a young boy does when he picks up what he thinks is a toy gun? He points it at someone, in this case his brother, and pulls the trigger. It's a miracle someone wasn't shot."

We longed for the 'good old days' in Michigan.

My college teaching began in earnest, and I loved it. Good thing. There needed to be some compensation, some trade-off for what we had sacrificed in coming here. Little by little we all made our peace with living in Chicago. We grew to love the lakefront, the parks, and the culture the city offered. We did, however, spend quite a few weekends back in Michigan!

In addition to my college teaching I was hired as a part-time choral director in our neighborhood Covenant church. My artistic plate was full. I was doing things I loved. Slowly our past years in Michigan faded from immediacy, but not from memory.

For three years we lived in school apartments, plural, having moved across the street in the second year. It was time to find a home of our own. We had lived in Chicago long enough to know house prices were considerably higher than we had experienced in Michigan. Finding something we could afford would be a challenge. Then there was that problem of only $300 in the bank coupled with my yearly salary of $9000.

I wanted to stay within walking distance of the campus. My position required long hours and I didn't want to spend needless time stuck in traffic at both ends of the day. I began walking the neighborhood surrounding the college once or twice each week, looking for sale signs. In those years houses sold rather quickly; it was important to be the first to spot a sign. Often houses sold the day of the sign's posting. The area was home to many Chicago-style bungalows and large two- or three-flat apartment buildings. I wasn't a fan of bungalows, and certainly didn't want any more apartment living. Many of the single family homes were quite outdated and in need of serious remodeling and updating. Furthermore, they had only two bedrooms and one bath, an unfinished basement, and unusable attic space. I checked out several, and the prices were much higher than I could afford, even those that needed a lot of work. My strolls through the area were frustrating.

However, there was one house I passed on each journey that I loved. It was not a bungalow. It was situated on a lot a bit larger than was typical for Chicago. It didn't look like any other house. I would stand in front of it every time and think to myself, *"I'd love to have this house."* But if bungalows were out of my price range there was no conceivable way I would ever be able to acquire this special place. It didn't matter; it wasn't for sale. That just added to my frustration.

This process continued for months. We soon came to the realization that purchasing a home in Chicago was out of the question. Without a home of our own a long-term commitment to North Park wasn't possible. I would have to return to Michigan and seek re-instatement into the position I had left three years earlier, or something similar. That was the only path to solvency and homeownership.

Every third or fourth weekend we traveled back to Michigan looking for a future position. It looked like we were going to have to rethink my 'call' to North Park and admit it may simply have been wishful thinking. During this process 'that house' on St. Louis Avenue continued to draw my admiration. We had just recently discovered the names of the owners: Dr. Fernly Johnson and his wife Grace. We also discovered they were back from the mission field in Africa and attended the church where I was on staff. We didn't know them by sight—only by name.

1969: The Miracle of the House

I had been praying regularly over our situation.

"God," I prayed, *"if you really want us to be here you'll have to make it known to me, and clearly. I can't afford a home. You'll have to make it possible."*

Rather than sit back and wait for the 'handwriting on the wall', I felt it necessary to be active. I knew from Scripture that the only time God 'wrote on the wall', it was a message of doom!

"God," I continued, *"I'm going to continue my search. If it is your will that I return to Michigan, then open some doors. If not, then close them and open some doors here. Make yourself known."* My prayers were becoming increasingly more specific.

One day my wife was invited to a Tupperware Party. Before it began someone mentioned to her that she had heard Dr. Fernly Johnson was returning to Africa. My wife left the gathering immediately, raced home, and told me what she had heard. *"You need to check it out,"* she said. I didn't know Dr. Johnson, so I called the Pastor of our church, Douglas Cedarleaf.

"Doug, I've heard Dr. Johnson is returning to Africa. What do you know about that?"

He said he hadn't heard but that he would call and find out, then let me know. A few minutes later he called back.

"Yes, Fernly is going back to Africa, but he didn't want anyone to know. He's surprised that someone found out. I told him of your interest in his house. He said his son's Father-in-law is going to give him the money for the home, so it won't be available."

Fernly's son was doing his internship as a medical doctor, so with his Father-in-law's help purchasing the home would be no problem. We were back to square one. The Chicago doors were closing. It was a sign to keep checking in Michigan, and so we did.

During this time I kept praying. I became ever more bold in my petitions, putting out the so-called 'fleece' as a specific sign of God's answer:

"God, if you want me to stay here at North Park, you're going to have to supply a home. Not just any home. Dr. Johnson's home!"

One Sunday evening, returning home after leaving the Ann Arbor area, the phone was ringing as I entered our apartment. It was Grace Johnson, Fernly's wife. I had never spoken with her or Fernly.

"Greg," she said, *"our son's Father-in-law can't part with the money at this time. Our son has not been able to acquire a loan. If you want the house, it yours."*

Many thoughts raced through my mind in a flash. *"If a soon-to-be doctor can't get a loan, what chance do I have with my meager salary and $300 in the bank?"* Also, I had never been in the house. I didn't know what the purchase price was. All I knew was that I had not been able to afford a bungalow. This was nearly twice the house. How would I ever be able to buy it?

On the other hand, what about my prayers? Was this an answer? Was this the open door God was providing? I had prayed in faith, believing. Now that the 'fleece' had provided an answer I had to apply the same faith in spite of the rational thought surrounding my financial circumstances.

"Yes. I'd love to buy your home." Sight unseen. Purchase price unknown.

"Stop by and let us show you around," she said.

It was truly a special place. The price was about twenty-five percent more than those bungalows I couldn't afford! I swallowed hard and proceeded.

It was time to secure a loan. I drove to my bank, then passed it by and headed to a different bank.

"Can I help you?"

"Yes, I'm here to inquire about a home mortgage loan."

"Is this your bank?"

"No."

"Why don't you go to your own bank? We hardly have enough available even for our own customers." With that I turned and proceeded toward the door.

"Don't I know you?" It was another person. I told him I'd never been in their bank before.

"Don't you teach at North Park?" I replied in the affirmative.

"Weren't you the director of the Oratorio Chorus?" Again, affirmative.

"I've heard your performances. I love North Park. What do you need?"

The Johnson home was selling for $34,500. I had $300 in savings, a $9000 yearly salary before deductions, and no collateral.

"$9000," I said. Why I said $9000 when I needed four times that much I don't know. It was the first figure that crossed my mind.

"How long do you need it?"

"I'll pay it back in 90 days." What was I thinking?

"It's yours."

That night I had a rehearsal with my church choir. Afterwards, one of my singers, Dr. Robert Hulburt, said,

"I hear you're buying Fernly's house."

"Well, I hope to, if I can get the money."

Bob then told me his recently deceased parents' estate had been settled and he was debating how to invest the money.

"I'll tell you what. How about if I loan you the money at six percent interest. That's better than I can get from a bank, and less than you'd pay if you could secure a mortgage."

He was right; banks were charging over eight percent with limited availability of funds.

"You can have whatever you need for as long as you need it." I wanted to be sure he was serious. He was.

"$22,000," I said, "for twenty years." He agreed.

Again, why did I say $22,000? I needed $3500 more than that, counting the $9000 from Ravenswood Bank. I'm good with numbers, and yet on this single day my math was screwy.

The very next day my mother-in-law called!

"Greg," she said, "I woke up this morning with the thought that you needed some money."

She knew nothing of our intent to purchase the Johnson house. I told her. I would never ask her for money, and told her that as well. She replied,

"I know you wouldn't, but I want to help you. What do you need?" I gave her the amount: $3500.

"It will be in the mail today. Don't tell your Father-in-law! This is just between you and me. You can pay it back whenever you can."

In two days the amount of the purchase price was in hand!

However, after several months I was fast approaching the end of my 90-day $9000 loan with the bank. Again, the phone rang. Again, it was my mother-in-law.

"I had another of those thoughts." I explained the situation. *"It will be in the mail. Don't tell your Father-in-law. You can pay it back whenever possible, at no interest."*

On the ninetieth day I walked into Ravenswood Bank to pay off their loan to me. The officer who had given me the money was astonished.

"I didn't expect you to pay it off on time. I was willing to extend it as long as you needed. Your credit is good here anytime."

I gave him the $9000 plus interest. That was the last time I was ever in that bank!

I owed my mother-in-law $12,500. My mortgage with Bob Hulburt was for twenty years. My monthly mortgage payment was under $150, less than I'd been paying North Park College for the rental apartment!

How many miracles does that make? But the story is not yet finished.

Several weeks later the phone rang. It was Eric Freudigman, a friend from my Michigan days. We had sung together in a professional choir out of Detroit conducted by his Father-in-law Kenneth Jewell. Eric told me a group of donors had made possible an experimental program in the Arts for High School students, called *Adventures in Creativity*, running for the next four summers, beginning immediately.

The premise behind the program was that young people with artistic talents are forced to make decisions about which art to pursue long before they should have to. The program was being established to give talented students the opportunity to explore several other art forms in addition to the one in which they had excelled. Was it possible they might exhibit similar if not greater abilities in another art form? Every student was to have private instruction with great professional artists in their chosen area, while pursuing two new art forms, also with professional instruction.

The program was housed at the *Cranbrook Institute* in Bloomfield Hills, Michigan. The Institute was a work of art in its own right, located on the private wooded estate of the Booth family, owners of the Detroit newspapers. The Finnish architect Saarinen had designed all the buildings; his wife and son had designed the furniture and table settings. Carl Milles, the Swedish sculptor, had his works on permanent display all over the campus.

Eric found professional instructors from across the United States in the areas of Dance, Theater, Music, Sculpture, Painting, Poetry, and Creative Writing. He needed someone to guide the teaching procedures of the professional artists, and offered that position to me. My family would be housed on the estate with all meals provided. The salary was highly professional. I said an enthusiastic yes.

For the next four summers I rented out my new home in Chicago, covering my mortgage payments and utilities. I had no expenses for those four summers, and banked the salary. At the end of the fourth summer, the final summer of the program, I paid back the $12,500 loan graciously extended to me by my wonderful Mother-in-law. I never touched the $300 that I had brought with me to Chicago when I joined the faculty at North Park College.

In subsequent years I received opportunities to leave North Park. I turned them down. God had made a commitment to me. I made a commitment to Him. North Park was truly my 'calling', and while there were occasions of frustration with the college, I never once doubted that I was where I was supposed to be. This was God's doing. 5247 North St. Louis Avenue in Chicago, where I have lived for forty-six years, is my 'miracle house'.

CHAPTER 23

1969: Cranbrook and the "Rock Mass"

Adventures in Creativity was just what it proposed to be. The students were extremely talented, as were the faculty. We all, students and faculty alike, ventured into art forms previously unexplored. I took up sculpture with great joy and a bit of success. Three works—two large wood sculptures and a clay self-portrait bust—remain part of my home's décor. Not only that; what I learned about myself as an artist, and what was revealed to me in a deepening spiritual posture, date to those attempts at sculpture, as will be recounted in the next chapter.

One day I mentioned to Eric Freudigman that it had been in my mind to write a *Latin Mass* in the *rock* idiom. Where that came from I don't know; I'm not a composer—that's not my gift—though I had written a few compositions just for fun, and several had been performed. *Rock* had taken over the *Pop* music scene; the Beatles were popular, but the idiom had not yet invaded the music climate of the Church. I wasn't a fan of either *popular music* or the *rock* genre; Big Bands appealed to me—groups like Stan Kenton, Billy May, Sauter-Finnegan, Count Basie, and Duke Ellington.

1969: Cranbrook and the "Rock Mass"

Whatever possessed me to think I knew enough about *rock* to even attempt a venture into that realm?

My 'cell group' of young, creative artists

Several weeks later Eric asked how the *Rock Mass* was coming. I had forgotten all about my casual comment to him in the busy-ness of the summer, and I told him so.

"Well, you'd better get started. I have a rock band coming to campus next week to start rehearsing."

The program was ending in two weeks! Eric was planning a final celebration event for students and their parents; the *Rock Mass* was to be part of the program. I began in earnest, and was still writing during the first rehearsal. The piece was written for *Lead Guitar, Bass Guitar, Keyboard, Drums*, and a *Unison Choir* singing in Latin. There had not been a choir during the summer, but one was hastily arranged with students and faculty participating. We set the *Ordinary of the Mass* to music: *Kyrie, Gloria, Credo, Sanctus-Benedictus*, and *Agnus Dei*. I had one rehearsal with the band, one rehearsal with the singers, and two with the combined forces. To everyone's surprise, including my own, it came together quite well.

The students absolutely loved the *Mass*. At our closing ceremony the performance was greeted with great enthusiasm. Rod Serling, writer and producer of *The Twilight Zone*, was in attendance, as his daughter was a participant in the program. He was a sweet man, and complimented me on the *Mass*.

No one slept that night. The tape recording of the *Mass* played constantly as students danced to its music and continued singing it randomly throughout the halls and gathering rooms until, exhausted, we sat down for our final breakfast. We made tapes for everyone as a 'farewell' gift, promising to mail them to their homes when the process was completed.

Student Amy's parents, Charles and Barbara Matthews, sent me a lovely note soon after returning home:

Dear Greg (as I am used to having Amy refer to you): We want to express personal thanks to you—more than anyone else on the "Creativity" staff—for awakening Amy to a much larger world in which she is beginning to see the value of her own resources. For the first time, I think she realizes she has a 'choice' as to how she uses her free time—whether with her friends or by herself developing some of

1969: Cranbrook and the "Rock Mass"

her many interests. She particularly enjoyed your *Comparative Arts Seminar.... Gratefully.*

A year later I received a letter from Helen Fingold of Pittsburgh, whose daughter Betty had been one of the singers in the *Rock Mass* performance:

Dear Mr. Athnos: In all the world Betty has no more treasured possession than her "Rock Mass" tape that you sent after last summer. Since we have no tape recorder on which to play it, she asked for her birthday if we'd have a record cut from the tape. I have guarded the tape with my life, I thought, only to discover now that the bag in which I was carrying it to town has somehow been lost. Before I lose my mind, I wonder is it possible to get another tape from you? I then will have the record made before Betty returns from Mt. Hermon school. I truly think nothing has ever made me feel as wretched as the loss of the tape. You cannot imagine everything that to her is tied up in this precious bit of music.... You were a most important part of the whole 'adventure' and gave her much that she treasures and remembers.... I will be eternally grateful....

Of course I was flattered by her note, and quickly sent another copy. Her daughter never knew of the dilemma.

The *Rock Mass* had a short performance lifespan, but it was fun. Over the next several years it was performed on three occasions: by the *Cranbrook Academy Choir* on their Spring concert; as the featured event at *Covenant High Congress* in upstate New York with me as conductor; and for the *Midwinter Conference of the Covenant Church* in Chicago, where the performers were pastors, students, and laypersons from around the country. Zenos Hawkinson, a colleague at North Park, was a member of the conference audience. In his typically clever fashion he wrote,

Eat in Harmony

The Mass was a mass, and it was good, and it did swing, and I did want to shout "Hallelujah!" and I didn't have the guts, but I was sorry I didn't, but even that didn't change the pleasure, and I'm glad I went and I hope the tape turned out because I'd like to hear it again. Thanks!

CHAPTER 24

Reflections: What I Learned From Beethoven and a Piece of Wood

My forays into the art of sculpture while teaching at the Cranbrook *Adventures in Creativity* produced more than the three works that resulted and grace my home. While seeking the 'image' embedded in the wood I was also blessed to discover what lay underneath the surface of my own spirituality and quest for a relationship with my Creator. Strangely, Beethoven's life played a role in the journey.

200 years ago one of the most gifted and promising composers who ever lived found himself deeply mired in the cauldron of despair. Before his genius had time to flower his greatest gift, his hearing, came under a monstrous assault. *"My ears whistle and buzz continually, day and night,"* he said. *"I am deaf."* Deafness—it was his worst nightmare; it was the condition from Hell! It was, for a composer, the most tragic flaw imaginable.

He was considering suicide; there was nothing left to live for. He had never had any true friends. Only music. Now the only 'true angel' of his life, that divine spark, had been taken away. Anna Kamienska, the Polish poet, wrote these words:

> *No one can know how lonely it is when an angel departs.*
> *The world is then immense, open and empty*
> *And the voice cannot describe it*
> *And no hand is friendly enough.*

If Beethoven had followed through with his suicide plans none of his greatest works, all composed *after* the onslaught of his deafness, would have been written. We would say of him he was filled with promise sadly unfulfilled.

He said he would *"take fate by the throat."* In a furious battle to preserve his life by preserving his art Beethoven again and again made reference in his letters to two concepts: *Assertion* and *Submission*. What was he suggesting?

All my life I have known what *Assertion* means: a certain willfulness, a strength or power of putting yourself or your positions forward no matter what. On the surface of things, that's Beethoven! But what does *Submission* have to do with *Assertion*? They seem opposed, contradictory.

I have also known *Submission*, and that was different for me. In my little church, all of my growing up years, I was told that *Submission* meant giving up my willfulness, emptying myself of pride, ego, identity—becoming a hollow vessel so that God could fill me up with *His* presence. Yes, I wanted that, but not at the expense of giving up who I was. I had pride, I was ME. So that emptying process never occurred—and for years I felt guilty about it. I was convinced I was not in the will of God because I couldn't become a 'hollow vessel'; I couldn't become *submissive*.

Reflections: What I Learned From Beethoven and a Piece of Wood

Submission and *Assertion*, those two juxtaposed concepts in Beethoven's letters, immediately captured my attention—not only because they both appeared, but primarily because he seemed to use them together—hyphenated, so to speak: *Assertion-Submission*. How could these two opposites inhabit one concept? I knew if I could understand what Beethoven meant by that fusion I might finally find the solution to my life-long feeling of guilt.

Then, in 1971, it happened. It was the third year of the experimental program in the arts for high school artists, *Adventure in Creativity*. That summer we were housed at Oakland University north of Detroit, a new and rather visually sterile campus of buildings and parking lots beautified by one stand of mature black walnut trees. Word came to us that the University was going to get rid of the trees to expand a parking lot. A pit would be dug and those precious trees bulldozed into it and buried.

The early 70's were times of radical activities and sit-ins. Our program was no exception. Some of us on the summer program faculty decided to confront the university President.

"How could you remove the only things of beauty on your campus? Build the parking lot around them."

Over our protests he was determined to proceed with his plans. We contacted several lumber mill owners who were willing to pay the university for the trees and remove them free of charge. They said the wood was worth a fortune on the black walnut veneer market. The President remained intransigent. Our attempts to stop the action were fruitless, but we had a fallback strategy.

We went into the nearby town of Rochester and rented as many chainsaws as we could. When the trees were bulldozed we planned to jump into the pit before they were buried and cut out as much of this wonderful sculpting wood as possible.

The day came. We were in the pit with our chainsaws. The bulldozers stood silent near the edge. The trees were cut into manageable segments so that they could be carried out and into our art studios. As I was wielding my chainsaw on a large tree trunk with three large branches, it came over me:

"I'll sculpt this piece myself!"

It was a rather brash thought. The last sculpting I had done was in elementary school, rolling out coils of clay and winding them into the shape of a pot! Now I was going to be working with a hundred pound piece of wood! I knew immediately what I would carve into it; I saw the image even as I was cutting it. It took three of us to lift the wood out of the pit.

It was time to begin. Mike Kapitan, one of the sculptors on the faculty, showed me the tools.

"First," he said, *"remove all the bark."* (Did he even have to tell me?)

It was more difficult than I imagined. Using a heavy maple mallet and a gouge I attacked the first phase. Not used to working with my hands in manual activities my fingers began to swell up. It became difficult to hold the instruments. The shock waves of the gouge against the wood responding to the whistling maple mallet ran up my arms into my shoulders. All the joints of my hands and arms were aching, and I as yet hadn't removed all the bark.

"Now remove the pulp wood."

A two-inch thick band of white pulp surrounded the black walnut meat. The painful process continued. For two days I had worked on the bark and the pulp and hadn't begun the process of sculpting the image into the tree, that image I had seen while working with a chainsaw in the pit. But over those days the image reinforced itself in my mind and in my intent.

Finally I was ready to start with the black walnut. I began outlining the image that had burned itself into my consciousness. Frustration! I was making a mess of it. Hours of sweat were producing a totally unsatisfying result.

At long last Mike came by. He was 6'6" tall, and gangly. I had been one of Mike's teachers when he was in high school. He and all his siblings had IQ's that could not be measured; they were all genius offspring of a school janitor. Mike, who earned his degrees in Art History and Sculpture from Harvard, had left me alone for several days, but was quietly observing my progress. I think he was hoping I'd learn an important lesson. At last he came by. Sensing my frustration, he leaned his tall frame over me, and whispered into my ear,

"Greg, you must listen to the wood." Then he walked away.

"What does he mean, listen to the wood?"

I left the studio and walked around the sterile campus. I had a sleepless night, tossing and turning, with Mike's words running on an imaginary tape loop and the image of the wood in my mind. I got up early, went back to the studio in the quiet of the morning, and sat in silence, staring at the wood.

The image I had seen days earlier was still there, but not in the way I had envisioned it. I began to see the grain flow of the wood; it was saying, 'follow me'. The image had been in the wood all along! I didn't have to *impose* the image on the tree; I simply had to *release* it. "Don't go against the grain," which I had indeed been doing according to *my* plan for the wood, took on meaning beyond my previous use of that phrase!

Then the light dawned. Beethoven's *Assertion-Submission* powered its way into my awareness. Now I knew what he meant!

Greg 'listening to the wood'

The tree had its own idea, but it needed me to bring it to light, to release it. The tree wouldn't sculpt itself. While it may have preferred Michelangelo, it got me instead. It needed the strength of me, not my weakness. It didn't want the emptiness of me, the hollowness of me; it wanted my complete identity. It needed the best of what I could bring to it. It needed my *assertiveness*, my determination, but not that alone. It also needed my awareness of *its* identity. The tree's grain flow had been asserting itself intransigently against my own assertiveness to our mutual detriment.

I began to see it: *Submission* was not the emptiness and weakness of me put up against the fullness and strength of the tree, nor was it the tree submitting itself completely, entirely to my fullness and strength. It was strength against strength coupled with submission against submission. It was my power and ability made compatible with the will of the tree. I understood it now: *Submission* was really *Assertion* hand in hand with another's *Assertion*. *Submission*, in the way I previously understood it, had relegated me to the status of audience to someone else's solo. *Submission* as I now understood it placed me in the position of partnership in a 'great duet'.

Put another way, 'If I was the hand, the tree was the glove'. They needed to fit each other. So it is between my Creator and me. He is the glove; I am the hand. He made my hand to fit His glove perfectly. His glove is never too large, nor will it ever restrict me by being too small. It is just right for who I am with my strengths and weaknesses, my gifts and my capabilities. Though exceedingly less than Michelangelo's hand, where God's glove was exceedingly large, God's 'glove' for me was appropriate for the smallness of my gift. God uses gifts of all sizes, hands large and small. He only requires that we put our fullness, our hands, whatever their limitations, into the full employ of His perfectly tailored glove.

Beethoven became clearer to me than ever before. I now understood the man behind the music in a way that made it impossible to separate one from the other, the person from the promise. Beethoven the man was completely embedded into and wedded with his music. When I hear his music I cannot help but see him and his victory over his condition.

Another problem arose in my work with the wood. A huge knot, a gigantic flaw, protruded from the side of the piece. I had tried to work around it or disguise it, with no success. This was disconcerting; I didn't want any flaw in *my* sculpture! I tried to remove it, but soon learned that knots are not surface blemishes; they are infused deep into the wood. Furthermore, the longer I tried to get rid of it the more I realized knots are the toughest part of the tree. Gouges were constantly being dulled in the process of my attempts at removal.

Another light dawned, at least as significant as when Beethoven's *Assertion-Submission* had become clear to me. The 'flaw' made the piece of wood unique. Without this knot, this 'flaw', the piece would be no different than any other trunk with three protruding limbs, and there must be tens of thousands, perhaps tens of millions like that. I realized that this particular 'flaw'—its size, shape, and location—was not only unique to *this* piece—it needed to become a major part of my sculpture. No hiding it. Feature it!

The flaw was the tree's special gift!

I looked at my own life. I had always seen my flaws in a negative light. I had apologized for them. I had used them as excuses; I had used my flaws to cover up my unwillingness to do what, deep inside my heart, I knew I was called to do. How many do that? Think of Moses trying to use his speech impediment to escape God's call to lead his people out of Egypt. King David was greatly flawed, yet God used him.

Now I realized my 'flaws' were gifts. My flaws make me special, unique. I am one of a kind, like no other. I am God's creation. He knew from the foundation of the world how I would be made and who I would become. As James the Apostle said, referring to tests and challenges:

Don't get thrown off course. Every desirable and beneficial gift comes out of Heaven.

God knew from the beginning He could use me just the way He created me. Making myself 'empty' of what God had placed there was wrong. To deny my flaws, or try to cover them up, or consider myself a victim of them, was to deny God's perfect creation as well as His unique purpose for my life. How audacious would it be for me to disavow myself of God's personalized 'investment'.

God's 'glove' fits my flaws perfectly. Gloves do not force themselves onto flaws. Flaws, by the decision of the flawed, need to make the first move. Offer them back in service to the Giver.

Flaws are only flaws if we consider them to be flaws. They need to be seen as gifts.

So it was with Beethoven. In my opinion his deafness, his 'tragic flaw', became his greatest gift. In the isolation forced by his deafness, the flower that was Beethoven—*The tranquil blossom on the tortured stem*, as Edna St. Vincent Millay wrote in her poem, 'On Listening to a Symphony of Beethoven'—was released from the conditioning and culture of the world around him. It was freed to grow in its own soil—unique, special, unlike the creations of his contemporaries in the most profound ways. Beethoven would have been the greatest composer of his age with or without his 'flaw', but not that much different from the others. His 'flaw' created a great distance, completely relegating his contemporaries to significantly lesser status in the historical accounts. In his battle with Fate he put his trust in the God of Creation. He put his hand in the glove God had intended for him. He created a music that transcends his age and speaks directly to the grace of God. His *Submission* gave way to the power of the human spirit under fire through his *Assertive* determination. If a deaf man can write some of the greatest music ever written, then nothing we might consider 'flawed' is beyond the human spirit's overcoming when coupled with God's redemptive power.

Two remarkable and life-changing discoveries occurred that summer: a new view of what it means to be *assertively submissive*, and a determination to see my *flaws* as gifts.

I finished the sculpture. Ironically, it is a figure of Christ rising from the tomb, coiled in anticipation, suspended between his death (my death) and his resurrection (my promise). The work isn't all that great, but it isn't the work itself that is important. Rather, all that matters is what I discovered about myself, my flaws, and my relationship with the Creator God. The work sits in my home, a constant reminder of that very powerful moment of awareness and transformation in my life.

Who would ever have thought such a grand, life-changing moment could result from the letters of Beethoven and a piece of discarded, flawed wood!

Completed sculpture

CHAPTER 25

1969: The New Song

The closing of North Park Academy in the spring of 1969 constituted a disappointment reaching beyond the walls of the rehearsal room. Students from the North Park neighborhood who had looked forward to their own future participation in Varsity Singers felt robbed of their dreams; they had wanted the excitement they witnessed in others. A group of them came pleading for me to start a choir that would meet at North Park Covenant Church where I was on staff as director of Adult Choirs. I told them my schedule, between the church and the college, was too busy.

Having just completed my first summer with *Adventure in Creativity*, and having dabbled in the *rock* idiom through the *Rock Mass*, I offered them an alternative.

"Let me encourage you to start a group that writes its own lyrics and music. Can you find kids who play guitar? I won't do the work, but I'll encourage your creativity. What do you think?"

The result was *The New Song*. If not the first church group to begin the *Christian Contemporary Music* movement, it was at least one of the earliest. We sat in the Youth Room of North Park Covenant Church once a week for about a month waiting for the first spark of creativity to ignite what I hoped would become a firestorm. At first no one came forward with either lyrics or melodies. I became bored with the repetitions of *Michael Row the Boat Ashore* and other folk songs, but was patient and determined to wait them out.

Finally two girls from the group of fifteen Middle School and High School students sheepishly volunteered that they had written some lyrics and a melody with a few guitar chords. Judy Hawkinson and Linda Bergquist shared their creative idea with the group. That's all it took. Within weeks fully half the group were writing music and lyrics. Whatever instruments they played we used, regardless of their proficiency. We ended up with five guitars, one trombone, drums, and me on electric bass guitar (I had never played guitar before this).

The New Song began to participate in Sunday worship services, sharing once a month from their growing repertoire of musical creativity. Not everyone in the church was pleased with what they called 'an intrusion' into the so-called sanctity of traditional worship. I heard of a few people peeking into the sanctuary before the service began to see whether there was a guitar and an amp on the chancel platform; if there was, they went home. I could never understand that response. These were their 'kids', eager to participate in the church and its worship, contrasting dramatically with the growing secularization of young people across the country. These 'kids' were examining their lives and their faith, giving creative voice to their quest for spiritual meaning. Those 'adult' responses were both puzzling and rude.

1969: The New Song

Sunday morning service at their home church, North Park Covenant in Chicago

It marked an early episode in the 'worship wars' that have spread like a virus throughout Protestantism in recent decades, and continue even now. More churches have been split over 'musical styles' than 'theological differences'. These wars reflect a high degree of selfishness on both sides of the 'worship aisle'. Each side wants it their way, refusing to acknowledge that people are 'fed' by different worship languages. The Church needs to speak to all, yet rarely does it happen. Tragic. I have experienced more than one 'worship war', having witnessed the battle in every church where I have been a volunteer in the music program over the forty-six years since the beginning of the *New Song*.

In spite of some opposition to *The New Song*, their influence grew. In our second year, the monthly journal of the Covenant Church, the *Covenant Companion*, asked me to write an article capturing what was happening in this creative movement in our church. It read,

Put twenty-one people into two stations wagons and a VW bus; add five guitars, a bass guitar and amplifier, trombone and drums, a dozen maxi-dresses and a thousand programs containing the musical and lyrical creativity of 15- and 16-year-olds; travel 1500 miles through the greater Midwest singing for five enthusiastic Covenant audiences; shake, stir, and mix curious youth and adults for one hour; add a pinch of incredulity; allow the enthusiasm of creative dust to settle; frost lavishly with applause and standing ovations, and you have 'The New Song' from North Park Covenant Church in Chicago on their very successful Spring Tour.

'The New Song' has for the last two years been writing its own music and lyrics in a folk-pop-rock idiom. In its short existence the group has been in great demand in the Midwest. In addition to the performances in many Chicago area Covenant churches, they have provided 'creative workshops' for the Covenant Youth Ministry Workshop in Grand Rapids, Michigan, and the Chicago area Methodist Youth Ministry Workshop. They have performed for the Central Conference Covenant Women and for the Covenant Annual Meeting. Their recent tour took them to Moline, Illinois; Lincoln and Omaha, Nebraska; Rochester, Minnesota; and Madison, Wisconsin.

> *Thank you, God, for giving me life.*
> *Thank you, God, for liberty.*
> *Thank you, God, for giving me a mind,*
> *But most of all, thanks for Love.* *

'The New Song's' lyrics continually point out this beautiful recognition. They have also discovered who they are as persons through this group endeavor, and I'd like to make you aware of the process.

As for me, I am their 'Maypole', a stationary figure around whom they run free. My role is encouragement, enthusiasm, faith, and waiting—waiting for them to come to terms with themselves as individuals and as a community; waiting for them to probe their spirits and make a creative statement about 'Life'. Sometimes the wait is long and hard. The 'adult' in me, or the 'musician' in me screams to do it for them, or short-circuit the creative process. More often than not I am a study in concealed frustration.

> *Thank you, God, for flowers and trees.*
> *Thank you, God, for friends that care.*
> *Thank you, God, for giving me a home.*
> *But most of all, thanks for Love.**

But they are free! Free to succeed or fail in what they do; free to settle for mediocrity or strive for more; free to wait for 'inspiration' or diligently pursue their ideas; free to accept or reject the contributions of others. Sometimes for them the freedom is hard, and they wait for me to assume the creative responsibility. But more often than not 'The New Song' is a beautiful study in the discipline of creative freedom, and their bond of friendship and acceptance grows daily.

> *Thanks for people who take me as I am.*
> *Thanks for people who don't.*
> *Thanks for people who care about the other guy.*
> *And I will pray for those who won't.**

If you were to visit a rehearsal you might be appalled! You'd find sixteen young people sitting in various contorted postures around the Youth Lounge talking about any topic of interest to teenagers. Some would be toying with their guitars and others singing a tune from 'Jesus Christ Superstar'. You'd find me there, too, bass guitar silently in hand, waiting. To the casual observer the atmosphere would appear to be chaotic. An hour later the kids are heading for home and their 'Maypole', me, is heading down the stairs to a structured Chancel

Choir rehearsal where, because of my formal musical background, I feel secure. Next week's rehearsal could be an instant replay but having gone through this agonizing process week after week I have become comfortably assured that eventually someone is going to arrive with lyrics, melody and chords for a new song. Then the creative juices will flow! The melody will be taught by rote to everyone and when they know it well they will begin to improvise harmonies until several 'good' parts take shape. They may decide to try humming, whistling, or adding certain instrumental effects. The process will be slow, but it will be their own! In a rehearsal or two a song will be born of their brains and spirits. This birth process has occurred about thirty times since the advent of the group. Each time it has been slow and painful, but always worth it. Birth is like that.

I have lived with these kids for the past two years. I know them well and have shared moments of joy and frustration in their physical and spiritual 'growing up'. What they have stated in the composition of their many songs is a real witness to the fact that they HAVE grown! Their lyrics have moved from 'protest' to 'proclamation', from secular issues to Scriptural truths, and back and forth between the simply profound and the profoundly simple.

And they are interested in the Church. They know that what they are doing is the most creative endeavor to hit their Church in a long time. They know they are setting an example for the rest of us on what it means to 'bring-give-share' from the guts of the spirit. They know what it means to be accepted and rejected. Not everyone likes what they do, but these kids are dauntless. More than once I have seen them 'key' in on a person in the audience whose expression betrayed doubt or disdain, look him straight in the eye and turn on a most charming smile until their subject's dour expression melted into acceptance.

1969: The New Song

What, then, can we learn from 'The New Song'? That the expression of youthful idealism, when encouraged and accepted, can manifest itself in a beautifully artistic and positive fashion; that our young people seriously want to become a respected part of the Church community and are willing to give tremendously of themselves for its welfare; that, given a chance, they can spark a feeling of discomfort in the average Church member's traditional role of 'receiving', forcing all of us to explore avenues of creative giving.

> *Thank you, God, for showing me the Light.*
> *Thank you, God, for answering my prayer.*
> *Thank you, God, for sending down your Son.*
> *And most of all, thanks for Love.**
> *(* "Thanks for Love", lyrics and music by Cindy Hulburt of the New Song)*

Their 'thing' is music, but the expressive capabilities of the Church as a body of Christian individuals are indeed phenomenal; I have learned this through them.

Life is like that. 'The New Song' has provided us a joyful encounter with 'Life', the big and the little of it. What an affirmation!

The New Song lasted three years and in that time those creative young people wrote over forty original songs. I never had to vacate my role as 'maypole'; I simply sat by and marveled at, and guided their creative talents.

I left North Park Covenant Church as Director of Choirs to concentrate on my College teaching and prepare for my first Sabbatical leave. Sadly, no one volunteered to continue with the group. The creative 'spark plugs' of *The New Song* graduated from high school and went on to college and their lives. It had been a remarkable journey, for them and for me. They can be pleased with their accomplishments. They can look back with pride, knowing they were among the first to open a new path, a 'new song' leading generations of creative young people into broadening the 'worship language' of the Church of Jesus Christ.

CHAPTER 26

1972: The First Foreign Study Initiative

Earlier I wrote of my interest in the Renaissance, how, in my second year, the Chamber Singers had been formed to specialize in the sacred choral music of that Age. Now, five years later, I found myself exploring more than the music. The great visual artists Massaccio, Ghiberti, Brunelleschi, Leonardo, Botticelli, and Michelangelo had become fascinating to me along with the dominant philosophy during the *Florentine Renaissance: Neo-Platonism* (though not all artists subscribed to it). Dabbling in the Renaissance was no longer enough for me; I wanted a deeper awareness of that profound period in Western History not only for myself but for my students as well.

I had an idea. Why not use a *North Park College Project Period* for study purposes rather than an excuse to hit the beaches of Florida? Why not give students an opportunity to discover the Renaissance in the place of its birth? Mentioning it to a number of students I found a growing interest in such a venture. To make it work I'd need several other professors on the team. Two immediately came to mind.

Zenos Hawkinson was Professor of History and a brilliant classroom teacher. It was said of him that when he described the *Battle at Gettysburg* his students smelled the gunpowder. Zenos was well-rounded and loved Art and Music as much as History. He would be perfect. I would have to do the 'heavy lifting' for the study project because Zenos was not well organized. However, his knowledge and enthusiastic teaching would be worth the extra work.

The second to come to mind was Hans Mollenhauer. Hans was one of those 'renaissance men' whose interests and knowledge covered a vast landscape. In addition to his brilliance, he spoke fluent Italian.

Both were true 'liberal arts' proponents. Zenos and Hans became enthusiastic about the project. Together, we refined the educational objective of the trip: *A study of the men and events that shaped and guided the humanistic flowering that was the Renaissance, from St. Francis through Michelangelo.*

The three of us shared in preparing and leading nine pre-tour seminars:

- *The Byzantine Foundation*
- *St. Francis and Religious Humanism: Seeds of the Renaissance Spirit*
- *Dante and Giotto: Conception of Renaissance Artistic Ideals*
- *The Medici Family and Lorenzo the Magnificent*
- *Florence and Siena: The Struggle for Supremacy*
- *Leonarda da Vinci, Raphael, and Michelangelo*
- *Josquin des Prez and Palestrina: Sacred Music's Synthesis*

1972: The First Foreign Study Initiative

- *Monteverdi and the Italian Madrigal: Secular Bridge to the Baroque*

- *St. Peter's and the Vatican: Renaissance to Baroque*

Entirely self-funded, our trip cost the institution nothing, and the students missed only one half day of classes.

Twenty-four students and a college librarian traveled with the three of us on our study tour. We began in Florence, traveled to Pisa, Siena, and Assisi, ending in Rome. Our daily discussions were extremely stimulat-

Zenos, Greg, and Hans enjoying Tartuffo in the Renaissance Piazza Navona, Rome

ing, almost to the point of overload. A 'new world' was dawning in the minds of the students, and we didn't want to waste much time sleeping.

Much to our surprise, the most moving and captivating moments were rooted in Assisi, so much so that we stayed up all that night huddled together in one of our hotel rooms trying to make sense of what had happened to us. We felt we had been 'invaded' by a kind of intellectual and spiritual '*stigmata*'. St. Francis' words, prayers, and canticles provoked hours of revelation, weeping, taking time to write our thoughts in prose and poetry, and silence; above all silence.

Susan Rabe, who went on to earn her doctorate and become a

History professor at North Park, taking up the mantle of her mentor Zenos Hawkinson, wrote:

How can I deny the faith which moved these men?
 I am confronted by a force, a presence,
 A spirit that draws me irresistibly, from which I cannot withdraw.
I try to understand, rationally, intellectually—I cannot in a world so tuned as this.
So I accept it unquestioningly—a comfortable choice!
 And yet, I think, a valid one; because in acceptance,
 In entering into it openly, I find a deeper understanding.
 A spiritual comprehension which evades me intellectually
 And yet holds me unremittingly: a more profound communion.
"The Spirit himself intercedes for us with sighs too deep for words…"
 I am made aware.
"For when a man's will is ready to believe, he loves the truth he believes…"
 I am comforted.
I cannot compete with the forces of science, with objective denials by reason and fact;
I am no match for cynics.
And yet—I see my evidence:
 The masterpiece of men,
 And the greater work of God: The Soul in Faith!

Hans Mollenhauer sat in a circle with Pat Gorman, Tim Czarnecki, and librarian Beverly Zimmerman, and wrote their thoughts together, the last stanza of which reads,

 The tomb in the vault,
 Medieval and cold,
 froze all of my expectations;

> *Yet an inner longing never here told,*
> *Vibrated my soul like the wings of a dove,*
> *Not far from Francesco's redeeming and love.*

Linda Zeagler's thoughts were expressed in these words,

> *In quiet cold stillness, in smoothed stones*
> *And courtyards old, walked by pilgrims,*
> *Voices once silenced cry out in tones,*
> *Alleluias imagined only in realms of seraphim.*
> *The chains of death, they bind not there,*
> *But in a laugh, a joyful tone*
> *They call to each, a weight to bear*
> *Whose cause is dear, whose Master's known.*
> *I am the penitent who seeks release,*
> *Thomas am I. Doubting reunion*
> *I come in worship, needing increase,*
> *And find, unsought, communion.*
> *I come to Assisi and find not I alone,*
> *But parts of me which had stayed too long unknown.*

And the last six lines from the first poem Nancy Eggert ever wrote,

> *He was such a gentle man, feeding birds,*
> *Preaching, and bleeding as Christ himself bled—*
> *Yet never complaining, though he suffered much*
> *And found peace in God in death.*
> *And though I wept at his tomb, the tears*
> *Are not for him, but for me and what I am.*

Every one of us that night contributed something from deep within, some expressing themselves in a manner that surprised them. I compiled our writings upon our return to North Park and sent copies to all of them, accompanied by my words of thanks to them:

Dear Renaissance Compatriots: For me our Renaissance experience was life-bending. The reasons are more than culture, art, and citizenry, although I couldn't begin to communicate to you how they altered and enhanced my view. Equally as startling as all of these was what I recognized as the beauty of 'you': the community of spirits and sensitivities. You brought down mightily upon my head once again my belief in and commitment to this place North Park, the quality of persons who share here and the promise that has just begun to shed its shackles. I am greatly indebted to all of you.

Like so many of you, I could not escape the bombardment of challenges, and spent many long nights wrestling with poetic ideas. I must say one final word: even now as I have spent the afternoon typing your contributions I am moved by your genuine-ness and eloquence, simple and profound. You have made my life much the better.

Our Spring Break *Italian Renaissance Project* was the first foreign study tour in North Park's history. It paved the way for programs that eventually became part of North Park's offerings.

CHAPTER 27

Reflections: What My Imagination Told Me

Those of us examining the *Italian Renaissance* were students and faculty engaged in an intellectual pursuit. What we discovered in Assisi took us to another place, and the realm we explored there revealed a world set apart: a world unknowable and intangible unless intellect ceases its reign as the dominant agenda.

Faith in the unknowable or intangible should be easier for artists than for others. Artists sense there is no contradiction between matter and spirit. Artists are capable of moving freely between these two worlds, because for them the material and spiritual worlds are 'one'. When the artist creates, the material being used is not destroyed or eliminated. It retains its properties in a very recognizable way: stone remains stone, wood remains wood, pigment remains pigment, sound remains sound, and words remain words. There is, however, one remarkable difference: the spiritual properties, formerly trapped or hidden within the material, under the artist's hand are released and transcend it. Its physical property remains, but the 'message' the artist discovers rises above it. Our challenge is to create the means by which the message 'rises above' or 'transcends' the commonness of the ingredients.

In the 'real' world trees are simply trees. Often, the more we confront this 'real' world the less attention we pay to it. For instance, can we describe the trees between our house and the nearest corner, even though we have 'lived' with them for years, walked by them, climbed them, raked their leaves, or sat in their shade? Here is the paradox: it appears the more we confront the 'real' world the less significant it becomes; on the other hand, the more we confront the artist's rendering of the 'real' world through his imagination, the more significant it becomes. When we approach the artist's painting of a tree, we are *first* drawn to the work's spirit, *then* to its physical properties. Were it not for the painting's spirit there would be little reason to linger over it or be compelled to examine it. This spiritual connection causes us to identify with the 'tree' in ways that profoundly affect our senses, our emotions, and our hearts. Isn't it interesting that we can often describe in great detail and emotion a painting we have seen only once. It appears that only when the material and spiritual worlds intersect is it possible for us to achieve what I prefer to call a 'memory of the heart'.

The sheer, overwhelming power of music tugs at our hearts before our minds rationalize that it is only vibrations, the same 'stuff' embodied in traffic noise or the sound of fingernails on a blackboard. And 'words' notwithstanding, *Hamlet* has nothing in common with the nightly weather report. Words and vibrations in the hands of the artist become transcendent and spiritual. They create 'heart memories'.

This is important: the artist's act of creation is, in the human sphere, a mirrored reflection of God's Divine intention in His creation—spirit and matter are fused, and matter is redeemed from its mundane and common nature. Viewed from a Christian perspective, creativity comes from God; it is His gift to us, and He knows what it is because He was the first to exercise it. Creativity is an act of respect and profound love for God's spiritual promise. Mark Driscoll wrote:

To be made in the image and likeness of God is to yearn for the creation of beauty that reflects our Creator.

That was the world we uncovered in viewing the works of Cimabue and Giotto and the life of St. Francis in our journey to Assisi. We were, at least for that brief moment through the night of self-discovery, poetry, and silence, captivated by our 'imaginings', by the fusion of faith and intellect, and by the symbiosis of spirit and flesh.

Teach me to know joy
To speak unspeakable lays
To dance as poets
(GA)

CHAPTER 28

1972: The Holy Mountain

My uncle, Monk Cleomenis Mastaropoulos, Icon Painter

While looking for my uncle I found myself lost in the mountains. Why had I set out on this preposterous journey?

It was August, 1972. My wife, twin fourteen-year-old sons, and I had been vacationing in Greece. Our journey had taken us first to Crete. The highlight of the island was the cave, high in the mountains, in which legend has it Zeus was hidden by his mother to escape being eaten by his father Kronos. We wound our way up a treacherous dirt and gravel road, sometimes one lane, with no guard-rails to protect us from the thousand-foot drops. The boys were laying on the floor of the back seat, afraid to look out the windows. I would have joined them, but someone had to drive!

After stops at several other islands we explored Athens, Delphi and areas of the Peloponnese—Mycenae, Olympia, Naufplion and the magnificent amphitheater of Epidavros—before heading north to Meteora and its monasteries. Then on to Salonika where the Apostle Paul had journeyed on several occasions and later penned his letters to the burgeoning Church.

Salonika was to be our starting point for a venture east through the Halkidiki Peninsula to the last edge of modern civilization before arriving at *Agios Oros*, the Holy Mountain. From here it would be my solo journey one thousand years back in time while my family enjoyed the beaches of Ouranopoulos for ten days.

I was searching for Cleomenis, my father's brother, a Greek Orthodox monk who had journeyed to the Holy Mountain to become an Icon painter. While my father had pursued his visions of America, his younger brother had other desires. I had no idea whether Cleomenis (he preferred to be called Clonos) was still alive. My distant cousins living a stone's throw from Olympia wouldn't tell me. Their refrain to my repeated inquiries was, *"He left the world. Why do you care?"*

The history of the Holy Mountain is recorded in ancient accounts going back to Herodotus and Aeschylus; Homer mentions it in the *Iliad*. It has always been a wild place. Its highest mountain, *Mount Athos*, reaches up from the Aegean Sea by steep, densely forested slopes to nearly 7000 feet. The sea surrounding the peninsula is often violent and unpredictable, providing the Holy Mountain protection from marauders. (Two years later I would discover that sudden violence for myself in a raging storm while huddled below deck on a small fishing boat thinking my life was soon to be over).

Athos, mentioned in Greek Mythology, was the name of one of the Giants that challenged the Greek gods. According to the story, the Giant threw an enormous rock against Poseidon. It fell into the Aegean Sea and became *Mount Athos*.

Another legend has it that the Virgin Mary, accompanied by St. John, was on her way to visit Lazarus, who had been raised to life by Jesus. When the ship was blown off course it was forced to land on the peninsula of *Athos*. The Virgin, seeing the beauty of the mountain, blessed it and asked her Son to grant it to her as a garden. A voice was heard,

"Let this place be your inheritance and your garden, a paradise and a haven of salvation."

From that moment the 'Virgin's Garden' was not to be accessible to other women. The tradition holds today. Only men are allowed to set foot on *Athos*, and even female domestic animals are forbidden.

Historians are convinced that monks have inhabited the peninsula since the 4th century, perhaps earlier. At first both Christians and pagans lived there side by side. Under Julian the Apostate (361-363 AD) churches were destroyed and the Christians fled into the woods of the mountain. As the Islamic conquests swept their way from Egypt to Constantinople beginning in the 8th century Orthodox monks took their treasures to the safe havens of *Athos*.

Records indicate that monks from *Athos* participated in the 7th *Ecumenical Council of Nicaea* of AD 787, and in AD 885 the peninsula was declared a place for monks only. In AD 963 the *Great Lavra*, the largest monastery on the peninsula, situated near the top of the mountain, was established. On this mountainous stretch of land, thirty-five miles long and five miles wide, dozens of monasteries were built, some of them housing over 1000 monks. I had heard that many of them were now deserted, and the population of monks diminished as the world had become more secular.

Documentation from the Greek Government and the Greek Police was necessary for entrance into that medieval world. I had obtained them and, along with a hand drawn map, made my way into the past.

We arrived at Ouranopoulos at night, after the hotel restaurant was closed. My last meal had been an early lunch in Salonika. I rose before dawn the next morning to catch a fishing boat to the monastic port of Dafni. The only way onto the Holy Mountain was by sea. I was too early for breakfast, and purchased two Hershey bars from a vending machine. I put them into my backpack, along with a small thermos of water.

Arriving at the Dafni port I boarded a rickety bus, the only vehicle on the peninsula, and journeyed up the road to Karyes, the small city comprised of emissaries of the remaining inhabited monasteries. The bus was the only nod to the 20th century. There was no electricity on the peninsula. No toilets—only two footprints and a hole in the floor. I had stepped back one thousand years to life as it was lived in the early Middle Ages.

By the time I arrived the temperature had climbed to nearly 100 degrees. Speaking no Greek, I was nonetheless able to communicate that I wanted to see the records of monks who had entered the monasteries since 1905. I assumed that my uncle Clonos would have been an early teenager by then, the youngest age at which a novice can explore the monastic life. Handwritten in Greek script the records were difficult for me to read. My approach was to look for the name of the village of Krestana, my father's birthplace. Next, look for the family name: Athanasopoulos. I was able to read those two words. To my dismay I was unable to find anyone of that name from Krestana. There were entries from that village, but none bearing my family name. (I would learn later that Clonos had used his mother's maiden name, Mastaropoulos. Had I known that, chances are I would have found him. It was a great disappointment.) Not being successful would make my quest almost impossible. Where would I begin? Which monastery would I visit? How would I communicate?

The process was tedious and slow. The presiding monk grew impatient; it was, after all, siesta time in the extreme heat of the day, now over one hundred degrees and climbing. He rather brusquely ushered me out of the room. I was not allowed to stay in Karyes. I would have to find my way through the forest to another monastery.

Standing at the edge of the monastic complex of Karyes I checked my crude map and looked for a path. None were marked. Choosing a direction, I set out.

It was about one o'clock in the afternoon. The forest path was winding and the trees sometimes so dense I felt claustrophobic. My wanderings were fruitless; I saw no signs of life—no monasteries, no sketes or hovels where solitary monks chose to spend their life in silence. After about an hour I realized the path had brought me back to where I had started. I was wandering in a circle!

I set off again, this time making my own path. I was climbing higher, and that was a good sign. It meant I was proceeding up the mountains, crossing the peninsula to the north.

Somewhat more fruitful than my previous sojourn I saw a few dwellings, large and small. My heart leaped. At last, I thought; here

1972: The Holy Mountain

is a place to begin. As I drew closer it was only to discover that the places were deserted. My heart sank. This continued for a long time until, finally, I had reached the pinnacle of the mountain. Stretched out before me was the Aegean Sea on the north side of the peninsula. The path became easier but the temperature was still climbing. I was already soaked in perspiration.

I continued to find dwellings, but like the earlier sightings, they were all deserted. I was exhausted. It was now after five o'clock. I had been climbing for four hours in that incredible heat. I was drenched in sweat. My eyes were stinging from the salt. Nearly half way down the north side of the mountain I looked into the distance to my right. There was a large monastery just off the beach bordering the edge of the forest. Again, my heart began to pound. I raced down the last few hundred yards of the path, across the beach, and splashed nearly thigh deep into the sea to cool off.

Slowly walking the beach toward the monastery I became disillusioned once again. It appeared to be deserted. The gate was slightly open and hanging somewhat loosely from its hinges. Some of the roof tiles were missing. The monastery walls were covered with overgrowth. There was no sign of life; I hadn't seen life since leaving the monk in the archives of Karyes. Disillusionment began to border on fear. What would I do now? I had absolutely no energy left; I couldn't go any further. I rued my decision to come here.

Walking through the open gate I found a shade tree in the monastery courtyard next to a well. I sat down for the first time since Karyes. Hanging from a large chain on the side of the well was a small wooden bucket. I lowered it into the well hoping for water and became excited when it splashed some feet down. Finding a small, hand hammered metal cup attached to a chain, I drank. The thought crossed my mind—actually it was more of a question: *"I wonder how many monks have tasted water from this cup over the centuries."* It felt like a communion of sorts.

Exhausted, I reclined in the shade for what felt like the better part of an hour. When I looked at my watch only one minute had gone by! Something was happening to me, something strange and bewildering. *"I'm not dumb,"* I thought. *"I can tell the difference between an hour and a minute."* It was dizzying. I was disoriented.

The sun was beginning to disappear behind the mountains to the west. I couldn't go further. I would have to stay here for the night and set out again in the morning. But where should I sleep? I needed protection, enclosure, sanctuary. Yes, sanctuary—the monastery's church! There it was, the various domes each with a different style cross reflecting the multitude of cultural and political influences coursing through history over the centuries. The entry way was low and I ducked to enter, leaving the bright Greek sunlight for the dark interior.

What transpired next happened in just a few seconds time, the time it takes for one's eyes to adjust from bright light to darkness. But it was playing out in slow motion, like playing an old 78 recording on 33 1/3, or viewing a film taken at very high speed at an extremely slow playback. Each of the next experiences was like viewing the film one frame at a time.

First came the darkness; utter blackness, rendering me temporarily blind.

Then the smell of incense embedded in the walls from centuries of sacred rites; I was in a holy place and that was a comforting thought.

Haloes! Haloes surrounded me, those golden circles painted around the frescoed heads of the Prophets and Saints of Scripture throughout the ages of Orthodoxy. It was as if I had entered the pages of the Bible, literally.

Faces appeared under the haloed frescoes; I struggled to give them names.

What happened next was stunning. As my eyes adjusted to the dark through the stages just mentioned, I saw, seated in hand-crafted wooden high-backed chairs surrounding the entire perimeter of the Church, black-hooded, grey bearded monks, all staring at me through the silence. The second I recognized there was life in this place they started to sing the ancient chants. The sounds were of heaven but the language was Russian. There is no vocabulary to express what happened to my spirit at that instant! I was transported in just that physically short but psychologically long interim from dispirited bleakness to exalted sublimity. That was not the end of it, however.

Immediately upon hearing the 'music of heaven' a vision appeared directly in front of me. I couldn't look upon it; I didn't want to. It was at the same time ferocious and gentle. I turned away but it remained always before me. I could feel its warm breath on my face—a slow, rhythmic breathing. Minute by minute, hour by hour through the night of singing and the liturgical choreography that unfolded as the monks worshiped, the image enfolded my vision inescapably. Don't ask me to tell you who or what it was. A *Theophany*? I dare not venture a response. Honestly, I don't know. I can hardly imagine anyone ever believing my report and, in fact, very few people over the past forty-three years have heard my story.

While the unearthly vision possessed my consciousness another image, part of the real world of monasticism I was experiencing, heightened the 'paradise'. An enormous hand-hammered circular golden chandelier hung from the central dome. It was embedded with precious stones and Icons. Hand made candles, perhaps thirty of them, formed the circle. The officiating Prelate took his Shepherd's crook, grabbed hold of the chandelier and pulled it as far to one side of the sanctuary dome as he could. With a powerful action he thrust it into a slow arc, circling around the extreme edges of the sacred space. The candle flames sputtered audibly as they fought for survival. The slow, sputtering candle-flight, accompanied by the ancient Russian Orthodox chants, continued while the 'vision' implanted its own 'breath' on my face. Was this Heaven? Had I entered Paradise?

With the appearance of the early morning light the worship was complete and the monks headed back to their cells. The vision left me. I felt drained, empty, yet startlingly full. One of the monks escorted me to a small room and offered me the welcome afforded all who venture into the monastery: a small glass of wine, a piece of crusty bread, a bowl of broth, and two *loukoumi*, gelatin-like candies covered in powdered sugar. It was nearly forty hours since I had last eaten anything, yet this small offering seemed a feast to me.

I had intended to stay on the peninsula for ten days. My permit made possible my stay with the monks in whatever monasteries I visited, my meals with them, a small cell with a small bed, and the opportunity to worship with them throughout the days and nights. I learned this was the *Iviron Monastery*, one of several Russian Orthodox enclaves on *Agios Oros*.

The other-worldly experience of the night just passed had been intense—I was confused and baffled by it; what did it all mean? I doubted I would be able to withstand any further otherworldly confrontation; my world was far too small to either encompass or embrace the possibility of further excursions into such mysteries and epiphanies. I decided to leave my cell and return to Ouranopoulos and my family.

Back down the beach toward the west and then up the same path I had forged the day before, my course was set. The welcome treat had seemed to replenish my energy. It hadn't been much, but somehow my body seemed satisfied. As it turns out, it had been my spirit that was rejuvenated by the 'image', not my flesh by the food, and I began to wear down.

Short breaks were needed as I made my way up the mountain. The breaks became more frequent, sometimes after only ten or twelve steps, and their frequency was accompanied by greater length. Finally it became impossible to continue on. I wouldn't make it across the mountain today. Perhaps tomorrow, I thought, and began looking for some new place to rest, some small skete or hovel. I had passed several deserted places yesterday. Sitting on a rock alongside the path I surveyed my surroundings.

There was a shuffling sound in the distance, faint at first, and growing in my awareness. Up the path about fifty yards was an old, grey bearded monk making his way toward me. His feet didn't leave the ground as he shuffled. Rather, one foot would slide along a few inches followed by the other, and so on as he approached. When he was only a few yards from me, perhaps ten or so, I saw the reason for his slow progress and shuffling. He was blind. I stared at him in silence. He was completely unaware of my presence. At last he was just a few steps away.

Then I remembered. I had two Hershey bars and a small thermos of water in my backpack. I stood up, took it off, and retrieved them. The monk stopped, confused by the noise. Unwrapping one Hershey bar—it was completely melted into the wrapper—I pressed it not to my mouth, but to his. Startled at first, he quickly grabbed the wrapper and began licking it, getting chocolate all over his hands as well as his grey beard. I watched with some mixture of pleasure and amusement. Finished, he dropped the wrapper and stood there. I unwrapped the second bar. He devoured it in similar fashion.

No words were exchanged between us. While this was happening I unscrewed the top from the thermos and, after he dropped the second wrapper, pressed the container to his mouth. He took it himself and drank it dry, water cascading down his chocolate-covered beard. When the water was gone he dropped the thermos and continued shuffling down the path without so much as a nod or an *efxaristó*. I watched in silence until he disappeared around a bend.

"What did I just experience? Was he real, or another 'vision'?"

I didn't really know for sure. Yes, the Hershey bars were gone, their empty wrappers littering the ground; the thermos was empty. I hadn't partaken of them. It had to have been true. He was not another 'visitation'. Or was he?

Suddenly a verse from Scripture crept into my consciousness:

"Inasmuch as you have done this to the least of these, my brethren, you have done it unto me."

The monk had been real. Was it coincidence? I think not. He had been there for a purpose. I took encouragement from his presence. Here he was, a blind, elderly monk, making his way in a hostile environment, exhibiting complete trust in his God to direct his steps. When he needed nourishment God had provided that as well.

1972: The Holy Mountain

Having given his life to God, God had given life to him, guiding and protecting him in his sojourn. Their wedded-ness didn't need a verbal acknowledgment.

If he could manage under these conditions why couldn't I? I had needed encouragement and God provided it. He had needed sustenance and God had provided that as well. It had been a double-edged blessing.

When I realized the significance of this encounter I began sensing a surge of energy coursing its way throughout my body. I charged up the mountain, stopping for nothing. Reaching the crest I headed down toward Karyes, took the same old rickety bus to the port at Dafni, boarded a fishing boat and headed back toward Ouranopoulos.

A young German was on board. For him, it was his yearly pilgrimage on the Holy Mountain as he found himself growing closer to God. It was particularly important this year, Dietrich said, as he was to be engaged in heading up the world-wide television communication for the Munich Olympics, and needed the spiritual refreshing he found on the peninsula. I could sense something 'otherworldly' in his spirit and countenance and wondered if he too had been taken to 'another place'. Neither of us mentioned anything of our experiences on that sacred space; for me it was too personal as well as confusing.

Our conversation focused on his life as a German, a child of a soldier in the Third Reich. Like many from his generation he found it difficult to reconcile his love for his father and his country with the atrocities committed by his father's generation. Dietrich was excited about the 1972 Olympics in Munich, the first to be hosted by the Germans since the infamous 1936 games, where Hitler became infuriated with the successes of Jesse Owens. It was to be a time of reconciliation and healing for the German nation.

Only a few weeks later I would wonder what his life was like as he connected the watching world to the slaughter by the 'Black September' Palestinian terrorists of eleven Israeli athletes abducted from their compound at the games. Did his experience on the Holy Mountain sustain him and guide him through that tragic event?

Arriving at Ouranopoulos I saw my sons Erik and Jonathan down the beach; one was burying the other in the sand. They didn't see me. I entered our hotel room, startling my wife who hadn't expected me back for days. Seeing me, she burst into tears. I didn't wonder, as my return was certainly a surprise. Also, I looked a wreck. I hadn't shaved, bathed, or changed out of my sweaty, dirty clothes. My arms were sunburned, but not my face. Rather, my facial skin was like parchment; it crinkled when I touched it (what was that all about?). I was physically dirty from head to foot. Almost without food for two whole days and part of a third, and hiking in the intense hundred-degree heat, I had lost nearly twenty pounds.

"Don't cry," I said. *"I'm really fine in spite of how I must look. I'm sorry to have startled you."*

"No," she said through her sobs, *"it's your eyes. It's something about your eyes. The intensity, the brightness; I can't look at them."*

I looked into a mirror and saw nothing of what she saw.

That was August, 1972. I didn't know what this all meant, and even today I sometimes give in to my doubts and wonder if it was a figment of my imagination. Did I dream it? Did I make it up? Was it an hallucination? I tried for a time to find a reasonable, logical, scientific or medical explanation. Some say when a person is deprived of food, or suffers heat exhaustion or stress (I had experienced all three) hallucinations often result. That may be, but what explains what she saw in my eyes or my crinkled rather than sunburned face? I felt then, and still feel today that something 'of heaven' occurred, for what reason or purpose I didn't know at the time it happened.

Looking back, I remain convinced it was a preparation for what would take place two years later in another set of 'coincidences' that would change the course of my life. I would become certain that I had indeed been transformed for a new 'mission' by that visit to *Agios Oros*, the Holy Mountain.

> *Once reflections fade*
> *Vanishing apparitions*
> *Flee the failing night*
> *The new song is played*
> *Banishing last renditions*
> *In regaling flight*
> *Bright dawnings displayed*
> *Ravishing transpositions*
> *Incandescent light*
> (GA)

CHAPTER 29

Reflections: What the Arts Tell Me

The material world I had left behind when entering the monastic world of *Agios Oros* had given way to the underlying Divine Presence that inhabits our world unawares. The material world the artist transcends crosses a similar boundary and takes on once again the essence of the Divine Presence locked into it from the beginning.

Now let's be clear on this: the artist is not a savior of the fallen, material world, nor is art. Artists simply tug at their curiosity in a search for *Truth*, in a quest to reveal or release the *Truth*. Art is not divine, but has the capability to point us to the Divine. I believe that art has the power to constitute an initial step leading us to realize our need for reconciliation between the divided worlds of flesh and spirit.

Through the creative process the redeemed material world can open the portals of heaven. The arts transfigure the created things of earth and give back to them something reflecting the magnificence of God's intended purpose.

Christian artists must, I say *must* be convinced, persuaded that the material world is a gift from the Creator God. The 17th century poet, John Dryden, in the face of an increasingly secular and scientific worldview, defended the certainty of a Creator God when he penned these words:

> *This is a piece too fair*
> *to be the child of Chance, and not of Care.*
> *No atoms casually together hurl'd*
> *could e'er produce so beautifull a world.*
> (John Dryden, 1631-1700, "Design")

Two centuries later another poet refined the words of Dryden in a further declaration that artistic endeavors for the Christian are a consciously God-driven creative act:

> *Earth's crammed with heaven,*
> *And every common bush afire with God;*
> *But only he who sees, takes off his shoes....*
> (Elizabeth Barrett Browning, 1806-1861, "Glory in the Commonplace")

CHAPTER 30

1974: Sabbatical: From Norway to the Catacombs

My first Sabbatical was granted right on schedule. It was my seventh year on the North Park faculty and I chose to take the second semester and the following summer for my project. In January I would be going back to Norway!

I intended to continue my studies into the music of Edvard Grieg and its relation to Norwegian folk music. Central to the study was a further examination of that *Piano Trio* manuscript I uncovered in the Grieg archives in Bergen; I thought it had implications for the psychological turning point in the composer's life. I began that work in the summer of 1967 at the University of Oslo, working with several members of the Grieg Committee of Norway who were at that time on the faculty of the University's *International Summer School*. It appeared my initial research was being met with some interest, and that the Grieg Committee was open to my offering the world premier performance of the *Piano Trio*. A letter arrived from Kjell Skyllstad, one of my professors, which read:

1974: Sabbatical: From Norway to the Catacombs

Dear Gregory: There is no excuse for my long silence, except that I sent your manuscript to the Grieg Committee for appraisal and did not get it back till very recently. Of course, your work goes far beyond what we would consider sufficient.... When Schjelderup-Ebbe returns to Norway this fall to resume duties here, it will be very interesting to see his reaction to this new angle to an old problem.... The Grieg Committee has no objection to your performing the work at North Park College.... Hope we shall meet again very soon.

Then everything I had planned for seven years fell apart.

When I wrote to them about my leave and my intentions to return to Norway I assumed they would welcome my continuing research into their most famous composer. To my surprise the Grieg committee decided not to let me have access to the archives, presumably because I was no longer a student of theirs, nor was I a Norwegian citizen. Without that permission it was futile to go to Norway. This was a dilemma—my Sabbatical had been granted, but now I had no project!

I asked myself why I wanted to go to Norway in the middle of the winter anyway? Why not a place with a warmer climate? Greece immediately came to mind. I had been there twice before, first in 1965, that wonderful summer when I met one of the descendants of Felix Mendelssohn and re-united a broken family line, and again in 1972 when *Agios Oros* bent my reality. I had fallen in love with the place. My father had come from Greece as a sixteen year old, arriving by himself in 1907. All of his family, my second and third cousins, still lived there. His brother Athanasius, who accompanied him, fell ill on the journey, was turned back, and died before arriving home. The Atlantic is his burial place.

This, I thought, would be the perfect place to blend work and pleasure. But what work? Little significant classical music has come out of Greece since the *Hymn to Apollo* on the temple at Delphi dating to the 7th century BC. Why not study something else, I thought, something that was important in Greek history and would also appeal to my interest in religious art? Byzantine art, the art of the Greek Christian world from 400 AD to 1400 AD came to mind. I knew very little about it, but was challenged and intrigued by the project. Adding spice to the mix, my uncle Cleomenis (Clonos), whom I had never met, lived on Mt. Athos—*Agios Oros*, the Holy Mountain. My search for him in 1972, as recounted previously, was aborted and cut short by 'visions'. Perhaps I would have another opportunity to search for him. My new research project gained approval from the North Park Sabbatical Committee. I was on my way.

In January, 1974, I flew to Athens, moved into my third cousin's apartment and began my studies. For three months I read in the *Gennadion Library* and examined Byzantine icons in the *Byzantine Museum* and in significant churches throughout the Greek world of the first one and a half millennia AD. It was an exciting time. I ventured into central Turkey to explore the religious cave paintings that were subject to attacks by 8th century *iconoclasts*. My wonderful yet nearly fatal excursion into Cappadocia will be told in the next chapter.

Byzantine art was beautiful, the study was fascinating, but the art was too highly developed and stylized. I had been hoping to discover something of the evolution of Christian art, and it appeared to me that Byzantine art was too far along the developmental scale. I wanted to get to the actual beginnings of the Christian visual aesthetic. Greece was not the place. I assumed, I guessed, that Rome would provide some answers.

1974: Sabbatical: From Norway to the Catacombs

In May I flew to Rome. I had no idea where to begin, nor did I have a letter of introduction or credentials of any kind. My first attempt was to speak to the director of the Vatican Museum; I figured it was better to start at the top and work my way down! Who knows, I might get lucky! And I did!

I was granted an appointment with the museum director, the late Professor Enrico Josi. I didn't know it at the time, but he was a renowned scholar of early Christian art. It was Professor Josi, as a member of the Pontifical Institute of Archeology, who had discovered the bones of St. Peter under the Basilica named for the saint. I was very honest with him, explaining that I was a novice with no background in early Christian art. But two things I brought to the study, I said, were a deep curiosity and a deep commitment to the Christian faith. To my amazement Professor Josi welcomed me and made arrangements for me to work in the *Paleo-Christian Collection* of the Vatican Museum, not then open to the public, on the condition that he accompany me on every visit. What an offer! I was going to be introduced to the finest treasures of early Christian art by the world's leading expert!

I was also introduced to Vatican archeologists, and was given access to the Vatican Library. It was an incredible experience to show my pass and walk by the Swiss Guards every day on my way into the Vatican State.

Most important of all, I was granted the privilege of studying in the archives of the Roman catacombs housed in the Priscilla Convent on Via Salaria, the ancient salt road leading into the city.

Convent over the Catacomba di Priscilla, Rome

The convent was built over the oldest Christian catacomb yet discovered. Sister Maria Francesca Antongiovanni, Chief Archivist of the Catacombs was to be my host and mentor. At this point I began to sense a force greater than I was at work in my life, moving me in directions beyond my comprehension. Music, the arena of my life where I had contacts, credentials and expertise had led nowhere; but in this study where I was a stranger and a novice with nothing going for me but curiosity, every door imaginable was thrown open—doors I wouldn't even have thought of.

My journey thus far had seemed like a long maze of frustrations and dead-ends. Now I began to sense a purposeful and direct leading into a study intended by God to have significance in my life.

I arrived at the Priscilla Convent with some trepidation. What was it going to be like to be ushered into the inner sanctum of a monastic order of nuns? I think they had a few trepidations as well. What would it be like for them to have a non-clerical male (and a Protestant to boot) invading their very private sanctuary? My concerns were quickly alleviated. The elderly Sisters were gracious, though reserved, and tiny Sister Maria Francesca possessed an immediate warm smile that made me feel completely welcome. Communication was going to be a challenge; she spoke only a little English, and I spoke no Italian. But seeing we were both driven by a common interest the challenge was met with relative ease.

Sister Maria Francesca and Greg

I entered into the catacomb archives with certain predispositions. What I knew of the early Christians led me to believe that art would be of very little importance to them. Generally speaking they were, at least in the early years, imported slaves from the Greek-speaking world and the unskilled working class of Rome. They labored under the threat and occasionally the brutal realities of persecution from day to day. They worked from sun-rise to sun-set seven days a week. What inclination or time, not to mention ability, would such people have to produce works of art? For that matter, why should anyone expect to see art of any kind in burial places? Cemeteries are the last place one would look for aesthetic inspiration!

My second predisposition was that if there were art of any type it would be dark and despairing, with a sense of melancholy in keeping with what I perceived to be the nature of their lives. Living and suffering as they did under Roman persecution I expected death themes and crosses—especially crosses. If the cross is an important symbol today, I thought, ubiquitous as it is throughout our churches and cemeteries, what must it have been in that traumatic age?

I began studying the albums of photographs, the entire collection of known catacomb art works. I was stunned! My first predisposition couldn't have been more wrong. There were thousands of works or remaining fragments of works, from crude scratchings in the plaster sealing the graves, to frescoes of meager artistic merit, to elegantly carved burial sarcophagi.

Even more astounding than the number of works was the absence of any subject matter having to do with death! Both of my predispositions were wrong! Before the legalization of Christianity in 313 AD not a single death theme exists anywhere in catacomb art. Not only is the theme of death absent, there is no work which is despairing, or dark, or melancholy, or morose. This fact stands in stark contrast to the practices of Evangelical Christians over the last fifteen hundred years. While the resurrection of Jesus is part of every true Christian's faith, one cannot help but observe that our greater energies are spent on the suffering and death of Jesus. A 'Good Friday mood' seems to reign supreme over our corporate gatherings, from hymns to testimonies, prayers, sermons, to the particular catch phrases so much a part of Christian vocabulary that focus on the death of Christ. That isn't what we claim to believe, nor is it the truth of Holy Scripture, but it is the way we generally comport ourselves in our Christian communities and places of worship. I began to observe a disconnect between what Christians 'profess' and what Christians 'practice'.

What I was seeing prompted many questions:

If 'resurrection' was the mainstay of the early, persecuted Church, why is it so diminished in the contemporary Evangelical Church? Where does the resurrection fit? What role does it play, if all we really are professing is our need for the sacrificial and atoning death of Jesus? Was our hope both initiated and brought to completion through the sacrifice of Jesus on the cross? Is the resurrection merely 'frosting on the cake' and nothing of greater significance?

These were not hollow questions. On the basis of my own life in the Church I too had come to regard the Church's emphasis on suffering and death as mandated by the Scriptures. What kind of theology was this I was confronting for the first time in the Roman catacombs? What kind of theology was this that portrayed nothing of death even though it had every reason to?

And what about crosses? Shocking as it may seem, only three crosses exist prior to the mid-4th century and none before the legalization of Christianity in 313 AD! Imagine it: at most only three crosses and no death themes out of thousands of Christian works!

Every story in catacomb art is a tale of salvation, a tale of the powerlessness of death and the certainty of the resurrection. God delivers us from the consequences of death situations and gives us life instead. Isn't it interesting that all these acts of God's intervention are portrayed thousands of times in catacomb art, but the one act of intervention in which the Christian Church for the last thousand years has placed so much weight and significance—the cross, the crucifixion—appears at most three times, and then in crude form!

The entire collection of catacomb art forced me to ask the difficult question: did the sacrifice of Jesus on the cross hold greater significance than his resurrection for the early Christians, as it appears to do for us? Or was it the opposite?

That was the point at which I began. I had to get to the bottom of this chasm between the Good Friday emphasis of the contemporary western Church and the centrality of the Easter Jesus that seemed to be at the heart of the early Church.

With this exceedingly great visual and theological treasure covering the first three centuries of the Christian era I needed to ask the question why it had been completely overlooked? How did we miss it? I ventured two possibilities.

First, catacomb art has been overlooked by art historians primarily because it is not considered worthy of very much attention. Their calling is to elaborate on art for art's sake. Most art historians refer to catacomb art as a watered down, less than worthy version of the more admired Roman Imperial art. The result is that catacomb art has been almost completely dismissed from consideration in the total scheme of the history of art.

Theologians study theology. They examine the Scriptures and other primary sources written by the important early Fathers of the Church. Their primary task is to elaborate on the authenticity, meaning, and application of the great theological treatises of history. Art does not enter into their considerations; consequently, the significance of catacomb art has been missed by theologians as well as by art historians. Our great early Christian aesthetic witness, buried under the soil of Rome, has been overlooked by both the secular and the religious worlds.

While I agree with the art historians that catacomb art is not great art, it is none-the-less great theology. Were it not for this subterranean treasure we most likely would have no idea regarding the sustaining faith of the early believers who, apart from the few well-known writers and theologians of the day, were otherwise illiterate. The only way they could express their hearts was through the medium of art, crude though it was. My study of this crude art was transformative in my understanding of the rock solid promise of the resurrection of Jesus in the total scheme of faith.

We live on this side of the resurrection, yet we act as if we are on the far side of the crucifixion. We direct our activities to the cross while circumventing, or detouring around the event that gave it meaning. What I saw in the catacombs jarred me into a new reality. Reclaiming the power of Jesus' resurrection became the single, fervent challenge of my study and, even more, the new challenge of my life.

I examined those treasures of the catacombs, and it has been life changing and exciting, to the point that nine years later, 1983, I would return on a second Sabbatical to continue my research. It became clear to me that the 'message' of catacomb art was potentially life-changing for the Church as well. To that end my studies continued, even while I was fully employed as a musician-conductor at North Park.

Years later I would take early retirement to begin writing the books that had been 'calling out' to me since my first visit in 1974. In 2011 I completed the writing, and self-published two books:

The Art of the Roman Catacombs: Themes of Deliverance in the Age of Persecution, and *The Easter Jesus and the Good Friday Church: Reclaiming the Centrality of the Resurrection.* The response to them was heartening; both won awards.

Had the Grieg Committee of Norway accepted my Sabbatical project none of this would have happened. The path of my life would have continued on a straight trajectory of music and, more than likely, I would have been thoroughly satisfied, not knowing what I may have missed. As it is, I am a better person for having been denied by them. Accident? Coincidence? I don't believe in either. And what about those 'visions' two years earlier on *Agios Oros*? Was that moment of 'bent reality' a preparation?

There is a Purpose we can't always predict or discern while we're in the middle of the journey. Our best response, the one I've attempted to embrace in my life, is to get up off the ground of rejection and eagerly run the course laid out for us even without knowing where it will lead or end. Twenty-four years later I would again be called upon to put that practice into action, leading to an entirely new career and life path. Faith has been my guide in that process; without faith the failure of my own 'plans' to return to Norway and the music of Edvard Grieg would have constituted an ending rather than what turned out to be a wonderful beginning.

CHAPTER 31

1974: Almost Murdered in an Underground City

Here I was on a rather decrepit, 'fragrant' bus filled with Turkish women carrying live chickens on their laps, careening across the bleak landscape of central Turkey. Every ten minutes, sometimes more frequently depending on the odor, the Bus Attendant came down the aisle sprinkling rose water from a rubber-nippled Coke bottle onto the outstretched hands of the passengers. Not only was the bus alive with rather pungent body odor and chicken droppings, it was unbearably hot—not a good combination.

The year was 1974. Having intended my Sabbatical leave from university teaching to take me to Norway and the music of Grieg, how strange it was to find myself in Greece studying Byzantine art. Little did I realize at this time that I would soon find myself in the Catacombs of Rome. Byzantine studies had led me to undertake research on the *Iconoclastic Period*, pointing me to Turkey. Hence this four hour bus ride south from Ankara into *Nevsehir Province* on the *Anatolian Plain*, home to one of the most unusual regions I had ever visited: *Cappadocia*, home to one of the seven churches of Asia Minor mentioned in the New Testament.

In contrast to the flatness of the *Anatolian Plain,* the *Cappadocian* landscape seemed utterly other-worldly, one more easily imagined on another planet. The *Fairy Chimneys* in Urgüp, and the *Rock Formations* in Goréme are the stuff of dreams and visions rather than reality, more in tune with Salvador Dali's *surrealism* than Rembrandt's *realism.* My fear of heights notwithstanding, I spent an entire day climbing in, up, and around a host of provocative and amazingly beautiful geological formations in this visually delicious valley. The geology was great in itself, but over the centuries people had carved out dwellings as well as churches into the interiors of these huge spires of rock. I saw part of what I had come for: religious frescoes on the walls. But that was not the ultimate goal of my journey.

Fairy Chimneys, Cappadocia, Turkey

I was seeking the deserted underground cities I had discovered in my readings in the *Gennadion Library* in Athens. Only recently discovered by accident in 1963, they were dug out of the volcanic earth by the Hittites as early as 1400 BC. Later they were expanded by one group of Christians as sanctuaries or safe havens from the persecution by another group of Christians, a conflict referred to as the *Iconoclastic Controversy*. Some of these cities extended as many as twenty levels underground. Complete with ventilation shafts, cisterns to collect water, and protective stones to seal passageways, the sanctuaries were able to accommodate as many as 20,000 people underground for long periods of time. Though there are many such cities on the *Anatolian Plain*, some say as many as forty, two were the objects of my search: Derenkuyu and Kaymakli, connected by a seven-mile underground tunnel. All I knew was that they were located somewhere near the town of Nevsehir.

As my study had evolved backwards from the late Byzantine Period toward Early Christian Art, I was curious about the nature of Christian art that had been the seedbed of the *Iconoclastic Controversy*.

In the Byzantine Empire *Iconoclasm* began with Emperor Leo III in the early 8th century. Iconoclasts were those against any creation of religious images as, in their opinion, they were an assault on the Second Commandment forbidding graven images. The *Iconoclastic* agenda was generally supported by the poorer, non-Greek citizens of the Empire, primarily in the eastern provinces far away from the center of Byzantium in Constantinople.

On the other hand the wealthier Greeks of Constantinople as well as citizens of the Balkans and the Italian provinces supported the placement and veneration of religious images. An image of Jesus had been placed over the ceremonial entrance to the Great Palace of Constantinople, center of the Empire. Leo III ordered it removed, but the *Iconodules* (those in favor of images) murdered those assigned the task of their removal.

In the West Pope Gregory III, in the synod of 730 AD, formally condemned *Iconoclasm* and excommunicated its supporters. However, his Papal letter was intercepted by the Byzantines in Sicily before it could reach Constantinople.

Fifty years later another Council was called, this time by Constantine VI and his mother, Empress Irene. Again *Iconoclasm* was condemned, but before completion of the proceedings soldiers faithful to *Iconoclasm* disrupted the Council.

Seven years later, in the Second Council of Nicaea, 787, the policy condemning *Iconoclasm* was adopted. In the document the following excerpts can be found:

Representational art is in harmony with the history and spread of the Gospel, as it provides confirmation that the 'becoming man' of the Word of God was real and not just imaginary…. Things that mutually illustrate one another undoubtedly possess one another's message…. The revered and holy images, whether painted or made of mosaic or of other suitable material, are the images of our Lord, God, and Savior Jesus Christ; the more frequently they are seen in representational art, the more are those who see them drawn to remember and long for those who serve as models…. Certainly this is not the full adoration in accordance with our faith, which is properly paid only to the divine nature, but it resembles that given to the figure….

The *Iconoclasts* countered with these arguments against images:

The only real religious image must be an exact likeness of the prototype and of the same substance. That is impossible, as wood and paint are void of spirit and life…. Any true image of Jesus must be able to represent his dual nature; that is, human and divine. An icon is considered to be separating his two natures, since only the human nature can be depicted.... Icons are Satanic and mislead men into worshipping the creature rather than the Creator.

Back and forth the arguments continued for nearly a century. All the while assaults and murders continued, with the *Iconoclasts* attacking and the *Iconodules* hiding, protecting themselves in the underground cities of *Central Anatolia*.

In 1974, the year of my travel to Turkey, Nevsehir was a small town. Tourism had not yet discovered central Turkey, so hotels were sparse and primitive by Western standards. I had not arrived on a fancy bus with other tourists but, as I said, on a contraption smelling of body odor, chicken droppings, and rose water. I found a small hotel in the process of being built. Several rooms were finished, and we settled in for a brief stay. One day was given to sightseeing, and the next was to attempt to find the underground sanctuaries.

While I would discover years later that some underground sanctuaries had recently been opened for public visits sometime in the late 1960's, during my stay no one seemed to know anything about them. The owners of the small hotel found a local with a car—a 1957 Chevrolet, no less—and after going home to retrieve his taxi driver's hat to make it official, the driver set out with us in tow.

Around the environs of Nevsehir we drove, stopping periodically to inquire whether anyone knew of the sanctuaries. No one did. Finally we left the roads behind and set off across the fields.

We came to a small set of hills. A young 'twenty-something' man was standing nearby. Our driver approached him and asked the question that had been unanswered countless times. The young man nodded. Finally, it was a good sign. We exited the Chevy; the driver said he would return after a time, and set off to find something to drink.

Our 'guide' was dressed in typical Turkish adult male fashion, with un-pressed pants, an old sport coat that had seen better days, and an open neck white shirt. Curiously, he had a dim flashlight (yes, it was curious, I thought at the time). Approaching the hill he was able to find an opening in the brush, and we entered into the labyrinth. Little did I know just how much of a labyrinth this was going to be, not only in its physical layout, but also in the labyrinthian drama about to be played out.

We descended slowly into the dark passageways, one level, then two levels underground. What a remarkable feat of human engineering! These tunnels were nearly 1400 years old and were still structurally intact. Here a cistern; there a shaft letting in air and a bit of light. Occasionally a large circular stone lay to one side of the passage with a carved track allowing it to slide into place blocking the passageway from *iconoclastic* intruders.

The underground tunnels of Central Turkey

My fascination soon began to be shoved aside by another feeling. The further we went into the deserted underground city, the more bizarre the young man's behavior became. He kept pushing me aside to get closer to my wife. Finally succeeding at this, he grabbed her from behind and, pulling her close to his body with an iron grip thrust his pelvis into her backside over and over again. I forced myself between them. We should have gotten out of there quickly, but he seemed to settle down a bit and we continued. I would regret that decision.

Then it happened again. Again I intervened, this time forcefully. Now he became angry. We were in a passage that had a small wall about two feet tall running along one side. He stooped down, picked up a small stone, and while staring at me with a strange look on his face, dropped it over the other side of the wall. I didn't hear it strike anything. There apparently was a deep pit opposite our path. He reached into his pocket, pulled out a knife and charged toward me.

"Run," I shouted to my wife. *"Run. Get out of here."*

She began stumbling in the relative darkness back the way we had come. The 'guide' and I were struggling with each other. He was trying to force me over the wall into the void of the pit. I was able to shed his grasp, during which he dropped the knife. I began scrambling back the path. I could hear my wife ahead of me, and the 'guide', now presumably with the knife back in his hand, behind me. The distances between the three of us were not wide, but just enough to keep him trailing behind until, finally, we found ourselves exiting the tunnels into daylight.

What now? My wife was about fifteen yards outside the entrance when I exited. As I tried to catch up with her, around the curve of the hill came our driver! What providential timing! Just as he stopped in front of us the 'guide' entered the daylight. Seeing another Turk he stopped abruptly, put both his hands, including the one with the knife, behind his back, and smiled.

We were in the car now and the driver started to pull away. He had no idea what had just happened.

"Stop," I said. *"Back up."* He did.

"Wait here." I grabbed my camera, got out of the car, and took a picture of the man who tried to kill me. I still have it.

Everything in Kaymakli had happened so quickly I hadn't had time to be afraid. Adrenaline and self-preservation had taken charge. The nightmare of it began to register as we made our way back to the hotel.

I thought to myself, *"What would have happened had he succeeded?"*

We were supposed to be in Athens. We were in Turkey. No one knew our whereabouts! Had the 'guide' been successful in doing away with us we would simply have vanished from the face of the earth, literally. Someone may have uncovered our flight arrangements to Ankara, but the trail would have stopped there. No one would ever have heard from us again. No one would have ever discovered our bodies. Our twin 16-year-old sons would have grown up without us. The adrenaline having left my body, weakness took over, and I trembled at the thought.

The next day we were to take the bus back to Ankara. Three well-dressed Turks were checking out of the hotel when we approached the desk.

"Where are you going?", asked one of them in perfect English.

"Ankara."

"How are you getting there?"

"We're taking the bus."

"No. We're going to Ankara. You come with us."

I had had my fill of Turks at that point. We barely survived one situation; I wasn't going to put us in another potentially difficult situation.

"*No,*" I said, "*but thank you very much. We are happy taking the bus.*"

With that, two of the Turks grabbed our suitcases, walked out the door, and put them in the trunk of a very large Nash Ambassador. I could do nothing to deter them. On our way out of Nevsehir they stopped at a restaurant with us in tow. In addition to the food—which they kindly shared with us—each of them consumed a small bottle of Raki. I didn't know of Raki, but I do know Ouzo, the Greek equivalent. And I knew that one or two shots of Ouzo were enough to disrupt one's equilibrium. A whole bottle each! This was not going to be good.

Back in the Ambassador we headed toward Ankara. The three of them sat across the front seat. The driver was Ömür. We never learned the names of the other two, but the one in the middle they called the 'Godfather'. 'Godfather' had enormous jeweled rings on every finger. Some of the jewels were knuckle-big.

They began smoking unfiltered Bulgarian cigarettes, two at a time! My wife accepted their offer and began the same ritual. Four people smoking eight cigarettes at a time was too much for me. Cigarette after cigarette, endlessly. The car was filling up with smoke. I'm allergic to cigarette smoke. My eyes began to water. My nose was dripping constantly. The pungent odor was overpowering. They were driving 80 miles an hour down the rough Turkish back roads, fueled by Raki. "*We're going to die,*" I was certain.

At one point they asked my wife if she needed a bathroom. She did. They stopped the car, opened the trunk, and pulled out four poles and a large, white sheet. Putting the poles in the ground, they wrapped the sheet around them. "*There,*" they said. To my surprise she used the makeshift facility.

Several hours later we approached Ankara, much to my relief. We were still alive!

"Where are you staying?"

"We were going to find a hotel after we arrived back," I said.

Without any further discussion they drove into the main center of Ankara and pulled up in front of one of the fanciest, priciest hotels in the city. *"Oh, no,"* I said under my breath. *"We'll never be able to afford this."* We had been traveling on a tight budget and three star hotels were a luxury for us. This was far more than that. I thought if we got out of the car with our luggage we could wait until they left and then leave this high priced area for a more reasonable location. As I tried to open the car door I was interrupted.

"Wait here," Ömür said, while 'Godfather' and the third person grabbed our luggage and entered the hotel.

"This entire week has been a disaster," I said quietly to my wife, who agreed.

Some minutes later the two men returned. 'Godfather' spoke:

"You have a room in this hotel. I have scheduled a time for your dinner and breakfast. A taxi has been arranged to take you to the airport. It is all paid for. I hope you've had a nice time in Turkey."

Later that summer I received a letter postmarked Ankara. It was from Ömür Olfaz, the driver:

"Warm greetings.... I hope you can come to Turkey again. I want to learn what did your friends thought [sic] *about the memories of Turkey…but please do not tell about the 'Station without resting place'*

1974: Almost Murdered in an Underground City

[referring to the makeshift 'toilet'].... *I want to go to U.S. but it does not seem possible right now, because of my practice about architecture.... If you want something from Turkey please write me...."*

As Shakespeare said: *All's well that ends well.*

CHAPTER 32

February, 1974: My Father's Funeral

Some weeks later, returning to my home base of Athens from spending time in Israel, I found a telegram under my apartment door. My father had died. There was no mention of the exact date, nor any word about funeral arrangements.

He had been in a nursing home. On my last visit with him we knew, without speaking about it, that he might pass away before my return from Europe. He had been pleased I would be spending time in the country of his birth. We said our 'goodbyes' in a subtle way. My mother had given her blessing and permission for me stay in Europe and miss the services if my Dad died before my homecoming. She later told me that after I left his room he wept inconsolably. He knew.

In 1974 the oil embargo had greatly diminished air travel, but when I read the telegram my decision was made. I would try to get home, even if I missed the services, if for no other reason than to support my mother and pay my respects to the man who had made incredible sacrifices for me. The least I could do was to make even this minor sacrifice for him.

February, 1974: My Father's Funeral

I couldn't get a flight because so many had been curtailed. I sought the help of the U. S. Embassy in Athens. Each week I had visited the U. S. Embassy to let them know of my whereabouts and keep up with the current situation in the struggle between Greece and Turkey. In 1974 Greece was being ruled by a Military Junta. The conflict between Greeks and Turks on the isle of Cyprus was escalating. In addition there had been heated arguments over several islands in the north Aegean.

I knew there were military flights twice a week to Washington D.C. for Embassy staff and others. Explaining my situation I asked if I could arrange passage on a flight. They were absolutely resolute in their response: *"No. We only take care of our own."*

"I am 'your own'," I replied. *"My tax dollars give you this comfortable life with all its luxuries here in Athens."* They were not pleased by my confrontation. *"Can you at least be of assistance in finding a flight?"*

"No. We only take care of our own," they reiterated. Apparently I, a United States taxpaying citizen, was not 'their own', and that thought infuriated me.

On an earlier visit to the Embassy I had been told of potential trouble for me personally. As I showed my passport the attendant had casually remarked about my name:

"I see you are of Greek descent."

"Yes," I replied, *"my father was born here."*

"Your passport says you entered Greece three months ago."

"Yes, it was three months yesterday."

"You're in trouble. The next time you try to leave the country you'll be stopped and forced to spend two years in the Greek army."

"I'm a U.S. citizen," I protested. *"I was born in America. My father left Greece in 1906 and became a U.S. citizen in 1919."*

"That's where they have you. Unless your father became a citizen before 1913 he is still considered a Greek citizen. His male children are considered Greek citizens and are subject to military service after three months residence in Greece."

I told him I was ready to fight that ridiculous law. He said the Embassy was not able to come to my aid (again infuriating), but at least he, a Greek National in the employ of the embassy, advised me how to proceed on my own. For the next week I went from office to office in Athens, as no one claimed to have the authority to waive the requirement. Finally I ended up in the first office I had visited. By now I was extremely angry, having had this entire week taken away from my research. Normally a quiet person, and gentle—the typical middle child—I slammed my palms on the desk of the supervisor and yelled,

"If you don't give me the waiver I'm going to open that window, sit on the ledge, and yell how stupid your laws are to everyone on the street below."

It was a Greek standoff, and after three months in Athens I was learning how to play the game. Not wanting to make a scene, he opened his desk drawer, grabbed several stamps and pounded them on a document to place in my passport. I had no idea what it said. Shoving the passport back to me, he scowled and told me to leave. I did, in haste.

But now, weeks later, standing in front of the officer in the Embassy, the military law was the last thing on my mind. I needed assistance to get home for my father's funeral, and they were not willing to assist or even recommend avenues of pursuit.

I went to the Egyptian Embassy. I had traveled twice to Egypt in recent weeks. They referred me to Egypt Air offices in Athens. Nagi M. Aly, the Financial Representative, went to work on my behalf. Through the kindness of his staff they were able to arrange a series of flights that would get me to Chicago, and then on to La Crosse, Wisconsin: six flights taking nearly thirty hours!

I left immediately for the Athens airport. Standing in the Passport Control line at the airport, I wondered what would happen. I had the stamped waiver document folded inside my passport. The guard grabbed the document, read it, looked at me, read it again, and hesitated. I could see the wheels turning in his mind: should he let me go or pull me out of the line? At long last, with a snarl he motioned me through the control point. There would be no Greek army for me. I was finally on my sad journey home to bury my father.

Some weeks later the Military Junta was overthrown and the former Premier Karamanlis, deposed and living in exile in Paris, was brought back to lead the country. While I thought he wiped the ridiculous law off the books, I have recently learned it is still standard operating procedure.

My flight to Chicago, the fifth of six, left Oslo. Thinking of my father during the entire journey I wrote a 'memory requiem' while flying over Iceland:

Over Iceland, February 15, 1974:
Requiem for a Hamburger Houdini

**A Greek immigrant restaurant owner with six sons, whose restaurant was named: "Eat in Harmony Café".
Over the entrance was a sign reading,
"Through this portal enter the greatest people in the world: my customers".**

*Love was many things
And he wore many faces.
    It was wisdom in a whisper
    Teaching in the thunder
    Traditions of toys
    Persuasions of parades
    Watching a bobber
        That never went under.
Love was a Saturday Solomon
    Always eager for Monday
    Who created the gospel:
        "Twelve shiny shoes on Sunday".
Love was many things
And he wore many faces.
    A peddler of pancakes
    A fish fry philosopher
    A hamburger Houdini
    Who knew the power
        Of peanut butter and prayer.
    Love was always forgetting your name
    But knew how you liked your eggs.
Love was many things
And he wore many faces.
    It burned
        A small simple flame*

February, 1974: My Father's Funeral

That warmed many hands
Like an accumulation of candles.
Love has risen
A buttermilk batter resurrection
Through that portal
The great people enter.
Love has risen
Like the aroma of incense
And coffee urns.
The multitudinous choirs
Have known no greater Harmony.

One of the flights lost my luggage, but I arrived home an hour before the funeral service. Borrowing a tie from my brother I attended in the clothes I'd been wearing for two days. I had made it, no thanks to my own Embassy, but with great thanks to Mr. Ali and the Egyptian connections in Athens.

In June, 1974, Nagi sent me a handwritten note, mailed to my home in Chicago:

"I hope that you spent a nice time in your return back.... I hope you remember Egypt and the Egyptians. Thank you."

Would that I had received the same courtesy from those who should have come to my aid. Though I consider myself a Patriot it was a lesson well-learned, one that taught me to honor 'people' first—not 'cultures', not 'nations', not 'ideologies'—just people, those who at the deepest levels of the heart give to others with compassion what they desire for themselves.

Following the funeral I returned to Greece to continue my research. My mother returned to her now empty home. Going through her deceased husband's things searching for memories to sustain her in her grief, she uncovered a handwritten note from 1929, the year she had become a waitress in his restaurant. It was written on a Harmony Café menu in his immigrant scrawl, and was perhaps the most poignant and treasured gift she could have hoped to find. Tears flowed, coupling sadness and joy when she most needed their union. It read:

I think I'm falling in love with this new girl.

CHAPTER 33

1975: Building An Orchestra

Returning from my sabbatical, nine years into my North Park College career I was finally given my first promotion, having been hired as an Assistant Professor. I now held the rank of Associate Professor. In addition I was granted tenure. Life at North Park was reasonably rewarding, though not without its frustrations. Institutional life moved too slowly for me. I was an 'idea person'—an innovator—and often found myself careening into the brick walls of the 'comfortable status quo'. North Park seemed introverted, caught up in the 'small pond' of its Swedish-ness even though the vast majority of students were no longer of that heritage.

The College Choir performed annually in Orchestra Hall, home to the renowned Chicago Symphony. It was North Park's May tradition going back thirty years, yet no one had thought of taking out an ad or an announcement in the Chicago Tribune or on local radio. We seemed satisfied with our own little Covenant audience. Here we were in the middle of Chicago, with a stellar Music Department, yet practically no one in the media knew we existed. It was as if North Park was content with its 'inferiority complex'. I didn't feel we should settle for that.

Fortunately for me, my boss, the Chairman of the Fine Arts Division, Monroe Olson, trusted my instincts. I was the idea person; he knew how to push them through the academic hoops and implement them. We were a good team.

The Music Department had an excellent reputation, to be sure, but was significantly one-sided in its offerings. We were focused on Vocal Performance and Choral Music. The College Choir ruled the roost. Through my perseverance the Chamber Singers had joined the departmental 'pantheon'. The Wind Ensemble had been in existence for decades but always took a back seat. We were looking for singers, not instrumentalists (that was the unspoken mantra). If they came our way, fine, but we weren't actively seeking them. That, to me, seemed tragic and shortsighted.

In the Fall of 1975 another idea crossed my mind. It was time for North Park's music program to be balanced. Why not establish a Chamber Orchestra program? I approached Monroe with the idea. His first reaction was skepticism. There had been several attempts over the years to start such a program, without success. The ventures had been abandoned, remaining non-existent since before my joining the faculty in 1966. We simply couldn't compete with the other schools in our area that had active, successful orchestras, he said. How could we recruit good string players when all we could offer them was a promise? It would be unfair to aspiring young musicians.

While I agreed that we would be doing string majors a disservice by drawing them into a program with no guarantee of success, there was another way. I suggested a different approach.

In my experience with public school instrumental music programs it was often true that our best performers chose college majors outside of music. I knew that music departments needed to service their majors as their highest priorities. Others, performance capabilities notwithstanding, would be lower priorities, placed toward the back of the section if, indeed, there was even room for them in the orchestra.

I had seen some of our best high school performers go off to college and put their instruments in the closet. That was unacceptable to me, and now I had an idea that would keep such talented non-majors involved in something they loved.

"Monroe, let's build an orchestra with string players not being recruited by other schools; let's go after the non-music majors. But (and here was the part of my approach I feared would stop the idea in its tracks) *let's treat them as if they were music majors. I want to be able to offer them free private instruction with the teacher of their choice in the Chicago area. If teachers are willing to take our students into their studios we should pay for the lessons as part of their scholarship, even if those teachers are members of the Chicago Symphony Orchestra!"*

We had nothing to lose by recruiting these students. Even if the orchestra program didn't succeed, they would still be studying in their chosen fields, and North Park had many outstanding programs and courses of study from which to choose.

Monroe was able to shepherd the idea through the scholarship committees. I was given the 'green light' to create an orchestra of non-majors.

We began with a String Quartet the first year. I was actively recruiting on my own time, something our department had never done.

Each year saw substantial growth, and by our fifth year we had a Chamber Orchestra of nearly forty players. High School orchestra directors, upon hearing of our program, began calling me. They had those wonderful performers whom they feared would stop playing their instruments, and were thrilled to see what we were doing. The word spread, and recruiting became easier; they were finding *us*!

Soon the Chamber Orchestra began attracting music majors. Word of our growing success in building an orchestra spread, resulting in my being asked to write another article for the May, 1980 edition of the *Covenant Companion*. In it I focused on several of our recruits:

People make successful programs—people like Tom, Steve, Wendy, and Kerby. While bricks and mortar and courses of study are important, and increasing enrollment and numbers of concerts are amazing, nothing gives our music faculty more pride than our people, our students.

Tom, for example—when I first heard this talented Massachusetts Covenanter play the violin, he was a senior in high school and was not interested in North Park. We had just made a decision to create a string program and were looking for students willing to come into a new program and help build it. Tom knew the orchestra would be small at first. He understood that it wouldn't provide the challenge he'd get in a more developed ensemble. It might take several years, or it might not ever materialize. All we could promise was our commitment to its development. What DID appeal to him, as we talked, was the opportunity to study violin with the teacher of his choice in the city. He also came to realize that North Park could offer him a high quality, diversified course of study; that really appealed to his many talents and interests. Tom took a chance on us and came to North Park. He was the kind of person and the kind of player around whom we could build our string program. Now, three years later, Tom is studying violin with a teacher he thinks is 'fantastic'. He is concertmaster of the Chamber Orchestra, which now has attracted many fine players from around the country—all-state players from Illinois; concertmasters from various high school orchestras;

1975: Building An Orchestra

and several string players from the Civic Orchestra of Chicago, feeder orchestra for the world-renowned Chicago Symphony. The success of the Chamber Orchestra is North Park's surprise of the decade. Tom's faith in us was rewarded—so was our faith in him.

Two years ago I was vacationing in Florida and had made arrangements to audition another violinist from just outside Miami who was a national 'Arion Music Award' winner. When I called from St. Petersburg to confirm our appointment he asked if a friend of his could also audition. That's how I met Steve, who was an excellent student in addition to being a very fine clarinetist. Neither Steve nor his friend had ever heard of North Park, much less the Covenant Church! Steve had applied to the Curtis Institute in Philadelphia, one of the best music schools in the world, but his parents were uneasy about having him live in an apartment there. They were impressed with North Park, especially the personal concern they saw in the faculty; they appreciated the opportunities for private study with some of the world's finest clarinetists. Also, the Music Department had determined to recruit enough fine instrumentalists to make its ensembles of high quality, but not more than it could offer effective and personalized educational and musical experiences. Steve liked the idea that, because he would be one of only a few clarinet players, he would have maximum opportunity for both solo and ensemble performance from the very first day he stepped onto our campus. Steve's coming to North Park was a pleasant accident. He is principal clarinetist in both the Wind Ensemble and Chamber Orchestra, and is an associate in the Civic Orchestra of Chicago. He also plays Krummhorn in the Early Music Consort. Steve's dedication to excellence makes teaching a pleasure.

Wendy, one of my first recruits, is a senior nursing student, but she could easily have been a violin major. She chose North Park because of the excellent reputation of its nursing program and also because we offered her a violin scholarship even though she wasn't going to major in music. North Park may be the only school in the country to offer music scholarships to excellent performers regardless of major field of study. We established this unique scholarship program for one important reason: we think outstanding musicians should be encouraged to continue to develop their talents—not only those preparing for a musical career, but also those for whom performance can remain a source of inspiration and joy throughout their lives. Wendy has found her continuation in music to be the one thing that brings relaxation and balance to an otherwise harried and demanding life as a nursing student. And with a talent like hers it would have been a shame to give up the violin simply because she wasn't going to be a music major. If I had an orchestra filled with Wendys, I'd be extremely fortunate.

There is a cliché that says, "After God made so-and-so, he broke the mold." It could have been said of Kerby, a student from a small town in Pennsylvania. Kerby is an excellent bassoonist, an associate member of the Civic Orchestra, and a private student of the principal bassoonist of the Lyric Opera Orchestra. He is good enough to have been asked by the Lyric Opera to accompany them on their recent Mexican tour. But Kerby was born 500 years too late. What really excites him is the music of the Renaissance. He has become an expert on many instruments from that historical period.

When Kerby visited our campus to meet with me, he brought along his bassoon and a Serpent that he himself had made. The Serpent was the predecessor of the Tuba. Its serpentine shape is fingered like a Recorder, but has a brass mouthpiece. Kerby made it based on photographs, but he didn't know how to play it. I promised him that if he chose North Park I'd work with him to create a fingering chart and also assist him with brass mouthpiece techniques. Kerby chose North Park because it offered opportunities for performance in the traditional ensembles and also the unusual, like our Early Music Consort. In this group students learn to play all those funny-sounding, strangely named, weird-looking instruments that are so important to Kerby. He was also attracted by the wealth of the experiences available in a major city like Chicago. Here he could tap into all sorts of professional opportunities and experiences, while retaining that very important personality which is the hallmark of a small school like North Park. Kerby's remarkable individuality could retain its freshness and distinctiveness; it wouldn't be swallowed up in the huge sea of anonymity sometimes associated with a large university.

Tom, Steve, Wendy, and Kerby are only four of many talented young people from around the country who have not only gained immeasurably from their studies at North Park, but have also contributed much to the institution. They are just a few of the people who make our program successful.

Chamber Orchestra Strings, second year, 1976

I made the decision that we would not use non-students, or 'hired ringers' in our performances. We would only play music that fit our personnel. Nonetheless, our repertoire was broad and challenging, speaking to the growing success of our idea, encompassing great works from the Baroque to the Twentieth Century:

Corelli:	Concerto Grosso in g minor, Opus 6 #8 (Christmas)
Vivaldi:	Gloria, RV 589
Bach:	Orchestral Suite #2 in b minor, BWV 1067
	Wachet Auf, Cantata #140
	Brandenburg Concerto Grosso #3 in G Major, BWV 1048
	Brandenburg Concerto Grosso #5 in D Major, BWV 1050
	Concerto for Two Violins and Orchestra
Handel:	Messiah
	Concerto Grosso in Bb, Opus 6/7
Haydn:	Symphony #104 in D Major, Hoboken 1/104
Mozart:	Eine Kleine Nachtmusik in G Major, K. 525
	Symphony #35 in D Major, K. 385 (Haffner)
	Clarinet Concerto
Beethoven:	Symphony #1
	Symphony #2 in D Major, Opus 36
	Symphony #8 in F Major, Opus 93
	Piano Concerto #4 in G Major, Opus 58
Weber:	Concertino for Clarinet and Orchestra
Schubert:	Mass in G
	Symphony #5 in Bb
	Symphony #8 (Unfinished)
Mendelssohn:	Symphony #4 (Italian) in A Major, Opus 90
Dvorak:	Serenade for Strings in E Major, Opus 22
Tschaikowsky:	Serenade for Strings in C Major, Opus 48

1975: Building An Orchestra

Grieg:	*Holberg Suite for Strings*
Borodin:	*Polovtsian Dances from the opera 'Prince Igor'*
Verdi:	*Messa da Requiem (with the College Choir)*
Saint-Saens:	*Carnival of the Animals*
Bizet:	*Choruses and Arias from the opera 'Carmen'*
Ives:	*The Unanswered Question*
Prokofieff:	*Peter and the Wolf, Opus 67*
Bartok:	*Rumanian Folk Dances*
	Rhapsodie for Cello and Orchestra
Gershwin:	*Rhapsody in Blue*
Copland:	*Appalachian Spring (original version for 13 instruments)*
	Excerpts from 'Rodeo' (Ballet Score)

Early on the orchestra's success was reflected in letters we received. This letter came in the middle of our third year:

I would like to personally congratulate your orchestra. Last Friday night my friend and I were overwhelmed by the performance.

Another came in response to one of our concerts in Minneapolis:

In rehearsal. Christopher French, cellist, became principal cellist of the Houston Symphony Orchestra

Please express our sincere thanks to the Director and the Chamber Orchestra for the beautiful evening they shared with us in Minneapolis last Saturday night. The program was perfect, the talent superb, and the performance and commitment inspiring.

North Park's acting President, Arthur A. R. Nelson, sent me a hand-written note:

Thanks so much for the inspiring moments you gave us last night in Orchestra Hall. You have enabled miracles in your work with the Chamber Orchestra and have contributed greatly to making North Park's musical contribution and image of the finest quality.

Now that our Chamber Orchestra was established, successful and on a par with the vocal/choral program at North Park I decided it was time to unite the programs through offering a *Do-It-Yourself Messiah* to our community. Our voice majors and voice faculty were to be the soloists for the *arias* and *recitatives*, my Chamber Singers the foundation for the *choruses*, the Orchestra the *accompaniment*, and whatever audience we could assemble would add power and enthusiasm to the mix.

Our first attempt took place on the North Park campus in the Lecture-Hall Auditorium. We advertised in our community and throughout the Covenant Churches in the greater Chicago area. People were encouraged to bring *Messiah* scores; we would provide a few if necessary. The nearly 500 seats in the auditorium were roped off, with singing participants seated in sections and the listeners seated behind them.

We had no idea how many would show up. To our great delight, the auditorium filled to capacity! We had ample singers for each voice part, including tenors! The orchestra and soloists had rehearsed, but apart from that the work would proceed with whatever results came

1975: Building An Orchestra

from the unrehearsed and assembled group. I conducted, turning my attention to the audience for the singing of the choruses to make sure each section's entrances were indicated.

We were astounded at the result. It sounded as if the singers had been rehearsing all fall! I'm quite certain there have been rehearsed performances that weren't as musically rewarding as what happened that night.

Leading the chorus in North Park's first 'Do It Yourself Messiah'

On the basis of our first success we offered another *Do-It-Yourself Messiah* the next year. In addition, we were invited to bring our North Park forces to St. Joseph, Michigan to be the foundation for their first such attempt, sponsored by the *Berrien County*

Council of Churches, the *Gast Manufacturing Company*, and *Weldun International*. Again, it was a great delight. I received a copy of a letter sent to the sponsoring agencies:

I would like to thank you and your sponsors in industry for promoting the "Do-It-Yourself" Messiah.... It was a real thrill to sing it again, particularly in the company of such talented musicians and director—the last time I sang it was 39 years ago with the Apollo Chorus in Chicago.... I am looking forward to a repeat performance next year as, I am sure, everyone of the chorus does. Merry Christmas! Signed, Florence Zylstra, Benton Harbor, Michigan

In the spring of our sixth year, 1981, the orchestra tackled the demanding and treacherous Giuseppi Verdi *Requiem*, accompanying North Park's virtuoso College Choir. This was the only performance in our history where we hired extra players. We had always relied on our own student performers, but this musical score required three additional paid musicians: one bassoonist, one cellist, and one string bass. Much to the credit of North Park's fine music school, all the vocal soloists were our own voice majors or minors. It was a stellar event. To think that our orchestra had, in six years, grown from a string quartet to an ensemble capable of playing Verdi's *Requiem* is quite astounding.

I was the Founder and Conductor of the Chamber Orchestra for its first seven years. I had done what I set out to do. Now that the program was established on a solid footing it was time to hire a conductor who, unlike me, had experience as a string player.

My final performance with the Chamber Orchestra was on the stage of Chicago's Orchestra Hall. The program included one movement from Bela Bartok's *Rhapsodie for Cello and Orchestra* with student Christopher French as soloist; Carl Maria von Weber's *Concertino*

1975: Building An Orchestra

for Clarinet and Orchestra with Steven Hanusofski as soloist; George Gershwin's *Rhapsody in Blue*, Deborah Reckowsky, pianist; and arias and choruses from Georges Bizet's *Carmen*, with soloists Leslie Windmiller, Pat Cook, Joy Graham, Joel Ross, Jay Jingst, and Dan Harper. It was a fitting 'farewell', and I left the stage that night with enormous pride in what North Park had accomplished by taking a chance with my 'out of the box' idea.

My final performance with the Chamber Orchestra, Orchestra Hall, Chicago

My last class of recruits included three who went immediately upon graduation to professional orchestras: bassoon player Kerby Nelson joined the Hong Kong Symphony; clarinet player Steve Hanusofsky went to the Phoenix Symphony; cellist Christopher French went to the Honolulu Symphony and then to the Houston Symphony where he became principal cellist. Trumpet player Yvonne Toll went to Eastman School of Music, then to Atlanta where she is principal trumpet of the Atlanta Opera and participates with the Atlanta Symphony as an adjunct member. Not bad for a program that was still in its infancy.

Over the next twelve years North Park's Chamber Orchestra would see many directors come and go. My replacement was Tom Wilkins who went from North Park to become Associate Conductor of the Detroit Symphony, and on from there. Joseph Glymph was next in line, followed by Alan Heatherington, who became Founding Director of the Ars Viva Symphony, a highly regarded and praised orchestra in the Chicago Area. Alan's reputation is of the highest order; the music critics love his work. He was succeeded by Steven Alltop, now the Artistic Director of the Apollo Chorus in Chicago and conductor of the Elmhurst Symphony, one of the fine regional orchestras in the Chicago metroplex. Last in the line was Jim Fellenbaum, whose tenure was brief.

All of them were superb musician/conductors, more highly qualified than I, but were not inclined to do the hard work of recruiting. Consequently the program diminished in size and had to be supplemented by hired performers brought in for the last rehearsal before the concerts. In my years with the orchestra we had hired only three 'ringers' for one performance, the Verdi *Requiem*. Now, each concert was augmented by hired musicians; sometimes the 'ringers' comprised over one-third of the orchestra. While the performances were of high quality it was not without consequences for the integrity of the program; our students never experienced the fullness of the music until the 'ringers' joined them the day before the event.

Eventually North Park found Tom Zelle, an eager young conductor from Germany who worked hard to restore the organization to its original footing. His outreach to the surrounding community of young musicians is exemplary. Tom is perfect for the program; I'm pleased to know the program is in his hands.

As for me, I'm grateful for Monroe Olson's aggressive support. He took a chance on my idea. I don't think I let him down.

CHAPTER 34

Reflections: What I See In the Mud and Scum of Things

The Chamber Orchestra's evolution proved that great things can indeed be accomplished when a person aggressively tackles a dream. I knew there had to be a way forward, but I must confess that the evolution greatly outdistanced even my wildest fancies. Again, a lesson was learned in the process: pursuing a vision beyond one's current reality, even with no guarantee of fulfillment, is the only way growth can happen. It's a 'faith thing'.

To see or hear more than is physically, actually there is the desire of artists. They dream wildly. That was certainly true in the contemplation of developing an orchestra where everything mitigated against its creation. An artist's idle curiosity contains the seeds of future glories that are heard in their hearts if not in their minds. Artists initiate a process of transformation of materials, as did their ancient ancestors. The long-term consequences of their dreamings may well outdistance both their imagination and their life. For example, blowing against two blades of grass, creating an obnoxious squawking and grating on the ear, grew over millenia into the oboes and resurrection trumpets of Bach's *B Minor Mass*. Little did the original dreamer know what would eventually result from his innocent dreaming and squawking. And he probably experienced as much sheer joy and pleasure over his newly discovered squawk as we do from listening to Bach. When you stop to think about it, all that separates the modern orchestra from the blowing against two blades of grass and the thumping on hollow logs is the creative mind and centuries of innovation and technology.

All that could kill my dream of an orchestra and keep it from its fulfillment was inertia, ambivalence, or doubt. Those words were not part of my vocabulary.

Pursuing a dream takes courage and a willingness to see progress in little things. I was encouraged by what I believed about the inevitability of an idea to reach great heights, as I had observed within the context of history itself. A piling of rocks, created often in the Hebrew Scriptures to commemorate a miracle of God's activity in the world, seemed nothing compared to Pericles' *Parthenon* or the *Cathedral of Notre Dame*, yet the spirit it contained was the equal of them. The stones became more than stones, while remaining stones. Leonardo's *Last Supper* was prefigured in the first satisfying rubbings of leaves, bark, blood and soft stones. The Angel's question to the women at the empty tomb—*Quem Queritas?* ("Whom do you seek?")—contained all the theatrical elements for the first Christian liturgical drama. That is the paradox and the beauty of art. The role of an artist is to seek out that beauty which is hidden in the most ordinary of things; as the poet said:

> *Every common bush is afire with God.*

Another poet, Ralph Waldo Emerson, also encouraged this quest when he wrote:

> ....*In the darkest, meanest things there always, always,*
> *something sings....*
> ....*In the mud and scum of things there always, always,*
> *something sings....*
> (Ralph Waldo Emerson, 1803-1882, "Music")

In art, in being an artist, one brings fusion between the common and the extraordinary, the absurd and the sublime. In art, in being an artist, one sees the possibility of unraveling the greatest and deepest human contradictions. In art one becomes witness to images of God's miraculous healing of the cosmic split in our fallen nature.

Could it be that Boethius was right? That music is more than sound? That words are more than interchange? That pigment on canvas does more than set our optic nerves vibrating? Have we not experienced our most profoundly moving moments when we became vulnerable to a beautiful sunset, or a night sky possessed it seemed of 'anthracite and diamonds', or our child's first song, or a hymn that changed our life? What about those tears shed over a Chopin Etude or the poetry of John Donne?

Why did God give us the physiological capacity to move our voices across a wide span of pitches, far more than any other of His creatures? Why the unbelievable variety of vocal colors in our human voices? Why are our ears able to respond to this multitude of nuances? Why did He endow us with the capability to shout, or whisper? Why did He connect our ears and our eyes, our touch and our smell with our emotions—or give us emotions in the first place, so that such aural and visual effects and inflections would move us, or touch us in the most incredible ways? Our God was a Creator—an Artist; that's why! Five times in Genesis 1 it is said that God 'made', five times that He 'created'.

The Bible doesn't begin with a definition of who God is, but rather what God does.

Some have said that God is presented in the Christian revelation as more of a living and creative artist than as a philosopher or theologian. When God interrupted eternity with a desire for companionship His first act was one of a Creator, the supreme Artist. Determined to create a path of profound communication between Himself and us, as I said earlier, He created us in his marvelous image, and chose to endow us with a creative spirit like His. How many times and in how many ways have the arts brought us close to the loving, powerful presence of the Living God? What a brilliant God He is! What an immense gift He has given to us!

As for me, I want to dream wildly and fully use whatever gift I have graciously been given to guide my dreams to their fulfillment, holding nothing back, ever.

CHAPTER 35

1976: Hosting a Soviet Dissident

The phone rang. It was Byron Gustafson, a former student who had lived in our basement apartment for several years during his student days and his tenure at Chicago's Auditorium Theater. Byron had made possible my soirees in the theater dressing rooms with Dietrich Fischer-Dieskau, Isaac Stern, and others following their concerts. Now he was in management with Columbia Artists in New York, where he would eventually become a Vice President.

"Greg, I have a favor to ask of you."

It was unlike Byron to ask anything that would be an imposition, so I knew right away something compelling was in the offing.

"We are scheduling a Carnegie Hall concert for a Russian violin virtuoso who has fled the Soviet Union. It will be his first American performance. We want to schedule a trial run concert out of New York. Would you be willing to make arrangements in North Park's Lecture Hall Auditorium?"

The violinist was Gidon Kremer, born in Riga, Latvia in 1947, and student of the virtuoso violinist David Oistrakh. Denied permission to travel abroad by the Soviets, he nonetheless escaped, making his debut in Vienna in 1970. After winning the most prestigious competition awards, legendary conductor Herbert von Karajan proclaimed him the 'greatest violinist in the world' in 1976, the year he was finally to make his American debut.

It didn't take much convincing. Even before asking North Park's permission I said a hearty 'yes'.

Byron detailed the procedures. Mr. Kremer and his wife, who was also his accompanist, would be flown to O'Hare. I was to pick them up, take them to dinner, and set up their accommodations in the North Park College Hotel in the Campus Center. After entertaining them again at breakfast we would proceed to the Lecture Hall Auditorium for a rehearsal. Someone from Milwaukee was to meet us there to lend Mr. Kremer a Stradivarius violin to use in the preparatory recital as well as Carnegie Hall. The concert would be scheduled for the afternoon, after which I would take them to dinner and to the airport for their return to New York. Columbia Artists Management would reimburse me for any expenses.

We were not to do any advertising other than 'word of mouth', as the 'official' premier performance in Carnegie Hall was not to be overshadowed. I made a series of phone calls and asked North Park's Elizabeth Buccheri, Professor of Piano, to spread the word at Orchestra Hall to encourage Chicago Symphony string players to attend. Her husband John, Professor of Music Theory at Northwestern University, spread the word there.

Our Hall was packed. Many CSO players were in attendance, carrying their instrument cases, as they would leave immediately for Orchestra Hall for their own performance later that day. They were well aware of the reputation of the young Soviet dissident and wanted to hear him for themselves.

My time with Mr. Kremer was exciting, though brief. He was interested in my trip to Leningrad in 1965 and wanted to know what it was like for a westerner to visit during those rather troubling years. However, it was obvious he was distracted by this whirlwind of preparation for his debut. I respected their privacy and asked no questions about their escape from the Soviet Union. They were gracious and expressed sincere gratitude for my efforts and the willingness of North Park to host them.

We made a surreptitious cassette recording of his concert on our campus. No one other than me has ever heard it in these intervening thirty-nine years. I still have it. I remain grateful to Byron for trusting North Park to be discreet in these arrangements, and have been thankful that he felt he could trust me as well to be of assistance. It remains startling to think that North Park College was the site of the stellar Gidon Kremer's 'real' American debut!

A post-rehearsal phone call was the last time I spoke with Byron. Tragically, he died way too young of ALS, *Lou Gehrig's* disease.

The next year Gidon Kremer performed with the Chicago Symphony Orchestra.

CHAPTER 36

August, 1981: A Breakup

After twenty-four years of marriage my wife ran off with a mutual friend. My life came crashing down on top of me.

My entire life I had felt divorce was wrong. More than that, I was convinced it was a sin. Now that it had happened to me I was embarrassed and ashamed. I stopped going to church because of the humiliation, and didn't want to expose myself to what I thought might be 'clucking tongues'. At work I gave my all, then retreated into the privacy of my home, shying away from all human contact. My students were respectful of my time outside the rehearsal room.

Deep down inside I wished someone would break the silence and simply engage me as a friend. As I walked to work one day one of the Covenant pastors waved at me from across the street, gave me his greeting, and suggested he'd call me to have a cup of coffee. Encouraged, I waited anxiously for the call that never came. Several weeks later he again confirmed he would call. It never happened. I knew divorce was quite rare in evangelical circles at that time, and surmised that people just didn't know what to say to the victims of a breakup. It was safer to ignore them than to engage them. Nonetheless, I continued sitting by the phone. It remained silent.

Even though I was the abused victim of the abandonment I felt as if I was the abuser. "*It must have been my fault.*" I was convinced of it. The guilt was overwhelming, fortifying my reclusivity. In my darkest moments I was reassured through my Christian faith that there was an escape from this deep pit that was swallowing me alive, but the pathway seemed elusive. A few years earlier I had written a poem while standing in front of a small painting on the north wall of the *Duomo* in Florence, in which Dante stands against a background of the three levels of his *Divine Comedy*. Now, in my disconsolate state, I recalled the sentiment expressing the hope I now needed to claim:

While Thinking of Dante

Though planets churn and groan through space
In agonized spinning
    Their moons again are full
And the Crest
Breaking as quickly as it gathers
    Taken in tow becomes resurgent
The lowering sky
Its shades drawn down in darkness
    Awaits with wonder the warmth of sun
The throbbing
Coursing pulse of cycles and seasons
    Will not be broken
So the languished soul in night's entombment
Is caught and cradled by the eye of God
    In dawnings of each day's Paradise

(GA)

My hope was just that—hope. There was no reason, apart from prayer and faith, to expect anything to come of it; one hopes nonetheless, and with prayer and faith one hopes confidently. Without

August, 1981: A Breakup

it what could I expect to assuage the barren landscape that surrounded me? And so I hoped. More than that, I believed, and belief kept the doors from slamming shut completely and permanently. Life was about to change, and it came much sooner than my hope had anticipated.

CHAPTER 37

1981: Medieval France Meets Country Western

After a time I began trying to put my life back together by going to concerts and plays, sometimes at the spur of the moment, just to take my mind off my situation. If I could get a ticket, fine; if not, I'd simply go back home. At the beginning it helped, but it also constituted a continuation of my loneliness; at intermissions everyone around me was engaged in a conversation with their companions while I twiddled my thumbs waiting for *Act Two*. The events were wonderful, but my isolation in the midst of them contributed to my depression.

I decided to seek someone to accompany me on occasion—just a friendly relationship, with no intention of ever becoming 'romantically involved' or, horrors, to ever marry again. Gradually I was making my accommodation to 'singleness'. I didn't want to risk another chance of being abandoned.

But, who? I didn't know any single women who might share my same interest in the arts, and I didn't want to join any singles clubs! At age forty-five I was too old for that. Furthermore, there was to be no 'heart entanglement' ever again.

1981: Medieval France Meets Country Western

One day I picked up the College Faculty Directory and began casually going through it, looking for someone who I might not have remembered. Names of married faculty were accompanied by the names of their spouses. Beginning with 'A' I thumbed through with growing frustration. I was half way through the alphabet and no compatible name had surfaced. I continued on. Finally I reached 'S', and *'Steele, Doy—Theater'* caught my attention. She was single. She was involved in the arts.

"Well," I thought, *"at last, someone with a common interest."*

She was new to the faculty, in her second year; I had never met her, nor did I remember what she looked like. I checked the yearbook for a photo. She was attractive, to be sure, but so young.

"Well," I thought again, *"what difference does it make? It's only for an occasional concert or theater event."* I tucked her name away in my memory.

That very day an announcement came in the faculty mail, asking me to attend a meeting the next day with a small group of student advisors. Doy Steele's name was on the list. I decided to go early, wait until she sat down, seat myself next to her and strike up a conversation to see if she was easy to talk with. She was.

"Someday I'll ask her to attend an event," I said to myself. No urgency. Future companionship was not part of any equation.

That was Tuesday, November 3, 1981. The next day a flyer came in the mail announcing a concert at University of Chicago of *12th – 14th Century Music from France*. I had an interest as well as experience in *Early Music*, having organized a group of students interested in playing instruments of the Medieval and Renaissance eras. We performed on campus and had taken a summer-long tour of the western United

States. I knew the genre, so I decided to attend. The idea came to me; why not see if Ms. Steele would like to go with me? That night I called her, apologizing for the late date of the call. It was, after all, November 4th and the concert was just two days away.

"Oh my gosh, a music professor is calling me asking me to go to a concert of 12th through 14th century music from France!", she thought to herself on the other end of the phone (she recounted this to me weeks later). *"How am I going to tell him I listen to Country Western?"* She smiled into the phone and said, *"I'd love to go, but I don't know anything about it."*

I said I didn't know anything about it either. I lied, just to set her at ease, and was upset with myself for doing so. After the divorce I had determined never again to hide my feelings, or shade the truth merely for the sake of survival and self-preservation, yet I had done it. To my surprise, she agreed to go. After hanging up the phone it struck me—

"What have I done? I haven't dated anyone in a quarter of a century! What do I do now?" I was terrified. Really, I mean it; terrified.

Doy at the waterfall

Friday, November 6 arrived. I was extremely nervous as I knocked on her apartment door on Carmen Avenue a block from the campus. When she opened it my first thought was,

"Why does she have to look so beautiful?"

This was supposed to be just an occasional 'no strings attached' event. Her appearance was making it difficult. We started our drive south on Kimball Avenue to Irving Park Boulevard, then headed left toward Lake Shore Drive. At that moment a powerful, overwhelming, frightening thought came into my mind:

"You are going to marry this woman."

"No way," I said back. *"Never."*

Again the words, *"You're going to marry this woman."* Again I said no.

I looked at my watch; it had been only twelve minutes since we left her apartment! I wanted to turn the car around and take her back home, saying,

"Sorry, Doy, but this isn't the time. I can't do this."

Not wanting to be embarrassed, or to embarrass her, I continued on.

We had a wonderful time. Funny, but I don't remember a thing about the music! At intermission I spied a poster announcing a Chekhov play, *The Seagull*, the next weekend. Doy said she had read the play but had never seen it. I asked if she'd like to see it if I could get tickets. *"Yes,"* was her reply.

After the concert we went to the Red Star inn just off the Eden's expressway in Old Irving Park (it doesn't exist anymore, unfortunately). I ordered a Black Russian. I don't know what possessed me. I had never ordered one before! I hardly drink! Overwhelming nerves, I guess.

The next week passed slowly. Too slowly. I found myself constantly looking at my watch wondering why the hands weren't moving quickly enough. Then came Friday, the 13th, an evening with Chekhov. Again, we had a great time.

The evening of the 14th I went to a play at the college. Doy was there, but with another man. They looked good together. It dawned on me that she was much too young for me—sixteen years younger to be exact; she needed someone her own age. It was a disappointment, but also a stark reality. What had that image in the car been about? Intuitions have played a significant part in my life. I have always trusted them. More often than not my trust in them has been confirmed. Was this one of those rare occasions? Had it been more 'wishful thinking' than 'intuition'?

We had previously arranged to attend a performance the next night by a Greek Folk Dance group I had seen in Athens. I decided that would be the final time we would meet. I would find a way to break it off, which I did at intermission. I told her I was enjoying the times with her, but that we shouldn't let it go on. The second half of the performance I was miserable. I hadn't told Doy the truth. Afterwards I confessed my lie and my true feelings toward her.

"He's a recently divorced man," she reflected to herself. *"I shouldn't touch him with a ten foot pole. But something is here. Be patient. Take it slowly."*

Thanksgiving was eleven days away. I was going to visit my mother in Wisconsin during our short teaching break. I sent a hand printed note to Doy asking her to go with me:

1981: Medieval France Meets Country Western

> 11/11 a.m.
>
> Doy —
> Seriously, now
> Why not
> cancel
> your Thanksgiving plans, and
> Go
> with This Turkey
> To 'God's Country'.
> (Truth is —
> I
> need
> To be with
> you.)
>
> Greg

Note to Doy, November, 1981

She had plans to go with a friend to visit other friends in Ohio. At the last minute Doy changed her mind and decided to fly home to Grand Prairie, Texas, to be with her mom. Before we both left to go our separate directions, I asked if I could pick her up at O'Hare Sunday evening. She agreed.

I wonder if the topic of conversation in both cities was the same? I know mine centered on Doy. Was it reasonable to marry someone that much younger? Should I even risk another relationship? My mother encouraged me, reminding me that she was 20 years younger than my father and it had been wonderful.

"Live life today," she suggested, *"tomorrow will take care of itself. If love bathes the relationship age differences can be surmounted."*

That seemed reflective of what her mother had said regarding their ten children sharing one bedroom: *"A hundred angels can live on the blade of a knife where there is love."* My mother had married a much older man. Yes, her older husband had become infirm, but there was enough love to meet and surpass the challenge.

Soon after Doy exited the plane and entered the terminal I asked, *"Will you marry me?"* She said *"Yes".*

Wedding Day, May, 1982

1981: Medieval France Meets Country Western

The first time I had ever spoken to Doy was November 3rd. Before the month had come to its conclusion we had agreed to get married. Six months later we were. Thirty-three years later it is still like the night of *12th to 14th Century Music From France*. The man whose career was dressed in *concert tails* and the woman whose passion was *Patsy Cline and cowboy boots* joined hearts and hands. Who said *Medieval Music* and *Country Western* couldn't make a sublime duet?

CHAPTER 38

November, 1981: A Healing

While Thinking of Dante had opened the door to hope. Meeting Doy opened the door to healing and a relationship that turned my life from depression to a brightness that challenged everything I had known about love. It prompted these poems to Doy:

To Doy: Love, and Only Love, Is Right

You have interrupted my melancholy symphony
    A woven shroud repelling demons
Better to be kept without wings
    Than falter in flight.
You have intruded upon the boredom
    Worn like a protective cloak
    To shut out shivering.
Better to be dumb to suffering
    Than bright.
You have descended deep wells I carved
    To linger in oblivion
    Baked brittle as potter's clay.
Better the abyss
    Than the failure of height.
You have laid siege the towers I built

November, 1981: A Healing

> To escape barbed spears
>   Infecting my solitude with false hope.
> Better loneliness
>   Than the agony of spite.
> You have resurrected the death I inhabited
>   A book of sealed up spells
>   Plaguing tomorrows.
> Better to live in darkness
>   Than witness the dying of light.
> You, my Love, have become my Love.
>   Better your dreams than my feeble sight.
>   Better your exalting than my debasing fright.
>   Love, and only Love, is right.

Greg and Doy

Love is...

Love is a drawing down of blinds
Obliterating what the heart knows is haunting
Love is to awaken wellsprings of warmth
in stone-cold cisterns of sorrow
Love is a reconciliation of splendor
once as elusive as luscious fruit in barren deserts
Love is to know a loosing of laughter
to desire Desire
to shudder resplendent at a touch
to shout and not hear echoes
Love is an end to reaching, grasping emptiness
discovering anew what had not been missed
Love is being loved for no reason
But to withstand a winnowing of wonder
Truly for the sake of love
At the reconciling and resilient point of love
Love is a drawing down of blinds

CHAPTER 39

1983: If I Forget Thee, O Jerusalem...

Life was good. I was newly and happily married to a wonderful woman who continued her work in North Park's Theater program. We collaborated on two musicals: *The Fantasticks* and *The Portable Pioneer and Prairie Show*. Doy did the heavy lifting; I merely prepared the musical aspects. I marveled at her brilliance as a director. It was 'just plain fun' to stand aside and witness the unfolding of theatrical excellence under her compelling leadership. It was obvious her students loved her.

My second Sabbatical had been granted, this time to continue my research into the art of the Roman catacombs I had stumbled into nine years earlier. Once again I would travel to Rome and throughout the Middle East, gaining perspective and adding verification to support my developing thesis of *'Resurrection Centrality in the Early Church'*.

It was Palm Sunday, 1983. We were in Jerusalem as part of a ten-day trip to the Holy Land. The sound of a cock crowing had awakened us, as it had every day. It was as if each morning began with this ritual reminder.

Holy Week was upon us, and all the events of that most tragic and blessed Messianic pilgrimage tumbled in our minds like loose pieces of an often-worked puzzle. We knew how they fit, but how was it possible to make sense of them? The perennial questions surfaced once again: Who were those participants in the most significant drama of the ages? How could the disciples sleep while Jesus agonized nearby? Judas saw Jesus' life and miracles—what possessed him to become a traitor? Peter's denials didn't make sense. Pilate's wife seemed to be the only one who defended the Master. And Mary, poor Mary, losing her beloved Son. Where were the words I was seeking to make it real?

> *"Not my will but Thine"*
> *In blood-dropped Gethsemanes*
> *All men know sorrow*
> (GA)

We witnessed the Palm Sunday Procession from atop the city walls

To be in this place where the tragic *Pageant* had unfolded, I confessed, was hard to comprehend. We sat atop the city wall observing the *Palm Sunday Procession* winding its way down the hills of Midian, entering the old city of Jerusalem directly beneath our feet. We could see the place where Jesus agonized and prayed *"Not my will but Thine"* while his disciples slept, oblivious to the encroaching threat. But for now the Palm Sunday singing and shouts of 'hosannas' were glorious; we added our own to the myriad languages of the pilgrims.

On my previous visit to Jerusalem nine years earlier I had crossed the *Kidron Valley,* climbed the *Mount of Olives*, and prayed quietly in the *Garden of Gethsemane*. The *Upper Room* had been empty, yet it seemed full in my imagination. I had carried the Cross through the crooked and winding streets of Jerusalem as part of the Franciscan Monks' *Good Friday Via Dolorosa*. The empty *Garden Tomb* as well as the burial site in the *Church of the Holy Sepulchre* had provoked my silence. That which I had imagined and pictured from decades of Sunday School story telling and Scripture was being brought to its zenith and robbed of its mystery simultaneously.

Even now I mourned the loss of my childhood images while reveling in concrete reality. Joy and disappointment mingled, while in the distance that cock crowed.

> *Fireside bitterness*
> *Clashing cockcrow denials*
> *Symphony of smoke*
> (GA)

I had become so accustomed to that sound over these six days that it no longer registered in my consciousness. Rather, it was merely one small tile in an elaborate mosaic that was Jerusalem. Seated only a stone's throw from the *Courtyard of the High Priest Caiaphas*, scene of Peter's denial, the memory of it was deafening, his words reverberating throughout my entire being—denial, denial, denial. I had been searching for some 'handle', some word to attach to the confusion and disillusionment I had experienced in this holy land, but 'denial' was not it.

I had often been mesmerized by the Muslim *adhan* as ubiquitous as the crowing cocks. This chanting by the *Muezzin* from the minaret as he faced the direction of the *Kabah* in Mecca called the faithful to prayer five times a day; it was disconcerting to hear it in this land of Jesus. But that was not what plagued me. Nor was it the sound of Sabbath prayers at the *Wailing Wall* where I had stood in reverence and wept with those longing for the return of the Temple.

I reflected on my previous trip to Israel in 1974. The conflict between the various Christian religions in the *Church of the Holy Sepulchre* —Protestant, Roman Catholic, Eastern Orthodox— fighting over space, had made me angry. Christians have enough difficulties without fighting each other, I had growled under my breath. Why here, especially in this most sacred space built and dedicated by the mother of Emperor Constantine shortly after the legalization of Christianity in the early 4th century? (Strangely, the church was first called the *Church of the Resurrection*, but that's a story for another time).

I remembered spending several hours in the back of an olive wood shop in Bethlehem, speaking with the Palestinian Christians carving angels and figures for the *Bethlehem Child's* crèche. They sent me to a hillside overlooking the shepherd's field with a young Palestinian boy taking olive wood shavings to his mother for use in their outdoor earthen oven. She baked bread while we sat talking in their small home, the caves of the shepherds of the Gospels just outside our door. The smell of baking bread wafted into our conversation as her children reveled in this occasion to demonstrate their new knitting machine to this friendly stranger from America. She offered the fresh hot loaf along with tea—a secular *Eucharist* of sorts. Bethlehem was primarily a Christian town then. No more. Tragically, less and less is left of the Christian community in all the holy places associated with Jesus.

Some days later, driving through the *Golan Heights* in northern Israel I had been startled by heat lightning in the distance and remarked that it didn't seem hot enough for that. Arriving at our destination our hosts were shocked, explaining that we had just driven through an area being bombed in a random attack by the Syrian enemies of Israel. A *Cease Fire* agreement was signed later that year.

That was the real Israel, not the land of my childhood memories. Enemies modern and ancient crisscrossed my mind: the 20th century *Golan Heights,* the 1st century *Place of the Skull,* and the ancient *Babylonian Captivity*—Israel was home to a timeless tragedy.

Back in the Old City that same year, on February 25th an event had occurred which was then described in the *Jerusalem Post* the following day:

Actually, young Israeli soldiers with Uzis had converged on it from several directions, only partially able to muzzle its blast. I was standing no more than sixty feet from it.

Each day in Jerusalem I had

> **Bomb explodes near Western Wall**
> Jerusalem Post Reporter
> An explosive device went off yesterday on the steps leading to the Western Wall. No one was injured.
> A police spokesman said the device consisting of 150 grams of explosives and a timing device was hidden inside a water canteen which was left on the steps inside a nylon sack along with some oranges. A passerby who thought the sack suspicious, called a policeman. The bomb went off before the policeman reached it.

Bomb Explodes at
the Wailing Wall, Jerusalem

wandered out the Western Gate from the Old City across the 'no man's land' from the war for Jewish nationhood. My destination was the *Safrai Gallery* where I engaged in passionate conversations with the owner, Menachim Safrai. Our topics were varied, but many centered around the *Six Day War* with Egypt just seven years earlier. He couldn't understand why so many of his Palestinian friends, whom he had entertained in his home, whose children he had hired and supported, would no longer speak with him. He was heartbroken. Several Israeli lithographs I purchased from him depicted scenes from the Hebrew Scriptures' account of the *Abraham and Isaac Sacrifice.* The artist, Shraga Weil, had lost a son in that recent war, and this theme, a metaphor of his own sacrifice, came to possess his life. The story he painted over and over again was perhaps his pathway to a hopeful future. I think that must have been his consolation.

So now, in the Holy Land nine years later, I was still trying to decipher my own feelings about this conflicted place. The conflicts were not only *between* the Christians, Palestinians, and Jews; they were also *within* each of the religious communities, and my conversations with people from each camp revealed a seemingly unanswerable dilemma; peace was utterly elusive. That's why I was searching for a word, a thought, an image that would take me to a place of personal understanding and personal reconciliation.

Thus it was that Doy and I left the Old City through the *Zion Gate,* still pockmarked with bullet holes from the Zionist soldiers' attack on the Old City in the 1948 war for Jewish statehood. Sitting on a southern hillside blazing with wild flowers near the house of *Caiaphas the High Priest,* the place of Peter's denials, we cherished the peace the moment afforded. At the bottom of the hill the *Kidron Valley* ran its course past the golden city walls toward the *Mount of Olives* and the *Garden of Gethsemane.* We could see it clearly looking past the *Pinnacle of the Temple*. The scene was pregnant with the Gospel remembrances of the Passion of Jesus.

Crowing and chanting were, for the moment, silent. All was quiet now, save for the church bells whose constant tolling marks the Holy City. Here was the serenity we had sought for days, a place away from the crowds, the noise, and above all, the constant harangue of hawkers with their postcards and olive wood.

A shepherd boy, whose age we guessed at ten, brought his charge of seven goats to graze in our field. Caught between choice flowers and curiosity, the animals one by one paid us a visit, sniffing at our shoes and rubbing their heads against our legs. Their young master lay in the grass nearby idly pelting imaginary 'Goliaths' hiding in the pine trees with stones from his slingshot.

This was the image I was seeking! Away from all the trappings of the modern world and its cacophony we were being transported back to the pages of the Hebrew Scriptures. What shepherd boy had not relieved his boredom by doing what we were witnessing just a short stone's throw away? We were sharing a field with *David the shepherd boy, David the giant killer, David the King of Israel, David the Psalm-singer, David the progenitor of Messiah Yeshua, all the 'Davids' that had sacrificed over the centuries to preserve and reclaim Israel's 'divine blessing'.*

This was the Israel imbedded in my preferred memory—a land of inheritance, a land of covenant, a land of promise, a land of future fulfillment. At last I had found words for the true meaning and desire of Jerusalem and the whole of creation. They rang joyously in my heart, more loudly than the incessant bells and chants and explosions rocking the stability and sanity of this holy place. A contemporary Psalm joined the sacred lexicon of David's poetry:

Jerusalem, City of Peace. The New Jerusalem of John's Revelation. Jerusalem, my highest joy. I added my own:

> *O Jerusalem*
> *How many have wept for you*
> *I kneel on their stains*
>
> (GA)

CHAPTER 40

Reflections: When I Questioned Tertullian and Mentioned Beauty

And you shall make holy garments for Aaron your brother, for glory and for beauty.
(Exodus 28: 2)

If what I have been saying is true, then we are compelled to believe that the entire artistic offering of our lives should be haloed by the creative beauty God made possible and intended from the very beginning. Why is it frequently absent from our endeavors? Why do those most aligned with the Scriptures harbor suspicions towards the arts? One of the early church Fathers, Tertullian, asked the question,

> *What has Athens to do with Jerusalem?*

What he meant was, '*what has Reason to do with Faith?*' We could rephrase the question and ask,

> *What does Beauty have to do with Theology?*

Unfortunately, such questions perpetuate the fracture in the union God intended.

The Christian world was not always so suspicious of art. As a matter of fact, from the legalization of Christianity in the 4th century and continuing for more than a thousand years, the Church was the chief patron of the arts. It gathered into its fold the greatest artists of its age and fostered the highest excellence in artistic expression. It provided the most precious materials. The cathedrals themselves were immense and stunning in their architectural symbolism. The frescoes, mosaics, or stained glass magnificently told the stories of the Bible to the masses who couldn't read. Their reverent and otherworldly music was remarkably different from the music of the streets. Even the richness of the clergy's vestments, echoing the vestments of the Priests of the Old Covenant, as well as the choreography of the liturgy, spoke to the peasantry of the treasures and pageantry of Heaven. In all this visual and aural splendor they knew they were in the presence of God and His Son. To enter such a space was to leave the world for a time and experience the promise of Eternity.

In pre-Christian Russia, Vladimir, Prince of Kiev, sent his followers in search of the true religion. They traveled first to the Muslim Bulgars of the Volga, but found no joy in the religion; only, as they said, mournfulness and a great smell. Then they went to Germany and to Rome, and found the worship more satisfactory but still lacking something. Finally they found their way to Constantinople. Attending the Church of the Holy Wisdom, *Hagia Sophia*, they found what they were looking for. Returning to Kiev they told Prince Vladimir,

We knew not whether we were in heaven or on earth, for surely there is no such splendor or beauty anywhere upon earth. We cannot describe it

to you. Only this we know, that God dwells there among men, and that their service surpasses the worship of all other places, for we cannot forget that beauty. (Timothy Ware, <u>The Orthodox Church</u>, Baltimore, Penguin, 1963, p. 269)

For glory AND for beauty: that's a worthy creed for life, my life, as well as art.

CHAPTER 41

1983: Another Harbinger

Doy in Greece

My Sabbatical was coming to an end. Doy and I had traveled to Greece, Israel and Turkey while headquartered in Rome. Our Mediterranean cruise had proved to be just the respite we needed in the midst of my study frenzy. Though we didn't know it at the time, the ship was also the 'point of origin' for the saga of our son Trifon!

My second prolonged study in the catacombs only confirmed and enhanced the conclusions I had drawn nine years earlier during my first Sabbatical. There was no doubt that the themes of 'deliverance' and 'resurrection' dominated the frescoes in the burial chambers, and in addition seemed to permeate the entire fabric of the first three centuries AD. I knew then what I purposed to do with the rest of my life, apart from music, if ever I had the opportunity.

It was time to return our lease car to Brussels. But first we headed to the small town of Mittersill in Austria. We had made arrangements to spend three weeks there following my Rome sojourn in order to organize my approach to writing the books I felt were needed by the Church.

Schloss Mittersill, Austria

Our residence was *Schloss Mittersill*, a small castle on a hill overlooking the village. Run by IFES, the *International Federation of Evangelical Students*, it served double duty as a series of student bunk rooms for conferences in one wing, and a very upscale hotel in the other. Our room had been the honeymoon suite of Queen Juliana of the Netherlands, with windows overlooking the tallest of the Austrian Alps. We took 'full board'. A gourmet chef prepared all our meals, including gargantuan picnic lunches for our journeys into the surrounding beauty of Austria. In three weeks we had no duplicate meals!

Occasionally, we sat on a small decoratively painted bench outside the *Schloss* walls looking across the valley into the towering mountains just beyond. The great 20th century composer, Anton Webern, a resident of Mittersill, had spent many hours on this very bench gaining inspiration for his compositions. Tragically, he was shot and killed on his front porch while lighting a cigarette during the curfew at the end of the World War II. In the village we worshiped with other believers on the two Sundays we resided on the hill. Several had known the composer and gave us deeper insights into his untimely death.

Doy felt a bit quesy during our stay. We wondered. A pregnancy kit confirmed our suspicion. We two were about to become three!

We decided to celebrate the good news on our return to Brussels by spending a day in Lucerne, Switzerland. Flowers for Doy; a stroll across the *Kapellbrücke* covered wooden foot bridge with its beautifully painted adornments; then on to our lovely hotel with a balcony looking across the Reuss River and the *Kapellbrücke* toward a magnificent church with wide steps leading down to the river.

1983: Another Harbinger

Doy in Lucerne

Then, standing on our balcony, we witnessed a most amazing and wonderful sight. Three Alpine horn players stood at the top step with the bells of their long wooden horns curving upward near the water's edge. The music was sublime. It was another of those moments you wish could be frozen and then thawed in times of great turbulence to provide solace, comfort, and peacefulness. We were captured in awe of the music cascading down the cathedral steps and across the river in our direction.

Standing in a silent embrace we noticed a lamentation of swans slowly floating their way from various directions on the river toward the Alpine horns, equally drawn by the same beauty that had infected us. Then, at water's edge they gathered and the scene was caught in revery. The mellifluent sounds of the three instruments blended in a harmonious trio both otherworldly and reverent. *"Please don't stop—ever,"* I remember thinking to myself.

The significance and symbolism of that moment didn't register immediately. Clarity often comes in hindsight, and perhaps it's better that way: Swans! It was the third time in my life that beautiful creature had framed a beginning.

Some years later I reflected on my experiences, first with Camille Saint-Saens' *Swan* as a four-year-old boy, where I knew in my 'knowing' that music was to be my life. Then the *Swan of Tuonela* had invaded my consciousness while sitting at the graveside of Sibelius. I was twenty-nine years old and wondered what my future would hold. That summer, 1965, and that event marked a new episode leading to my position at North Park where I would spend the major part of my career in new endeavors far more rewarding than I could have imagined.

Now, in my look back, the swans of Lucerne had heralded another monumental change in the contour of my future life. Fatherhood, a second time, with its challenges and blessings, was to add depth and dimension as well as a counterbalance providing the equilibrium that every life needs. It was to be music of a different sort, but music nonetheless. Again, as I remembered in Finland, serenity above the surface of the water was to be juxtaposed against the unseen turbulence beneath it. Serenity and turbulence: both necessary to a fulfilled life.

I would revisit the first *Swan* again years later in my final concert as director of the North Park Chamber Orchestra. There would be yet another, a fourth, taking me by surprise. It would mark another transition in my life, though one possessed by sorrow.

CHAPTER 42

October, 1984: North Park College Chapel A Service of Commitment

One year after returning from my second Sabbatical North Park was on the brink of financial collapse. Word circulated around the campus that we might have to close our doors. There was considerable question whether the institution could survive without drastic measures being enacted. All of us, faculty and staff together, were concerned about our futures. We had given our lives to this place; I was in my eighteenth year. Many others equaled or surpassed that tenure. We had believed in its purpose and its ministry, though our zeal had grown dim over the years. Now the threat of extinction weighed heavily on us. A special Chapel was hastily arranged for the next morning; I received a call the night before the event from campus Chaplain Tim Heintzelman, asking if I would speak a word to the gathered community. I was never clear on the reasons for my choice; others had served far longer than I. It was a rather sleepless night spent wrestling with my thoughts:

Meditation: Encouragement and Praise
Greg Athnos

When Tim called me and asked if I would participate in today's Chapel my first thought was, "What words can I possibly utter that might contribute to the transforming of the North Park Community?" As I prepared my thoughts, my mind and heart were besieged by fragments and snippets. I was confused by the sheer number of things that could be said, but I must confess that even now I'm not sure I can make any sense of them.

The events of the last few weeks have imposed a kind of death on North Park, from the news of our financial dilemma to the now already infamous Chapel announcement that angered and confused so many of us. People all over campus feel threatened and insecure. I, however, want to give thanks to God for allowing us to suffer in these ways. If we are to accept Scripture we must consider whether He is chastening us whom He loves in order to bring us to the fulfillment of His plan. In this potential death of ours Jesus becomes the model. He, in order to gain victory over death, had to submit to its consequences, recognize it, embrace it and feel it. Yes, the act of evil men killed Him—but God raised Him up. Therein lies OUR hope.

One line from Luther's great hymn that we just sang has been with me since the early morning hours:

"If we in our own strength confide our striving would be losing."

I'm thankful for you, my colleagues at North Park. I believe we have an outstanding collection of faculty persons—talented, energetic, able, and dedicated. When I thought about you last night I realized that we represent over one thousand years of service to this institution. That's impressive! It also speaks of commitment. But perhaps we have relied too much on our own abilities, great as they are. For all our striving, have we added one brick to this place in the last fifteen years? Have we overcome the perpetual money worries? Have we been able to convince even those who support us of the real quality that is North Park? I believe we have fallen into the trap of being 'church-related' rather than 'Christian'. I also believe that apart from our Christian calling to serve God's Kingdom there is no reason whatsoever for our existence. There are many fine academic institutions with facilities greater than ours, with teaching equal to ours, with a greater variety of programs and courses to offer, and with better equipment. If we closed our doors tomorrow would the world miss us? Would Chicago? Would the Covenant Church? Our students, all of them, could be absorbed into other schools overnight.

I am grateful to God for bombarding us in these days with these questions. I believe that He is calling us to 'translation' and 'transformation'.

This call for 'translation' would have us turn 'belief' into 'confession': 'Jesus is Lord'; 'God raised Him'; through this we state our own salvation. Belief is internal; confession reaches out to others.

'Transformation' would see our community propelled into understanding that all we do must be haloed by the over-riding and underlying truth that the Kingdom of God needs to be at stake in our endeavors.

The promise of God is sure to them that trust in Him, that believe in Him, that confess Him.

Two questions must be raised and answered: First, what are our dreams and desires for North Park? Second, what can each of us offer by way of praise to God for what He is doing in our midst this very moment? Only by insuring that North Park continues to exist for the purpose of excellence given over completely to the furthering of God's Kingdom can we legitimately lay claim to our future.

Had I overstepped my bounds? I was certain there were a number of colleagues who were offended by my remarks. For years I had heard the comment, *"Our Christian mission is the responsibility of the religion faculty and the campus pastor, not me. I'm called to teach. Period."*

The only emotion I had at the conclusion was relief; what was said was said. I had spoken from my heart. Whatever consequences issued from my words I determined to accept. The next day a note came from a colleague:

Thank you for what you said in Chapel. I was very moved by your words.

I was grateful for the affirmation. North Park survived, but not without a major diminishment of faculty and staff, including my wife Doy.

CHAPTER 43

Reflections: What the History of Christianity Told Me

Looking back on North Park's short history it is possible to see the gradual erosion of its 'first principles'. Formed in the 1890's as a two-year institution to educate students from the Swedish heritage and the newly formed Covenant Church, it gradually broadened its outreach. In the early 1960's it became a four-year liberal arts institution. Its relationship with the denomination continued, but the student body became less and less Swedish and Covenant. The temptation was to diminish the 'church-related' and Christian role North Park had maintained from its foundation. Overt Christian profession became more covert. While still hired on the basis of a Christian profession of faith as well as educational qualifications, the faculty took a more neutral stance in the classroom. Issues of Faith were left to the Chaplain and the Religion faculty. The result was that the sponsoring denomination, sensing faith's diminishment, was becoming less and less inclined to send its students our way.

North Park's cornerstone displays the phrase: *"In Thy Light shall we see light."* Faith was seen as the portal to knowledge. Sixteen centuries earlier Augustine of Hippo (354 – 430 AD), a North African bishop, had said:

Therefore do not seek to understand in order to believe, but believe that thou mayest understand.

Anselm of Canterbury (c. 1033-1109 AD) repeated similar words seven hundred years later. Both theologians understood reason and faith to be companions, not enemies—but faith came first. At its founding, North Park recognized the virtue and scriptural veracity of that order—hence the cornerstone: First *Light*, then 'light'. Slowly the sentiment permeating the faculty and administration began to herald a different posture. How many other institutions of higher learning here and abroad gradually abandoned their 'first principles', as North Park was unwittingly doing in a slow and debasing diminishment?

We were undergoing and experiencing the same diminution of faith locally as Christian Eduction had undergone globally and historically. A lesson could have been learned had we been astute enough to see how what was happening was to our detriment. We should have started our search for meaning and understanding with Augustine and Anselm.

We could also have avoided our 'drift' by observing what had happened in the realm of art. Luther's Reformation was followed by the Enlightenment, resulting in a shift in religious thinking. That which touched our aesthetic spirit gave way to that which touched our minds, without the distractions of the visual. The accompanying theology shifted from 'the God who creates' to 'the God who spoke'. Ever since, the primary tendency in *Evangelicalism* has been to focus on worship as a cerebral act, engaging reason and the intellect as the pathway to the heart. What *made* worship was the sermon. All else was *preliminary* if not *secondary*, and in this context there was little need or use for the arts or an artistic vision.

The changing character of artistic creativity throughout the Christian era seems a metaphor of the historic controversies that had surrounded the divinity or humanity of Christ.

One heresy, *Gnosticism*, insisted Jesus was only divine, never really human. The *Apostle's Creed,* derived from the *Rule of Faith*, reinforced Jesus' humanity in balance with His divinity and defeated the Gnostic heresy.

Another heresy, *Arianism*, made Him only human, not divine. The *Nicene Creed* of the fourth century focused on Jesus' Divinity, thus driving out the *Arian* aberration.

Here is the parallel: any Christian artist's creative view or style that focuses exclusively on the transcendent, or otherworldly, runs the risk of stressing Jesus' divinity, and, like *Gnosticism,* can make Him appear inaccessible to our humanity. We may then feel far removed from the possibility of personal forgiveness, and end up trapped in our guilt consciousness.

Conversely, Christian creativity lacking the environment of the transcendent, like *Arianism,* runs the risk of making Jesus too human, too much like us, too much our 'good buddy in the sky'. Our sense of sinfulness can easily become diminished, and Grace then becomes cheapened.

Each side of this polarity misses something of the dual nature of Christ and continues the division in the 'wholeness' God desires for

His creation. One, the transcendent, emphasizes faith and minimizes reason. The other causes reason to render faith less necessary.

Do we really want a bifurcated Jesus? I want both; I need both the fully divine and fully human Jesus. I want both; I need both the imminent and transcendent Christ to be reflected in my worship of Him. I want spiritual *Light* to inform my academic *light*.

North Park needed both the imminent and the transcendent Christ to be infused with academic excellence, making sure its students benefited from the absolute integration of faith with learning. It needed to 'flesh out' that motto on its cornerstone: *In Thy Light shall we see light.*

The poet Norman Nicholson in his poem *The Burning Bush* wrote the following lines addressing the conflict between faith and reason, transcendence and imminence; in the end he abandons his first inclination and opens the door to transcendence:

> *When Moses, musing in the desert, found*
> *The thorn bush spiking up from the hot ground,*
> *And saw the branches, on a sudden, bear*
> *The crackling yellow barberries of fire,*
> *He searched his learning and imagination*
> *For any logical, neat explanation,*
> *And turned to go, but turned again and stayed,*
> *And faced the fire and knew it for his God.*
> (Norman Nicholson, born 1914, "The Burning Bush")

CHAPTER 44

1985: Bach's Lunch

The College News, February, 1985: North Park College will bring classical composer Johann Sebastian Bach "back to the people" with a series of noon concerts featuring his works in honor of the 300th anniversary of his birth.

Titled "Bach's Lunch", the four concerts will be performed by North Park College music students and faculty. Concert-goers are invited to bring a sack lunch or buy a "Bach's Lunch" at the concert.

Designed and coordinated by Gregory Athnos, North Park music professor, the concerts are scheduled for noon February 14, 21, March 14 and 21 in Carlson Tower Lobby, Foster and Kedzie Avenues.

The Bach celebrations will culminate March 21 on Bach's birthday with "Bach Around the Clock", when hourly lectures and performances are slated from 9 a.m. to 4 p.m. The college will offer music students the option of attending a Bach event in lieu of class. At noon a birthday cake will be served. "Bach's Lunch" and "Bach Around the Clock" are free and open to the public.

On the musical menu for "Bach's Lunch" are the following works:

February 14: North Park Chamber Singers and Instrumentalists performing Cantata No. 51, "Jauchzet Gott in allen Landen"; Cantata no. 140, "Wachet Auf", and selections from Cantata No. 78, "Jesu der du meine Seele".

February 21: North Park Chamber Orchestra performing Bach's d minor Double Violin Concerto.

March 14: North Park's keyboard faculty performing representative harpsichord works by the master.

March 21: North Park Chamber Orchestra, Bach's Brandenburg Concerto Grosso No. 5, and the College Choir with Cantata No. 50, "Nun is das Heil".

Born in Eisenach, Germany, in 1685, Johann Sebastian Bach is considered the master of Baroque music. A prolific composer, Bach was only known as an outstanding church organist in his day. A devout Christian who did not draw a distinction between vocation and faith, Bach rendered all of his compositions as "a gift to God".

"Because of the degree of craftsmanship Bach achieved in his compositions, there is a universality about his music which stands outside of time," states Athnos, coordinator of the Bach celebration.

Bach's compositions remained undiscovered and unperformed until 1829 when German composer Felix Mendelssohn found the works and presented them to the musical world.

I absolutely loved working on this project! It isn't often that major celebrations of the births of major figures in history present such an opportunity, and I wasn't about to miss it. We had the forces to make it special, and it cost the institution nothing to sponsor it. My department became enthusiastic about the idea and cooperated

1985: Bach's Lunch

fully in it; every music faculty member took part. The only question was whether anyone would bother to show up. We shouldn't have worried. After the final event on Bach's birthday the Faculty/Staff Newsletter wrote the following:

A noontime birthday bash complete with a candle-lit rainbow-frosted series of seven cakes spelling <u>B A C H 3 0 0</u> topped off the two-month concerts honoring Baroque composer Bach's 300th anniversary.

The North Park concerts titled "Bach's Lunch" were the inspiration of Gregory Athnos, music professor.

The concerts consistently drew a lunch crowd of around 200 crammed into the Carlson Tower Lobby. The final concert on March 21st not only increased the number of listeners to about 350 but also attracted the interest of WGN-TV and the Chicago Tribune, Sun-Times and Lerner Newspapers.

I remember holding my one-year-old son Trifon as the cameras whirled around us and into Chicagoland homes via television that night.

Many comments came in the mail:

The "Bach's Lunch" was terrific! I had such a good time. I hope you will again put your creative talents to such wonderful endeavors. Great stuff!

It was the highlight of my Winter.

What a super job!

Thanks for the marvelous "Bach Revisited". It was a wonderful idea and was professionally done.

It was a delightful experience in every way and I'm grateful to you for your inspiration which led to the series and for your many efforts in bringing it off so successfully.

Those of us from the Board of Directors who were able to attend "Bach's Lunch" last Thursday thoroughly enjoyed ourselves. What a terrific opportunity it provided for us to allow Board members to relax while reveling in the musicianship of our students! I particularly want to thank you for your leadership role in this (and so many other) projects.... The concert helped make this meeting of the Board an inspirational and uplifting one. Again, many thanks. Bill Hausman, President of North Park.

CHAPTER 45

Reflections: Bach: The Man Who Made All the Wrong Decisions

In my personal journey to reflect Christ in my profession as an artist/teacher, no one had served as an inspiration quite like Johann Sebastian Bach. He stood against the growing secularization of his day at great personal and professional cost. Bach was eventually vindicated, but not during his lifetime. Only by digging deeply into his life, beyond the biographies, did I come to fully understand him and benefit from his spiritual choices. His story remains my inspiration.

Were it not for Felix Mendelssohn Bach may have continued to languish in obscurity, un-cherished and un-played, just as he did in his lifetime. His is a story both poignant and inspiring. It also serves as a powerful reminder of the providence of God, who preserves greatness and truth despite the machinations of an age that either attempts to suppress them or is unable to recognize them. The supreme lesson of Bach is commitment to what is known by the 'heart' even though it stands against the 'reason' of the mind.

The world into which Johann Sebastian Bach was born in 1685 was a secular age. The *Enlightenment* glorified human mind and achievement. It was the age of Voltaire, born nine years after Bach, and Frederick the Great of Prussia, both of whom embodied the spirit of the *German Enlightenment*. Within this world, accompanied by the burgeoning of Science, empiricism stood at the forefront. Only that which could be proved was worth knowing, hence matters of faith held little sway. An enlightened person was one who cast aside the 'superstitious follies' of organized religion. The result was that church population diminished, and few educated persons made a habit of attendance. The secular leanings of the culture were reflected also in the arts: fewer religious subjects found their way onto the canvasses or manuscripts of great artists than had been true in the recent past. It was not a good time to give one's life to the service of God; to do so was to stand outside the culture and sensibility of the day. Yet that is precisely what Bach did.

His choice did not elicit an easy roadmap. Whatever constituted the desire of his heart was stymied and thwarted at every turn. People were willing to cede to him the title of 'world's greatest organist'. However, his compositional skills were either rebuked or ignored, being considered 'old fashioned' or 'out of date'. Finally, after waiting twenty-three years to fulfill his youthful desire to give his services to his God, life continued down the path of neglect. The Leipzig Town Council had said, upon hiring him,

Since we cannot hire the best person, we will have to settle for a mediocre one.

In spite of his troublesome situation in Leipzig Bach stayed twenty-seven years until his death in 1750.

After his death the reaction of the Town Council and *Thomas*

Kirchen, the center of his musical life in Leipzig, continued to demonstrate the utter disregard they had held for him throughout his career there. The church's death register for Friday, July 31, 1750, noted in two brief lines the death of their Kapellmeister Bach. The pulpit announcement the following Sunday stated in five short lines his name, his title, and that he had died and was buried. There was no eulogy, not from the church or from the Town Council: a final insult for the man who had served them for twenty-seven years!

One eulogy of sorts arrived some months later from Georg Philip Telemann of Hamburg, the man Leipzig had most wanted and favored over Bach. Even in this tribute the point of Bach's great musical genius was missed. Like all the others, Telemann's regard for the compositions of Bach was minimal. Only his organ mastery stands out, along with the compositional greatness of several of Bach's sons. Yes, Bach was a great organist and a great teacher, but not a great composer, he said. It is the sad truth that, at this time, to mention the name of Bach meant sons Carl Philipp Emmanuel in Berlin, and Johann Christian in London. Johann Sebastian was not then, nor had he ever been recognized for the powerful musical poetry he put to pen and paper. Telemann's eulogy read,

> *Departed Bach! Long since thy splendid organ playing*
> *Alone brought thee the noble cognomen 'the Great'…*
> *The pupils thou hast trained, and those they train in turn*
> *Prepare thy future crown of glory brightly glowing.*
> *Thy children's hands adorn it with its jewels bright,*
> *But what shall cause thy true worth to be judged aright*
> *Berlin to us now in a worthy son is showing.*

Almost overnight the music of Bach disappeared from the scene. His manuscripts were distributed to his family, according to the custom of the day, as the new Kapellmeister would be responsible for the music to be performed henceforth. The nature of Church composition was that your music was only used where you were; when you moved it went with you. When you died it ceased to be heard except on 'rare occasions'. By choosing to give his life to the Church, Bach had opted for oblivion. His music, tragically disregarded in life, was now to be even more tragically abandoned in his death. Almost overnight the name of Sebastian Bach was forgotten.

It was Felix Mendelssohn who resurrected the greatness Bach's music deserved. The young genius, Jewish by birth and later Christian by choice, accepted the post of conductor of the *Gewandhaus Orchestra* of Leipzig. That put him in the place where Bach had spent the last three decades of his life; if there was any chance of stumbling upon his music, it was here in Leipzig. And if anyone was to recognize the greatness of Bach it was Mendelssohn, who knew greatness when he heard it, and was disposed by his new Christian faith not to discard works imbued with that same faith.

Apocryphal stories abound how Mendelssohn first discovered the music manuscript of Bach in fish wrappings from a local market. However he discovered the Kapellmeister's music, he was overwhelmed by it, and the call went out all over Europe to find music of the Baroque master and send it to him in Leipzig.

Few of Bach's vocal works were known when the twenty-year-old Mendelssohn mounted the first performance of the *St. Matthew Passion* on March 11, 1829, seventy-nine years after the death of the composer. It was, to the astonishment of the public who considered Bach nothing more than an indecipherable musical mathematician, a smashing success.

From Mendelssohn's baton to the concert halls of the world, Bach's music began to take root and flourish. From the time of

Mendelssohn forward, Bach's compositional technique became the teaching tool for aspiring composers. That remains true today in every music school and conservatory on the planet. I, too, was taught to put pen to paper by studying his music.

Somewhere in the world, at this very moment, the music of Bach is either being rehearsed or performed: church choirs, high schools and universities, organists, harpsichordists and pianists, amateur and professional soloists, choirs, and orchestras, all engaged with the power and majesty of his art. Twenty-four hours a day, every day of the year, the world is being bathed by the music of Johann Sebastian Bach; this is a statement that can be said of few if any other composers: not Handel, not Mozart, not Beethoven, not Brahms—I can't think of one.

In Bach's day his contemporary Handel was the towering giant—rich, and famous on both sides of the Atlantic. Were it not for *Messiah* and the recent resurgence of several of his operas, Handel's music would rarely grace concert programs in our age.

Bach's music, heard only where he lived and worked during his lifetime, and residing in oblivion for three quarters of a century after his death, now has become universal. A 'nobody' in his age, he has now become the 'Everyman' of the musical arts. In the time capsule sent to the outer reaches of space, Bach's music and only his music is represented as the pinnacle and definition of the art of the human race. It reflects the genius of the mind, the passion of the heart, and the wonder of earthly existence itself.

So it is that the music of the 'man of faith', the man 'who made all the wrong decisions' triumphed over the great grinding-wheel of the *Enlightenment*. The *Age of Reason* did not eradicate the 'unreasonable choice' Bach made to give his life to the worship of God in the Church. Providence saw to it that the incredible truth embodied in the work of this man of faith was not relegated to the 'oblivion' that seemed to mark his life's choice.

The famous scientist of the generation before Bach, Blaise Pascal (1623-1662), who, like Mendelssohn, also chose to become a Christian, made a profound statement to justify his own position as a man of Faith in a world of Reason. He said,

The heart has its reasons, about which Reason knows nothing.

It could easily have been said by Bach, or about him. It is just as much a creed for modeling one's life today as it was 300 years ago. It has become my heart's desire.

Soli Deo Gloria

Recapitulation: Culmination
1986 – 1998

*Following the careful examination of themes
in the Development Section
they are re-assembled with new meaning
and a breath of fresh understanding
in the Recapitulation.*

My 'Sonata' Came With a Twist:
A New Theme

Another Career Change

Resurrected Excellence

A 20th Century Life-Changing Drama

A Sad But Promising Departure

CHAPTER 46

1986: The Reluctant Choirmaster

Two weeks into the fall semester of the 1986 school year my department head, Monroe Olson, pulled me aside.

"Greg, you need to be ready to take over the College Choir in two days. David Thorburn is going to resign today."

There had been no rehearsals of the College Choir at that point in the new semester. Their director said he was still auditioning singers. I thought it was strange, as he had never taken so long to establish his roster. My Chamber Singers auditions were finished before classes began and we were already in rehearsal. Why not his choir?

That afternoon (it was Monday of the third week) the note was posted: the College Choir was to have its first rehearsal. Enthusiasm ran high. DT, as his students affectionately called him, walked into the rehearsal room, told them he was resigning from the position, and walked out. Shock and tears filled the room.

My response to Monroe had been an emphatic 'no'. DT was a 'lion', a 'giant' to his students. They idolized him. He was a brilliant choirmaster. Over his twenty years as choral director he had built a virtuosic ensemble.

"Monroe, I have nothing to gain by taking the position; but I do have everything to lose. The students will see me as a demotion from the excellence they're used to. I'm not nearly the equal of DT. Let me continue my work with the Chamber Singers; that's where my reputation was built and that's where it belongs. Why don't you take the position?"

"Greg, I'm not asking you. I'm telling you. On Wednesday you need to be in that room as their new director."

I told him I'd think about it. That night I told Doy of my predicament and my reluctance to take the position. She gave me good advice, as I knew she would:

"Tell Monroe you'll take the position on a trial basis for one year. If, at the end of that time, you decide not to continue he'll have time to look for someone else. Look at it this way—if you don't like it, you will at least have given it a chance. If you say 'no', Monroe will hire someone else and then, somewhere down the road, it will be too late to reconsider—you'll kick yourself for not having taken the opportunity. You'll wonder if you could have succeeded with it."

Monroe accepted the proposition.

On Wednesday I walked into the rehearsal room and found forty women and eight men! When I walked into the room for my second rehearsal half the forty women had dropped out because of their loyalty to the previous conductor. The next several weeks I tried to build up the personnel, with some small success, but it was not a good choir and we all knew it. Virtuosity had crashed and burned almost overnight. My reputation as a musician and choral conductor, stellar heretofore, was caught in the conflagration. I was not happy with my decision, yet it was necessary for me to project confidence and enthusiasm in spite of what we all knew was the truth.

The students made valiant efforts to work with me, but were not able to become part of this new conductor's team. Again, their loyalties to DT were not easily dismissed.

Our concerts went on as in past years. The lack of quality was embarrassing to all of us. Complicating the already marginalized year was the looming East Coast Spring Tour scheduled for Spring Break.

It was a pathetic series of concerts as we made our way toward the eastern states. Then the choir was smitten by illness; an article in one of the local newspapers along our itinerary blamed the outbreak on tainted drinking water. Already limited in size, we became decimated by sickness. On any given night nearly one third of the choir was not on the risers. There was no doubt in my mind that I would terminate my role with them at the end of the school year. This had not been a good experience. I loved the students. In their own way they tried to love me back, but it wasn't working. Loyalties are strange things. Longing for DT they weren't able to cross that difficult bridge into a new existence.

Then something akin to a miracle took place. The singing remained weak, but the pre-concert prayers of the choir became stronger. The singers began to realize that unless we truly became of 'one heart' there was no way to survive the trip and the illnesses with our spirits in tact. First they began to lift each other up. Then they turned their attention to me. The miracle was not evident in the sounds emanating from the group, but it was overwhelmingly evident in the 'spiritual' essence that filled the room at each concert. What remained musically mediocre nonetheless became blessedly 'moving'.

1986: The Reluctant Choirmaster

We came to the conclusion that if we concentrated solely on the 'sound' of our singing, which we had been doing with unsatisfying results, we would miss the 'music' of it. Our audiences also felt something profound coming from the choral risers, and it was mentioned following our concerts.

After our last concert, on our way home, we stopped by *Ancilla Domini Convent*, tucked away in a grove of trees in the middle of an Indiana cornfield. I had performed there many times with my Chamber Singers; our wonderful recording was made in that blessed space. In an empty chapel with magnificent acoustics and Biblical texts embedded in the walls, we sang just for ourselves. Several nuns lingered prayerfully in the *Triforium Gallery* surrounding the *Nave*. Singing there surrounded by praying nuns was a Benediction placed upon our spiritual pilgrimage of the previous ten days and we all sensed it.

College choir stops at Ancilla to sing for themselves after tour

By JEFFERY G. SMITH
P-N Staff Writer

DONALDSON — The North Park College Choir's youthful voices filled the little Ancilla Domini Chapel to its vaulted ceilings with harmonies that soothed the ear. The chapel walls reverberated with powerful, then a gentle mixture of voices.

Choral director Gregory Athnos said the group was just returning to its home in Chicago after touring six states from Illinois to the East Coast.

"We came (to Ancilla) to sing for ourselves. A lot (of the students) wanted to go home, but now no one wants to go home," he said. " I've come to love this place and the people."

That love showed through in their informal performance. There were no costumes and no tickets were taken at the door. It was just a group of 18-22 year-olds in jeans and sweatshirts having a little fun and absorbing the soothing atmosphere.

"You kind of get caught up in the reverance," Athnos said. "We just came to experience this place and do something for ourselves. We have been singing for everyone else, now it was time we sang for us."

Most of the choral group hugged and prayed after the practice attended by a smattering of sisters and students.

"A lot of these kids are pretty serious about their faith. That's the kind of people they are," Athnos said.

Athnos explained that the tour was plagued with sickness from the start 12 days ago in Chicago. Most of the illnesses were minor sore throats and colds. A one time seven to eight people had to sit out of the performances on the tour because they were too sick.

At the end of the Ancilla practice one girl, Elizabeth Westburg, fainted and had to be carried to the back of the chapel. She recovered later.

Athnos said it had been a very difficult year for the group. Before leaving Chicago, Athnos said the choir did not sing as a group and they were not "his" choir. After this tour Athnos felt they had melted into a real choir.

The choir will be returning to the area on April 24 at 8 p.m. The group is sponsored by the Evangelical Covenant Church in Donaldson. Call 936-8354 for ticket information.

College Choir stops at Ancilla Domini Convent Chapel

We returned to campus revitalized, having come to see the 'promise' of the future, not the 'failure' of the past. Fortuitously, waiting for me when I returned to campus was a letter from Elsie Stone. Elsie, recently retired, had been Secretary of the Music Department for many years, pre-dating my joining the faculty in 1966. Her letter played a role in the decision I soon needed to make regarding my future with the College Choir. It read:

Dear Greg: This is a voice from your past and is long overdue.... When I first read in the 'North Parker' of your being made director of the Choir I wanted to write immediately how happy I am for you. I don't know who deserves it more. The Lord has vindicated you—and I am so thankful for your achievement. You will do a good job, and more— be an example of Christian love and excellence to the students. I wish you God's richest blessings and many years of joy in directing.... Then Easter week came your wonderful devotions [in the Covenant Home Altar]. *Each day seemed richer in content than the day before! At the time I was still very weak from the operation so Clarence sat by me and read it—then we prayed often with tears. 'He is risen—Hallelujah". Your devotions...sealed the good news to us again. You wrote as though you have experienced some new touch from the Lord. Sincerely, Elsie*

Our annual Orchestra Hall concert occurred as planned; it was my first as conductor of the College Choir. The spiritual essence we had sensed hovering over our last few tour performances continued, even on that hallowed stage. Again, the musical aspect was not up to the virtuosic standards of the past—not anywhere close—but that deficiency was overshadowed by the 'aura' everyone felt, from the risers to the last row of the gallery. Something special was taking place in our midst, in our hearts, and we took great courage from it. The year that had begun in misery ended in gratitude for the hope of the future.

I did not resign at the end of the year. Elsie's encouraging letter helped me view the illnesses—with the potential to destroy what little sense of pride we had left after a year of misery—not as a curse, but rather as a blessing. I'm convinced even to this day that we would not have been transformed without sickness invading our ranks. God indeed moves in 'mysterious ways His wonders to perform'.

College Choir, 1987-88

My second year with the choir began by giving the first six weeks to the Norwegian composer/conductor Knut Nystedt, who served as *Artist in Residence* for the Music Department. I had been somewhat reluctant to relinquish the lead role now that we were about to turn the corner on the previous year's debacle, but the opportunity to have my singers work with this renowned composer was too good to pass up. At the end of his residency he conducted a program of his own compositions, including the American premiere of a major work: *Ave Maria* for Choir and Solo Violin. Five years later, in 1993, we would feature that wonderful work on our European tour to Sweden, Russia, and Estonia.

Mr. Nystedt and I had a great time together. When he returned to Oslo he wrote a letter to me:

Dua and I want to thank you so much for the 'Nachspiel' at your wonderful home after my final concert. I am glad the concert went so well. It has been great to work with such a fine group of enthusiastic young people.

Thank you, Greg, for all the help you gave me in my work. I enjoyed also being together with you at 'Satyagraha' [we had attended the Philip Glass opera].

Enclosed you will find a couple of motets, among them "Now Is Christ Risen!", your favorite subject!

Sincerely, Dua and Knut

Sometimes it's the small things that have impact on the character of a group. That was certainly true at the end of our second year together. We were on the stage of Orchestra Hall in the spring of 1988 for our final performance of the year. Gradually, the choir was gaining confidence in itself, and placing their trust in me. I had attempted to instill in them a sense of security in self-governing, sometimes walking away from the conductor's chair in rehearsals to let them continue singing without direction, relying on their group discipline and musical integrity.

That night on stage it paid off. One of our altos had stayed in the sun too long that afternoon. She was standing on the end of the top step of the choral risers. We were performing Pavel Chesnokov's eight-part *Salvation is Created*, one of the most beautiful, exquisite pieces from the Russian Orthodox choral legacy. I noticed she was unsteady. Her eyes were closed. She wasn't singing. On instinct I motioned to the choir to keep singing, left the conductor's podium, walked slowly in her direction, arriving at the precise moment she fainted and fell off the top step. I caught her mid-flight. The choir kept singing as if nothing had happened. I slowly made my way to the stage door, pushed it open with my foot, walked through, gently laid her on the floor, slowly made my way back to the conductor's podium, and continued conducting. It had been seamless. No panic, no indecision, no hesitancy—just beautiful singing. All this in front of a thousand people gathered in the hall. After the performance that was the moment on everyone's lips.

> Dear Greg,
>
> Congratulations on your 2nd successful Orchestra Hall concert -- and the fine performances given by your students. I especially appreciated the way in which you helped the student off-stage who didn't feel well and the human compassion and class you evidenced in that moment.
>
> best wishes,
> Patti Wigand

Note from Patti Wigand

Yes, the concert had been musically rich, but performance was secondary to what the students displayed. It was *their* class that carried the moment. During those sixty seconds a bond that had been initiated in *Ancilla Domini Convent Chapel* one year earlier became set in stone. That night absolute trust and confidence in one another and in me, so difficult to imagine when I faced a disconsolate group of singers in my first rehearsal as their conductor, forged our future together. Insignificant? I don't think so.

The next year, 1988-89, on the stage of Orchestra Hall

One year later North Park would have one of the finest choirs in its history. In June of 1989, my third year as conductor, we would encounter a life-changing 20th century drama.

CHAPTER 47

1989: Hymnathon
Twenty-Four Hours of Success
A Fund-Raising Event for the
Hungary-Poland Choir Tour

It was to be North Park Choir's first foreign tour since 1965. I had pushed hard for it and was finally given permission to pursue the idea provided the institution would have no financial obligations. I agreed. In order to take the 'edge' off the students' cost I needed an idea. Then it came to me: the Covenant Church loves its Hymnal. Why not mount an event that would draw the attention of the denomination. We decided to sing our way through the entire hymnal, singing two verses of each hymn in one twenty-four hour period. I had timed out each hymn. We invited people to join in the singing, or simply come and listen. We were able to advertise that if people loved the Christmas hymns we would be at that point in the hymnal at a certain hour. We did the same for all the seasons and festivals of the Church year.

The entire Choir began on Friday evening at 7:00 and sang together until 8:00. Then we broke up into small groups of four to eight singers taking it in turn every hour through the night and next day. The entire Choir came back together at 6:00 on Saturday evening as we completed the journey.

We were amazed at the interest. People came from the neighborhood and from Covenant Churches in the metropolitan area of Chicago. Some sang along. Others listened. Still others brought food and beverages. It was a wonderful celebration! We raised $7,000! One of our singers, Tristan Melvie, wrote this article for the College News, Friday, April 21, 1989:

Last Friday, April 14, began 24 hours of an event so crazy only the choir members would volunteer to participate in it. Their incredible feat was to not only sing for the full 24 hours but to sing through the entire Covenant Hymnal, something that has probably never been done before, and probably never will be again.

For those of you who missed your opportunity to stop and observe the Hymnathon it is difficult to describe the event. Friday night was festive as the entire choir and many guests gathered to sing for the first hour. From then until 6:00 Saturday night, the singing was split into sections with a choir member from each voice part singing. Saturday night everyone returned to sing the last section including the Threefold Amen and the traditional Choral Benediction.

This may sound simply crazy and not extremely fun; however, most of the choir members would agree that it was actually a good time. The spirit was great throughout the entire night, which was surprising from students forced to get up and sing at 2:30 in the morning, or leave the beautiful day outside and sit in the Chapel instead. A positive side to the event was its casual atmosphere—no tuxedos on these tired bodies; the choir members actually got to sing in sweats or pajamas.

You may be wondering why in the heck the choir would do something

1989 Hymnathon Twenty-Four Hours of Success A Fund-Raising Event for the Hungary-Poland Choir Tour

this extraordinary. Most of you are aware of the upcoming tour of Poland and Hungary, beginning May 28. The Hymnathon was another fundraiser for our tour, and it successfully brought in just under $7,000. [My note: We would resurrect this idea again for our 1993 tour to Sweden, Russia and Estonia. We publicized it throughout the national Covenant Church. It raised $43,000!]

The Hymnathon was not only a fundraiser, though. It was a test of each member's patience and endurance, a time to discover new enjoyable hymns, or struggle through difficult harmonies on others. There were a few members who participated in out-of-the-ordinary ways, such as Walter DuMelle who sang through the entire night. Greg certified Walter as an official 'Covie' after his tiring night of singing. Whatever qualms the choir members had about the Hymnathon were soon lost in the spirit of the event, and it was a memorable 24 hours for all. [Note: Walter was not from the Covenant Church. He was a voice major and the lead bass in the choir. Walter went on to a successful singing career in New York City, and now resides in San Diego where he manages a successful concert venue].

As we approached the end of the school year the Administration became increasingly nervous about funding for the trip. We had crossed the 'point of no return', where arrangements were set and perhaps irrevocable. What if the fund raising was not sufficient; would the institution be responsible for the shortfall when I had received permission for the venture based solely upon the guarantee of self-funding?

Provost Rob Johnston called me into his office. I could tell he was in a tight spot.

"Greg, tell me how your fund raising is going. Will you make it, or do we have to consider pulling out?"

"Rob, we needed to raise $120,000."

The Provost was nervously waiting for the 'second shoe to fall'.

"To date we have raised $118,000, but I think we can make up the difference in the three weeks we have left."

Rob was ecstatic. More than that, he was relieved and amazed. After expressing his appreciation for what the choir and I had accomplished, he said,

"Greg, I want you to stop your fund raising efforts and turn your attention to your own musical preparations for the trip. I'll cover the last $2000 from my discretionary funds."

I was grateful. I had exhausted every avenue for funding that I could think of, and wondered if I needed to cover the remainder out of my own pocket to fulfill my pledge to the institution. That was the first and one of two times any institutional funds were contributed to the nearly one hundred weeks of tours I organized during my three decades leading the Chamber Singers, the Chamber Orchestra, and the Choir.

CHAPTER 48

1989: Hungary & Poland: Cathedral, Crucifix, and Congregation

Dear Mr. Athnos: Your article in the October issue of the Covenant Companion entitled 'Singing of Hope and Victory' stirred me emotionally and spiritually, as I have read it again and again. What a testimony! I congratulate you, Mr. Athnos, for your devotion to 'Him whom to know is Life Eternal' and for your work at North Park College. The Choir bears the stamp of excellence, to be sure. There is hope for our world when young people who have the privilege of attending North Park go out from there equipped with the 'Good News'. God Bless! Bernice Nelson

Ms. Nelson was referring to this following description of the North Park College Choir's tour of Poland and Hungary in the spring of 1989:

We sat in a stuffy, cramped hotel lobby in Copenhagen sharing our life-changing experiences of the previous sixteen days. We were the sixty members of the North Park College Choir, now dear friends bonded to each other by having lived with the people of Hungary and Poland at the most dramatic period of their countries' turbulent 20th century history. The world events leading up to our concert tour no longer tumbled through our minds as random or isolated situations. Instead, we saw clearly the pattern of destiny in them, and the unmatchable providence of God in allowing us to be a part of the Polish and Hungarian peoples' lives at that moment.

Poland and Hungary hadn't been in my initial plans. This was to be the first foreign tour by the College Choir since 1965, the year before I joined the faculty. I had determined to give a series of concerts in Germany and Austria, countries with a rich tradition of great choral singing. I wanted my choir to have both the pressure and the thrill of performing in front of musically discriminating audiences.

For several months in the Spring and Fall of 1988 I worked with a concert management company in California. We set the itinerary to include perhaps as many as ten performances in those countries.

Then everything changed. I began to have this very strong feeling—call it an intuition—that something monumental was going to happen in Europe during our travel dates, and it wasn't going to be along our itinerary. My whole life I have listened to my intuitions. Eastern Europe began to dominate my thoughts.

I dropped the plans with the California group, much to their dismay. My singers were none too happy either. I began searching for a company that had contacts in Eastern Europe. I found *Friendship Ambassadors Foundation* in New Jersey.

I told them I wanted to leave Chicago on May 26th and spend one week in Hungary. I was very specific about entering into Poland on June 2nd and giving concerts there for nine days. We submitted audition tapes in hopes of securing the support of the best agencies in the two countries. Then I proceeded to choose music for the concert tour. Little did I know at the time just how prescient my intuition was; we were going to experience one of the most powerful moments in 20th century history.

In Eastern Europe 1989 witnessed the birth of freedom, beginning in Poland and spreading like a grass fire throughout those countries trapped in the stranglehold of Communism. Witness these events: in May the barbed wire fence that had separated Hungary from the West began to be dismantled. A few days later Soviet troops initiated their withdrawal from Hungarian soil. This was followed by the Communist Party's confession that Imre Nagy, Premier of Hungary during the 1956 uprising who had been hanged for treason against the State and buried in an unmarked grave, was a martyred hero of the Hungarian People. His body would be exhumed and given a ceremonial entombment befitting a hero of the State.

Meanwhile, in April, the Polish Communist government agreed to allow the first free elections in the history of Communism, to be held on June 4th. In May the Roman Catholic Church was finally granted legal status by the Communist government. The Solidarity Party was officially recognized. Within days the Polish coalition began accusing the Russians of the 1940 massacre of 15,000 Polish officers and intelligentsia in the Katyn Forest, an atrocity that the Russians had blamed on the Germans in their quest to stamp out the future hope of Poland.

It was into these emotionally charged and turbulently changing countries that the 60-voice North Park College Choir of Chicago, Illinois, under my direction, began its concert tour. The choir was accompanied by two mothers of choristers, and two elderly Jewish widows whose relatives had not survived the horrible consequences of being Jewish in a Nazi-occupied country. In spite of our anticipation, preparation and study, little could we know just how stunned we would be by the experiences of history, culture, and faith that were about to envelop us in relentless fashion.

We left Chicago and, with a seven-hour layover in Copenhagen, arrived in Budapest the next evening. I dreaded the effect jet lag would have on us, as the next evening was to be our first concert of the tour in the beautiful and historic *Cathedral of Matthias (Matyas Templom)* on Castle Hill overlooking the Danube. It was in this historic Cathedral that all the Kings of Hungary had been coronated.

The choir had not rehearsed for two weeks because of final exams, and that, coupled with jet lag didn't bode well for our first venture. Yet in the middle of a violent and prolonged thunderstorm the choir sang magnificently—one of the best performances of the tour. I knew then that on the musical level this was going to be fun! I slept much better Sunday night than I had Saturday night!

Matyas Templom, Budapest, Hungary

Fun gave way to something of greater significance the next evening. We had traveled to the small town of Kiskunhalas in the south of Hungary, home to a large Soviet army base. It was from here the Soviet troop withdrawals had begun a few days earlier. That afternoon, in the Baroque *Church of Saints Peter and Paul,* we encountered for the first time the profound emotional outpouring that would mark every Cathedral concert for the duration of the tour.

The audience was an ecumenical mix, with clergy and laity from the conservative and evangelical community sitting amidst Roman

1989: Hungary & Poland: Cathedral, Crucifix, and Congregation

Catholics, a sight rarely seen in generations. During the concert we could hear the rumble of Soviet tanks as they exited Kiskunhalas via the street along side the Cathedral. The juxtaposed sounds of war machines and sacred music provoked profound emotions. At the end of the concert we sang, unannounced and in Hungarian, their most beloved nationalistic hymn, *Hymnusz*, which entreats God to look with favor, power, and preservation on the people of Hungary in order to keep them from oppression. Such a text as this would mean little to people who had never felt the heel of the oppressor. But for those who had suffered, fought, lost loved ones and now were on the brink of the text's fulfillment it was as if a bombshell went off in the Cathedral. The people rose immediately to their feet. As the hymn progressed, so did their weeping. When the final chord dissipated in the long nave, on impulse I sent the choir down the center and side aisles to greet the people. I said,

"Don't let anybody leave without shaking their hand and thanking them for coming."

Handshakes quickly gave way to tearful embraces. A Protestant clergyman approached me and related how he had come expecting a concert and received instead an outpouring of the Holy Spirit; I would hear that refrain many times over the next two weeks. It was a long time, and hundreds of autographed programs, before the people left.

I sensed that night, as did the choir, a power greater than our own working in us and through us. We were not on a tour, but rather, a mission.

After a secular concert in Szeged, on the border of Yugoslavia and Rumania, I met with a Baptist minister and a doctor from his congregation. For two hours we discussed religious persecution in

Hungary, the spiritual awakening in the churches of Hungary (both Roman Catholic and Protestant), and the overtures to the Church by the Communist Party. The Party, they said, was desperate for the Church's help in overcoming the results of moral decay in the country—particularly alcoholism, divorce, and suicide; this was the Soviet legacy in Hungary.

We returned to Budapest to perform for *Faculty Honors Day* at the *University of Budapest*.

Faculty Honors Day Concert, University of Budapest

Following the concert I was invited by the President of the University to join him and six Deans of the various colleges in a small, but elegant reception. After a few minutes of formalities regarding the concert they sat forward in their chairs, almost as if rehearsed, and began with the real reason for the gathering:

"What are your perceptions about the political climate of our country?"

"Of all the places you could have toured, why did you choose Hungary?"

"Are people in the United States aware through their press of our struggle for freedom?"

We talked about the aborted uprising of 1956, their feeling of being abandoned by the West, the barbed wire being removed, the 'resurrection', so to speak, of Imre Nagy, the departure of Soviet troops, and the rewriting of the Hungarian Constitution. And then a most surprising commentary not only because it was being asked in an academic, intellectual, secular environment, but also because it was being initiated by a man I presumed to be Jewish He said,

"I have the feeling that your students come from many religious backgrounds. Yet they sang your concert of Christian music as if with one voice, one spirit. How is that possible?"

This opening led to a statement by me of what constitutes the core of the Christian faith. While there may be differences of dogma, almost all the singers, I said, were united in that core of faith. Several, but not all heads nodded, if not in agreement, at least in understanding.

As our *soiree* drew to its conclusion the President wanted me to know that two of the six Deans present were on the National Committee rewriting the Hungarian Constitution, excising all Communist ideology and influence. As a gift they gave me a medallion commemorating the 350th anniversary of the founding of the University, the oldest existing in Hungary.

That night, after a delay of seven hours, our plane to Krakow never showed up, so we spent another night in Budapest, arriving in Poland a day late after only about four hours sleep.

Hungary had seemed remarkably Western with its surplus of quality goods and plentiful food. We hardly felt, apart from the language, that we were in a different culture, much less a foreign social/political structure. Also, we had stayed in hotels, making separation from the strains of culture shock possible.

Poland was different. Here was a country ravaged by wars and invaders throughout its entire history. Often the political leadership of Poland has not been Polish. As recently as the 19th century there was no territory on world maps called Poland. Other nations, in order to dominate the territory, have tried everything from outlawing the Polish language to genocide of the Polish people. Through all of this the Roman Catholic Church became, in addition to a spiritual force, a major center of Polish culture and Polish nationalism. The Church became everything that was necessary for the preservation of Poland. The Roman Catholic Church in Poland *is* Poland. We couldn't begin to comprehend Poland without first understanding this.

So it was greatly in our favor that the organization that invited us and sponsored us was the *KIK*, the *Catholic Club of Intellectuals*. The *KIK*, we learned, had been from the early 1950's until the formation of *Solidarity* in 1980, the underground opposition to the Communist party in Poland. Their ties go deep into the heart of the Polish Roman Catholic Church. We were to have access, through the *KIK,* to many wonderful people and historically important Cathedral concert sites in Poland.

The bus ride from the airport into Krakow revealed an agricultural system that was archaic, factories which were decrepit and grossly polluting, and a people with few possessions or amenities for living—all this the Communist legacy in Poland.

It was June 3rd. Our first stop was a regional *Solidarity* headquarters in Krakow. Walking with our luggage through Market Square we passed many booths set up by the election candidates to dispense their flyers and lapel pins. Great crowds of people surrounded every *Solidarity* booth, while not a single person appeared at the Communist booths.

At *Solidarity* headquarters we were introduced to our host families who were members of *KIK, Solidarity*, or both. This opportunity for living in Polish homes had been one of the great attractions of the tour, but now, as it came time to actually enter into the experience, having had a glimpse of the poverty in Poland, we were nervous, maybe even terrified of what lay ahead. We had hoped to room in pairs, so at least each student would have another for moral support. We now realized few hosts would be able to care for more than one guest. It was a quiet, somber group of young people that left the center of Krakow that rainy afternoon.

We gathered in rehearsal for our first concert in Poland in the great *Mariacki Cathedral*.

This was the spot where, six centuries earlier, a trumpeter had signaled a warning from the bell tower that the ancient capital was under siege. His trumpet signal was cut short by an arrow that pierced his throat. Krakow survived, and from that day to this a trumpeter signals the same tune in four directions every hour around the clock, stopping abruptly at the same 'mortal' spot in the tune. Incidentally, my host, a boyhood friend of Pope John Paul II, lived in an apartment directly across a small courtyard from the

Rehearsal in Mariacki Cathedral, Krakow

Cathedral and its bell tower. I was serenaded nightly for three nights, every hour on the hour, by the trumpeter of Krakow!

The coming together the next morning of my 'troops' trumpeted a different tune. Everyone was in great spirits. They had already been drawn close by their Polish hosts, who proved to be more than hospitable. As we would experience throughout Poland, our hosts were sacrificial in their outpourings to us, almost to the point of our embarrassment. We said it to each other many times: if Americans gave as graciously and willingly out of our bounty the societal ills of our country, and perhaps the world, could be addressed almost overnight. We learned from our Polish hosts the true meaning of giving from a full heart with a joyful spirit. One of my singers, Tristan Melvie, wrote this:

Throughout our countless experiences in Hungary and Poland, what fascinated me most were the people. I still cannot believe the incredible warmth and generosity seen wherever we went. Most of our host families, living at the poverty level by our standards, spent at least one month's salary on us for food and gifts, and did so joyfully. I was very moved as I entered a store in Poland and saw at least fifty people in line just to buy meat, which is rationed, and there was nothing but a little sausage and other meats we would consider very inexpensive. Often they leave empty handed. These people taught me a great deal about my own life and reminded me time and time again that true happiness and satisfaction cannot be found in things, but can only come from devotion and reverence to our God.

Another student, Nancy Wiebe, recounted her first night with her Polish host family:

When I was first greeted by Tomek Piekarz and his friend Rafael in our meeting place in Krakow, Poland, I had no idea what a treat was in store for me. Over the next few days I enjoyed some enlightening conversation. I found that the father, Tadeusz Piekarz, had been imprisoned in 1982-83 with Lech Walesa for their peaceful involvement in Poland's Solidarity movement. He had his passport taken at that time; it has never been returned. Yet the Piekarz's have remained faithful in spite of persecution. At one point they asked if I was 'Evangelical'. I wasn't sure what they meant, but I figured I was more so than not, so I said, "Yes," and asked if they were. They said, "No, we're Catholic." I laughed and said, "We worship the same God." We talked for an hour and a half about why Jesus means so much to me, when my parents don't force their beliefs on me, and when I live in a free country. We exchanged more than words that night; I saw their strength in the face of governmental opposition—hopefully they saw my weakness made strong only in Jesus. This opportunity to live with these new-found friends in Poland has been life-changing.

How interesting it was for me to spend election night in *Solidarity* Headquarters in Krakow listening to world opinion through *Radio Free Europe,* the *BBC,* and *Voice of America,* all the while conversing with the director, a descendent of a long line of Polish Princes. How thrilled we were on two occasions to have lunch with two newly elected Senators from the *Solidarity Party.*

During our stay in Poland the North Park College Choir lived with 150 different Polish families. My Polish host families brought the world history surrounding my own life into a deeper, more personalized focus. This was particularly true in Wroclaw, where I stayed with Dr. Professor Jan Slek and his wife Ludwicka following our concert in *St. Michael's Church.* Jan was conductor of the Opera and musical director of the Philharmonia in addition to his professorship at the State Academy of Music. Ludwicka was Professor of Philology at the University. Over a marvelous dinner Jan related to me how he had been sent to Dachau concentration camp at age 13 simply because he was Polish. His two older brothers were sent to Ravensbruck, accused of being underground partisans against the Germans. His oldest brother died in the camp. The other brother survived, but when the Russians 'liberated' the camp they threw him into a Russian prison camp accused of collaborating with the Germans. Sentenced to death, he somehow survived and was released ten years later. Jan Slek was released to a German farmer after three months in Dachau and survived the war on a farm near Augsburg. In 2009 he was awarded the *Austrian Cross of Honor* for his promotion of Viennese music in Poland.

This conversation, just one day after witnessing Auschwitz and Birkenau, transferred the horrors of the 40's from the written pages of history to the indelible memory of my being.

1989: Hungary & Poland: Cathedral, Crucifix, and Congregation

Auschwitz

Anne Wahlstedt wrote this in her journal:

When we arrived at Auschwitz and got out of the bus we were all quiet because of just knowing where we were; but I don't think the impact had really hit us fully. The gate those innocent and confused people walked through was lined on both sides with two rows of electrical fences. Above the gate were the deceitful, lying words, "Work makes free". As we went from bunker to bunker seeing photographs and actual piles and piles of human hair, eyeglasses, brushes, suitcases and clothing we couldn't help but realize that what happened here wasn't so long ago; it was definitely impossible to ignore. In a deeply felt, but feeble effort to show our respect and compassion, the choir sang the Choral Benediction at the place where 20,000 innocent victims, standing naked, were shot in the back of the head:

> *The Lord spoke to Moses, saying, "Speak to Aaron and his sons, saying, Thus you shall bless the people of Israel: you shall say to them,*

The Lord bless you and keep you;

The Lord make his face to shine upon you and be gracious to you;

The Lord lift up his countenance upon you and give you peace.

Bea's recitation of a Hebrew mourner's Kaddish from her deceased husband's Prayer Book, and our singing made us truly feel the immense sadness of that place, which is all we can hope to do now—really feel it so something even close to that won't happen again.

Anne's friend, Tracy Dvorak, had this to say:

Personally, I was overwhelmed by our singing at the wall where people were shot, and I literally had no control over my crying. I went straight outside just to look at the concentration camp—and I noticed everyone did the same thing. Not one person said anything to anyone for a long time.

Many journal entries reflected on this experience. Katrina Ahlquist wrote:

Some of us went from Auschwitz to Birkenau, the larger concentration camp. The crude, inhumane barracks just kept going on and on forever, row after row. Many of us sat alone, thinking, praying, asking why. I have asked so many times. What an incredible period of time the world had to go through. O Lord, I hope through all of this we have at least learned some sort of lesson.

Other journals recounted more pleasant experiences. Thaïs Johnson had this to say:

One family told me they could see freedom in my face because my eyes were constantly shining; and they could hear freedom in my voice because it sounded happy. They also said I represented something they are struggling for. This made me take a look at myself. I thought about all those times I wanted more than I had, and how these people have so much less than I could ever have imagined, yet gave everything they had to me. It has made me far more appreciative of my freedom.

Scott Meyer recounted a most interesting moment with his host family:

My family in Warsaw viewed America as the next best thing to Heaven. They want to come to America so badly, to work or even to visit, that they have spent ten years of hard work actually building a large yacht so that they can sail to America. It sounds like a movie, but it's real. The mother told us in broken English: 'Life is easier on the boat!' This is the same family that brought out a puzzle of the United States and were teaching their 5-year old daughter the names of all the States. It really made me think.

As we were leaving Wroclaw for Czestochowa, where we would sing at the unveiling of the iconic *Black Madonna*, Jan Slek drove me to the departure site in his rickety Russian Fiat. *"Don't leave until I return,"* he said, and left in a fog of burning oil. Our bus driver was in a hurry, but I insisted we wait. Twenty minutes later Jan returned, drove up onto the lawn and hurried out to give me a bag full of apples. He had searched for some fruit for our journey and it hadn't been easy to find. While the apples were somewhat shriveled and small, I don't know that I've ever savored a more loving treat than on the way to Poland's greatest treasure.

Three days later my Warsaw host family, a retired couple, related how they helped rebuild the totally devastated city brick by brick after having seen it systematically dynamited by the Germans as a final act of retribution. Out of the rubble, chiseling mortar off the old bricks, Warsaw literally was raised from the ashes. They, too, had been incarcerated by the Russians as potentially dangerous counter-revolutionaries. Our conversation spun its way back through Poland's World War II history and ended at the Katyn forest massacre. As we talked about the terrible loss of Polish leadership in that atrocity, my host revealed to me that his brother was one of the murdered officers.

This wonderful couple, like all the other hosts, gave sacrificially. I had six meals with them—three breakfasts and three dinners, consisting of bread, cheese, tomatoes, cucumbers, marmalade, tea and cold cuts. I noticed they didn't eat the cold cuts but insisted every meal that I have more. They wouldn't have said it, but I knew that meat is rationed, expensive, and often unavailable. They gave me everything they had. The last day they gave me a gift of a book, in Polish, with hundreds of photographs of the destruction of Warsaw. I know it was expensive. They wanted me not only to remember them, but also their beloved city that they had helped redeem with their bare hands.

Election Day Concert! Church of St. Casimir, Nowy Sacz

But I have digressed ahead of the story. Sunday, June 4, was a monumental day marked worldwide by tragedy and triumph. Communism was falling apart. Its ideologies had misread the human spirit. Its legacy was, at the very least, inertia, while at the other end of the spectrum lay despair and hopelessness. All that was now changing. On this first Sunday of June, 1989, polar opposites took place in the Communist world: violent repression in Tienanmen Square (which I would visit as conductor of a Chinese choir nineteen years later for the Beijing Pre-Olympic Festival), and peaceful, free elections in Poland.

The North Park College Choir was in Poland on election day! Our timing and my intuition were perfect. Given their history, especially the last forty-two years under the Communist yoke, their triumph in gaining a free election was in need of a point for emotional catharsis. And there we were. As they turned away from Soviet Russia and looked toward the West an initial contact was needed. And there we were, 60 musicians eager to share our music, our faith, our encouragement and our support. And we did, not only through our concerts, but especially in our willingness to reach out physically, sharing in both laughter and tears their sweet, precious moment of victory.

Our concert that day was in the *Church of St. Casimir* in Nowy Sacz. One of my students wrote this in her journal:

Today is June 4th. Election day! But it was not spent in Krakow; we travelled to the small town of Nowy Sacz. It was here where we first sang "Boze Cos Polske", and Professor Athnos invited the congregation to sing with us. I was completely overcome with emotion: pride, heartache, and mostly, because today was election day, joy. Something which really struck me as I looked out at the crowd was the children. Today is for them. All that the Polish people have struggled for, these hearty people who belted this song out to us with beaming smiles and tears in their eyes, all that they have prayed for, has begun to take place today. And it's the children who sang this song, who gave us flowers, and later today the children who stood in line with us for ice-cream and who threw a Frisbee for the first time—it's for them. They will see the fruits of their parents' work, people like my host father, Mr. Rieger, who will stay up all night tonight counting the ballots; people who freely and unhesitatingly dedicate their lives to see that their country will someday, once again be their own. They are giving their children a future with freedom and a promise.

Many members of our host families in Krakow, Wroclaw and Warsaw were involved in counting the ballots by hand. Each of the nine days we were in Poland revealed just a little more about how total and complete was the victory of Solidarity and the humiliation of the Communists. In each of our five concerts in Poland the emotional outpouring became magnified or intensified by the growing awareness of the people's success. It was almost too much to bear at times, for them and for us as well. How long could we sustain this emotional momentum night after night, without flying apart?

Concerts became more than concerts. Each became a mirror of history in the making. Each became a point of release for the pent-up, too-long trapped emotions of the enormous crowds of people gathered in the Cathedrals to hear us. It was as if they hadn't come to the concerts for the music. Why should they have come at all, especially at this time when the focus of the entire country was anywhere but on choral music? And who were we? How could we really understand what they were going through? They needed us, it seems, to be for them a channel through which their emotions could flow freely and openly.

That each concert was merely a chapter in the same book, one growing out of the previous and into the next, unfolding the same theme, was borne out by the responses of the Priests in the Cathedrals. Each night they came to me—different men, different cities, different days—and said the same words. Not the words a conductor normally hears following a concert—words of thanks or praise. Instead, these words:

The Holy Spirit was working among us tonight.

These profoundly religious Polish people were savoring their political victory in the spiritual institution that had sustained them in tragedy. Their political triumph needed the higher validation to be found only in the Church. Their motivation of the heart intersected with our prayers, sparks flew, and we were all caught up in the ensuing fire. We were privileged to be part of their first steps into the world of freedom.

A moment of relief from the hyper-emotions of our cathedral concerts came through our performance of excerpts from George Gershwin's opera *Porgy and Bess* in the famous Warsaw Castle. My student soloists were superb, especially Elizabeth Magnusson and Walter DuMelle, both of whom went on to successful oratorio and opera careers. The audience absolutely loved the music; so did we. It was not lost on anyone that the last, intentionally chosen lyrics of our performance were reflective of what the Polish people had just accomplished in their historic election:

"I'm on my way to the Promised Land."

My most vivid memory grows out of the performance in the Warsaw *Cathedral of St. John*, our final concert. For almost 600 years it had stood as a symbol of the Christian faith. Then, in 1945, it was consciously and viciously destroyed, only part of one wall left standing. On one wall had been a large crucifix, the metal figure of Christ hanging on a wooden cross. The soldiers shot it to pieces. The torso of Christ was riddled with gaping bullet holes; one arm was blown off, leaving the figure hanging precariously by part of the remaining arm. It was as if Christ had been crucified a second time. After the war the remains of the crucifix were found in the rubble. The Cathedral was lovingly rebuilt (my Warsaw hosts had helped) and the crucifix was again mounted on the wall, exactly as it had been found, as a reminder of the past. This figure of Christ in His 'second resurrection' became a powerful image for us that night. I remember whispering to the choir, gathered in the chancel of this magnificent Cathedral,

"This Cathedral knew a tragic death. It also has experienced a glorious resurrection."

Warsaw Cathedral, dynamited by the Germans as an act of retribution

In my mind the Cathedral, the Crucifix, and the Congregation became tangled in the same resurrection metaphor. As Christ had been raised so now in this re-born Cathedral the hopes of the Polish nation stood on the brink of a new life; it was a triple resurrection! Choristers told me how they focused on those words and the resurrected crucifix throughout the entire concert and how waves of emotion swept over them. It was not our best concert musically because it was a turmoil of unbridled passion and tears, but I shall never forget the 'spiritual' electricity that surged like surf and undertow alternately between the congregation and the choir, with me in the middle, drenched by their energies at the point of collision.

People were sitting on folding chairs, sitting in the aisles and standing everywhere—even crowded into the pulpit and the stairs leading up to it. During the performance there were times when the applause was so enthusiastic and sustained that it was almost impossible to continue. One of the Cathedral Priests, with whom I met again when he visited Chicago a month later, said he had never seen anything like it; never had applause for a concert been so loud or long.

I noticed an older gentleman sitting in a folding chair right next to me. Throughout the evening his applause was especially boisterous. When our final piece from the printed program ended he clasped his hands together and shook them up and down vigorously in front of my face, saying, *"Please, please."* He didn't want the evening to end—neither did I.

In Poland, as in Hungary, we proceeded unannounced to a patriotic hymn: *"Boze Cos Polske"*. Written in the 19th century when Poland 'didn't exist' on the maps of Europe, it begins with the words, "*God save Poland*", and ends with the phrase,

Give us back the freedom we once had.

We had learned that this piece was one of the single most unifying elements in the Polish nation. It had been sung as a prayer and also as an act of defiance against oppressors.

During the German occupation of Poland the hymn was outlawed. Many citizens had been imprisoned for singing it, but they continued in spite of the consequences. The story was told to me of a Christmas Eve Mass in one of the Cathedrals, crowded with worshippers. When German troops entered the Cathedral, violating its sanctity, in defiance the people rose to their feet and began singing the forbidden melody.

After the war, knowing they couldn't keep the Poles from singing this hymn, the Russians changed the concluding words from, *Give us back the freedom we one had,* to,

Help us retain the freedom we now have.

As a matter of fact the copy I was given to teach the choir used that Russian ending. But as my copy was written in phonetic pronunciation of the Polish, with no translation, I had no idea what it said, nor did I know anything of the hymn and its history.

Fortunately, I went to the *Polish National Alliance* headquarters in Chicago for help in pronunciation of the Polish. Wojciech Wierzewski, editor of *Zgoda*, the national Polish newspaper, had difficulty with the text as well because it wasn't in the Polish language nor was it in English; it was, as I said, phonetic. After a few minutes of struggle he looked up, slammed his fists on his desk and shouted,

"No, you cannot sing this song; it will be an insult to the Polish people!"

I was greatly relieved to have sought his help. He then explained to me the history of the hymn. I asked his advice. He asked,

"How brave are you?"

"What do you mean?" I inquired.

"Are you willing to sing the forbidden text?"

He suggested there was no way of knowing the response that might come our way. I said we would take our chances; we would be singing our concerts at the time of the free elections, and I doubted the outcome would favor the Communists. Mr. Wierzewski cautioned me that it wouldn't be the first time an election had been 'rigged'. We changed the concluding words back to their original:

Give us back the freedom we once had.

We began singing *"Boze Cos Polske"* with the previously forbidden text. At first, as in the other concerts, the audience froze, perhaps wondering how it would end. The effect was dramatic. People leaped to their feet at that concluding line and, as we had witnessed throughout Poland during this week in which they had achieved with stunning success the first step on the road to the hymn's fulfillment, they raised their arms and fingers in the sign of victory. Tears began to flow, both theirs and ours.

When we finished, I turned to Mr. Wojtek Sawicki, who had been our facilitator in Warsaw, and asked him to have the congregation sing it with us as we had done in previous concerts. He hesitated, saying, *"No, you're the professionals."* I kept asking and he kept hesitating. Finally I said that we weren't going to leave the Chancel of the Cathedral unless he asked the people to sing it with us as a gesture of union between our two nations. The audience leaped to its feet. It was one of the great moments in my life to conduct this sea of nearly 1000 weeping citizens as they sang freedom's song. In this historic, resurrected, packed Cathedral the combination of their voices with ours was heart-wrenching, majestic, and heavenly.

The procession of flowers and gifts began—some planned by our hosts, the *KIK*, as had been true at every concert—but many more; simply spontaneous or personal gestures of good will and appreciation from young and old alike, not only to me but to members of the choir as well. That night I received flowers of every description, hand written music manuscripts from several Polish composers in attendance, and many hugs and kisses.

One gift in particular stands out in my memory. A bent and ancient lady, dressed in black from her babushka to her shoes, whose facial lines and creases told a tragic tale of 20th century Polish history, made her way slowly to the front, embraced me with kisses and pressed into my hands a small religious pamphlet with a picture of Jesus on one side. It was all she had and she gave it from her heart. I shall never forget her.

I was surrounded by people at the end. The older gentleman who had pleadingly clasped his hands turned out to be the Director of Choral Music at the *Academy of Music* in Warsaw. He couldn't speak much English, but said again and again in German,

"*Meisterstücke, meisterstücke*"—masterpiece, masterpiece.

Here again the Cathedral Priest said,

"*The Holy Spirit was present tonight.*"

A couple who had arrived just the day before from the Netherlands, saw our concert poster and came, said to me,

"*We were expecting a concert. What we received instead was a spiritual experience.*"

One of my students wrote this to me:

I walked home hand-in-hand with my host lady after that last concert. We were not able to speak one word to each other, but words weren't needed. We were bonded together by our common faith and hope and holding hands was the best form of communication imaginable.

Dennis Hunt, one of the administrators of *Friendship Ambassadors Foundation*, the organization that made our tour arrangements, wrote this to me one month after our return:

I was in Poland immediately following your tour and spoke with Wojtek Sawicki of the KIK…. He described the filled Cathedrals and emotional outpouring of the people in response to your choir's performance. This is the kind of exchange we hope for, but I must say, what he described was especially rich. Rarely are Priests on hand to welcome groups or to offer appreciation on behalf of the community. Obviously the 'spiritual dimension' of this connection was deeply felt.

Our mission was over, and here we were in this cramped hotel lobby. The fifteen minutes we had planned to spend turned into several hours trying to find words that would provide an adequate focus and closure before we parted for the last time. One student after another spoke of their admiration for the people they had come to love. Voices cracked as they realized how important freedom was for these people, and how much we Americans have taken it for granted. Tears flowed as students, impressed by the strong faith of the Polish people, began to reconsider a stronger commitment to their own faith. One student took a first, tenuous step toward the Christian faith.

We had seen and done many things. We had been at the center of an historic whirlwind. We had been raised to great heights by the love and goodwill of our audiences and host families. We had talked a mile a minute in any language that would work: English, German,

French; and had walked alone and in a provoked silence through the gas chambers of Auschwitz and barracks of Birkenau. We had wept as we sang the *Choral Benediction* at Auschwitz following the reading by one of our Jewish ladies of a Hebrew prayer for the dead from her deceased husband's Prayer Book. I had observed with great pride how our students extended themselves without hesitation or reservation to the people we met—in love, concern, prayer, and compassion. One of my students left a hand-written Bible verse on the kitchen table of her hosts each morning, choosing a passage she thought would speak to their needs as expressed in conversation the night before.

We received from the Polish people far more than we gave, and were changed by the experience. In a country overwhelmed by physical poverty and hardship, we had been in the presence of a people blessed with a richness of spirit. We discovered how truly fragile and precious freedom is, and through seeing the determination of the Polish people we have come to more greatly appreciate and treasure that which we too often take lightly.

Yes, at the professional level the tour was a musical and personal triumph. I doubted I would ever again experience the respect from fellow musicians and conductors or the exultation from audiences I was accorded in those countries. It was humorous at times. On several occasions I was asked how many awards and national honors I had received, because, they suggested,

Certainly someone whose choir is so outstanding must be a national treasure!

How could I tell them that most people even within my own city have never heard of my college much less my choir.

One final journal entry deserves to serve as the final revelation of this life-changing experience for me and my student singers. Elizabeth Aguilar, a senior, wrote this very poignant summation:

Tonight in Warsaw was our last concert in Europe and my last concert with the North Park choir. When Greg said, "God—is—here—now", right before we began our first song, it sent chills up my spine. He was right; God was there. In fact, God has been with us from the very beginning. Never before have I felt God's presence with me as I have in the concerts here in Poland. This last concert in particular was very special, mainly because my host family was in the audience. This Polish family made me feel a part of their household, and so I felt as if my own family was there. We communicated through Kate, the 21-year old daughter who spoke a little English. They have treated me as if I were a Queen. They've fed me, hugged me, smiled, laughed and cried with me. I told them how important it is for us to share this special time in their history with them, and I stressed how appreciative I felt for their generosity toward me.

Little did I know that a flood of emotions were to follow this. Kate began to cry and said she was sad because she cannot find this happiness in her parents or in herself. We were silent after this. After breakfast today she and her mother began to cry again, right out of the blue. I thought I had said or done something wrong. Kate explained that I hadn't. Instead they were crying because they were so happy to have had me as a guest! My time with this last family has been an emotional one, one that has challenged me to look closer at what I do have, at what my responsibility is as a Christian, and at my own future. All I can say after this entire trip is that God has been with us, and has put us in the hands of very kind people. For this I will be eternally grateful to the North Park Choir, to Greg, and above all, to God.

In April of the next year, 1990, I wrote letters to our contacts in the four cathedrals that hosted our concerts—Krakow, Nowy Sacz,

Wroclaw, and Warsaw—and to our host sponsor, the Catholic Club of Intellectuals. It read,

Dear Friends,

The North Park College Choir remembers with great joy and gratitude our time in your Church and your homes during our concert tour of Poland last summer. Your generosity and kindness was a gift to us that we will never forget. Also, it was a great privilege to be with you during your victorious elections. Your country's courage over the years has led to a promising future, not only in Poland but also throughout all of Central Europe.

We continue to follow the news in your country. My students write to their host families occasionally. As we share our experiences here at home people are moved, often to tears. I have received many letters and phone calls from strangers who have heard the story we witnessed during that momentous occasion of June, 1989.

While we were in your country we tape-recorded all our concerts. A cassette tape was made. Over 2000 tapes were sold. My singers requested that the profit from the sale be sent as a gift to all the Churches who sponsored us. In addition we want to give a gift to the Catholic Club of Intellectuals for their work in arranging our tour.

$500 (U.S.) is being given to each of you. We have thought of several suggestions for using the gift: 1) to purchase music for the choirs of the churches; 2) to support families with great need during this time of high inflation and difficulty; 3) to purchase something greatly needed by your Church for use in your ministry and worship. You may have other ideas for use of the gift. We want you to distribute the gift in ways that seem best for your people.

The gifts are being delivered to Wojtek Sawicki, formerly of the KIK in Warsaw and newly elected Secretary for the Solidarity Party. He is

making arrangements to forward the gift to you. It is only a small way to say 'thank you' for all you did for us.

'Boze cos Polske'.

We received many notes and letters in response, including the following from Dr. Filaber, the renowned Polish choirmaster and Music Director of the Warsaw Cathedral:

**CHÓR
ARCHIKATEDRY WARSZAWSKIEJ**
DYR. KS. ANDRZEJ FILABER
00-278 WARSZAWA, UL. ŚWIĘTOJAŃSKA 8 - TEL. 31-96-62

Warszawa, May 21st, 1990

Mr Gregory S. Athnos
Director
North Park College

Dear Sir,

I would like to thank you with all my heart in the name of our team, of the Cathedral parish and my own for your gift that is to serve the Warsaw Cathedral. We are agreeably surprised and very grateful.

We also have a pleasant memory of your stay in Warsaw and the two splendid concerts. Enclosed please find a notice from "Ruch Muzyczny" ("Music Movement"), the most serious music periodical in Poland.

There is still one timid request. During our meeting you promised to me some recordings of negro spirituals sung by your choir. I would very much appreciate it if you could send me a record or a cassette with that music ("Ain't Got Time to Die" and other). We are now preparing a few compositions of this kind and such recording could be a great aid as far as rendition is concerned.

Thanking you once more for your nice letter and for the present received through Mr W. Sawicki, I send my most cordial greetings to you and your whole Choir and wish you further success in the artistic realm.

Yours truly,

A. Filaber

Warsaw Cathedral letter

Eat in Harmony

Our tour administrator in Warsaw, Wojtek Sawicki, was elected to the new Polish Senate on June 4th. He then became Secretary of the Solidarity Party. His letter came one year later in response to our gifts to the churches in Poland:

SZEF
KANCELARII SENATU

Warszawa, dn 11. June 1990 r.

Dear Gregory,

    First, I must apologize for not having written for such a long time. There is no excuse for it, the only one is that I usually stay in my Senate office from 8 am till 8 pm. I got your letters with the gifts. All of them were already passed to the churches in Cracow, Wrocław, Nowy Sącz and Warsaw and to KIK. I would like to thank to you and all members of the choir for your help and assistance.

    I still remember your marvellous concert in Warsaw Cathedral and in the Royal Castle. It was really great to be there together with you. Do you think it could be possible to get one copy of cassette you made with recordings of your concerts in Poland. I would appreciate it.

    Please give my best wishes to all members of your choir. With very warm greetings to yourself.

Sincerely,

Wojtek Sawicki

Letter from Senator Wojtek Sawicki

1989: Hungary & Poland: Cathedral, Crucifix, and Congregation

This historic concert tour rose to cultural and spiritual heights beyond all that we could have wished for or dreamed. *Bose Cos Polske!* God bless Poland!

CHAPTER 49

Olga, Dimitri, Smolny: Soviet Union 1965, Russia 1993

Four years later our second foreign tour took us to Sweden, Russia, and Estonia. On our previous tour we had been in the center of the whirlwind that brought the first break in the armor of the Soviet Union. Now we were about to enter a changed Russia as well as its liberated satellite—Estonia.

I was standing at 50 Borovaya Street in St. Petersburg, Russia, looking for the *Temple of the Gospel*, but all I could see was a dilapidated and boarded up hulk. We were scheduled to sing in their morning worship service the next day, but it appeared this church was no longer in existence. Had we come to the wrong location? Once a grand Russian Orthodox Church, this building had lost all its onion domes. Most of its brick veneer was gone, exposing the rough masonry. The wood doors were rotted and bolted shut.

Finding an opening in a makeshift corrugated metal fence surrounding the building I noticed a small wooden shack propped up next to the old church. As I pushed against its door an elderly man opened it. He was Stepanovich. Explaining my search I noticed his

Olga, Dimitri, Smolny: Soviet Union 1965, Russia 1993

face begin to light up. Yes, he was the caretaker and this was the *Temple of the Gospel*.

Temple of the Gospel, St. Petersburg, Russia

He led me through the garbage-littered courtyard into a back entrance and through a dark, narrow corridor. Rounding a corner we entered with great surprise into a brightly lit, freshly painted, beautiful gem of a sanctuary. The pews were handcrafted, as was the wrap-around balcony. Through the altar screen was a lovely fresco of Christ. Mr. Stepanovich told me that after the Bolshevik revolution the church had been converted into a picture frame factory. The turrets and onion domes were knocked down, the exterior brick façade was stripped away to be used for other purposes, and the interior was completely gutted. The walls, once painted with frescoes, had been destroyed or painted over. During those 70 years of occupation all remembrances of the building's former dedication to God had vanished.

After the fall of Communism in the Soviet Union, Gorbachev gave the building to a group of several dozen Christians. Within two years the new evangelical work had grown to become the largest such group in St. Petersburg. They completely rebuilt the interior, and were able to save one of the frescoes that had been painted over. The church now has over 500 members, with new seekers in attendance every time the doors open. They have a seminary of 40 students, and import faculty from American seminaries to teach mini-courses. The pastor, Sergei Nikolayev, is building a library of Christian theological and devotional books that will serve as a center for learning and spiritual growth for the entire evangelical community of the St. Petersburg area.

Within half an hour I had been taken from a world of desolation and desertion to one of vibrancy, life, and promise for the future. The church seemed yet another metaphor of the Christian faith: the battered and worn life of the severely persecuted flesh housed the temple of the inner spirit, the beautiful life of hope that propelled people into taking great risks for the sake of the Gospel. Through seven decades the faithful prayed and perservered. They were the remnant God promises. The *Temple of the Gospel* is a testimony to that glorious fact.

This one experience is a microcosm of life in Russia today. Coming soon after the North Park College Choir's entrance into the country, it became a guide for understanding the forces of change and the conflict apparent in everyday existence for the Russian people. Their's is not an easy life; we could see it etched on their faces. However, in spite of their dark and oppressive history we were able to see a love and a passion for life lurking behind their somber countenances. Our days in Russia would be marked by contrasts between physical deprivation and a wonderful and absolute zest for life. Were it not for that great renewed seeking after life in its fullness, our time in Russia would have been unbearable. As it was, we struggled daily against living conditions that tested our mettle and endurance. It was not pleasant for us rather spoiled Americans.

It was easy to look back on Sweden with great fondness. Things worked there, like the plumbing. Food was plentiful, recognizable, and familiar. We had strong ties with Sweden through our Covenant roots. Fully one-third of our singers had relatives with whom they stayed along the journey. Even the landscape looked like home. Almost everyone spoke English or understood it. People attending our concerts had reason to be there, and to like us; we were part of them in a strongly tangible way. Following a banquet hosted by the Governor of Uppsala our final concert was the in magnificent Uppsala Cathedral, one of the largest cathedrals in northern Europe. The sound in that space was glorious. Our recording from that evening is truly inspiring, even all these years later. Sweden was fun.

Russia, however, was markedly different. The enormous emotional weight of the truth of Russia quickly exhausted the capacity of our intellectual preparation. We thought we were prepared, but we could recount hundreds of experiences in a jumble of recollections and still be left trying to create a composite picture that makes sense. Russia is beyond our sensibility, and perhaps always will be.

I had been in the Soviet Union twenty-eight years earlier, in the summer of 1965, one of the first Americans let in after the thaw in the Cold War. Krushchev had recently been in power, the one who banged his shoe on the table at the UN and declared, "We will bury you." It was shortly after he and John F. Kennedy had had their war of nerves with fingers poised near the red nuclear buttons over the Cuban situation. Less than two years earlier our President had been assassinated under very mysterious circumstances. Many in the States thought the Soviet Union was behind it. Suspicions running in both directions didn't bode well for my excursion into this 'lion's den'. I was followed constantly by men in uniform with rifles; bayonets fixed. No adults dared speak to me. No one smiled, ever. Shops were empty. People had money but there was nothing to buy. If there was a line they joined it without knowing what was at the other end. Who knew, perhaps it was something they could use. The lines were longer than the goods were plentiful.

Rubble from World War II still remained in the streets; the buildings were pockmarked from shells. The great *Hermitage Museum*, with one of most auspicious art collections in the world, had its windows severely taped to keep glass from cutting masterpieces in the event of an explosion. Many sculptures were encircled by sandbags. On the streets suspicion was written on every face—only the young children appeared innocent of it, as they constantly begged for chewing gum and ballpoint pens. Even they were wary, and approached me only after I turned a corner, running up to me before anyone who might be following me could see them.

Retreating to my hotel proved not to be a sanctuary. Hotel Sovetskaya, though relatively new, was a hash of incompetence and intrigue. Nothing worked, not elevators, telephones, the plumbing—nothing. Buxom matrons with harsh countenances sternly controlled desks at the end of every corridor, supposedly to be of assistance to their clients. In reality they were there to keep control of their maids, who were desperate to exchange aprons full of rubles for American made clothes, jeans especially. Entering my room one maid flashed hands full of currency and begged for anything I could give her. Wanting to comply I hesitated, having heard rumors of 'plants' intending to catch 'black market Americans'. It didn't take long to fall prey to suspicion and paranoia, the very attitudes etched on the faces of countless people on the streets.

Churches were museums, if they existed at all. The great Kazan Cathedral, formerly the wedding place of the Czars, had been converted into a museum dedicated to atheism and anti-U.S. propaganda. I had found it on my own, as my guide Ludmilla wouldn't tell me how to get there. I wasn't supposed to be on my own, but constantly broke away to see the 'real' Soviet Union. Here, in this great Cathedral of the Czars, there was nothing left that suggested faith had ever been on display. Instead, there were two major themes. One was a presentation of the United States, with pictures of depression era bread lines and poverty, followed by images from the civil rights era with African-Americans being attacked by dogs or being blown down by fire hoses. The other theme depicted the successes of the Russian space program with photos of Yuri Gagarin and his statement, *"There is no God; we have been to the heavens and he isn't there."* This was four years before our own successes: John Glenn, Neil Armstrong, and the moon landing. How strange that a space once dedicated to God and the declaration that we all share a common creation was now a citadel of anti-religion and anti-U.S. propaganda.

With Ludmilla I had learned to look left when she said to look right; what she wanted me to see, I soon came to discover, was less important, really, than what she didn't want me to see.

I remember going to *Peter the Great's Summer Palace* on the only rainless day of my visit. The fountains weren't working, and hadn't since the war. The palace itself was gleaming with fresh paint and gold leaf; it was dazzling.

"Ludmilla," I asked, *"let's go inside."*

"No," she replied, and shrugged it off suggesting there was really nothing to see.

It was a casual remark intended to dissuade me from further inquiry. Again, I broke away, approached a window and looked inside. She had been more right than her casual remark had indicated. There was literally nothing inside; it was an empty shell. I later learned the Germans had used it as a stable for horses. Here again, the *Summer Palace* was a symbol of what I had surmised about the Soviet Union: all show on the outside, and emptiness within.

There were few cars on the streets, only people walking aimlessly down one side of Leningrad's major street, *Nevsky Prospekt*, back the other, and then beginning the circle again, crowded together in a lethargic, restless sea of humanity. It was depressing.

On the final night of my visit in 1965 I learned the Moscow Circus was in Leningrad. I decided to go, and took the trolley to the event, leaving Ludmilla behind. Fantastic! What absolute brilliance! What fun! Most remarkable was that this was the first and only time in my week-long stay I saw people smile and actually laugh.

Back on the trolley it dawned on me that I had not experienced the 'night life' of Leningrad, and wondered if indeed there was any. I approached a young man approximately my own age (29) and tried to strike up a conversation. He struggled with a few English words. Some elderly women sitting next to where we were standing laughed at him and, embarrassed, he walked away. Not to be denied, I waited a few seconds and followed him, starting our conversation once again. It so happened we had ended up next to a boy with a Russian-English dictionary. Whenever words failed either of us the boy looked them up.

"Do you like Jazz," I asked (I had heard that Russians liked Jazz).

"Russian Jazz no goot (good)," he replied.

"No, do you like American Jazz."

He grinned widely, and said, *"Ah, Gershwin, Armstrong."*

That began our inquiry into each other's professions. He learned I was a musician; I learned he was a shipbuilder in the Leningrad shipyards. As we continued our struggle with language I noticed that the trolley had passed by my hotel, and I had not yet asked about experiencing the city's night life. Rather than pursue it I decided simply to return to my hotel.

"Bol'shoe spasibo," I said. *"Thank you very much,"* and stepped down out of the trolley.

As my feet hit the bottom step I was grabbed from behind by two burly arms and dragged back up into the trolley.

"No," I panicked, *"I'm finally going to be caught for breaking away from the guide,"* which I had been doing all week. Being followed was now giving way to being apprehended.

The burly arms turned me around; they belonged to the young man with whom I had conversed. He pulled me close, gave me a giant bear hug, and whispered into my ear,

"I listen to Radio Free Europe."

Now, fifty years later, that moment still brings tears to my eyes. He was saying that while ideologies separate common men from common men, we were still brothers in the human race. We shared the same hopes and dreams. We shared a similar humanity. We had demonstrated that by crossing the artificial barriers put there by people with other motives in their hearts, even as we conversed on the trolley. In that single gesture I was made aware of a beauty that existed in Russia that would have eluded me had the conversation not taken place. I would only have seen the bleak Russia of the Soviet Union, the grey-ness, the somberness, the depression of the human spirit, the unsmiling face of a debilitating ideology. Those six words, following our genuine attempt to learn of each other, changed everything.

This was now my second visit, twenty-eight years later, 1993. Communism had been delivered a severe setback. There was no Soviet Union. I was anxious to see how much had changed. The value of currency was the first change that struck me. In 1965 one ruble equaled one dollar, and as recently as 1991 this was still true. The collapse of the Soviet system changed everything, starting with hyperinflation. Two weeks before we left Chicago, mid-May, the exchange rate was 800 rubles to the dollar. By the time we entered Russia after Sweden, it was over 1100. Imagine a dollar you earned in 1991 being worth one dime two years later. We were told that the average Russian worker earned about $15 a month in buying power, down from $150 a month in buying power one year ago. Is it any wonder life is hard? Retired people feel their lives are over.

Their money has become worthless. We saw many elderly people begging on the streets.

"We had it better under the Soviets", was a common litany I heard every day from the elderly.

I now understand why the faces populating our television screens in Russian protests against Boris Yeltsin are the faces of the elderly. The reality of their monetary dilemma became most vividly clear in Moscow at the world's largest McDonald's, located near the Kremlin. Here our students could buy two big Macs, a large order of fries and a large coke for two dollars, a bargain for us, but about one-seventh of the average Russian's monthly income. He would have to work four and a half days for that single meal. And if he had a wife and two children he'd spend half of one month's salary for just one family meal at McDonald's. It was a sobering thought. Yes, there are goods in the stores and food on the grocery shelves. The shocking reality of Russia today is that people can't afford to buy them.

I was struck most of all by the change in spirit. Not that it was either brighter or darker, but that whatever people felt, they could express freely, without fear of reprisal.

For many of us our most anticipated concert was to be with a Russian orchestra in the Smolny Cathedral in St. Petersburg with me as conductor.

It was in the Smolny Convent with its immense cathedral that Lenin and his cohorts plotted the October 1917 revolution that established Communism in Russia and led to the abandonment and persecution of the Christian faith. I had asked the conductor of the orchestra to select the choral-orchestral works they would prefer. To my astonishment he requested excerpts from Handel's *Messiah*, apparently because he could now do so without fear of reprisal. As far as we could determine the *Messiah* had not been officially performed in Russia since the Bolshevik Revolution of 1917. To sing this magnificent composition based on the prophecies of the birth, life, and Second Coming of the Savior of the world, a work so familiar to all of us in the West but totally unfamiliar to those for whom we would sing, was both a challenge and an honor. It was also ministry.

Smolny Cathedral, St. Petersburg, Russia

Olga, Dimitri, Smolny: Soviet Union 1965, Russia 1993

My rehearsals with the Russian orchestra were dreadful. I wondered why I had agreed to do this. I could be with my students, I thought to myself, experiencing the beauty of the city of Peter the Great. Instead, here I was in the middle of this horrible, messy project. No one in the orchestra had ever played any part of the work. They knew nothing of the piece or even the style of the Baroque period. They were used to playing 19th century Russian music: bombastic, romantic, big vibrato music. The concertmaster was intractable; he wanted to control everything: tempo, dynamics, style. It was miserable, and I was equally miserable. Complicating my task was the fact that I had no translator to assist me until my last rehearsal with them. What I wanted from their playing I had to sing for them. In six hours of rehearsal over three days, little by little, they began to catch on. Our final rehearsal with the choir in the Smolny Cathedral went fairly well. After all this effort, and much frustration, I felt we might just put it together.

To my shock it was not to be. At the very first note of *Messiah* the orchestra reverted back to the way they played at our first rehearsal. The concertmaster became a wild man, slinging his bow around like it was a sword. The orchestra never came in on my downbeats. When they did, it was at a different tempo than I had established. The one concert we had most looked forward to, most prayed about, was the worst performance of our tour, maybe the worst performance of my entire career as a musician/conductor, even worse than those concerts of my first year with the choir. The evening seemed interminable and I wondered if my plight would ever end!

Yet we could feel that God was still at work among us and through us. His message was still being powerfully proclaimed through the printed text as well as the spiritual commitment of our singers and the prayers of our state-side prayer warriors. We found ourselves surprisingly moved by the experience, and we could feel that from the audience as well. It was a great lesson: God doesn't demand perfection, only dedication. We are not called to be successful, only faithful. So, in spite of everything going wrong that could have gone wrong we found ourselves blessed nonetheless.

That night will stand out in our memories. Lenin was dead; we would see his body in Moscow. Communism, which had brought untold misery to countless millions of people, was being abandoned all over the globe. In the Smolny Cathedral, the place of the first Communist denial of God and the birthplace of Soviet atheism, we brought back into existence that night the message of the One who reigns as 'King of kings, and Lord of lords'.

I was told to stay after the concert and wait for a visit from a Russia citizen:

"Do what he tells you and go where he takes you. You must hear his story."

I was still in my conductor's 'tails' as Dimitri Korolian introduced himself to me and invited me to his apartment to meet his wife Natalia and have dinner with them. Across the Neva River and up several flights of dimly lit stairs smelling of disinfectant, and through several locked steel doors, we entered their apartment. It had a tiny kitchen, a bathroom, their daughter's small bedroom little larger than a closet, and their own bedroom, which also served as their dining room, living room, and study. As we sat on and around the bed where a large piece of plywood had been placed to convert it into a table, we ate a delicious treat prepared by Natalia. Dimitri told me his story.

Dimitri had been sent to the Soviet Military Academy to be trained as an officer. Upon graduation he began serving in the military as a teacher of future officers, but he didn't believe everything he had been taught. He knew much of the propaganda wasn't true. He knew he was lying to his men. Deep down inside he felt what he was doing was morally wrong, which struck me as surprising given his life in an amoral political system. Dimitri told his superior officers he could no longer continue lying to his men. They drove him out of the military, considering him untrustworthy. Because of the stigma attached to his discharge he couldn't get a job. He couldn't support his family. Guilt weighed heavily on him. He had few friends. Desperate for money he fell prey to the Russian 'mafia' (they were the first to come to power after the Soviet collapse) who assigned him the task of controlling the prostitutes in several St. Petersburg hotels. After several months he informed the 'mafia' that he didn't feel right working with prostitution; it was immoral. To test his loyalty they ordered him to kill an informant. When Dimitri balked at this assignment and wanted 'out' they threatened his family. He owed them $200; if he could pay up, he would be given his release. $200 was a fortune to him, almost one and a half year's wages if he could get a job. He didn't have the money. He didn't have a job.

Dimitri became despondent. One day he was sitting on a park bench near the Neva River outside the *Hermitage Museum* contemplating suicide. That seemed the only way to spare his family from the threats of the 'mafia', he thought. As he was sitting there an elderly American woman came running up to him, sobbing that she had become separated from her husband and didn't know what to do. Instinctively, Dimitri, who speaks wonderful English, began questioning her. They were part of a tour group gathered at the edge of the park ready to leave, but her husband had not returned. Dimitri was able to locate him and reunite him with his wife and the tour group. That being accomplished he went back to his park bench. One of the Americans in the tour group came to thank him. Noticing that Dimitri seemed despondent, the man asked what was wrong and if he could be of any help.

It was, Dimitri told me, the first time in his life anyone had ever shown any interest in him and his feelings. Normally a very private person, he poured out his situation to the stranger, with tears. The man consoled him, then left. A few minutes later the American returned, gave him $200 and told him to pay off the 'mafia' and go back to his family. He gave him a Bible and pointed out several marked passages he thought would be of help. It was the first time Dimitri had ever held a Bible in his hands. He went back to his apartment and began reading. That very night Dimitri and his wife Natalia embraced Christ and the Christian faith. His life had been changed.

The reason Dimitri wanted to tell his story was that he wanted me to assist him to come to America and go to Seminary. He wanted to be trained for the ministry in order to bring the message of the Gospel back to his people. I was moved by his story and promised to do what I could. Eventually he was able to make contact with the man who had given him the $200, attended Seminary in Florida, and returned to St. Petersburg.

All this to say that the Word of God is one of the most powerful elements at work in the new Russia. For three generations the Bible had been kept from the people. Mainly it is only the oldest citizens of Russia who remember things religious or spiritual. Most people had never even seen a Bible. By the time of our 1993 visit there were few remaining restraints on the Gospel message.

Our choir distributed 700 Gospels of Mark and 200 Bibles to our host families, churches, and other people we met in Russia. I told my students any time someone did them a favor, or treated them kindly, to give them a Bible. As we recounted our tales of distribution, three responses seemed typical. First, recipients would press the Bible to their chests, smile from ear to ear, and continue following the student until that was no longer possible. Second, they would immediately sit down wherever they were and begin reading. The third response was weeping; a Bible was a long forbidden treasure!

Olga, our Russian translator and tour manager, observed us giving Bibles to our hosts as well as people on the street. We had several long conversations while traveling between cities. She herself had never had access to a Bible. Her parents had gone along with the Party line for fear of recrimination. God was never mentioned in her home. Like so many of the Russians we met, Olga was naïve about the Christian faith. She knew none of the stories so commonplace in our experience. She had no understanding of the claims of Jesus or who He was. She only knew there was such a thing as Christianity, but knew absolutely nothing about it. Olga had many questions. She was open and inquisitive in our conversations. Day after day she observed us in our concerts, our attitudes, our behaviors with each other and the people we met along the way. More than once she mentioned how different we were from other groups she had accompanied. She sensed power in the music we sang. But, always the professional, Olga maintained her business-like demeanor. On our very last day, as we made our way to the train station in Moscow to set off for Estonia, Olga put her professionalism aside while we sat together on the bus for the last time. I asked her to deliver several Bible Commentaries to the *Temple of the Gospel*, and gave them to her. This opened the door for her. She said,

"I know your choir has given many Bibles to people here in Russia. Is there a chance you have one left for me?"

Little did she know I had saved one just on the possibility that she would ask, and had already written a note to her inside the cover. I said a silent prayer over that Bible as I handed it to her. The choir had planted a seed. It is up to God to look after it.

Crossing the border into Estonia was like breathing fresh air for the first time. Though the Estonians had lived under Soviet rule for fifty years, and had seen the disintegration of their economy and infrastructure like all the others who had been enslaved, it felt different. Hopefulness was everywhere. In St. Petersburg physical decay was abundant; in Estonia renovation was taking place at a rapid pace in spite of the lack of funds. Had we gone to Estonia from Sweden we would have felt like we were stepping backwards into a more deprived situation, but coming from Russia Estonia was more like home. And we were ready for home!

Messiah with the State Symphony of Estonia

Our final concert in Philharmonic Hall with the Estonian State Symphony Orchestra, again performing *Messiah* after fifty years of absence, was magnificent. What a great way to end a most exhausting, exhilarating concert tour!

I was indeed proud of our choristers and their commitment to the music and its ministry. They were wonderful representatives of North Park University, America, and especially the Christian faith. It was touching to see how they embraced and cared for people we met along the way. And they cared for each other. I never heard a cross word between singers. Even though they suffered from jet lag, different beds every night, strange cultures, occasionally unpalatable food, lack of sleep and the stress of concerts night after night, I never heard them complain. As tough as it was, they knew that any Russian would gladly have traded places with them in an instant. They, and I, came to realize how truly privileged and blessed we are in our lives. I think we have come to appreciate the many things we formerly took for granted, not the least of which is our heritage of the Christian faith.

God is still at work in the world. We saw the results of His powerful actions first hand. And in a very real way we had become, for a brief time, His instruments and messengers of His glorious Gospel.

CHAPTER 50

Another Commitment Call

It had been fifteen years since the near demise of North Park and my remarks in the hastily called Chapel to address our concerns as a faculty. Whatever commitment we made to expressing our faith in the context of our teaching had once again faltered. In late February of 1996 the question of the integration of faith and learning once again was under consideration at 'Community Day' on our campus. It seemed the majority opinion was that matters of faith should be left to the Religion faculty; it was a reprise of the dilemma of the early 1980's with the same flagging result. Some of us were disturbed by the dialogue. What did it reflect about our wavering commitment to the faith we professed? I again felt the necessity to express what I had spoken in that earlier Chapel and had an article published in the March 1, 1996 College News:

Community Day offered the opportunity for dialogue and increased understanding of our increasingly pluralistic campus, for which I was grateful. North Park benefits from this wonderful cross-section of cultures and faiths. However, such diversity presents a challenge: "What does it mean to be a Christian College with an open admissions policy?"

Freedom. *North Park has a 'special calling' to accept students of any or* no faith posture. I support the openness and freedom we allow students to choose or not choose participation in the religious life on campus. However, we have chosen the most difficult way, both in terms of how we comport ourselves as Christians and how we hold on to our mission.

How can we maintain students' freedom while remaining true to our Christian mission? How do we respect student diversity without dishonoring Christ? Coercion is not the answer. Nor is spiritual laxity. If anything, the more we insist on 'freedom' for our students the more disciplined must be our Christian example and witness.

Faculty freedom and commitment. We as faculty and administrators do not honor either our students or Christ if we profess to be a Christian institution and then proceed in the 'name' without any visible evidence. It is not enough simply to 'show respect and concern for students', a statement on our Teacher Evaluation Form that has been misconstrued as evidence of Christian teaching. To be the best teacher one can be is the call of the profession itself and contains nothing distinctively Christian. Any dedicated teacher would have those qualities, whether Buddhist, Muslim, Hindu, Atheist, Christian or any other.

We profess to be men and women of the Christian faith. To acknowledge the Christian faith and be in agreement with the Mission Statement of the College places a corresponding responsibility to proceed with the commitment in tangible and definitive ways. Surely we must at some point have considered how our academic disciplines and our faith impact each other! Surely we must have discovered ways in which to demonstrate our Christian faith within the context of our own particular disciplines! We have the responsibility to bring the same zeal to both our academic disciplines and our Christian profession. Anything less is dishonest.

Freedom to be Christian. If we insist on students' freedom to choose *what they want to believe, shouldn't the institution be allowed the same freedom to be what it is called to believe, and fully so? To respect another's opinion does not mandate putting a wet blanket on your own. Christianity inhibits freedom only when it is dogmatic, and acts out of coercion and insensitivity instead of love.*

North Park has tended over the years to remain relatively silent in its mission for fear of offending those of other faiths. Consequently, we are asking of ourselves what we would not ask of others who take their faith seriously—that is, to live a watered down commitment to a watered down faith. The New Testament is critical of such 'lukewarm' Christians.

Students know North Park is a Christian college but they come anyway for a variety of reasons. They're willing to 'put up with' our Christian stance for the sake of the excellent education they'll receive. No one has been deceived. It amazes me, then, that we are so apologetic about participating in our mission. Are we or are we not a Christian institution? If we truly are, and manifest it with sensitivity and love, our students will respect us for our seriousness of commitment, even if they don't ascribe to it themselves. We will have been faithful to our call, and God will honor our faithfulness. However, if what we say we are and what we actually demonstrate do not harmonize would we not merit our students' contempt?

'Freedom' can easily degenerate into license or laxity if it is not marked by discipline in our commitment and courage in our witness. Apart from our Christian calling to serve God's purposes in the world through Christian higher education there is no special reason for North Park's existence. Perhaps we drift aimlessly because we have not taken the initiative to define what we mean by 'Christian faith'. It is imperative that we discover the essential basis of what it means to be Christian, without confusing or muddying the foundation with petty dogmas or

personal preferences. We can live with many denominational expressions as long as there is one Lord with whom we agree and on whom we depend.

Freedom in Christ. *We say we believe God exists. We say and believe Jesus Christ is the Son of God, just as he claimed. A true God doesn't lie: we have no choice but to accept his claims and his teachings. If he was not the Son of God, but just an honest, upright, decent, moral person, we could use his life as a model while disregarding his words about forgiveness, salvation, and eternity; the Christian faith would not be special, distinctive, or unique, and we could keep our belief to ourselves. This question of who Jesus is constitutes the knife-edge dilemma of faith for those who call themselves Christians. He said his way was narrow; he said he was 'the Way, the Truth, and the Life', not one among many. These are hard words, especially in our pluralistic world, but to be Christian is to acknowledge them as true and the basis of Christian belief. He also commanded us to love our neighbors. If we really love our neighbors and believe the words of Jesus are true, would love be exercised by withholding the truth? Would not our silence constitute a condemnation of those we profess to love? Christians are called to witness with a loving heart and a compassionate spirit. Such a life as this is not offensive, but compelling.*

When men and women of all other religions are compelled to live out their faith openly, honestly, respectfully, compassionately, and unabashedly—and we become provoked when they don't—should Christians do less? Are we so concerned about the path to a so-called 'campus harmony' that we are willing to abandon Truth? We wouldn't consider being intolerant of others' beliefs; we wouldn't tolerate abandoning Truth in our disciplines; why would we tolerate abandoning the Truth of our faith? Tolerance is not a one-way street.

According to our Scriptures, belief in Christ, acceptance of his teachings, and heeding his call to be 'witnesses' constitute the 'freeing path'. May we follow it as we continue to welcome and embrace men and women of other faiths who live among us, and who, as part of our community, have become our 'family'.

CHAPTER 51

1998: Departing North Park
All Good Things Come To An End

Even at the half-way point of my thirty-second year on the North Park faculty, five years after our trip to Russia, I was unaware it would be my last. I was simply continuing my work in the classroom and rehearsal room, and enjoying every minute of it. Retirement had always been off my radar. I loved teaching. I loved rehearsals. I loved touring with my students. My off-campus engagements were stimulating. Friendships with colleagues and my students were immensely satisfying and fulfilling. I was lucky to have my job and was keenly aware of my good fortune every day, and knew there were many musicians more qualified than I who would give anything to hold the job I had. It had long been my intention to continue on without interruption; often I said, purely in jest, mind you, my goal was to stay on doing what I loved until I dropped dead in the middle of a Beethoven lecture! What happened mid-year in 1998 caught me by surprise.

Yes, on the surface my life at North Park, both on and off campus, was rewarding, but only one promotion in nearly thirty-two years had been tough to take. In North Park's history no one had come close to that ignominious record. I had waited nine years for my first promotion, longer than anyone in North Park's tenure-track history. Now I had waited another twenty-two years.

I had fulfilled all that was asked of me. My initiatives were all successful with little if any outside financial assistance or other support: the Academy Varsity Singers; the Chamber Singers; the Early Music Consort; the Chamber Orchestra; Arts in Chicago; the first Foreign Study project; the first foreign music tours in a quarter of a century; all the fundraising to support each of those programs; every tour ending with a surplus. I had re-invigorated the College Choir after its great disappointment in losing their former conductor. In addition, my student classroom reviews were stellar, and my collegial reviews were among the highest on the faculty. I was the Music Department's 'point person' for building the new Anderson Chapel, working with the architects and acousticians as well as the denominational panel assigned to the task. The Chapel project was a huge success. I served one semester as interim Fine Arts Coordinator during Karen Bauer's sabbatical and received high praise for my work.

I often had waiting lists for my *Introduction to Music* classes. Some students who had taken the class as freshmen asked permission to sit in on the classes in their senior years, wanting to end their undergraduate programs with what they thought was a valuable summation and cohesion of all they had studied. I had the reputation of 'making cultural connections' and assembling the 'loose ends' of their educational process. Many called the class *Lessons in Life*. Hardly a week went by during my three decade tenure without a note or two of gratitude or thanks, signed or anonymous, tacked on my office door.

1998: Departing North Park All Good Things Come To An End

President David Horner, whose musical tastes were somewhat limited, was nonetheless pragmatic. Though music was low on his personal priority list, he recognized the denomination's keen interest in hearing our performing groups, and voiced support for our touring agenda (though no financial or planning support). His son, center on the basketball team, was one of my *Introduction to Music* students. One day the President called me,

"What are you doing to my son?"

Knowing that many of the campus athletes resented having to take any Fine Arts courses, I wondered what I might have done to upset his son Mark.

"I called my son's dorm room. When the phone was answered I heard Classical music in the background and hung up, thinking I had misdialed. This couldn't be my son. He won't go near Classical music. I dialed once more. Again I heard Classical music, and then my son came on the line. I asked him what he was listening to. 'Mozart', he said. I asked why. He told me that listening to Classical music while he studied helped him focus his mind. I thought you might like to know you've made a convert in my son."

My 'academic portfolio' should have been sufficient to be promoted to Full Professor. In addition I was awarded the *Sears-Roebuck Foundation "Teaching Excellence and Campus Leadership Award"* (now called the *Zenos Hawkinson Award*) in 1990, the second North Park faculty member so honored, and one of 700 college/university faculty members nationwide to be recognized. Regarding the award, Provost Robert Johnston wrote to the faculty,

Professor Athnos has been an important member of our music faculty since 1966. In addition to consistently superb classroom instruction, Greg founded a chamber orchestra, founded and still directs a chamber

singers group that has travelled internationally, and he presently is director of the College Choir. The choir's historic tour of Poland and Hungary last summer was the single result of his efforts. North Park's success is dependent upon such outstanding faculty as Professor Athnos. We salute him.

The *Faculty Personnel Committee Report*, when addressing my *Evaluation for Promotion to Full Professor,* included a number of recommendations that should have cemented my request for promotion. My Chairperson's report stated:

[Mr. Olson] is highly positive about Mr. Athnos' teaching abilities and accomplishments, and also about his overall contributions to the college. Noteworthy comments include the following: "His classroom performance is brilliant"; "It is impossible to say any one person is invaluable to the school, but Greg comes close to that"; "Most of the new ideas from the Music Department have come from Greg."

The committee's final recommendation read:

Mr. Athnos is one of the most effective teachers on the North Park campus, particularly in his capacity to arouse a high level of student interest in music and to integrate faith and learning. He is also one of the campus' most creative thinkers and innovators of new approaches and programs. In his work at North Park he has given unsparingly of his time and efforts to the college, to the point of considerable self-sacrifice. This campus community has been his life and he has greatly enriched it.

In light of the above, the final line of the recommendation was baffling:

Therefore, the Committee recommends that Mr. Athnos be promoted to Professor contingent upon the completion of his doctorate or its equivalent.

In spite of every issue that spoke to my competence and my standing with students and faculty, I was not promoted. I had started the doctoral program at Michigan years earlier, completing most of the course work, but decided not to continue. I felt the time away from North Park was not commensurate with the value from doctoral studies to be used in my classroom teaching. As I spent most of my class time with non-music majors very little of what I researched would ever be usable. That was not a good trade-off in my opinion. I would benefit, both in title and salary, but my students would not, and they were my highest priority. So it was never my intention to go back.

Furthermore, faculty members are subject to the *Faculty Handbook* under which they were hired. In the *Handbook* operable at the time of my joining the faculty in 1966 the doctorate was not a prerequisite for promotion to Full Professor. I suggested to the President that two of my colleagues in the music department, hired under the same *Handbook*, had been promoted to the highest rank without a doctorate. I possessed exactly the same credentials, and perhaps surpassed them in contributions at large to the institution as well as its national constituency. The President was determined to discount the *Handbook*; he wanted everyone on the faculty to have doctorates.

As if lack of promotion wasn't enough to frustrate me, for several years leading up to 1995 I had been asking for financial support to run the choral program. To that point I was receiving about $1000 a year, a ridiculously insufficient amount. Whatever money was needed for tuxes, dresses, music, and tours was my responsibility. That had not been the case before I became director of the College Choir; for my predecessors the institution had financially supported the program completely, and the Development Office planned and financed the tours. All that changed upon my promotion to the position for reasons that were never expressed.

Now I was asking for assistance. I wanted the equivalent of 'one tuition', about $15,000 per year. That was not enough for an organization considered the 'calling card' of the institution, but it was at least a start. I was asking for less than ten percent of what they gave the football program for eight games a year. My request was denied.

For about three years I had continued asking and received no response. In frustration I needed to get away from North Park, at least for a short time to reassess my situation. I talked with a former student of mine who was in charge of the *Scandinavian Studies Program*. North Park had a relationship with a Folkhögskola in Jönköping, Sweden, and sent one teacher each year to prepare Swedish students for the semester they would spend at North Park.

It turned out the exchange teacher for the following fall had backed out. I took his place. The fall of 1995 my wife and son accompanied me to Sweden. Doy and I would share the teaching while our son Trifon went to a Swedish Elementary school in accordance with Swedish law.

In my absence North Park hired an interim director for the College Choir. They decided not to ask him to be a fundraiser for the program and gave the choral program twice what I had been asking for and thirty times more than I had been receiving: $30,000! Furthermore it was decided that whatever remained at the end of the year would roll over into an accruing fund so that foreign tours would require less fundraising. That had also been part of my request. I had raised over $200,000 for the two foreign tours in 1989 and 1993. North Park's action was thoroughly upsetting.

While in Sweden the fax machine was getting a great workout

1998: Departing North Park All Good Things Come To An End

between North Park and me. Upon my return would I receive the same financial consideration as they were now giving to my replacement? North Park made no commitment to me. I could no longer take this two-pronged denial: no promotion and no funding of my programs. I sent a fax resigning from the directorship of the Choir.

Returning to the campus in January, 1996, I worked closely with William Snell, my replacement who had now been appointed Interim Conductor. I determined to be of whatever assistance I could to help him make the transition. I liked Bill. He appreciated my help.

That Spring marked the 50th anniversary of our yearly Orchestra Hall concerts. Only one organization other than the Chicago Symphony had sustained such a record; it was to be a monumental celebration. I had looked forward to leading the Choir in that event, but my decision to step aside brought the dream to an end. However, I was asked to write a script for the evening's celebration; it was a small consolation for what had promised to be a grand evening. While I took the stage as moderator for the event, it wasn't the same as mounting the conductor's podium.

Unfortunately, the string of fifty consecutive years of Orchestra Hall appearances was broken in the Spring of 1997.

In late Spring of that year, 1997, I was called into the President's office. He was getting complaints from choristers and others. Bill wasn't working out for the institution.

"Will you take the choir back?"

"You know I didn't resign from the choir because I didn't enjoy it. I loved working with them. I resigned because of a lack of financial assistance.

I'll take back the directorship under one condition. You must continue the practice instituted for Dr. Snell, giving the choral program $30,000 each year with the surplus rolling over for future use."

The President, the Academic Dean, and my Department Chairperson were in on the arrangement and the agreement was made. The following school year, 1997-98, I took the reins of the choir once again. The foreign tour plan I had put in place in 1989 with tours every four years, was set back by two years. We would delay our trip until the spring of 1999.

In the fall of 1997, after resuming the position of Choral Director, I asked my Chairperson to check on the balance of our account. We estimated that the money left over from Bill's last year, coupled with what had been saved from the previous year and what was anticipated for the current year would come to approximately $75,000. Adding the next year's stipend would total over $100,000, greatly diminishing the fundraising for the proposed tour to Korea and China. The next day Karen Bauer called me into her office. She appeared upset; that was not a good sign.

"There is no money in the account. Not one dime. They say we misunderstood the agreement. They intended to give us $30,000 each year as 'seed money' to be paid back as we progressed in our fundraising."

She knew as well as I that such an agreement was not made. The Academic Dean knew it as well.

I had also resumed pursuing promotion since returning to North Park from Sweden. Now there were two issues to work through.

Both issues plagued the last months of the 1997-98 school year. I sent notes to the President. I had meetings with him. It was not easy to maintain a positive attitude, but there were two domestic tours to plan as we approached the end of the semester: a Midwest tour for the University Choir and a California tour for the Chamber Singers. In addition, we had resumed our appearances at Orchestra Hall, now called Symphony Center. It would be our 51st concert in that hallowed space. There was a lot on my plate; I soldiered on.

A chorister wrote me this letter following the choir's March tour:

Dear Greg, It has only been two days since our return from the tour, and already I miss it more than any vacation. The spiritual high that I experienced towards the end of last week and the weekend was indescribable. You may not remember, but during the Rochester concert you looked at us and said, "We're very close to Heaven tonight." I keep coming back to those words as a reminder of how close I did feel to Heaven. The feelings that I have had since our return Sunday night can only be described as symptoms of withdrawal. When I finally got back to my dorm I was filled with so much excitement and joy that I couldn't even sleep. I rode my bike half way to Lake Michigan simply to expel some of the excitement within me. On Monday it was difficult to sit through my classes without the music drifting into my mind.

I cannot wait until the next time we perform this concert. It is such a thrill to worship through this music that has become ingrained in my soul. Thank you so much for the opportunity that you gave me, and the whole choir, to be a part of this tour. It is only my first year at North Park, but I feel that I have much to look forward to as a member of the choir and I am excited to see what the future holds for us. Yours in Christ, Stephen Sharkey [Steve went on to Seminary and then to the Pastorate]

The Chamber Singers had received an invitation to sing on the nationally televised morning services of Robert Schuller's *Crystal Cathedral* in California, and we built our tour around that invitation. This time North Park assisted in raising the money to fly our singers to the West Coast and rent two vans. The remaining expenses were my responsibility. We scheduled concerts each night in churches, with home-stays, starting in San Francisco. We worked our way down the coast, arriving in Los Angeles Saturday night.

Early Sunday we arrived at the *Crystal Cathedral* for the first of two services in which we would sing. Standing on the Chancel steps we began our first piece: the double-choir composition *Sing to the Lord a New Song*, by the Baroque composer Heinrich Schütz. It was a setting of *Psalm 98*, the same Psalm my father had read every morning while sitting at our kitchen table. When we ended, the congregation leaped to their feet and gave the group a thunderous ovation. I thought it unusual for a worship service. The same thing happened at the beginning of the second service as well.

Before we left, the Chairman of the Music Committee came to the Green Room to thank the singers. Pulling me aside, she asked if I knew their Music Director and Organist, Frederick Swann, was leaving the church. I had heard that several days earlier in Oakland. She said,

"We called a quick meeting of our committee between services, and they authorized me to ask whether you would consider applying for the position."

I told her I had a good job, but thanked her for the honor of being considered.

We left for San Diego and a series of concerts. I began to rethink her offer. North Park was ignoring my requests for financial support and promotion in spite of my exemplary career. I had proved myself for thirty-two years! Yet after hearing only three pieces of music by the Chamber Singers, and witnessing two standing ovations, the *Crystal Cathedral* wanted to pursue my talent for their program. The irony was not lost on me. While I'm certainly not worthy of being called a prophet, nonetheless that passage from Scripture about a prophet not being honored in his own country crossed my mind.

The *Crystal Cathedral* was on the way to our next concert as we headed back north from San Diego. I called the Chairperson suggesting a meeting with them. She wanted me to meet with Frederick Swann, who was campaigning for me to be his replacement.

Yet another 'swan' intersecting my path? I needed to pay attention.

During our meeting he cleared up my curiosity about the standing ovation:

"Do you know why your singers received a standing ovation? My Chancel Choir, seated behind you, seemed disinterested when your small group of college students took their place on the chancel steps; they were busy with each other. When your group began singing the Schütz double choir motet they sat bolt upright with their eyes wide open. When you finished they leaped to their feet, and the congregation followed. It was my choir that started it."

He said that of all who had applied to replace him, I was the person he wanted to recommend to the committee. Again, I was flattered, but still felt committed to North Park and my students. For all this to be happening—on the heels of my frustrating yearslong request for promotion and the refusal to honor an institutional promise to contribute subsidy for future tours—struck me as a microcosm of the lack of respect the leadership of North Park had for my work.

We returned to the campus; the school year was over, and summer would give me time to think. A few days later a letter arrived from Neva Penner, Worship Service Director, Crystal Cathedral:

Please let me say Thank You one more time to each one of you for joining us at the Crystal Cathedral.... It was a great performance in our morning services of worship and the prelude was so inspiring! .... You did an outstanding performance on "I'm Goin' to Sing", and "Steal Away"...and "Sing to the Lord a New Song".... Dr. Schuller and all of us who are involved in the planning of the services want to express our appreciation to you for sharing your wonderful talents.... May God richly bless you.... Sincerely in His service, Neva Penner

I had been asked to at least send a brief *bio* to the *Crystal Cathedral* music search committee, which I did, with no intention of doing anything further.

I received a letter dated June 16, 1998, from Mr. Swann:

Dear Greg: It was a distinct pleasure for me to meet and talk with you. I must tell you again how personally satisfying it was to have you and your fine choir sing for us. The Search Committee...wanted me to convey to you their deep appreciation for the consideration that you were willing to give to the position here....

As it turns out, in spite of my lack of pursuit of the position, I was one of three candidates in their final 'pool'.

I continued to speak with North Park's President about promotion. I was told when I completed the doctorate it would be granted. He knew that at age sixty-two I wasn't going back to school.

1998: Departing North Park All Good Things Come To An End

A sad decision

The silver swan, who, living, had no Note
When Death approached, unlocked her silent throat.
Leaning her breast against the reedy shore,
Thus sang her first and last, and sang no more:
"Farewell, all joys!..."

I had sung this Orlando Gibbons Madrigal on numerous occasions with my Chamber Singers and also with a small choral group I conducted at the 1967 International Summer School in Oslo. I knew it well; it was perhaps, from a musical standpoint, my favorite madrigal. Little did I realize how poignant the text would be in my decision regarding North Park.

For Gibbons, in his *First Set of Madrigals and Motets for Five Voices (1612),* the text was a commentary on the loss of the Elizabethan musical tradition in England, a metaphor depicting the end of an era.

For me it represented mourning over the decision I was about to make, and the loss of something that had been dear and precious in my life. How tragically fitting that my metaphor embraced another swan! My first encounter had forged in my tender mind a desire to bathe my life in the art of music. The second swan of importance in my life, confronted in a Finnish forest, had prepared me for a long and rewarding career at North Park. Another swan pointed me toward the joys of fatherhood following closely on our discovery that Doy was pregnant. Now, the fourth swan was, incongruously, prelude to an ending. I saw my entire life bracketed by the music that emerged from that magnificent, regal creation.

After a performance in the Warsaw Castle

It was my thirty-second year at North Park, my thirty-first year with the Chamber Singers, and my twelfth as conductor of the University Choir. It would be my last. I had felt 'called' to North Park, and many God-ordained confirmations of that 'call' over the years cemented my loyalty and commitment. I decided on the spur of the moment in August to leave North Park and enter into an entirely new phase of life and ministry. To have come to such a conclusion after having determined early in my career that North Park was 'my life until death' only underscores the immense and profound depth of my frustration and disappointment; I thought I deserved better. It was simultaneously enormously heartbreaking and freeing, in that order. I couldn't control my weeping as I bade farewell to my beloved student musicians.

Thy hope, thy confidence let nothing shake;

All now mysterious shall be bright at last.

Those words came back to me. Just as they had hinted at my future by the grave of Sibelius in 1965, so now, thirty-three years later, they were sealing the door to my past and offering a glimpse of a new hope for my coming years. I need not fear, they whispered:

In every change He faithful will remain…

1998: Departing North Park—All Good Things Co...

Be still, my soul: thy God doth undertake

To guide the future as He has the past...

I left my tears behind in H-23, the rehearsal room so much a part of my life at North Park—a place of musical and spiritual growth, a haven of delight with my musicians, a sanctuary where words and music formed a chemistry that changed our lives—tears that washed away the hurt of the recent past while watering the seeds of my future. I trusted God's promise.

Before I made this monumental personal decision a note came to me from Linnea Holmgren. It was almost as if she had a premonition of my departure, perhaps even before it registered in my own heart. Her words were, and remain, a comfort and consolation:

Dear Greg,

I know I told you last week that you have been one of those people to make a real difference in my life, but there is just nothing like a personal note. You know, I heard about you for years before I actually really got the opportunity to know you. I can remember listening to you talk about the catacombs or about resurrection scholarship—and in you I saw modeled a man dedicated to God, to his faith, to his wife and family, and to the passion God has given you for music. I saw that same passion visibly in choir during numerous rehearsals. I always knew walking into choir rehearsals that I was entering a time of praise and worship and that was never more evident than when you would remind us of the words we would form in our mouths. I have learned dedication and determination from you.... I can tell you that my life has been touched and marked in a way that will not easily leave me. You have influenced the person I continue to become, and for all of these reasons and more, I thank God for you and am eternally grateful to you. With my love, Linnea

; Rollo Dilworth for several years, preparing University Choir in the (unlikely) event I re-ed mentoring. He was a wonderful person as usician and colleague. On his first day in the 'ark once again began doing all the tour plan-ne $30,000!

The word of my leaving North Park traveled quickly. Perhaps the most heartwarming letter came from a former colleague from the English Department, Dr. Peter Fellowes. Peter had been a very quiet and subtle influence on me through his gentle spirit and his poetic heart. It had been a great disappointment to me and a great loss to North Park when he left to take over his family's business. Peter wrote,

Dear Greg, During my first year at North Park I formed a prayer in my heart before it ever became a prayer, that I could come to possess the radiance of spirit I saw in you, know the love of God I felt in your presence when you talked of music, performed it and otherwise expressed your faith. I don't know how close I got, but I do know that I took hold of my own faith with greater confidence and gladness knowing you.

This memory came back to me as I read the story of your retirement.... I couldn't help be sad at the thought of your leaving…knowing how many lives besides my own you have touched with a blessing over 32 years. God bless you, good friend.

CHAPTER 52

Reflections: What Post-Modernism Tells Me

Whatever was to come of my 'new life', I determined to continue my quest for 'wholeness' and the search for spiritual union between my profession in the arts and my personal profession of faith. North Park had allowed me such a union because of its declaration of faith as a guiding principle. Would I find it as easy in the secular world? I was soon to find out.

The Scriptures implore us to worship God *"in the beauty of holiness"* in every endeavor, in season and out of season, sacred setting or secular. This wonderful phrase seems to suggest a union between the aesthetic and the holy. Beauty is not enough; yet spirit-filled holiness needs the halo of the beautiful. We are 'scripturally commissioned' to seek their union, the same union Bezalel was commissioned to create in the building of the Tabernacle.

I believe this union is slowly being reclaimed in our day. The Postmodern world, in spite of some of its less desirable tendencies, is turning away from faith in Reason alone and is beginning to recognize the mysterious nature of the world. There is an emerging shift

he symbolic. People of Faith in our post-mod-
racted to the beauty of God and His creation
he existence of God.

aul II, in his 1999 *Letter to Artists* urged artists to,

…use your creative intuition to enter into the heart of the mystery of the Incarnate God and at the same time into the mystery of man.

He suggested that the artist's central image of beauty should arise from God's incarnation of Himself in the person of Christ. He wrote,

God is the Creator, and Artists are Craftsmen whose vocation is beauty.… Insofar as it seeks the beautiful…art is by its nature a kind of appeal to the mystery. Even when they explore the darkest depths of the soul or the most unsettling aspects of evil, artists give voice in a way to the universal desire for redemption. (Pope John Paul II, <u>Letter to Artists</u>, 4 April 1999, Regeneration Quarterly 5, no. 4, pp. 9-12)

Art, then, for Christian artists and musicians, is a calling to acknowledge the Supreme Creator who gave the gift. It is a calling to release the hidden powers within His creation with the best of the gifts He has given us. Such gifts as these carry with them an ordination for excellence. Such gifts are an anointing, as stated in God's charge to Moses in Exodus 28: 41, that the Priests, or the spiritual leaders of the people, be anointed, ordained, and consecrated to serve *Him*. God is our audience and we are gifted and set apart to lead people to Him "*for glory and for beauty*". We must fully recognize that creativity and artistic expression were not afterthoughts in the mind of God, nor were they in the actions of His chosen people. Above all, art is a calling to be surprised by the joy of the wind in the tall grass of all we create and know that it is not we, but God who sings! Our creative spirit is *from* God, *of* God, and has the power to lead us back *to* Him in reverence and praise.

Soli Deo Gloria

CODA: Reflections
1998 –

*Codas are optional endings intended to put an exclamation point on the inspiration that precedes them.
In my story the end has not yet been reached.
Rather, this 'Coda' exclamation point brings to an end simply the longest theme of my life.*

*Another Symphonic Exposition is being formed.
There are more themes to discover,
and I desire the wisdom to see God's plan at work in them.*

*That young boy,
peering over the balcony rail with visions of music's thrall,
has become the old man seated on the stage,
drawing the bow across the strings,
prompting the sweetness, tasting its harmony,
fully possessed of it,
never letting go.
Wonder of all wonders. Blessing of all blessings. I am he.*

CHAPTER 53

Reflections

North Park was now in the shadows. A new light was being created by my future. Looking back, I had been one of the most fortunate of men to have held my position at the college, and I knew it and gave thanks for it every day of my thirty-two years on the campus. The journey had been circuitous in some ways but straight-line direct in others. There was a 'Hand' greater than mine at play along the path; I felt it to be of God. I learned far more than I taught; I received far more than I gave. In some small yet profound way I had felt compelled to honor my calling and attempt to live up to it by acknowledging in my life and work that it was indeed a 'call'.

At North Park, in my own frail and feeble way, my desire was to stand in the shadow of God and express the beauty of His creation. I asked myself, *"Can I give Him every corner of my own creative heart?"* Whatever gift I had been given, it needed to be returned to the Giver; that was important to me.

I chose to seek and attempted to find the 'holy fire' latent in every facet and ingredient of art and communicate it to my students. I didn't want to ignore or walk away from the *'burning yet unconsumed bush'*; it was critical that I seek to embrace its mystery. My students came to expect more than just the facts, figures, and theoreticals of the subject matter. Every day for thirty-two years, as I walked the bleak Chicago alleys on the way to my office, one question was paramount: *"What is the most important 'life' concept to be imbedded in my teaching today?"*

Always willing to seek a better way, I chose to dance to the silent and elusive *music of the spheres* rather than stumble along the common, the ordinary, or the predictable path. *"What good questions did you ask today?",* words of wisdom from boyhood friend Terry Sharp's Jewish immigrant mother, caused me to be open to new modes of thinking about art and life. Bezalel was my model; his story in Exodus was an inspiration to me, and I knew God always is seeking someone who will give himself to His cause. I wanted to be such a person.

Even as, when a child, I crossed that gravel road on my Uncle Enoch's farm seeking the welcoming hay of his music-filled barn, so in my career at North Park I sought to leave behind 'earthly parlors' for a greater magnificence.

Desiring, yearning, feeling compelled, choosing, questioning, hoping, seeking joy—what greater motivation could there have been? God alone will judge how far along that path, by His grace and His alone, I have journeyed.

In our human arrogance and *hubris* we tend to see the cosmos through the eyes of our position in it. So easily do we see ourselves occupying the center, in total control of our destiny, when in truth we do not and are not. I fell prey to that same self-imposed seduction and delusion. Gradually, thankfully, I came to realize just how small and insignificant I was in the total scheme of things, while recognizing at the same time my life was intended to have purpose, to be of consequence. It was as if I had revisited that crisp Fall night in the northern Wisconsin woods, staring up at the vast accumulation of stars and thinking myself nothing; being aware of my nothingness confirmed to me that I was 'something' in the mind and heart of God. It was, you might say, my 'Boethius' moment. To be 'something' and 'nothing' simultaneously seems the ultimate 'God Plan'.

I knew then and know now that my path was not of my creating. I knew then and know now that I was not called to be successful, though I gave it everything I could. I was called to be faithful. Was I? Often, not. And when I was, did it make a difference in my life? Did I make a difference in the lives of my students? Was North Park a better place because I had given a third of a century and half my life to it?

Seeking answers to those questions, I thought back to my father and his '*eat in harmony*' philosophy.

His favorite Scripture, a great influence on his life and his treatment of others, was *Psalm 98*. It contains clues—mercy, salvation, the sea, and music—that reflect on his ocean crossing, his love of people, and the naming of the *Eat in Harmony Café*. He read it every morning out of his King James Bible:

O sing unto the Lord a new song; for he hath done marvelous things: his right hand, and his holy arm, hath gotten him the victory. The Lord hath made known his salvation: his righteousness hath he openly showed in the sight of the heathen. He hath remembered his mercy and his truth toward the house of Israel: all the ends of the earth have seen the salvation of our God. Make a joyful noise unto the Lord, all the earth: make a loud noise, and rejoice, and sing praise. Sing unto the Lord with the harp, with the harp and the voice of a psalm. With trumpets and sound of cornet make a joyful noise before the Lord, the King. Let the sea roar, and the fullness thereof; the world and they that dwell therein. Let the floods clap their hands: let the hills be joyful together before the Lord; for he cometh to judge the earth: with righteousness shall he judge the world, and the people with equity.

The sea had indeed roared in his crossing to America. His companion younger brother Athanasius had been denied entrance because of illness and died on the way back to Greece. The Atlantic is his burial ground. Yet my father had learned to 'sing' the praises of his new home and to show mercy as a reflection of the mercy God had granted him.

Each customer was like a brother to him, the brother he had lost in the crossing—now there were a thousand Athanasiuses. Countless regulars walked through the door that had the sign prominently displayed over the entrance that read:

'Through this door walk the greatest people in the world—my customers"

For nearly forty years the *Eat in Harmony Café* was a haven for nourishment of the body *and* the soul. He employed both his great talent and his heart. Then his health declined; he sold the restaurant. Within two years it ceased to exist. Why? The food may have been just as good, plentiful, and inexpensive, but something was missing: was it the aura of congeniality, good humor, and the aspect of 'harmonious gathering' that had given birth to his restaurant's name?

Stomachs crave refueling within hours. The feeding of souls lasts a lifetime. That 'silent music' of the soul being fed departed with him. Now, more than fifty years later, only a handful of elderly citizens remember Louie and his *Eat in Harmony Café*. Only two people who ever worked there are still alive: my brother David, and me, Louie's son, who manned the cash register and poured water for the Negro Leaguers that insisted on eating at the 'Harmony'. I last worked there in 1955, sixty years ago. While writing this book my mother passed away, just one month after her 104th birthday. She worked at the 'Harmony' in 1929, and later that year married the owner.

The 'Harmony' exists only in the historic register of the community, but no longer in the hearts and minds of the people. Was, then, his service for naught, just a blip on the radar screen of the ages? Did he change the world? Not really. Not much. Did he contribute to changed lives of those who sat a few feet away from his short order grill and kibbitzed with him while he scrambled eggs and flipped pancakes? Yes. Often. Did they, in turn, pass on his 'philosophy' in their own spheres of family and influence? Would anyone in succeeding generations be able to trace their manner of living and loving back to that Greek immigrant and his dreams of Ellis Island and the Lady in the Harbor? Who can measure? One only hopes that service and sacrifice have meaning beyond what can be weighed by the standard scales of society. That was his hope, and mine as well.

I would not inherit the restaurant business, nor would any of my brothers. He wouldn't have wanted us to follow his path. His desire was that we pursue the 'gifts' the 'Giver' of all good gifts had showered on us. He knew and was proud that music was my 'gift' and was to become my 'feast'. He knew I would spend my life serving it to others – 'flipping' and 'scrambling' the Bachs and Beethovens of history with a side order of faith. We both hoped the musical feast would be delicious.

Just as my father enthusiastically served the downtrodden of the Depression and welcomed the socially outcast Black American athletes to sit at his tables, so too I wanted to work with and inspire the musically lacking, the musical 'underdogs'. I would choose to impart my love of music to those who might not have envisioned their lives could be made more beautiful by partaking of it; it would be my determination and my joy to share its transforming power. I preferred that my university teaching colleagues produce tomorrow's performers. I determined to prepare their future audiences. The 'consonance' of music as well as its great nourishment to the soul became the inspiration behind my pursuit of life itself. I served a different banquet, hopefully equally satisfying. I think my father was deeply pleased by my choice.

I most certainly was affected by his life. I took upon myself the mantle of his philosophy, inspired to honor his life by translating it into my own professional 'language'. I hope I learned his lessons well and provided 'music for the soul' bathed in pools of 'harmonious living' with the transcendence only faith can inspire.

All I know is that our deeds—my deeds—are soon forgotten and lose their connection with their originator. Even these short seventeen years after departing North Park I walk on the campus totally unknown by the current students and remembered only by the few remaining colleagues from my generation. It serves as a humbling reminder that we are smaller than we think. My personal legacy is ephemeral, and remains alive only in the hearts of those whose lives were touched as I sojourned among them. And, over time, none will remain. Thankfully, many of my 'initiatives'—Chamber Singers, Orchestra, Foreign Study Programs to name just three—remain part of the university's curriculum, continuing to bless and inspire today's and tomorrow's students. They exist on their own merits, now separated from their 'initiator', led by other gifted people, and that is perhaps as it should be; I take pride and comfort in their continuation. Slowly I have come to realize that if life is for the living, then North Park is for its contemporaries.

Eat in Harmony

The fundamental lesson of service is marked not only by the effect it has on others, but also in how our own lives are impacted by serving. Using that barometer I was well served through giving my life to North Park. My life was changed by North Park; that is reward enough. I heeded the call of those 'swans' I encountered along the way beginning at age four; they were signal-post markers along my God-ordained journey. I pray God will continue to broaden my path, lengthen it, and inspire me to continue without wavering to explore it, because I have so much yet to learn, and still so many '*qvestions*' seeking answers. I pray I will never run out of 'swans'.

Eat in Harmony, my father said, and life will be full. I say the same.

> *And that will be heaven*
> *And that will be heaven*
> * At last   the first unclouded*
> * Seeing*
>
> *   To stand like the sunflower*
> *Turned full face to the sun   drenched*
> *   In light   in the still centre*
> *   Held   while the circling planets*
> *   Hum with an utter joy*
> *   Seeing and knowing*
> *   At last   In every particle*
> *   Seen and known*
> *   And not turning away*
> *   Never turning away*
> *   Again*
>
> (Evangeline Paterson, born 1928, 'And That Will Be Heaven')

CHAPTER 54

Looking Forward: Life After North Park

Following my departure from North Park University I was determined to continue in my desire to encourage people in the arts. No 'recliner' for me! What had been 'extra-curricular' for me during my years at the university now became central to my life. As it turns out, the past seventeen years have been consumed with everything I had been involved with at North Park; now my involvements are for people outside the institution. Lectures on art, working with choirs, leading tours to Europe, offering seminars on Catacomb Art and Resurrection—the very 'stuff' of my university career and more—continued. Every 'passion' that had driven my life heretofore was now part of my 'new life'—a 'recapitulation' of my career, so to speak, but more than that. A 'coda' in a manner of speaking, but not an ending. Yes, I look back; that's the prerogative of age. Yes, on occasion I reflect in gratitude for previous accomplishments. But I am also being 'born anew': all things of my life past and present were coalescing and forming a new future. As my dear and loving wife said,

"Greg took his 'show' on the road!"

CHAPTER 55

2008: China and the Pre-Olympic Festival

When I left North Park I assumed my conducting days were finished. That realization was bittersweet. I had to admit to myself I was blessed beyond measure to have served as conductor for nearly five decades, over three of them at North Park. Mine had been a completely rewarding and exciting life; the goal I set in my youth had been achieved. My North Park concerts numbered just over one thousand appearances in almost half the states in the U. S., and seven foreign countries, including appearances in major cathedrals of Europe, guest conductor experiences with the Chamber Orchestra of Pushkin, Russia, and the State Symphony of Estonia, twenty-five concerts on the stage of Orchestra Hall in Chicago, and five in Minneapolis Orchestra Hall. People wondered why I relinquished so highly valued a prize. I confess to having had similar questions.

Life was going to be vastly different and I wasn't sure how I would respond. I knew teaching remained part of my future; I already was engaged in many lecture venues off campus and planned to continue with them. It was that 'hole' created by vacating the conductor's podium that concerned me. It wasn't only the performances; I had always loved the preparations, the rehearsals, where we as a team explored the depth of the art and the power of the texts, seeking to discover the 'chemistry' between them. Might I find myself regretting my decision to retire, weeping over the loss?

My answer came rather quickly and it eliminated the worry over the questions. I was in a new church. The Minister of Music and Worship discovered my expertise and asked me to form a Chamber Choir to sing the sacred Classics. I readily agreed. We began with a group of about twelve singers; all of them were wonderful musicians, excellent readers, and fine singers. After several years the group had grown to about twenty-five. We rehearsed twice a month, just enough to enjoy without becoming a burden or putting a crimp in my lecture circuit. We sang one Sunday each month. They loved singing together. They loved leading worship. They loved our rehearsal times, and there was little they couldn't master in our limited schedule. The pressures were far less than at the university, the quality lesser as well, but the joy remained undiminished. I was doing what I had been gifted to do.

Then another opportunity arose; one that I almost turned down because it involved traveling to China.

China was the last place on my travel radar. Throughout my entire life I have not had an interest in the culture or music of the Far East. Put me in any museum of the world and I will walk right past the Asian collection without pausing for a single moment. I'm a Western civilization guy. That was my training. That's what I taught in secondary schools as well as the university. My world didn't include anything outside the western hemisphere. To my surprise I ended up in China! It became one of the most significant cultural and religious experiences of my life. How did it happen?

The Majesty Chorale was formed in October 2005 as part of the Majesty Multi-media Ministries. The Chorale had as its purpose ministry among the Chinese immigrant community of Chicago. Through the efforts of Mike Chan, President of both the Ministries and the Majesty Chorale, the organization was invited to participate in the China Pre-Olympic Festival during the summer of 2008. Professional groups from various countries around the world had been asked to participate by the Olympic Cultural Committee in Beijing. Here was this small, totally amateur group of Chinese immigrants that had just recently been formed. How did they manage an invitation?

Mr. Chan worked for the Immigration Office in Chicago and knew several of the staff persons at the Chinese Consulate. He inquired whether his group would be welcome to submit an application. As the conversation continued it was revealed that the Majesty Chorale was a Christian group and sang Christian Sacred Music.

"Would that be allowed?" he asked.

"Yes," was the response, *"provided you can justify that every piece you sing is representative of Western culture."*

That's hardly a Mount Everest to be conquered. The group began its preparations immediately after this formal invitation was extended:

Dear Mr. Chan,

This is indeed my great pleasure to extend our official invitation to the Majesty Chorale (or the Heavenly Sound "Tien Yue" in Chinese) to participate in many cultural events as prelude to the opening of the 2008 Olympics between June 23rd and July 15th, 2008.

We are pleased to learn that despite your recent formation, the Majesty

2008: China and the Pre-Olympic Festival

Chorale has already distinguished yourselves at a concert last October, attended by over 1,300 people in the Chicago metropolitan area. We are also quite impressed by the fact that the Majesty Chorale uniquely consists of Chinese Americans and Caucasians representing a wide spectrum of the American multi-ethnic population.

We look forward to your visit to China. Together with other international cultural entities, we would like to cultivate the spirit of world peace and good will between our people, as well as with many other countries.

During the festival, the Majesty Chorale will be featured to present your repertoire in Beijing, Tsingdao and Shanghai, joining other international groups in a series of cultural events to build up the momentum for the opening of the 2008 Olympics in China. Therefore, we eagerly await your arrival in 2008 to participate in this significant event that promotes international friendship.

Sincerely yours,

Wang Xiuqin, Deputy Director; Cultural Exchanges Division, China Performing Arts Agency

Then a near derailment took place. In 2007 their director resigned, and my name surfaced as a possible replacement. One of the singers said to the Board, *"I think my Bible teacher's husband is a musician."* They told her to check me out, and an email was sent asking whether I would be interested. As I had never been interested in cultural China my intention was to decline, but not by an email return. Seeing they had taken the trouble to find me, I thought the least I could do, the honorable thing, would be to meet them face-to-face and graciously remove myself from consideration. I met with their Board in Chinatown.

When I saw who they were, and began to understand their hearts for ministry, something registered in my own heart. I knew a number of missionaries who had served in China. I had followed somewhat closely the persecution of Christians around the world, particularly in China. I had read numerous reports of the explosive response to the Christian Gospel in spite of all attempts to repress it. When I realized their main purpose was to attempt to use their participation as a ministry opportunity I said an enthusiastic 'yes'. This would constitute an opportunity to see the explosion and repression of Christianity first hand. In the end it was not the culture and art of China that drew me; rather, it was faith and mission. Returning home I told Doy of my decision and she was shocked. For nearly a year between that moment and our departure for China she was exceedingly nervous; so was I.

We rehearsed once each month in Chinatown, Chicago, and as we moved closer to departure date we added more rehearsals. There were no professional musicians in the group. They simply loved to sing and loved to share the Gospel of Christ. The first few rehearsals were unremarkable to say the least. Diction, vocal color, and all sorts of other musical issues seemed insurmountable, as the Chinese vocal culture appeared incompatible with Western choral traditions. Changing the musical culture of the group was a tall order. These dear people were wonderful and willing to do whatever I asked, even when it seemed counter-intuitive to their background and musical understanding. Little by little they became a cohesive group. Whatever musical shortcomings remained were overshadowed by the enthusiasm and great heart behind their singing. Additionally, they had a huge advantage over non-sectarian singers; the words and the lyrics were part of who they were and what they believed. The 'sounds' came from another place, deeper and more profound. They didn't only sing the music; they lived the music. They *became* the music.

2008: China and the Pre-Olympic Festival

Our chorale consisted of twenty-two singers, about two thirds of them Chinese and the rest Anglos from my Chamber Choir at North Suburban Church in Deerfield, Illinois. Adding assistance in a variety of ways were five adjunct tour members: Doug Adams, who facilitated our daily schedule; Sarah Chan, Mike Chan's wife who served as our photographer; Betty Neerhof, wife of one of our singers who served as a most important prayer warrior; Dr. Stewart Yu, a retired Chinese doctor and evangelist; and Doy Athnos, my wife, who led us in daily devotions. Most of the Chinese were native Chinese speakers; that was to be of tremendous importance in the success of our ministry in China.

The Chinese Olympic Festival Committee had originally been open to our singing Sacred Music from the Christian tradition. As we drew nearer to our departure date they changed their minds. Apparently they feared an 'incident' would spoil their 'coming out party' to the world. There had been various demonstrations in the months leading up to the Summer of 2008, most prominent among them the *Free Tibet* movement. Now they began to take a closer look at this 'Christian' group from Chicago. Would we cause havoc over the perceived (and actual) suppression of the Church in China?

The email exchanges began. They stated we could sing no religious music at all—only two Chinese folk songs and one American Patriotic song. Though we argued this point in daily emails for the last three months before the Festival they would not be deterred. Our correspondence, emails from both sides, built up a huge dossier on our group. They really wanted to disinvite us, but didn't. To do so would be to 'lose face', something unacceptable in Chinese culture. They thought their insistence and our growing frustration would cause us to cancel the trip, saving them the disgrace. In one exasperated email they came close to breaking their cultural 'rule':

"Perhaps you would feel better if you stayed home."

And we almost did. Why should we spend all this money only to sing three pieces of music, and none of the sacred repertoire that had been the motivation behind our participation? What would the absence of Sacred music do to our ministry? Besides, three pieces is not a concert.

God gently caused us to realize we had been arrogant to think that ministry could take place only if we did it. I became convicted by my own lack of faith and, in humility, wrote this letter to the singers:

Dear Members of the Majesty Chorale:

Let me encourage you in our 'Mission' to China next summer. When we received the recent notice that our program had been put 'under the microscope' and that it might have to be changed, it was for me a bit disconcerting. But after thinking about it I have come away with a renewed commitment to our God-ordained ministry. Yes, it is God-ordained; how else could we have come this far, gathering sincere mission-oriented Believers from all over the greater Chicago area!

Two things have become paramount in my mind and heart: first, we need to serve our 'mission' to bring the Gospel to people in China; and second, we need to maintain our 'integrity' as a Christian chorale. I have felt from the beginning that while we wanted to proclaim the Gospel message through our Olympic Festival concerts, our greater role, far greater, would be in the ministries outside the Festival. That is still my feeling. While our program will of necessity be restructured to satisfy the concerns of the Festival organizers, most of it will remain intact. And the music we've been working on that will be removed from the Festival program will still be used in other venues. So, it is only in the Olympic venues that our program will change, but even then, only slightly.

2008: China and the Pre-Olympic Festival

In any case, whatever program changes are made one thing remains clear in my mind: We are God's ambassadors no matter what music we sing. We are called to be His witnesses. And if we are called, can we doubt that God will work in us and through us? Our ministry will, by God's grace, be powerful, and we must trust that the Holy Spirit will work in 'mysterious ways His wonders to perform', in spite of whatever attempts are made by the China officials to inhibit the message. God's message cannot be 'inhibited'; it is already at work powerfully in China. And we must also trust that in the opportunities we have with individuals at other occasions of ministry we will be able to share directly, one heart to another—strike the flint and let the Holy Spirit fan the flames.

So be encouraged. This is God's work, not ours. What we bring with us to China is 'full hearts' surrendered completely to His will and purpose. Share what you've been called to share, then stand aside, and see what God can do.

Your Director, Greg.

The Chorale voted to proceed with our plans and turn the ministry over to the working of the Spirit of God. It was the perfect decision; we were to become witnesses to God's power in daily miracles.

On our first full day in Beijing we had the privilege of attending a *Three Self Church*. The *National*

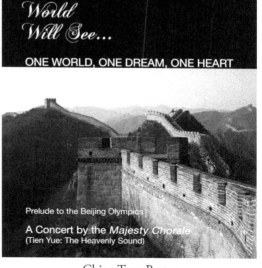

China Tour Poster

Committee of the Three-Self Patriotic Movement of the Protestant Churches in China is a Protestant Church movement in the People's Republic of China. They form the only state-sanctioned Protestant Church in the country. *Three Self* refers to the principles of self-governance, self-support independent from foreigners, and self-propagation. There can be no proselytizing outside the walls of their church, nor can there be any political discussion or dissent. We were told government spies are usually in attendance to verify compliance. The *Three Self Gangwashi Church* we were to visit had seen their Pastor literally dragged out of the pulpit during a worship service because of his breaking of the rules.

For months our request for this visit had been stonewalled by the Olympic Festival Committee. On the eve of our departure from Chicago we were granted permission to visit on a Thursday night: Youth Night. When we arrived about 45 minutes before the service was to begin, there were dozens of Chinese on their knees praying for the service. Apart from the leadership of *Gangwashi Church* no one knew we would be in attendance. By the time the service began the sanctuary was crowded to capacity. Latecomers were seated in an adjacent hall. Over 600 were there—on a Thursday night!

We sang a few hymns early in the service. Before the sermon the Moderator stood up and asked the congregation a question. I was seated toward the front of the church along with several other Anglos from my choir. We thought he asked, *"How many of you are here for the first time tonight? Please stand."* Over one hundred rose to their feet. *"Impressive and exciting,"* we thought. We later learned from our Chinese singers the full extent of the question: *"How many of you are here and for the first time are ready to express your faith in Jesus as your Savior?"* Fully one-fifth of those gathered stood to signal their desire! God was indeed at work, and I think He wanted us to see it and take confidence in His presence with us.

2008: China and the Pre-Olympic Festival

What an explosive way to begin our mission, and it was just the first day. There was much more to come.

Our second day in China we visited the Great Wall which was blanketed by dense, choking pollution. It's impossible to describe the enormity of that fabulous and stunning man-made creation. What impressed us daily, and it was on full display here at the Great Wall, was the friendliness of the Chinese people. I had not expected it. All I knew of China was what was available on the TV news and in journals: a provocative, authoritarian, militaristic presence, a Chinese version of the Russian "We will bury you" rant by Krushchev at the United Nations some decades earlier.

At the Great Wall of China

I was moved by what I observed here. They almost seemed 'Italian' in the way they drew close as they spoke quietly to me, gently touching my forearm or my shoulder. It was a gentleness and softness both disarming and endearing, and I found my heart softening in its attitude toward the Chinese people. I should have known from previous forays into 'enemy' countries, the Soviet Union first and foremost, that people are people. We have the same desires. We share the same hopes and dreams for lives of peace and security. Sadly, ideologies build walls and create enmity that keeps us from the brotherhood of humankind intended by the Creator. I was once again being reminded of this fact by the kindness of these Chinese 'strangers'.

Our concert schedule was about to begin. There would be nine concerts total. Our first performance at the *Concert Hall of the National Orchestra* was with the impressive *Harbin Military University Alumni Choir*.

Online photos of the *Alumni Choir* dressed in their Military uniforms circulated around our group the month before our departure. Very intimidating! Then, when we heard them in their rehearsal we were even more intimidated—enormous voices, filled with power. Our impression was that the Chinese Festival Committee wanted to completely blow away our small 22-voice Christian amateur choir. We would not be able to compete with their power or their size. We meekly followed them onto the stage for our own warm-up. I privately ruminated that we would be humbled by the musical comparison. To their credit they vacated the stage and sat in the auditorium quietly listening as we went through our procedures, clapping vigorously at each pause. Again I couldn't help being impressed with their genuine spirit of good will.

I had an idea. The final musical selection on our program was a famous and much loved Chinese folk song, *Mo Li Hwa* (Jasmine Flower), in a beautiful arrangement by composer and friend Gary Fry.

"Why not invite them to join us on stage after we've sung it to sing it again," I thought.

I went to the dressing room of their conductor and presented the invitation. To my surprise and delight he accepted.

My advice to our singers was to spread apart when they joined us so that their singers would be interspersed with ours in order to share the music. I told them that when the piece was finished they should do whatever came to their minds: handshakes or hugs, whatever felt right. I mentioned that if they felt comfortable sharing their Faith they should do so.

'Mo Li Hwa' with the Harbin Military University Choir

When the singing ended and the handshakes and hugs ensued it was magnificent to behold! Many from the audience, usually out the door quickly to get home, came up on to the stage to join in the celebration. No one wanted to be left out. The conversations lasted a long time, and I'm certain there was talk about the Gospel of Christ.

What had been intended to stifle our ministry by limiting our program to three pieces was really a gift to us. Had we been allowed to sing our entire program a second choir wouldn't have been added to fill out the time. Pairing us with a large Chinese Choir, intended to intimidate and overshadow us, turned out to be a powerful opportunity for witness. We knew that night God was in charge of our venture. If we had seen glimmers of it the night before at the *Gangwashi Three Self Church*, we saw it magnified this night. Imagine singing about a beautiful Jasmine flower with the *Harbin Choir*, men and women who, as former professors and students at China's most prominent Military University, had designed the weapons used by China, the perceived enemy of the United States!

Relieved by the success of our first concert venture we spent a lovely day at the foot of *Xishan Mountain* in Beijing visiting the Summer Palace. Originally called the *Garden of Clear Ripples*, it was built beginning in 1750 during emperor Qianlong's reign. The unique combination of natural beauty and exquisite architecture fully embodies the building style of ancient China's imperial gardens.

The Summer Palace in Beijing

An atmosphere of serenity permeates the scene. We were always attracted to the gentle, Confucius-like sayings we found at every turn: *Qianqing gong*, the Palace of Heavenly Purity; *Kunning gong*, the Palace of Earthly Tranquility; or *Taihe dian*, the Hall of Supreme Harmony. Most fetching was a statement which read:

A single act of carelessness leads to the eternal loss of beauty.

2008: China and the Pre-Olympic Festival

How true!

We marveled over the *Jade Belt Bridge, Longevity Hill,* and *Kunming Lake*. Inside a large garden was the smaller *Garden of Harmonious Interests*. Then there was the Grand Theater in the *Garden of Virtuous Harmony*, and a wonderful Covered Walkway. Reigning above the entire Summer Palace was the *Tower of Buddha Fragrance*. We loved the names, all of which were symbolic of peace and tranquility, hallmarks of ancient Chinese culture. The stark contrast between our pre-tour expectations and this pre-Mao picture of China was revelatory, and served as a prelude to yet another contrasting view of the real, contemporary People's Republic. The juxtaposition of 'China past' and 'China present' continually made us almost dizzy with confusion.

Finally, it was opening night at the new outdoor Olympic Festival Park. The event was to begin at 5:30 p.m., with the Majesty Chorale scheduled to perform at 6:30. When we arrived for a sound check

Greg and Doy at Olympic Park

there were about 40 people in orange T-shirts seated at the foot of the stage clapping plastic thunder sticks and chanting a short, recurring refrain. "*Such enthusiasm,*" I thought. They seemed immensely excited for the opening of the Festival Park, which heralded the official opening of the Olympic summer.

"Without the Communist Party there can be no new China"

As I stood smiling at the chanted refrain one of my Chinese singers asked me if I knew what they were saying:

"Without the Communist Party there can be no new China".

It appears they had been planted and organized to set the scene for the evening, directing the attention of the gathering crowd toward their political reality. Seated behind them were many officials from the government of Beijing. We think it was meant for intimidation, as they knew we were a Christian group. They needed to offset the potential conflict of ideologies.

Mike and I were introduced to 'Ashley'. She was the anonymous, unseen face behind all the intimidating emails of the previous three months. Here she was: dainty, petite, charming, smiling, eager to be photographed with us. Mike and I looked at each other and with a sort of subtle signal revealed our uniform impression:

2008: China and the Pre-Olympic Festival

Greg and Mike Chan with 'Ashley'

"Don't be fooled. This is one tough cookie."

We knew the battle would now be engaged in person. 'Ashley' would be tracking our moves.

An Olympic official approached me and said in fractured English, while shaking his finger in my face,

"Your group sing 5:30, not 6:30."

It appeared they wanted us out of the way before the park filled up. A few minutes later he returned and demanded, again wagging his finger at me,

"You introduce your group."

This was a dilemma; how was I to be honest about the Christian nature of my group without jeopardizing our concert mission? As I was trying to formulate my comments, he returned and shouted,

"You say nothing; we say."

It was apparent they simply didn't know what to do with this Christian group.

By now all our singers were submerged in a state of anxiety as they began mounting the stage. Their expressions were somber; what were we expecting after three months of e-mail intimidations, and now this, with the chanting and the wagging fingers?

The Moderator for the evening began his introduction, powerfully, and with a rather stentorian theatrical voice. All of a sudden my Chinese singers broke into smiles. Everything changed. It appears the Moderator had been given the *dossier* on our Majesty Chorale, thick with the reports and emails of our months-long battle with the Olympic Festival Committee. We think that without proof-reading anything he began reading the first page from the *dossier*— which turned out to be our first description of who we were and what our mission was! He read with great power:

"The Tien Yue (Majesty Chorale) is a group of Chinese Christian immigrants to Chicago USA, who have come to China to share their Christian message of love and hope with the people of China".

I would never have been bold enough to say that! It was only the first miracle of the night!

We sang our short program; it was met with great enthusiasm by the crowd. As a concession to our months-long request to have our entire program honored, they allowed us to sing two religious compositions. The first was a Mozart setting, in Latin, of a text praising the God of the universe and His Son. We decided the second should be Sir John Stainer's very familiar and much loved English setting of John 3: 16,

God so loved the world that He gave His only begotten Son, that whosoever believes in Him will not perish but have everlasting life.

To our surprise the Moderator granted our request that the texts of both pieces be read to the crowd in Chinese, and he did so in the same stentorian, authoritative voice. It was the second miracle of the evening.

Opening night at the Olympic Park in Beijing

We left the stage to prolonged applause and boarded our bus to leave. The second performing group was proceeding to the stage. Immediately a huge thunderstorm hit the park, wiping out the rest of the evening. Had the officials left our performance at 6:30 as intended we wouldn't have performed at all. As it turned out we were the only group the audience heard that night, and they left having only heard the 'good news' of Christ. What had been intended to stifle our ministry only served to shine a spotlight on it.

That was the third miracle and it reduced us to cheers, laughter, and tears as we sat on the bus, lightning flashing all around us. At that moment we knew beyond a shadow of doubt that God had taken full control of our mission. Everything would be all right.

On our last day in Beijing we participated in a worship service at the *International Christian Fellowship Church*. Needing government approval, these international congregations are nonetheless able to function without interference or control. They are open only to people showing their foreign Passports to Communist guards stationed at all the doors. No Chinese nationals can attend. The large gathering was made up of people from around the globe: businessmen and women, tourists or visitors to China, and others.

Gathered on our bus at the conclusion of the service we realized we were missing two of our singers. That was unusual, as the group had always been prompt. Mike Chan went to look for them. A few minutes later we saw the three of them walking out of the building, animated and smiling. Returning to the bus Kezia and Felicia, two of our native born Chinese singers, explained the reason for their delay. Upon leaving the sanctuary they each, spontaneously, turned to the Communist guards at the door and asked a question that, had it been asked by the church authorities and congregants, would have been cause to shut down their ministry:

"Has anyone ever told you about the love of Jesus?"

"No," was the response.

"Would you like to hear?"

"Yes." Then Felicia and Kezia told them the Gospel story in a nutshell.

"Would you like to embrace Jesus and become a Christian?"

"Yes." They knelt and each of the guards prayed a prayer of confession and acceptance.

This became a common theme throughout the trip. We found that most Chinese with whom we met had never heard about the Christian faith or the Person at the center, Jesus. No one ever refused to listen to the message when it was offered, one on one. Everyone embraced the message and the Person when the invitation was extended. The message of the Gospel is completely foreign to the Chinese, and offers them something completely missing in their own religious practices—hope for the present as well as for eternity. It appears that this powerful message is a universal desire of the human race, and here in China we understood why the Christian faith is exploding exponentially.

Kezia was an irrepressible witness to the merits of Christ. She never missed an opportunity to share from her heart. In our Beijing hotel she had been approached by one of the Bellhops; her slight features and more chiseled face caused him to think she was Japanese, not Chinese. He greeted her in Japanese. After a few formalities, Kezia asked the same question she asked everyone she met along the way,

"Has anyone ever told you of the love of Jesus?"

"No."

"Would you like to hear?"

"Yes," he replied, *"but not now. I'm on duty. I can come to work early tomorrow, if you like."*

Normally, that would appear to be a brush-off, but not in this case. The next morning, early, Kezia and the Bellhop met in a hallway and she shared the Good News. The Bellhop made the life-changing decision to listen to the call of Christ and become a Christian.

The morning of our departure from Beijing, as we boarded our bus, the Bellhop came on board. This had been his day off, but he had risen early and travelled from the other side of this enormous city to share a word with us. He thanked us for coming to China and then said,

"This was no accident that you came. You came so I might hear."

Tour Director Zhang Dongqiang "Dennis" became a Christian on our last day in China

The final person to respond to the message of Christ was one of our appointed Tour Directors, Zhang Dongqiang. "Dennis" made the decision to become a Christian on our last day of the tour, after many hours of subtle witness by members of the Majesty Chorale each day on

2008: China and the Pre-Olympic Festival

the bus. Wanting to improve his command of English, several of our singers sat with him and used the texts of our Sacred concert material as examples of understanding and pronunciation. Little by little he began to grasp the depth of the Gospel message. In a hotel room hours before our final checkout he embraced it for himself. He continues to grow in his new faith in Christ.

Leaving Beijing by train we arrived in Tsingdao and prepared for our concert in that city, site of the Olympic sailing events. Algae, driven by a storm from the China Sea, completely filled the harbor, causing concern that the events might have to be cancelled. Thousands of Tsingdao citizens, from children to the elderly, worked night and day, successfully, to collect it, clearing the bay. The sailing competitions were spared.

I asked Mike Chan what would happen if we began singing those Sacred Christian compositions the Olympic Festival Committee had banned from our program. Would we be stopped? Would 'Ashley' and the Committee refuse to let us continue in our concert schedule? Mike said he didn't know. I asked, *"Should we try it and see?"* Mike replied, *"Why not?"* We proceeded through our entire program. No one interfered.

I then asked what he thought would happen if we verbally translated our sacred music texts for our audiences (the Olympic Committee had refused to allow us to portray the texts in

Translating the texts of our Sacred Music

any form). Mike suggested we try that as well. We became a sort of theological 'tag team' as I delivered the message and Mike translated.

So beginning in Tsingdao we sang our entire program and began telling the audiences what the words said, and further, what they meant from a Christian perspective. Audiences seemed to listen carefully, and Mike and I became more and more bold as the concerts unfolded.

To our great surprise there was no 'push back' from any of the Festival authorities, including 'Ashley'. We shouldn't have been surprised; God had proven Himself active and present every step of the way, not only protecting us, but also providing opportunities for witness at every turn.

As I mentioned earlier, the Festival Committee had tried to overshadow the singing of the Majesty Chorale by putting very large and professional Chinese Choirs on our concert venues. They needed to build up the program, seeing they had intended to limit the number of compositions we were allowed to sing, eliminating all Christian texts.

Beginning here in Tsingdao we sang our entire repertoire. As it developed, we used that wonderful Chinese Folk Song *Mo Li Hwa* to invite the Chinese Choirs to join us at the end of our performances just as we had done in Beijing. Because it was the last number it opened the possibility for the Majesty Chorale singers to engage in conversations, often about matters of the Christian faith. We heard reports that many of our members were asking,

"Has anyone ever told you about Jesus?" "Would you like to know?"

As far as we could tell, everyone who was asked wanted to hear the story.

We saw again and again how the people of China are eager for a message which gives them hope and joy. That is precisely what the Christian faith is all about, and why it is making great headway in that magnificent country.

Our concert in Tsingdao was in the *Song and Dance Theater*, a venue completely out of the center of the city and difficult to find. We had the feeling the place had been chosen thinking no one would be able to find it. Wonder of wonders, the room was packed! We were joined by another very outstanding Chinese Choir, conducted by Jian Sru Yao. I introduced our program:

We have been privileged this week to experience Chinese culture, its long and great traditions, and its friendly people. And we are pleased to be in your beautiful city of Tsingdao. Since arriving yesterday I see this is a city that loves music: you even have a music park, Ying Yue Guang Chang, filled with sculptures of China's greatest composers. We in the West are not familiar with them, but I'd love to hear their music that has contributed to your great traditions. I'm very impressed to discover you honor them. We in America could learn from that.

We also have wonderful composers who have given beauty to our own Western culture, and we want to share some of their music with you tonight. Many of our finest composers have taken their inspiration from the Judeo-Christian foundations of Western culture.

In our first section we'd like to perform several compositions from the European tradition. Mozart is one of the West's greatest composers, who lived in the late 18th century. This piece describes with power and glory the Judeo-Christian God and His Son Jesus Christ. The second piece in this section, by the English composer John Stainer, is a musical setting of the most important text from the Christian's Holy Book. It tells us that God sent His Son Jesus Christ into our world to take away its sin.

Finally, the last composition tells us how we can be lifted up from our trials and troubles through embracing God's Son.

After performing those three, we continued:

Part of our American tradition comes from the African-American Spiritual. Spirituals always speak of a longing for Heaven while struggling for survival in this world. I see you have a lighthouse, Dung Ta, on your island called Shiao Teechin Dao, or Violin Island. Lighthouses point those at sea toward a safe harbor. In this Spiritual we sing of a Lighthouse that the African-Americans thought would take them into a safe harbor. That Lighthouse for them was Jesus Christ.

Then, before our final section:

Finally, we have chosen music from the great hymn tradition in both Europe and America. The three hymns we have chosen have been sung by millions of Christians in Europe and America for two hundred years; they have been part of Sunday worship in churches all across both continents. In the first hymn [Great Is Thy Faithfulness] the text tells us that God is faithful to meet all our needs, whatever they might be. And because God is faithful, our souls are satisfied [It is Well With My Soul]. We conclude with one of the most loved hymns of the West, "When I Survey the Wondrous Cross", which describes the sacrifice of Jesus Christ, who gave up His life for us by dying on a wooden cross, and what His sacrifice means for the possibility of being forgiven. When Jesus was raised from the dead we were given the hope for a new life, an everlasting life.

Thank you for letting us share this music which is loved very much by all of my singers. We hope you will see on our faces that we believe these texts are true.

Shanghai was our final stop and location of our two final concerts with excellent Chinese Choirs: the *Shanghai Symphony Chorus*, conducted by Wang Hai Ling, and the *Shanghai Conservatory of Music Choir*, conducted by Wang Jin.

As we had done from the beginning, we invited the choirs to join us at the end in the singing of that wonderful Chinese Folk Song. My singers continued their practice of engaging our guest singers in hugs and 'conversations'.

I continued my introductory remarks to these most sophisticated audiences of the Festival:

Greg with Wang Jin, conductor of the Shanghai Conservatory of Music Choir

As you can see, most of the singers in the Tien Yue are Chinese immigrants to the United States. They were born and grew up in your wonderful culture and now have grown to embrace another culture as well. They love beauty, they love music, and they love God. And it is these three aspects that define our Christian Culture.

In Tsingdao those of us new to the Chinese culture were introduced to your traditional instruments, so different from our Western instruments. They play melodies based upon scales different from the scales used in our music. In the West half-steps are part of every scale and it is these half-steps that create a tension which demands a resolution. Your music avoids these tensions; the result is a sound that is 'untroubled', 'peaceful' and 'serene'.

In your museums of Chinese art we observed that your paintings separate physical reality from a greater reality. Your canvases leave room for visual 'silence'. There is great space between what is near and present, and what is far and other-worldly. Again, peacefulness and serenity are created.

Slowly I have begun to understand your traditions. I see how your traditions make you who you are. I not only have begun to understand your traditions, I also honor them.

In the West we too are defined by our history of art and music and religion. Tonight we'd like to share music that not only defines us, but also inspires us. It is the great treasure of choral music giving voice to the Sacred writings of the Christian faith.

Again, like yours, our art points to a greater reality—one which all my singers embrace. This is a reality that transcends the reality of the world around us. It is a reality of the 'spirit', a reality of the heart. It brings us 'peace', it brings us 'serenity', but above all, it brings us 'hope'.

Relaxing on our last day in China

On our last Sunday we sang our entire program at the *International Church in Shanghai*. The church was completely filled for both services. It was a wonderful experience for me to lead the congregation in singing the marvelous hymn, "Great Is Thy Faithfulness".

The theme of our China

mission is best depicted by the title my wife Doy gave her meditation at the *International Church of Shanghai*: *"Look what God has done!"* We truly saw God at work in this magnificent and daunting country.

I have given an account of the miracles that were poured out in abundance along our path. Often we find ourselves asking for miracles—or at least for God's intervention in our affairs—then seem surprised when they occur! That may have been true for our journey as well—at least at first. That thunderstorm at our opening Olympic event in Beijing changed the contours of our hearts. There was no mistaking it for anything other than what it was: an absolutely profound statement revealing the presence of God in our midst. It was our 'parting of the Red Sea' moment, and God continued to provide 'manna' in the wilderness of our mission in China, day after miraculous day.

The Majesty Chorale disbanded after our China experience. It was known that might be the case; after all, the group was formed essentially for that mission. We have met a few times for dinner and conversation, remembering God's blessings and miracles. Who knows? Sometimes we wonder if there is yet another mission to draw us together once again.

To think my 'europe-centric' arrogance almost caused me to miss this God-given and God-inspired gift! It was an honor, a privilege, and a blessing to be part of it.

CHAPTER 56

Milwaukee Art Museum Lectures

In the Spring of 1993 Clarice Zucker attended one of my Elderhostel weeks at Geneva Bay Center in Lake Geneva, Wisconsin. Clarice was a long-time Docent at the Milwaukee Art Museum, but I didn't know it at the time. Clarice mentioned my name to Barbara Brown Lee, Director of Education at the museum, suggesting me as a speaker for one of their weekly Docent meetings. It didn't take long before I received an invitation to speak on March 31, 1994.

What was I to say to the Docents? They knew more about the visual arts than I did. It became clear, at least to me, that I should adopt the role of fusing the arts and culture. Could there be a new way to look at art if seen through a cultural prism? Was it possible, for example, to see the visual arts more clearly by talking about music? Or philosophy? Science? Theology? I suggested such an approach to Barbara. She agreed we needed to give it a try and see how the Docents would respond.

My presentation was entitled, *"Debussy Sounds Like Monet Looks"*. The day came. The Docents turned out in great numbers, almost filling the auditorium. I had a fabulous time and I think they did as well. Clarice wrote me a very kind note:

My thank you note might almost be redundant as I'm sure you're still remembering the exuberant expressions of appreciation you received from all of the Docents. It took me forever to get out of the museum because so many people had to tell me how great you were, to be sure to have you come back, and to thank me for arranging your visit.

I mean it sincerely when I say that you are a world-class communicator. You had the group in the palm of your hand. And I meant it when I described you as a Renaissance Man—your knowledge across the arts is impressive!

President Horner of North Park received a letter from Barbara Brown Lee that she then shared with me:

Dear President Horner: We were privileged to hear a presentation delivered by Gregory Athnos on "Impressionism: Debussy Sounds Like Monet Looks", at the Milwaukee Art Museum. Mr. Athnos came to our attention because one of our docents, Clarice Zucker, heard him at Lake Geneva. Clarice has raved about his knowledge and skills as a presenter.... As Director of Education at the Art Museum, heading a group of 157 Docents, I want to compliment your college for recognizing the quality of Mr. Athnos' breadth of knowledge across all the arts, and his excellence as a communicator. Our Docents have been exposed to many fine speakers over the years and Greg Athnos is right up there at the top. We wanted you to know how much we appreciated this outstanding program.

Thus began a wonderful relationship with Barbara and the Docent group. I have returned to the museum almost every year since, sometimes two and three times a year, delivering lectures on the arts and culture. I continue to be impressed with them as well as challenged to constantly consider new ways of thinking about and responding to art. It has been a completely fulfilling and rewarding relationship.

Every lecture stretches me, and I spend months preparing. One lecture in particular stands out in my memory. The museum was hosting a collection of European works that had recently been returned to Poland after having been stolen by the Germans during the war. The central work in the collection was Leonardo da Vinci's *Lady With An Ermine*. Barbara told me to take some time to frame a topic for this challenging collection. Without hesitation an idea came to me; actually a complete title sprang into my head:

When I Can Fly What Will I Need To Know?
Leonardo da Vinci, an Aristotelian 'Misfit' trapped in a Neo-Platonic World.

Barbara loved it. After I hung up the phone I said out loud to myself, "What have I done?"

The next five months I sweat over that topic. I knew the essence was correct. Leonardo was a man of *this world*, a follower of Aristotle's vision of *real things*. The period in which he lived, the Renaissance, was infatuated with Plato's *Ideal World* and the *realm of the Spirit or the 'other world'*. Though no one had ever said as much, I knew this to be true; you could see it in the contrast between Leonardo's works and the works of those great artists surrounding him: Botticelli, Raphael, Michelangelo. And I knew that Leonardo's relative neglect by his contemporaries was in part a result of this conflict. The question was how to put it together in a lecture format to convince the Docents of the idea's merit. After five months it still wasn't making sense to me. Then, in the last week before my Milwaukee presentation it came thundering into clarity. I received a standing ovation for that lecture, and breathed a huge sigh of relief.

Other equally challenging lectures have included the following:

Before and After the Great War: Revolutions and Revelations (1900-1930)

Art of the Roman Catacombs: Mythology Transformed, Judaism Embraced, Persecution Defeated, Christianity Enhanced, Eternity Assured

Flaws and Gifts: Beethoven's Journey from Classicism to Romanticism

From the Crusades to the Black Death & the Edge of the Renaissance

The Road to the Renaissance:
Plato, Aristotle, Aquinas, St. Francis, Dante

Baroque Transitions:
The Irresistible Modern vs. The Immovable Traditional

From Sacred to Secular: The Rise of Instrumental Music
J. S. Bach and the 'Art' of Making 'Wrong Decisions'

Enlightenment: Returning to Classical Principles

Through a Glass Darkly:
Visions and the Shifting Foundations of Aesthetic Truth

Rembrandt's Prodigals and Samaritans:
The Realm Between the Colors, the Silence Amidst the Sounds

The Finite and the Infinite:
O, How the Cosmos Churned and Groaned at the Birth of the Modern World

After the Revolution--Another Revolution:
Life, Liberty, and the Pursuit of Individuality

Wassily Kandinsky:
The Man Who Heard His Paintbox Hiss and Listened to the Music

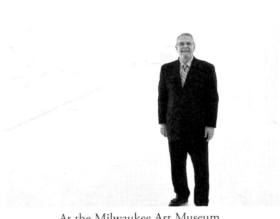

At the Milwaukee Art Museum
following one of my lectures

Barbara continued to invite me. I loved the opportunities to share with her Docent group. It is a privilege to speak to people who have knowledge of and love for the arts, and who are willing to consider new ways of thinking about them. And it doesn't hurt to receive compliments from Barbara!

As usual the Docents came away from your talk all enthused and excited. They rave about your lectures! We are so pleased you like to come and do this for us; you have so much to give and share.

And again,

How do you do it! Every time you come you are better and better—spellbinding! I have never known the Docents to give anyone a standing ovation! That is high praise!!! Thank you, thank you, thank you for giving us such a wonderful insight.... We love you! Barbara

CHAPTER 57

Elderhostel/Road Scholar Lectures

In 1974 two middle-aged men in New Hampshire were walking through a Dartmouth dormitory. Plastered on every bulletin board were notices of 'Youth Hostel' accommodations.

"Why does everything have to be for youth?" said one.

"Yeah. Why couldn't there be something for older people—elders like us?"

"Like 'Elderhostel'?"

And so the idea began. The first year, 1975, they established the program in several institutions of higher learning in New Hampshire. The essence of the program was educational. Intended for people over age 55, the program ran from Sunday evening to Friday noon. It included three lectures each day by three different presenters. Topics varied. Off-campus field trips were included, along with accommodations and meals. The price was reasonable. The program was an instant success.

The second year they decided to spread their wings and try sites across the country. North Park College had just hired a new administrator whose previous experience was in New Hampshire. He volunteered North Park as one of the 'Elderhostel' locations. When the request for teachers was announced I raised my hand. That's how it all began for me.

In the early years the program was confined to college and university campuses. Subjects were academic. Senior citizens attended in droves, but soon tired of sharing dormitory bathrooms 'down the hall'. Gradually the programs, though still sponsored by the universities, moved to other venues with private bathrooms.

The program expanded and now is international in scope with thousands of locations world-wide.

I am now about to enter my 40th year of Elderhostel teaching, having offered nearly 200 weeks of lectures on two of their sites: *Geneva Bay Center* on Lake Geneva in Wisconsin, and *Pilgrim Pines Conference Center* in West Swanzey, New Hampshire. Over those weeks my lectures, one and a half hours in length, total nearly 800, on probably 100 different topics derived from the *Arts of the Western World*. I've selected a sampling of fifteen topics with a few comments from participants.

"Musical Impressionism"

"I was spellbound"
"The best course I have ever had in analysis of musical composition."
"Outstanding in every aspect. Genuinely inspiring teacher, humanist, and philosopher."

Elderhostel/Road Scholar Lectures

"Go for Baroque"

"Learned more about music in this course than any in my lifetime."

"Greg is one of the best instructors at all of the Elderhostels we have attended."

"Western Musical Traditions, 1400 to the present"

"Magnificent! Electric! Inspiring. Inspirational. Well prepared. The hours flew by!"

"I have never heard a better presentation of a complex and complicated subject."

"I've majored in music, and none of my teachers made it so interesting."

"The Symphonies of Beethoven"

"A moving time - brought a familiar subject into a personal treasure."

"The most outstanding lecturer I've heard in Elderhostel or college."

"Vivacious in his presentation! His heart and soul is in his presentation each day!"

"Transitions in the Western World—Music and Art (double sessions)"

"A master teacher."

"It was a wonderful experience."

"Such an intellectual. Can make a potentially "dull" subject come alive."

"Musical Nationalism: From Crude Huts to Concert Halls"

"Among the few master teachers I've encountered in my entire

educational history."
"Greg Athnos is a spellbinder!"

"J. S. Bach: A Spiritual Man in a Secular World"

"A fantastic, enthusiastic teacher."
"He has a wonderful personality and comes across as a great human being."
"Excellent beyond belief. Want to hear more from this marvelous man."

"Musical Frontiers: From the Fall of Rome to 1600"

"Baroque Music and the Rise of the Modern World"

"The best music course I have ever attended."
"Outstanding in all respects. Great depth of understanding of subject."
"One of the best instructors I have heard in any environment, including three post-graduate degrees.

"Music & Art in the Western World"

"Able to communicate in layman's language. Stimulating."
"The perfect teacher."
"A truly gifted teacher. Bravo!"

Keyboard: Bach to the 20th Century

"I have run out of superlatives."
"Smashing."
"Athnos is a dazzling, brilliant teacher. I see a deep mind here."

Five Artists

"He is the 'best' of the best!"

"Creative program by a Renaissance man."
"Mesmerizing and truly learned and gifted. I love him."

Composers & Poets Look at War and Peace

"Perfect. Wonderful. Fervent."
"Enthusiasm is contagious."
"Is there <u>nothing</u> Greg can't make most worthwhile?"

Viva Italia

"Off the charts for excellence…the best."
"Fantastic. The best teacher I've ever experienced."
"So superb it changed my interest level in these 'arts'."

How to Listen to a Symphony

"Greg is absolutely the most outstanding and effective instructor I have ever heard."
"Wow! Perfection!"
"The greatest and most fascinating music appreciation presentation ever!"

Five German Composers

"Incredible. Perhaps the best teacher I have ever encountered. Speaks from the heart."
"Fantastic! I will never listen to the German Composers in quite the same way again."
"Absolutely outstanding presentation. Dynamic."

At St. Gauden's National Park, NH, during my Pilgrim Pines Road Scholar lectures

It would be an understatement to say that my involvement with *Elderhostel/Road Scholar* has been a delight. To teach subjects I love to people with a deep desire to learn is rewarding beyond measure. The old cliché, 'Education is wasted on the young', rarely applied to my college and university students; I was fortunate in that regard. Even more, Elderhostelers continually impress me with their zest for life and for learning.

I have been able to develop topics determined by my interest alone instead of those that must fit into a university curriculum. In this process I have continued to be a learner. I always told my students that when I ceased to be a learner I would stop being a teacher. Thank goodness, I'm still learning!

In 2005 Elderhostel celebrated its 30th anniversary year. As part of their celebration they decided to call it *The Year of the Teacher*,

Elderhostel/Road Scholar Lectures

and chose to honor twenty-four lecturers from across the country and from the thousands of instructors engaged in their program. Participant reviews were the sole criteria for selection. To my great surprise, and pleasure, I was selected, and was honored at a wonderful banquet in Chicago's *Natural History Museum*.

My goal is to continue in this program that has brought me such great personal rewards, and I'm praying that will be many years yet to come.

CHAPTER 58

European Arts Tours

Even before leaving North Park I took great delight in leading tours to Europe to talk about art and culture. That has continued. As with the tours of my North Park performance groups, I plan each itinerary along with the most important art venues. I have occasionally been invited by other university or community groups to accompany them on their performance tours as 'culture coordinator', taking interested students to major museums or art venues during their free time. On each tour my lectures cover the great artists and composers who lived and worked along the path of our journeys. Five itineraries cover the nature of my interests:

European Arts Tours

The Art Treasures of Italy: Venice, Ravenna, Florence and Rome

At the Trevi Fountain, Rome

In the Footsteps of Bach, Mozart, and Beethoven: Eisenach, Weimar, Leipzig, Prague, Salzburg, and Vienna

With Beethoven in Heiligenstadt near Vienna

Eat in Harmony

Gardens, Cathedrals, Museums, and Concerts:
Amsterdam, Brugge, Giverny, Chartres, Versailles, and Paris

Treasures of France River Cruise:
From Paris to Nice

Russia Revealed River Cruise:
Moscow, Uglich, Goritsy, Kizhi, Petrozavodsk,
Svir Stroi, and St. Petersburg

At the Summer Palace in St. Petersburg, Russia

CHAPTER 59

Author

Two books were self-published in 2011 through *Outskirts Press* after years of research beginning in 1974. They are available online or through any bookstore.

The Art of the Roman Catacombs:
Themes of Deliverance in the Age of Persecution

Every story in catacomb art is a tale of deliverance, of the powerlessness of death, and the certainty of the resurrection. This book, which includes more than fifty art plates, is an attempt to see these treasures as more than art; rather, as a theology of the early Church.

Reviewed by *Reader Views*, it was awarded 'First Place' in their *Literary Awards Competition* History category for self-published books from 2011. The review:

One would think that by reading a book about the art that adorns the Roman catacombs, one would purely concentrate on analyzing the style and technique of the ancient artists. However, author Gregory S. Athnos presents his thoughts on the subject from a unique and fascinating angle.

"The Art of the Roman Catacombs: Themes of Deliverance in the Age of Persecution" is not your typical Sunday school lecture.

"The Art of the Roman Catacombs" is an amazing journey into the subterranean world of early Christian tomb frescoes. While Athnos does make distinction between the rudimentary plaster scratchings and the sarcophagi carvings, he focuses mostly on the main themes of the artwork and how they differ from our current day Christian emphasis. Specifically, we tend to center our minds on the sacrifice—the crucifixion of Jesus Christ—when practicing Christianity. Athnos shows through example after surprising example that early Christians didn't include crosses or any references to sacrifice or death in their art. Instead, they emphasize the resurrection and the newfound power over death. The messages they left were of hope, of deliverance, and of eternal life.

I found the first appendix at the end of the book to be especially interesting. Athnos uses recorded astrological events, historical data, and seasonal information to pinpoint Jesus' birthday…and it's not what you think. I grew up believing what he explains although I only had the 'shepherds couldn't have been out in the fields at night in December' reasoning. Athnos not only presents this appendix with ample information to back up his theory but can even utilize the catacomb art to further justify it. I was simply blown away.

Athnos writes with an authoritative tone, speaking with intelligence and eloquence. His style is straightforward and organized which give the book a sense of direction and flow. He also succeeds in importing his enthusiasm on the subject to his readers. Overall, I found his novel way of interpreting the tomb art to be absolutely captivating. I think this would be a fantastic book for not only Bible historians but for small group Bible studies. Further, tourists looking to tour the catacombs would enjoy reading the book before visiting; I know I would have loved to have this before my travels there. It truly gives a fresh perspective on traditional Christianity.

"The Art of the Roman Catacombs" represents a thirst for greater knowledge, empathy for those early Christians living during the Age of Persecution, and a hope that those reading will have a better understanding of what the emphasis was in the religion's beginning. (Vicki Liston)

The Easter Jesus and the Good Friday Church: Reclaiming the Centrality of the Resurrection

"The Easter Jesus and the Good Friday Church" explores biblical evidence to support the centrality of the resurrection, and teaches readers how to read the New Testament with 'resurrection eyes'. What did the disciples believe about Jesus? What convinced them? What did Jesus have to say about his death and resurrection? What difference does the resurrection make?

Both books were also honored by *World Magazine* in their July, 14, 2012 Books Issue:

Authors send WORLD senior writer Susan Olasky about 200 self-published books each year, and twice a year she writes briefly about the 10 best.... Her list begins with two books by retired university professor Gregory Athnos, who traveled to Rome during one of his sabbaticals to study early Christian catacomb art. Granted access to the Vatican archives, Athnos discovered how early Christians emphasized the Resurrection in a way the modern church fails to do. In 'The Easter Jesus and the Good Friday Church' he unpacks a theology of resurrection. In 'The Art of the Roman Catacombs: Themes of Deliverance in the Age of Persecution', Athnos provides a guide through the art that inspired his research. Clear writing and illustrations make this an engaging guide to the art that arose from the early Christians' resurrection hope.

To my great delight, another honor was accorded *"The Easter Jesus and the Good Friday Church"*. In January, 2015, *"The Christian Author Awards Certificate of Achievement for 2014"* awarded the book First Place in the category of Theology.

CHAPTER 60

Others Look Back: Notes and Letters

Music 101: Introduction to Music"
"Creative Quality in Teaching"
from the 'North Parker', Summer, 1986

The following interview with one of North Park's creative teachers was conducted by editorial assistant Steve Elde

North Parker: *Greg, in your course "Introduction to Music", how do you make great music come alive for your students?*

Athnos: *This is the course I enjoy teaching more than any other. We have talented music majors and gifted faculty who can bring the best out of them, but these majors have nothing to look forward to if they don't have an audience. I attempt to create an audience for them by preparing the listeners of the future.*

In some cases I succeed, and in some I don't. Many of the students are taking the class because they have to. I acknowledge this on the first day of class because I realize most of them would rather be taking something more appropriate to their major. But I challenge them to think about what it means to live in this world by dealing with art and music.

It is my opinion that art mirrors life. Art has always been a mirror held up to its times, to the thought of its day, to those things most important in a particular age. By holding up that mirror to different periods in history we can better understand why we are where we are now.

North Parker: Do you bring together visual art and music as part of your teaching method?

Athnos: Many students tell me that the course should be called "Introduction to Life". We talk about everything. We talk about music, sculpture, and painting. We discuss poetry, literature, and theater. We talk about philosophy and science. Nothing exists in isolation, yet that's how courses are often taught. In my mind music isn't just frosting on the cake that you can do with or without—it's part of the whole fabric of existence. We look at art so we can understand life.

North Parker: How do you relate specific composers and their music to a period in history? At what point do I hear Beethoven or see Rubens…?

Athnos: Let me give you an example. When I talk about the Baroque period, I describe the general characteristics of that time: the thought of the day, what was happening in science, man's relationship to God…

North Parker: You provide a context.

Athnos: There is a context for everything. In the Baroque period we are dealing with a mechanistic universe where everything is orderly, everything organized. I ask, "What can you see in art that gives you a sense of this constant, swirling motion?" You can see it in the paintings of Rubens. You can hear it in the music of Bach—that machine-like drive. We look at the universe of atoms made up of particles, and then we look at a piece of music by Bach, discovering a tiny particle that's three notes long, and see how he created an entire universe of music out of those three notes. You see definite parallels between the painting, the music, and the thought of the day.

I always try to give my students the cultural framework, the intellectual framework. Then we hang the art on it.

North Parker: *In your course, then, you try to help your students see the integrated character of a period, to understand that nothing happens without something else also happening.*

Athnos: *Whatever barriers have been separating disciplines are artificial. Now, I would not like to undergo brain surgery by a surgeon who had studied the anatomy of the brain in the way I teach "Introduction to Music"! There are certain disciplines that have to be very specialized. I tell my students, "What happens in this class is not going to make or break your career. You don't need this to make a living, but it may influence what your career will become, and it will affect the quality of your life.*

North Parker: *You seem to take a personal interest in your students…*

Athnos: *I am interested in them. I'm interested in the quality of their life, in the fulfilling of their potential.*

North Parker: *There is a wholeness in your teaching. Art and faith come together…*

Athnos: *The very fact of creation is an example of wholeness. God made material substance out of his Spirit. Within the material substances all around us, within sound and paint, within stone and wood, is revealed the God who created them. An artist takes these mundane substances and reveals something of the Spirit. Art is the reconciliation of material and Spirit. In my teaching I try to bring them together.*

A Few Notes From 'Introduction to Music' Students

Dear Greg,

I just had to write you a note to thank you for Music 101 and to tell you how much I enjoyed it.... I've learned so much from your lectures—about music and LIFE!!! I looked forward to class everyday because no matter what kind of mood I was in, I would leave refreshed and positive. Some days it seemed as if God was speaking through you to give me new insights because of the tough time I was having with friends. Your "advice" was super and has helped a great deal. THANKS.

You have such a gift for sharing and inspiring—and use it well, knowing it is from God.... Thanks for all you put into it because what I'm walking out with, I could never repay. Thanks again. (Sue Chelgren)

Dear Mr. Athnos,

Music 101 has been the most enjoyable course I've had at North Park College, and, considering its scope, the most informative. Judging from my own experience, as well as from the remarks of others in the class, I think your efforts do not go unrewarded—both from the point of view of an increased appreciation of music and the students' very positive view of yourself. Your enthusiasm and genuine friendliness, among other things are not lost on most of them, and serves to increase their already considerable regard for you. You're due my sincere thanks for a course that has broadened me more consciously than any other I've taken at the four colleges I've attended in the past 22 years. Warm regards, (Brother Philip K., C.F.A.)

Dear Mr. Athnos,

Far too late I write you a little card from Europe. Still, I so very much want to thank you for sharing your great knowledge of music, but even more perhaps, for sharing yourself. Your words about "daring to be vulnerable" are so true; it is first when you wholly and fully dare to be yourself—good and bad—that you really live. You taught us all this in a very wonderful way—namely by being a good example. I really thank you for that. That you also opened the door to a fantastic world of music is also something I am so grateful for, as of course all of the other Swedish and American students are too. This was only a little, little thanks, but I hope I have been able to express some of the gratitude. With kindest and warmest regards. (Tina L., Swedish exchange student)

Dear Mr. Athnos,

Yes, it's hard to believe, almost frightening to believe what a good man you are. [Anonymous note left on my lectern after class]

Mr. Athnos,

A group of high school students from our church sat in on your Introduction to Music class during their pre-college weekend.... Your lecture on Beethoven was for me, and I believe for some of the young people as well, a real highlight of the weekend. Your outstanding lecture style made Beethoven into a very memorable person for me. (Director of Christian Education, Covenant Church, Lyndhurst, Ohio)

Dear Mr. Athnos

How can someone say that another person could produce a mind-shaking, dynamic explosion for them in just five short weeks? Your lecture on Beethoven's 'spiritual development' truly 'hit home'.... I felt as though I was plastered against the back wall.... At the end of your lecture I felt almost emotionally drained, but ready to really face reality. I think my basic reason for writing is, first, to show you the effect you have on people...and to say thank you. Sincerely, (Andrea M.)

Mr. Athnos

You're a very dynamic teacher because you have the gift of stirring our emotions and getting us to understand that 'gut feeling' deep inside all of us. Because of this you've gained the respect of every person in that classroom. I could tell that especially this morning because of the total silence as you were talking about J. S. Bach and his life...how we can relate to him in a way concerning important decisions that we are being faced with at this point in our lives.... Thank you for your witness and inspiration. Sincerely yours, (Carolyn Levander)

Mr. Athnos

You are truly a unique human being, one who believes that Life is made to live and to learn. Through your lectures your wisdom and knowledge is not taught or learned but sewn into young and eager minds so that the same thirst for knowledge is grown, and then cultivated.... You have rekindled the fire, so to speak, and once again, we 'live'. Love, respect, and friendship always, (Pat C. and Robbin S.)

Mr. Athnos

[A professor asked our group] what we were doing here. I couldn't answer that.... As the day went on that question must have gone through my mind at least a hundred times.... All of a sudden I felt very insecure...and I went out in the field last night and sat and cried.... When I walked into your class today I was pretty down. Then you started to put into words why you were here.... You brought everything back into perspective for me and I knew that God wanted me just where I am. I had lost sight of that in the confusion of these first few weeks. You are a very rare type of person.... You have taught me a new, deep appreciation of music, but much more than that you have taught me many valuable lessons about life. Thank you, (Karen Eklund)

G.E. 202, "Traditions of the West" Student Evaluations

(compiled by Dr. Charles Wiberg from class evaluations)

"The art and music portions, along with Mr. Athnos' lectures, were the most interesting.... Professor Athnos gave the most understandable and easy to follow lectures."

"Athnos: very interesting and enjoyable to listen to."

"Mr. Athnos' lectures and attitudes were fantastic. He was always very clear and also excited about what he was teaching."

"I like the team teaching style. I especially liked Mr. Athnos.... He was one of the best lecturers ever of my three years of college.

"Athnos: utterly dedicated.... Impressive...."

"I just wanted to say that I appreciated Mr. Athnos' inspiration and excitement. There was one day in particular, in which I was dealing with the recent (that week) suicide attempt of a friend of mine and was feeling quite burdened and guilty and heavy-hearted. It was the day we learned about Beethoven, and I remember thinking, 'Oh, (bleep), another suicide.'.... But the message that I got from that lecture was not one of despair, but of hope, and during the course of that hour, I was able to let go of the burden that was clouding my heart. The inspiration that I received from the lecture was just what I needed. I almost started crying in the middle of class. I don't know if you say those same things every year, or whether God just knew what I needed to hear, but I just wanted to thank you."

"Greg Athnos is awesome as the arts lecturer. His lectures were very interesting, clear, and precise."

"Mr. Athnos is the savior to 202! He is the best...in relating relevant info to the students."

"Mr. Athnos' lectures are very exciting. But besides his enthusiasm he seems to be on the level of the student and learning is shared, not handed down."

"The art and music portion of this course was very interesting and informative—partly because of the enthusiasm by which it was taught by Mr. Athnos. I would like to see this as a larger part of this class."

"Mr. Athnos is a great teacher, he makes every lecture very interesting."

"Athnos - Art and Music were very interesting and motivating. He spoke in a language that you could understand. His lectures were very clear and informative. He put energy and emotion and made his topic come to life. He changed my feelings toward classical music - I used to think it was for old people."

"Greg Athnos is a great professor - he gets you really excited about his subject!"

A Few Letters from Parents

Dear Professor Athnos,

We want to thank you for the role you played in Ben's maturing while at North Park College. As parents it has been gratifying to see Ben's interests mature from football to great music. While course work introduced him to good music, performance in the choir influenced his tastes as well.... We recognize your gift of taking ordinary students and forming them into a great choir. Ben's involvement with the choir was one of *the great experiences of his college career. Thank you for making such a wonderful opportunity available to him—and now, also, to Anna.*

We also want to thank you for the tremendous personal effort which you expended to plan and execute the Europe trip and the fund raising events preceding it. Our children's experiences on the trip will provide them with a perspective and memories for a lifetime. You gave so much of yourself for the benefit of the choir members and you have contributed significantly to the reputation of the college by your efforts. Sincerely, George and Judy Brinkman

Dear Greg,

Having left on vacation immediately following the Orchestra Hall concert, this is my first opportunity to thank you for an outstanding concert! The musicianship was excellent and your choice in programming certainly appealed to everyone.

Also a word of special thanks for your continuing support and friendship to Elizabeth. She has learned so much from you, not only in the field of music, but in the everyday living of life. Your being there, being available, has been a positive plus. Sincerely, Carole Magnusson [Her daughter Lyssa went on to an operatic career in Germany]

Dear Greg,

Thank you for your assistance in getting Gretchen home for her Grandpa Berry's funeral. You have been a very important God-given influence upon her life these past four years. Without your encouragement and training, she would have given up her future in music other than an occasional solo....

We really enjoyed being a part of the choir tour in Russia and Sweden. The choir members were all so kind and polite to us, and the music was outstanding.... Our favorite memories are those trips to Chicago each year at Christmas to hear the North Park Choir, Chamber Singers, and Orchestra perform at Queen of All Saints Basilica. What a soul-touching experience that has been each year! It has been the highlight of the season for us.

Thank you for being used of God in the moulding of Gretchen these years. Her life and ours will never be the same as a result of the opportunities and experiences you have afforded us.... Thank you for your part in our lives. Sincerely, Alan and Nancy Olson

Dear Greg:

This school year has been one of the highlights of my life, and I feel that I would be very remiss if I did not take the time to sit down and write this note to you. I have thoroughly enjoyed my 8+ months of 'traveling' with the choir through the Hymnal [the choir sang through the entire Covenant Hymnal in 24 hours as a fundraiser for our trip to Sweden, Russia, and Estonia] all the way to chapel a week ago [the final chapel before the trip]. The tone and the power of this choir is just awesome to me.

I praise God and thank you for what you have done for these young people and for what you are about to undertake. Please know that I look forward to not only bringing each of you before the Lord daily... but I will also make an attempt to time a very special prayer at the beginning of each performance. If my figuring is correct, there should even be a couple of 4:00 a.m.'s, and I will give it a try and trust the Lord to take it from there.

Have a wonderful trip. We will pray for everyone's safety, good health, and that God will be glorified. Most sincerely in Christ, Sally Searles

Dear Greg,

Thank you for the interest and impact you have had on Ryan's life. He values your wisdom and considers you a great friend. I recall meeting you for the first time thinking this person is someone God has placed in Ryan's life for a very special purpose.

It seems that so much of Ryan's time there has been filled with frustration but your friendship has been very special. No words could express my gratitude for such a gentleman.... Ryan is a better person for having known you and your family. Thank you and God bless you, Garry Olson

Appendix

Extra-Curricular Endeavors

Over my years at North Park I had opportunities for many speaking engagements off campus. Some were on behalf of North Park; most came my way as a result of recommendations from people outside our college community. I loved the variety of topics as well as the unique venues where my presentations took place. Here are a few:

Chicago Symphony Orchestra Symposium

Gregory Athnos, Associate Professor of Music at North Park College in Chicago, earlier this year was invited by the Junior Governing Board of the Chicago Symphony Orchestra to preside over a symposium for college students preceding a University Night concert at Orchestra Hall.

Joining Mr. Athnos on the symposium panel were two keyboard artists from the North Park College faculty (Elizabeth Buccheri and Richard Boldrey, who demonstrated the music being discussed); Adolph Herseth, principal trumpet with the CSO; Dale Clevenger, principal horn; Norman Schweikert, horn; and Ralph Zeitlin, recorder player from New York.

Focus of the symposium discussion was the CSO's performance for that evening, an all-Bach program conducted by Georg Solti, which included three Brandenburg Concerti.

The symposium was excellent, carefully planned and directed by Mr. Athnos so that each participant's contribution to the discussion was pertinent and illuminating, providing those in attendance with an understanding of the music that would enable them to more thoroughly enjoy the concert.

At the end of the concert season a questionnaire was distributed to our Student Subscribers which included a request that they indicate the symposium they considered the most informative and entertaining in the series of six. Winner of the survey was the symposium hosted by Mr. Athnos.

Mr. Athnos has been asked to return again this season and we are looking forward to another lively session. Signed, Marilyn K. Arado, Coordinator

I was thrilled to be asked to lead this symposium, and greatly honored to have been invited back. I am indebted to Elizabeth Buccheri, who recommended me to the Junior Governing Board, and who encouraged my outline and plan for the event. Today, April 14, 2013, as I read of the passing of Adolph Herseth, I am reminded of his brilliant trumpet performances for over 50 years with the Chicago Symphony. Most of all, I remember how he did everything I asked him to demonstrate with a genuinely lovely and humble spirit. That was important for me, as I also remember how intimidated I felt in his presence.

Appendix

Board of Education: Your High Schools Report, Highland Park-Deerfield High Schools

Athnos is one of five Artists-in-Residence sharing talents with District 113 students this school year. For his late fall lectures on "Revolutionaries in Music" the North Park College music professor played tapes, showed slides, and read poetry. Ask students how they liked Artist-in-Residence Greg Athnos: "What he knows—wow!" "He left space for your own opinions." "I hated poetry. Now I'm going to try my own." Or, as DHS humanities teacher Tom Silverwood put it, "It was instant two-way communication when Greg Athnos stepped in front of the class."

College Music Society: Wingspread Conference
As reported in the College News by Eric Lundberg, October, 1981:

Gregory Athnos, Assistant Professor of Music at North Park, was selected for a national committee on the teaching of music in General Education.... Sponsored by the College Music Society, the Wingspread Conference in Racine, Wisconsin, was planned for the purpose of seriously evaluating the teaching of music in colleges. Participants were chosen from around the country on the basis of recommendations submitted to the Society. Athnos was recommended by Elizabeth Buccheri [music department chairperson], Charles Wiberg [teaching partner in Traditions of the West], and by a representative of the Chicago Symphony Orchestra.

Athnos has been a regular participant in the symphony's pre-concert lecture series and, according to Buccheri, "is always at the top of the list when they take informal polls of which lecturer they liked." Along with the recommendations, Buccheri submitted several letters about Athnos which have come back to North Park from former students. "They all tell about how much his classes affected them," said Buccheri. "Not just how much they learned, but how it changed their lives. Some of those letters brought tears to my eyes."

Out of 130 nominees from around the country, only 25 were selected to attend the conference. Not surprisingly, Athnos was one of them.

The Wingspread Conference was primarily a brainstorming session, and focused mainly on the introductory level music course.... Athnos said it surprised him to see a new trend that offered a world-wide, cosmopolitan approach to music. Instead of concentrating on traditional western 'classical music', teachers were aiming for more 'world music'. Athnos expressed some reservations about this trend, saying, "If music reflects human tradition, and if we are products of our culture, and if the best way to understand one's self is to understand one's culture, then maybe OUR OWN music tradition and literature is where we should start.... One should understand one's self first, and THEN one's neighbors."

Athnos says that of all the things he does, the teaching of Introduction to Music is his favorite. "Introduction to Music is the most important thing I can do on this campus. While our music faculty does a fine job preparing the performers of the future, what's a performer without the listener? I prepare the listener." The popularity of Athnos' Intro classes (they are nearly always filled with a waiting list) attests to his dedication to the course. "When I make a breakthrough with a student", he says, "it is the most rewarding experience I know."

Representing North Park

Dear President Hausman: I have known Greg Athnos for many years and have always appreciated his creativity and sensitive interpretation of music. His relationship with the students is remarkable. But the word I want to say about Greg is his presentation of North Park to our people.... In all of the years that I have been in close contact with our school, I have never heard anyone make such an excellent presentation with such balance and accuracy as Greg made last Wednesday evening. He built his remarks on the sentence: "North Park is a Christian Liberal Arts College in the City". I would suggest that you sit down with him and just hear him out personally how he presents the school.... I can say not even with tongue in cheek that he outclassed the four presidents I have known, and every school representative, whether faculty or administration. That's saying an awful lot, but I mean every word of it. Sincerely, Norbert E. Johnson, Pastor, First Covenant Church, Omaha, Nebraska*

Mayor Daley's Chicago Prayer Breakfast

The North Park College Chamber Singers and College Choir were invited to provide special music for two separate Prayer Breakfasts.

Arts in Chicago

After several years at North Park it occurred to me that while the college was located in the city it seemed to pretend it wasn't. We were constantly in a state of denial, making apologies for our location when we should have been exploiting it. North Park is unique in many ways. Most Christian colleges are located in suburbia or even further removed from metropolitan centers. Often parents feel more secure sending their children to what are considered 'safer' environments. North Park seemed to be attempting to convince such parents we were like an 'oasis' sheltered from the city and its hazards. Poor North Park! We were originally far removed from the city, and to our great misfortune the city had grown and swallowed us up!

I felt that if we weren't going to identify with the city we should move. However, if the city was our home we should take advantage of it. As an artist, it struck me that Chicago offered great treasures that could make our location special and offer us recruitment bonuses unavailable to most other institutions like us. What came out of this awareness was an extracurricular program called 'Arts in Chicago'.

I assembled packages of cultural events throughout the city, including theater, opera, dance, and symphony. We ended up with two packages, one of six events and another of seven different events. A subscriber could take either or both packages.

Scheduling was difficult. I needed to work around our academic calendar: campus sporting events, concerts, plays, exams, breaks, and holidays. Working with the various arts organizations in the city I was able to arrange discount tickets.

We made the 'Arts in Chicago' packages available to faculty, staff, students, and people from the community. It was risky at first, as I had to predict how many we would sell and find ways to pay for the tickets not sold. But it was worth the risk.

In our second year nearly 100 people subscribed. An added bonus was that students and faculty developed a 'community spirit' by traveling together either in cars or by public transportation to the events, sometimes going out for dinner before the event or for dessert following. On occasion I offered pre-concert lectures.

It was a lot of work, but it was great fun: arranging the calendar, calling the arts agencies, printing the brochure, soliciting participants, collecting the money, and mailing the tickets. The program continued for three years and was exceedingly successful. After the third year I asked for some help. It was costing me much time, and a substantial amount of money. I felt the institution needed to take a certain degree of ownership in the program, even if it was as little as paying for my personal tickets to the events. North Park, purportedly for financial reasons, couldn't comply with my request. At the same time I was preparing for my first Sabbatical and would be out of the country for most of the next academic year. No one stepped up to take charge of the program in the interim. 'Arts in Chicago' was discontinued. Some years later the idea was resurrected and became part of the Freshman curriculum with several faculty members, led by me, participating.

Chapel Choir Initiative
North Park was blessed with many of its faculty and staff possessed of a love for choral singing. Why not enlist their talents in a small choir to participate in periodic Chapels? We began with a group of between fifteen and twenty singers; it was a joy for all of us. We rehearsed forty-five minutes before Chapel. They were quick 'readers', enabling me to choose sacred anthems without much concern for vocal limitations.

Unfortunately, our initiative lasted only the better part of one year. The character of the Chapel experience was moving toward the more contemporary Christian style, and student leadership took over the musical responsibilities. The wonderful pipe organ in Anderson Chapel fell silent, as did the voices of our faculty-staff singers.

Gospel Choir Initiative
Two students, one Caucasian and one African-American, came to Philosophy Professor David Gill and me asking for advice. There was a growing interest in Gospel Music and a groundswell of students

interested in forming a group. We were asked to support them by hosting an open forum to begin the process. They also asked if we would represent their initiative to the faculty and administration.

David and I were enthusiastic about the proposition, and shepherded the program into existence. Once established, a student conductor took charge. The Gospel Choir then progressed under its own energies, eventually becoming a major part of North Park's outreach.

Courses taught, Initiatives

Music Education: Elementary School Methods

Music Education: Secondary School Methods

Coordinator and Supervisor of Practice Teaching

Beginning Conducting

Sight-Singing and Ear-Training

Introduction to Music, a General Education course for non-majors

Introduction to Music Literature, for Freshman Music majors and Minors (*created by me*)

Music of the Baroque Period, for upper level Music Majors and Minors

Music of the Romantic Period, for upper level Music Majors and Minors

Wagner's "Ring Cycle", one-time course (*created by Elizabeth Buccheri and me*)

Traditions of the West, G.E. required course (*created by an interdisciplinary team, including me*)

Appendix

Oratorio Chorus (a community chorus)

Chapel Choir (*created by me* for faculty, staff, students to participate monthly in chapel services)

Chamber Singers (*created by me*)

Early Music Consort (*created by me*)

Chamber Orchestra (*created by me*)

College/University Choir

The Gospel Choir (*founding supporter*, along with Philosophy Professor David Gill)

CPSIA information can be obtained
at www.ICGtesting.com
Printed in the USA
BVHW040707290919
559704BV00007B/545/P